Theological Education
in the
Evangelical Tradition

Theological Education
in the
Evangelical Tradition

*Edited by D. G. Hart
and R. Albert Mohler, Jr.*

Baker Books

A Division of Baker Book House Co
Grand Rapids, Michigan 49516

Published by Baker Books
a division of Baker Book House Company
P.O. Box 6287, Grand Rapids, MI 49516-6287

Printed in the United States of America

Library of Congress Cataloging-in-Publication Data

Theological education in the Evangelical tradition / edited by D. G. Hart and R. Albert Mohler, Jr.
    p.   cm.
    Includes bibliographical references and index.
    ISBN 0-8010-2061-1 (pbk.)
    1. Theology—Study and teaching—History. 2. Evangelicalism—History.
I. Mohler, R. Albert, 1959– . II. Hart, D. G. (Darryl G.)
BV1640.T47   1996
207'.73—dc20   96-35212

Contents

97789

Foreword

Evangelical Christians have a record of uneasiness with theological education. Sometimes this uneasiness has been expressed in outright hostility toward theological schools. More frequently it has taken the form of a cautious, even slightly nervous, sponsorship of seminary education.

This uneasiness is quite understandable. Evangelicalism has often functioned as a protest movement within the larger Christian community, criticizing the dominant patterns of thought and practice of the day. This has meant that evangelical Christians have regularly been at odds with the mainstream of theological education. Evangelical uneasiness in this area is not directed, however, simply to the issues of specific theological controversies. It is an expression of motifs that run deep in evangelical spirituality. Evangelicalism is a strain of Protestantism that emphasizes the personal, transforming power of the gospel. We evangelicals worry about the kind of fascination with "head knowledge" that crowds out "heart knowledge."

It is good to worry about this kind of thing. A fear of an overintellectualized Christianity need not set us against the project of theological scholarship as such. But it can help us think clearly why it is that theological education is a good thing. We do not want to foster a clerical elitism that does not meet the spiritual needs of ordinary Christians and fails to support the crucial task of bringing the gospel to the lost.

The church's mission can only be healthy, however, when it is based on sound theology. Evangelicals have often rightly perceived the theological threat posed by various heterodoxies. But we have not always been clear about the ways in which a thoroughgoing pragmatism—always a strong presence in the evangelical movement—also poses dangers to the clear proclamation of the gospel. Learning how to "do" ministry is not enough. We must also learn to "be" ministers. This means being exposed to biblical scholarship, weighing theories of Christian practice, and learning to think systematically about the fundamental issues of the faith.

It also means being in conversation with the Christian past. And not the least of our interests in exploring past patterns of Christian thought and practice ought to be in studying the enterprise of theological education itself. What is the history of our practices of training people for ministry? How have various evangelical communities shaped their programs of seminary education? How can the lessons of the past provide guidance for the challenges of the present?

For all who care—or who ought to care—about these questions, this volume is a valuable resource. Scholars who have critically and lovingly studied the educational programs of the evangelical past here share with us the results of their labors. The issues discussed are of vital importance for the health of the evangelical movement. This is a book that deserves careful study and widespread discussion.

Richard J. Mouw

Introduction

Theological education is not a subject that readily comes to mind in connection when thinking about American evangelicalism. To be sure, in the lexicon of American church history evangelicalism has been commonly identified with certain doctrinal emphases, thus suggesting the need for theological education of some kind in the evangelical tradition. Yet, with its stress upon the new birth, vital piety, and holy living, evangelicalism has generally been distrustful of formal learning and academic institutions. From the eighteenth-century broadsides against overly educated ministers by George Whitefield and Gilbert and William Tennent, to recent criticisms of seminaries by megachurch and parachurch leaders, evangelicals have usually been somewhat suspicious of formal theological education and an overly scholarly exposition of the gospel. The remarks of one Methodist itinerant made during the early nineteenth century at the time of the Second Great Awakening expressed well the congenital evangelical suspicion of learning generally, and theological education specifically:

> What I insist, upon by brethren and sisters, is this: larnin isn't religion, and eddication don't give a man the power of the Spirit. It is grace and gifts that furnish the real live coals from off the altar. St. Peter was a fisherman—do you think he ever went to Yale College?[1]

Nevertheless, despite such ambivalence about the value and edification of formal theological training, evangelicals in North America support and rely upon a constellation of theological seminaries which comprise the largest segment of institutions that offer postbaccalaureate education for men and women training for the ministry. Indeed, the size of particular institutions, the number of evangelical seminaries, along with the large constituency of evangelical students studying theology at evangelical and mainline seminaries are remarkable facets of a movement whose identity more often revolves

---

1. Samuel Goodrich, *Recollections of a Lifetime*, 2 vols. (New York, 1856), 196–97, quoted in Nathan Hatch, *The Democratization of American Christianity* (New Haven: Yale University Press, 1989), 20.

around the individual's acceptance of Christ in the new birth as the royal road to truth.

According to recent statistics from the Association of Theological Schools, the body which sets the standards and regulates theological education in North America, roughly sixty-three evangelical seminaries (including six Southern Baptist institutions), offer degrees of one variety or another to more than thirty thousand students. While evangelical seminaries comprise only thirty percent of those schools accredited by ATS, the student body at these institutions makes up almost fifty (48) percent of the total enrollment at North American seminaries and divinity schools. The five largest seminaries in the United States are also evangelical: Southwestern Baptist Theological Seminary (Southern Baptist Convention) in Fort Worth, Texas with 3,364 students; Fuller Theological Seminary (nondenominational) in Pasadena, California with 2,868; Southern Baptist Theological Seminary (Southern Baptist Convention) in Louisville, Kentucky with 2,269; New Orleans Baptist Theological Seminary (Southern Baptist Convention) in Louisiana with 2,252 students; Trinity Evangelical Divinity School (Evangelical Free Church) in Deerfield, Illinois with 1,633 students; and Dallas Theological Seminary (non-denominational) in Texas with 1,125 students. (These five institutions alone account for twenty percent (13,511) of the total ATS student enrollment!)[2]

For the sake of comparison, mainstream Protestant seminaries account for almost half (46%) of the institutions in ATS, while enrollment at mainline institutions is approximately twenty-five thousand students (39%). The other large constituency within ATS is Roman Catholic, which accounts for twenty-six percent (51) of the accredited seminaries in North America and provides theological education to almost seven thousand students (11%). While figures do not describe the character or measure the influence of theological education provided by evangelical seminaries, they do demonstrate the exceptional presence of evangelical institutions within the world of theological education. Evangelicals have become the largest supporters and beneficiaries of formal, accredited theological education. To gain some perspective on these statistics, one needs to remember that two nondenominational evangelical seminaries, Fuller and Gordon-Conwell, train more Presbyterian ministers than all of the Presbyterian Church's official seminaries put together.[3]

The aim of this book is not to assess or document the current size and influence of contemporary evangelical seminaries. Rather, its subject is the history of evangelical theological education and, as such, its purpose is to pro-

---

2. Statistics compiled by Peter Wallace, from *Fact Book on Theological Education, 1992–1993* (Pittsburgh: ATS, 1993).
3. Ibid.

vide the historical perspective necessary for measuring the strength, vitality, and character, as well as the weaknesses and failures of evangelical theological institutions. (One weakness may, in fact, be an infatuation with numbers.) This book examines specifically the origins, distinctive contributions, and tensions within theological education in the evangelical tradition. In many respects this volume is an early foray into a neglected field of research. Though Protestant seminaries and divinity schools have been important components in American intellectual history, whether as the first institutions to offer graduate education or as the chief locus of learned discourse in the early American republic, with few exceptions they have not received adequate treatment, aside from conventional institutional histories. We offer and bring together in this book the firstfruits of historians who have been exploring various aspects of evangelical theological education in the hope that such work will stimulate more study of a topic whose importance and historical development has all too often been assumed, but seldom examined. For this reason we have purposefully designed this book to be used by the faculty and administrators of theological institutions who desire a historical perspective on many of the issues that continue to bedevil evangelical seminaries as they prepare for the twenty-first century.[4]

While one of the purposes of this book is to contribute to and spur interest in the history of theological education, it is also designed to add to the growing literature on the history of evangelicalism, but in this case from a quarter generally overlooked. Since the flowering of pietism in the seventeenth century and the revivals associated with the Great Awakenings of the next century, evangelicalism has most often been a dissenting religious movement. Along the way evangelicals have established a broad range of institutions, seminaries and theological colleges among them, whose purpose was to protest the direction of the religious establishment and nurture the beliefs and ideals thought necessary for genuine Christian faith and practice. And the institutions, which evangelicals founded to provide theological education, say a good deal about the character of their religious convictions and the resolve of their devotion. Not only did these schools, located as they were (at least initially) on the periphery of the educational establishment, require great sacrifice, but they also provided an education which embodied, or at least attempted to do so, those things that evangelicals believed were essential to the Christian religion and the way it should be communicated and lived.

4. On the contributions of theological seminaries in the world of nineteenth-century American learning, see William Warren Sweet, "The Rise of Theological Schools in America," *Church History* 6 (1937): 260–73; Natalie A. Naylor, "The Theological Seminary in the Configuration of American Higher Education: The Ante-Bellum Years," *History of Education Quarterly* 17 (1977): 17–30; Glenn T. Miller, *Piety and Intellect: The Aims and Purposes of Ante-Bellum Theological Education* (Atlanta: Scholars Press, 1990); and Bruce Kuklick, *Churchmen and Philosophers: From Jonathan Edwards to John Dewey* (New Haven: Yale University Press, 1985).

Though it is certainly an overstatement to say that seminaries are the key to comprehending evangelicalism, it is nonetheless legitimate to highlight the significance of theological education to the development of the evangelical movement. At pivotal moments in evangelical history, theological institutions came into existence whose purpose was to sustain evangelical identity. Yet, the importance of theological education to evangelicalism has often been slighted, if not ignored, because of evangelical convictions about the priority of "heart knowledge" over "head knowledge." This book should make clear that wherever evangelicals have prospered, they have relied to some degree upon theological education. Granted, such education may not have been up to the standards of the existing institutions. But in many cases this was precisely the point. Evangelicals, throughout their history, from Calvinists to Wesleyans, have founded theological schools because they believed the existing institutions were neglecting essential elements of Christian faith and witness. Consequently, in order to understand evangelicalism better, we need to come to terms with the role and significance of evangelical theological education.

Defining Evangelicalism

At the outset it is important to be clear about the term "evangelical," a word used with as much frequency as imprecision. The most common definition, the one used by neoevangelical leaders, pollsters, and historians has been a prescriptive and normative definition. By these criteria, an evangelical is one who holds a high view of canonical Scripture as the Word of God, believes that God can act and has acted in history, affirms the lordship of Christ and the centrality of his salvific work, and believes in the necessity of a personal experience of grace. Another way of describing evangelicalism theologically, one that captures well the movement's character, has been to highlight four key doctrines. The first is conversionism, the idea that a life-changing experience, a "new birth," is necessary to being a Christian. The second is biblicism, or a stress upon the Reformation doctrine of the Bible alone as the ultimate authority for religion. The third distinctive element of the evangelical tradition is activism, the notion that believers must always be engaged in sharing the faith and leading others to Christ. And finally, evangelicals have emphasized crucientism, or a focus upon Christ's redeeming death upon the cross and resurrection from the grave, as the defining moment of the Christian religion.[5]

5. Mark A. Noll, *Between Faith and Criticism: Evangelicals, Scholarship, and the Bible,* 2d ed. (Grand Rapids: Baker, 1991), 2, for instance, uses the former definition. David Bebbington, *Evangelicalism in Modern Britain: A History from the 1730s to the 1980s* (London: Unwin Hyman, 1989), 2–19 defines evangelicalism by the latter four impulses.

This definition has its usefulness, especially as a beginning for theological reflection and for setting confessional boundaries or establishing some order within a movement, organization, or institution. But it is not entirely adequate for the task of describing those people who identify themselves as evangelicals, a very amorphous group that find themselves in Catholic and Protestant churches, have high and low conceptions of the church, are loyal to denominations and advocate independency, come from charismatic and Reformed backgrounds, hold different conceptions of the end times, and work and worship within mainline and fundamentalist churches. Even the dominant emphases described above do not constitute evangelicalism as a Christian tradition on the order of Catholicism, Orthodoxy, Presbyterianism, or Pentecostalism. The movement has always been composed of shifting alliances, important personalities, and temporary associations. Thus, while a theological definition of evangelicalism yields conceptual clarity, it can prevent understanding why these believers who call themselves evangelicals have come to identify these doctrines as crucial, and why these believers who come from such diverse theological and ecclesiastical backgrounds prefer the company and fellowship of those who share these convictions.

Indeed, as the essays in this volume illustrate—contrary to its subtitle—no single evangelical tradition exists. Rather, evangelicals are heirs of a variety of ethnic and confessional traditions, from Scandinavian sectarian movements to Scotch-Irish Presbyterians. This book attempts to do justice to some of this diversity through the themes treated in each section, especially the one on the evangelical mosaic. Yet our purpose is not to further balkanize the evangelical world in the same way that contemporary debates about cultural diversity within American politics and education have divided the nation. Despite diversity, evangelicalism in its various manifestations is comprised of common elements and impulses, which we hope will become evident throughout the book as a whole.

Actually, the definition of evangelicalism that makes the most sense of the movement's diversity is one that is descriptive and historical. In this sense, twentieth-century evangelicalism is an organic family of movements and traditions which comprise the variety of evangelicals who support evangelists like Billy Graham, read *Christianity Today,* hire pastors trained at seminaries such as Fuller or Gordon-Conwell, and who belong to organizations like the National Association of Evangelicals.

Evangelicalism in a historical sense emerged during the Protestant Reformation of the sixteenth century. The very first believers to identify themselves as evangelicals were the early followers of Martin Luther. For these Protestants, whether Lutheran, Anglican, Reformed, or Anabaptist, the term evangelical implied the recovery of the evangel, the good news of salvation by grace. So in Europe today, and in the United States until the fundamentalist controversy of the 1920s, "evangelical" has been virtually synonymous with Protestant.[6]

Yet, even though Protestants from various denominations at the beginning of the twentieth century would have been comfortable with the label "evangelical," the term clearly has come to have a narrower meaning, one that stems as much from the kind of faith and practice that emerged in the seventeenth century among Pietists and Puritans as it does from the battles between modernists and fundamentalists during the 1920s. What characterizes evangelicalism in this broader historical sense is a reaction against the perceived formalism and rationalism of Protestant scholasticism and the established national churches. Pietism and Puritanism stressed conversion and experiential religion. This emphasis made important contributions by injecting a good deal of spiritual vitality into Protestant churches in Germany, Holland, England, and America. Both movements reasserted the necessity of the subjective and ethical aspects of Christianity against overly academic and corporate conceptions of the faith. Pietists and Puritans took seriously the Protestant doctrine of the priesthood of believers and encouraged the laity to study the Bible for themselves and to live godly lives. They also promoted and sponsored the first widespread missionary efforts.

North American Christianity has been shaped more specifically by revivalism, a distinctive brand of Pietism. Revivalism became prominent in America, thanks largely to the First Great Awakening of the 1740s and the Second Great Awakening of the first half of the nineteenth century. The first was led by the itinerant evangelist, George Whitefield, and the Puritan minister, Jonathan Edwards. Like Pietism, these revivals promoted the necessity of religious experience and godly living among ministers and especially among the laity. The revival also encouraged a new style of leadership, one that was direct, personal, popular, and depended much more on the speaker's appeal to the audience than upon his standing in the social hierarchy. In turn, revivalism undermined the power of the established churches. The routines of Christian devotion in the local congregation were still a significant part of the convert's religious life, but not as important as his or her personal decision to trust in Christ or private piety. The Second Great Awakening accelerated the immediacy and individualism of the First Great Awakening and helped to establish evangelical dominance in the new nation by furnishing a form of Christianity fully compatible with the ideals of the American republic and easily adapted to the new social and political realities of the United States.[7]

---

6. This and the following paragraphs follow Mark Noll's judicious assessment of evangelical history in *The Scandal of the Evangelical Mind* (Grand Rapids: Eerdmans, 1994), chap. 3.

7. On these developments, see especially Harry S. Stout, *The Divine Dramatist: George Whitefield and the Rise of Modern Evangelicalism* (Grand Rapids: Eerdmans, 1991); Hatch, *Democratization of American Christianity;* and Daniel Walker Howe, "The Evangelical Movement and Political Culture in the North during the Second Party System," *Journal of American History* 77 (1991): 1216–1239.

Evangelical Theological Education

Even though evangelicalism seemed to make systematic theology and a learned clergy unnecessary, if not an encumbrance to real and vital religion, evangelicals have never rejected the value of theological education outright. As this book shows, Pietists, Puritans, and Revivalists, all Protestants who stressed the necessity of the new birth and accompanying signs and testimonies of grace, have supported theological education actively, even if providing it in a form not approved by the theological and educational establishment. In fact, throughout the history of evangelicalism, institutions providing theological education to prospective ministers have been as important in the students they train as in giving conceptual identity to the movement.

The early model for theological education came from the great universities of western Europe where theological faculties, under the direction and patronage of the state, trained clergy for ministry in the national church. Though differences existed between Britain and the continent, and between Catholics and Protestants, theological education was part of the training that universities provided for the professions, which included law and medicine in addition to the ministry. The pattern of making the theological curriculum and faculty part of undergraduate education or including it within the university still prevails in the United Kingdom, Canada, and Europe. Seminaries, however, are a relatively recent phenomenon within the history of higher education and are particular to theological education in the United States. The forerunner of the seminary was the phenomenon of reading divinity, a form of theological education that prevailed in colonial America where college graduates intent upon the ministry served as apprentices to senior clergy. Reading divinity not only included observation and participation in the daily parish ministry, but also included a more intensive study of the Bible and theology than obtained in the colleges. The disciples of Jonathan Edwards, for instance, used this system to perpetuate a particular theology and form of ministry along the Connecticut River valley.[8]

With the founding of Andover in 1808 and Princeton in 1812, the institution of the seminary gradually replaced the older system of reading divinity. While some American universities would eventually sponsor divinity schools, Harvard and Yale being the first and most notable examples in 1815 and 1822 respectively, the model of the seminary prevailed by the mid-nineteenth century, focusing on training for the ministry at a separate institution after first receiving an undergraduate degree.[9]

---

8. See Miller, *Piety and Intellect*, chaps. 3–4.
9. Conrad Wright, "The Early Period (1811–1840)," in *The Harvard Divinity School*, ed. George Huntson Williams (Boston, 1954), chap. 1; and Roland H. Bainton, *Yale and the Ministry* (New York: Harper, 1957).

Thanks to the dominance of the seminary model in the United States, especially after the establishment in 1934 of a theological accrediting agency, the Association of Theological Schools, evangelical theological education has not differed fundamentally in institutional or formal characteristics from Protestant seminaries outside the evangelical orbit. In the antebellum era, Andover and Princeton shared with the more liberal Yale and Harvard most of the same standards for curriculum, faculty, administrators, and students as do Fuller and Southern Baptist today with Duke Divinity School and Andover–Newton. Yet, the ethos and style of evangelical seminaries has set them apart from the more established Protestant institutions and continues to do so. Attending an evangelical seminary as a student or being a member of the faculty at an evangelical school often involves becoming part of a network of congregations, denominations, and parachurch organizations that subscribe to an evangelical expression of Christianity in doctrine, conduct, and piety.[10]

Thus while evangelical theological education has not been different formally from that sponsored by established and mainline Protestants in North America and Europe, it has manifested a self-conscious identity or separateness that makes it distinct from other varieties of theological education. Indeed, evangelical training for the ministry has more often than not been a means for expressing dissatisfaction with the dominant patterns of church life and piety. As this book makes clear, evangelicals have been especially wary of religion that appears to be automatic or routine, and they have desired ministers and leaders who have experienced firsthand a vital and deep encounter with God's grace and who could instill and reproduce such characteristics within other believers.[11]

As a result, evangelicalism has sponsored a variety of institutions, from the followers of Edwards and New Side Presbyterians of the eighteenth century, evangelical Baptists in England, confessional Calvinists in the Netherlands, the American Methodist and Nazarene followers of John Wesley, to evangelical theological colleges in Canada. All of these efforts manifest the

10. Barbara Wheeler, "You Who Were Far Off: Religious Divisions and the Role of Religious Research," Paul Douglas lecture, Religious Research Association, fall 1995, makes this very point quite convincingly.

11. A companion project to this volume is the Fuller Consultation on the Aims and Purposes of Evangelical Theological Education, headed by Dr. Richard Mouw. There, the discussions have focused on the uniqueness of evangelical theological education and the aim is to produce a body of literature from an evangelical perspective which addresses some of the issues raised in such works as Edward Farley, *Theologia: The Fragmentation and Unity of Theological Education* (Philadelphia: Fortress Press, 1983); idem, *The Fragility of Knowledge: Theological Education in the Church and the University* (Philadelphia: Fortress Press, 1988); Joseph C. Hough, Jr., and John B. Cobb, Jr., *Christian Identity and Theological Education* (Atlanta: Scholars Press, 1985); Charles M. Wood, *Vision and Discernment: An Orientation in Theological Study* (Atlanta: Scholars Press, 1985); Joseph C. Hough, Jr., and Barbara G. Wheeler, eds., *Beyond Clericalism: The Congregation as a Focus for Theological Education* (Atlanta: Scholars Press, 1988); and David H. Kelsey, *Between Athens and Berlin: The Theological Education Debate* (Grand Rapids: Eerdmans, 1993).

same desire to provide an education and means of spiritual formation, which evangelicals believe to be necessary for genuine faith. What has been true in the past is also characteristic of evangelical theological education in the last three-quarters of the twentieth century when the term "evangelical" has taken on a more narrow meaning. Just as Puritan and Pietist programs for theological education were essential to the identity of these movements, so evangelical seminaries like Fuller, Dallas, and Trinity Evangelical Divinity School have been critical to defining the contemporary expression of evangelicalism. This is no less true for Southern Baptists, who bear all the marks of the evangelical tradition but are suspicious about the Yankee origins of the term, and where the quirks of denominational polity allow the creation of new theological institutions dedicated to many of the planks of a prescriptive evangelical platform.

The Shape of This Book

Even though this book is historical in orientation, we have arranged the chapters around specific themes, which are particularly germane to contemporary debates within the seminary community about the aims and purposes of theological education. As anachronistic as this method of organization may appear, it does highlight what we believe to be one of the merits of the essays presented here, that is, the relevance of historical study for understanding the present and preparing for the future. Each essay is able to stand on its own as a self-contained historical study. But collectively they speak to many of the issues that confront the contemporary evangelical seminary. And even though several of the chapters address pre-twentieth-century topics and institutions in evangelical theological education, the book as a whole shows that the problems seminaries face today are not dramatically different from those that confronted evangelical theological educators in the past. In fact, it is not an overstatement to claim that the so-called crisis in evangelical theological education in large measure stems from assumptions and norms established in the experience of previous generations of evangelicals.

One of the perennial debates in the history of evangelical theological education concerns the democratic, lay-oriented character of evangelicalism. One way of stating this issue is to ask what the relationship is between the populist, anti-elitist (whether clerical or academic) nature of evangelicalism and the formal structures, which theological education must of necessity take. While tensions between the laity and clergy have been evident throughout the history of the Christian church, the frequency with which this question is asked in evangelical circles may indicate that it is a defining element in the evangelical tradition and, therefore, in evangelical theological education. In contrast, for instance, the literature on mainline Protestant theological education gives little attention to this concern, and one doubts that it plagues those administrators and professors responsible for training Roman Catholic clergy. But, as readers will see, it comes up repeatedly in evangelical institutions no matter what the historical period or theological tradition. So, democratic appeals can be heard in the Wesleyan and Holiness world (e.g., Russell E. Richey's and Melvin E. Dieter's chapters), as well as in the creation of Baptist and Presbyterian seminaries (e.g., Timothy George's and Gary Scott Smith's chapters).

A related theme in the history of evangelical theological education concerns the relationship between evangelical piety or zeal and the life of the mind. Evangelicalism, of course, has a reputation for stressing the experience of conversion, or the new birth, as well as a concerned zeal for evangelism, missions, and clean living. Yet, for all of evangelicalism's enthusiasm, it has also been dependent upon and has nurtured concepts of knowledge associated with the Enlightenment. David Bebbington has argued persuasively that the evangelical movement has, since its origins, been permeated by the empiricist and inductive epistemology, which has dominated the natural sciences and intellectual life more generally since the eighteenth century.[12] Evangelicals, thus, look for evidence of grace and visible signs of conversion in ways remarkably similar to the methods scientists use to explore the natural world and human society. This insight suggests that historically there has not been an inherent antagonism between faith and reason in the evangelical tradition. It is also helpful for explaining why evangelicals have not bitterly retreated from the world of learning, but rather have endeavored to create their own institutions of higher learning. This also helps to explain why evangelical seminaries have often been called upon to do more than train ministers. Evangelical theological education, as shown particularly in the chapters by Nina Reid–Maroney, David Bebbington, James D. Bratt, and George A. Rawlyk, has also been concerned with cultivating intellectual leaders for the church beyond the clergy. To be sure, these efforts have not always proved successful and in some cases have detracted seminaries from the explicit task of training ministers and studying theology. But evangelical faculty and administrators who today feel pulled between the demands of the academy and the life of the church will find some consolation in the pages that follow from knowing that their frustrations are not new.

Another theme of this book is the relationship between evangelicalism and modernity. Despite the movement's reputation for being hostile to such forces of modernization as secularization and relativism, evangelicals have also been amazingly adept at using the fruits of modernity, such as technology, various organizational techniques, and the mechanisms of the market in communicating the claims of the gospel. While various evangelists and parachurch agencies come to mind as examples of this trait, seminaries in the

12. *Evangelicalism in Modern Britain*, 50–69.

evangelical tradition have also relied upon many of the elements and products of modernity. Evangelical seminaries, for instance, have shown a greater willingness to admit larger numbers of students, to use a variety of nontraditional methods for delivering theological education, and to use market forces to fund the training of Christian workers. This is only to say that the ethos of evangelical seminaries, despite the traditionalism of the instruction they provide, often has more the feel of a business enterprise than an ivory tower. The motives for the evangelical striving for numbers and size are not inherently crass. For, as many of the chapters that follow show (especially those in the first section on the evangelical mosaic), the zeal for influence and success has been rooted in a commitment to spreading the Word. Thus, evangelical theological education confirms the point that evangelicals have embraced many of the elements of modernity, if not with enthusiasm, at least for distinctly evangelistic ends.

While zeal for reaching the lost has been a latent impulse with evangelical theological education, so has a concern for inculcating a particular kind of piety. Indeed, one of the hallmarks of evangelicalism is that theological knowledge without godliness and piety is virtually meaningless. For this reason, theological instruction at evangelical seminaries has not only featured indoctrination in specific evangelical formulations of Christian theology, but it has also been marked by efforts to stimulate greater devotion within its students. Although recognizing this characteristic of evangelical theological education is important for understanding evangelicalism more generally, attention to the ways in which evangelicals have attempted to nurture Christian devotion is particularly poignant today when theological educators, both evangelical and mainline, Protestant and Catholic, are addressing the issue of spiritual formation at seminary. For this reason, we have devoted one whole section of the book to the theme of spiritual formation. And as the chapters by Richard A. Muller, David W. Kling, and James E. Bradley show, a concern for godly ministers is not just a contemporary issue, but extends back even into the period of Protestant scholasticism, an era considered by many to be responsible for the dead orthodoxy against which evangelicals have consistently railed.[13] And these papers also suggest, as does the book more generally, that the qualities of coldness and vitality are ultimately in the eye of the beholder. For the theological formulations, which some consider destructive of piety, are for others the very breath of spiritual health. Nevertheless, whatever disagreement there may be about the relationship between learning and piety, or between theology and experience, this book of-

---

13. For examples of the argument that Protestant scholasticism's influence has been unhealthy, especially with regard to evangelical views of the Bible, see Jack B. Rogers and Donald K. McKim, *The Authority and Interpretation of the Bible: An Historical Approach* (San Francisco: Harper and Row, 1979); and James Barr, *Fundamentalism* (Philadelphia: Westminster, 1977).

fers much for contemporary theological educators to ponder as they retool curricula and design programs for the purpose of forming the spirituality of students.

A final topic addressed throughout the chapters that follow concerns the curriculum or course of instruction in evangelical theological education. If, as Mark Noll contends, evangelicalism is not an "ism" like other Christian "isms," that is, if evangelicalism is not a tradition by itself, but is rather a renewal impulse within various Protestant traditions, then it is not likely that the actual instruction at an evangelical seminary is noticeably different from other Protestant seminaries.[14] Throughout the history of evangelical theological education, evangelicals have usually taught courses and assigned books that were commonly used by other Protestants, in which case it is not the content per se which makes evangelical theological education distinctive, but the ethos or culture of the instruction. Here, again, the point, not necessarily shared by all, is that what makes evangelicalism unique is the kind of piety or experience evangelicals believe to be indicative of genuine faith or true religion. And the importance of this point for our purposes is that evangelicals historically have been particularly concerned to make the cultivation of the proper kind of piety in prospective ministers and other Christian leaders a necessary ingredient in theological education.

Nevertheless, this book also shows that evangelicals, if they offer anything distinctive in the world of theological education, present a curriculum that still features a high regard for the centrality of the Bible as God's infallible Word. In recent discussions about the aims and purposes of theological education much has been made of the fourfold pattern in Protestant seminaries. This pattern divides theological instruction into four areas: the Bible, systematic theology, church history, and practical theology. And in much of the discussion it has been assumed that evangelicals, because of their particular understanding of Scripture, have a special attachment to the fourfold curriculum.[15] As Edward Farley argues, this way of dividing up the theological curriculum, is bound up with an understanding of theology which takes as its reference authoritative or "apodictically true texts."[16] While it is true that evangelicals still rely overwhelmingly on the fourfold pattern, this feature of evangelical theology stems as much from evangelical convictions about the Bible as it does from a particular fondness for the fourfold scheme. As Richard Mouw has written, "Evangelicals view Biblical authority as a foundational item. . . . The fourfold pattern seems to *comport* well with our theological convictions."[17] Though several of the chapters that follow allude

14. Noll, *The Scandal of the Evangelical Mind* (Grand Rapids: Eerdmans, 1994), 8.
15. For a critical assessment of the fourfold pattern, see Farley, *Theologia.*
16. Farley, *The Fragility of Knowledge,* 104.
17. Richard J. Mouw, "Evangelical Reflections on the 'Aims and Purposes' Literature," unpublished paper, 7.

to curricular matters, none takes up the topic explicitly. Yet, throughout the book, evangelical convictions about Scripture are evident, as are the implications of those convictions for the curriculum. For this reason, this volume is designed to identify what the aims and purposes of evangelical theological education have been historically, while also giving some guidance to ongoing discussions about the curriculum at evangelical seminaries.

Finally, we would like to take this opportunity to thank the Lilly Endowment, a foundation with a long tradition of support for theological education and reflection about the purposes of Protestant seminaries, which supplied a generous grant for the conference at which these chapters were first presented. This book is a testimony to the endowment's commitment to stimulate greater study of the definitions, purposes, benefits, and communities of theological education. We would also be remiss if we did not mention the debt we owe to the Institute for the Study of American Evangelicals, which sponsored the project from which these essays came. Edith Blumhofer, former director of the Institute and presently with the University of Chicago, and Larry Eskridge, assistant director, deserve high marks for hosting the conference and assisting with all of the logistical and administrative details related to the project. Finally, special thanks should be given to the members of the Fuller Consultation on the Aims and Purposes of Evangelical Theological Education: Richard Mouw, David Jones, Stephen Mott, James E. Massey, Ben Ollenburger, Paul Bassett, Rob Johnston, Daniel Aleshire, Linda Cannell, Cheryl Bridges Johns, David Kirkpatrick, Walter Liefeld, John Thompson, and Barbara Wheeler. This group gave us good direction in conceiving and implementing this project and insured that the past retrieved here would be a usable one for their peers in the task of theological education.

D. G. Hart and R. Albert Mohler, Jr.

Contributors

David W. Bebbington is senior lecturer in history at the University of Stirling (Scotland).

James E. Bradley is professor of church history at Fuller Theological Seminary.

James D. Bratt is professor of history at Calvin College.

Virginia Lieson Brereton is co-director of the Women and Twentieth-Century Protestantism Project at Andover-Newton Theological School.

Melvin E. Dieter is emeritus professor of church history at Asbury Theological Seminary.

Gabriel Fackre is Abbot Professor of Christian Theology at Andover-Newton Theological School.

Karin Gedge is assistant professor of history at Eastern Michigan University.

Timothy George is academic dean of the Beeson Divinity School, Samford University.

D. G. Hart is librarian and associate professor of church history and theological bibiliography at Westminster Theological Seminary (PA).

David W. Kling is assistant professor of religious studies at Miami University.

Nina-Reid Maroney received her Ph.D. in history from the University of Toronto.

R. Albert Mohler, Jr. is president of the Southern Baptist Theological Seminary.

Richard J. Mouw is president of Fuller Theological Seminary.

Richard A. Muller is the P. J. Zondervan Professor of Historical Theology at Calvin Theological Seminary.

George A. Rawlyk was professor of history at Queen's University (Ontario).

Russell E. Richey is associate dean and professor of church history at the Divinity School, Duke University.

Gary Scott Smith is professor of sociology at Grove City College.

David F. Wells is the Andrew Mutch Professor of Historical and Systematic Theology at Gordon-Conwell Theological Seminary.

Part 1

The Evangelical Mosaic and Theological Education

In recent years it has become almost a truism to say that evangelicalism is a diverse movement in American Protestantism. Twenty years ago, according to most scholars and observers of American religion, Protestantism was divided in two with the mainline on the left and evangelicals on the right. But as the scholarly literature on American religion has exploded, so have conventional notions about the lay of the Protestant land.

The first section of this book reflects this change in the understanding of evangelicalism and examines the diversity of institutions and theology in evangelical theological education. It should go without saying that this would make for a very long book to cover all of the variety of evangelical theological education. In other words, what follows is a sampler. Nevertheless, no matter how selective, the chapters in this part make the helpful reminder that when making generalizations about evangelical theological education we need to remember that many of the seminaries associated with the movement have peculiar stories, reflecting unique ecclesiastical circumstances, specific doctrinal struggles, and particular stages in the evolution of seminary education. While some observers of the seminary world today express concern about the number of theological institutions, especially in the light of scarce resources, the diversity of evangelical seminaries serves notice that theology and beliefs have mattered to American evangelicals. To an outsider, one particular seminary may appear to be providing the exact same education as another theological institution one hundred miles away. But the convictions that these schools inculcate and the histories they represent usually disprove the appearance of similarity. Indeed, by highlighting the diversity within the world of evangelical theological education, this book merely extends to the whole of evangelical seminaries what Glenn Miller wrote of antebellum American theological education, that evangelicals believe "doctrinal differences to be eternally significant."[1]

In the first chapter, Timothy George provides a survey of Baptist theological education, both North and South. While George highlights some of the unique features of Baptist seminaries, which stem from Baptist convictions, his essay also serves as a helpful commentary on the difficulties confronting all seminaries that seek to be culturally relevant and theologically faithful. Russell E. Richey also surveys the development of Methodist theological education and the doctrinal distinctives that prompted this history. But at the same time, he explores the variety of ways that Methodists prepared individuals for ministry and reminds us that formal instruction in a classroom is not the only aspect of theological education. In the next chapter, Melvin E. Dieter explores the history of theological education in the Holiness tradition, and in the process highlights a perennial tension within evangelical theological education more generally. Repeatedly, evangelicals have established schools as a means of protesting developments in existing church bodies and of calling for greater faithfulness. But these institutions eventually face the task of consolidating and perpetuating a given set of convictions and thus move from a posture of reform to one of maintenance. Dieter illustrates well how the Holiness tradition has negotiated these sometimes conflicting goals. Finally, Gary Scott Smith compares theological education within the Methodist and Presbyterian traditions at a time when theological modernism grew to prominence. Presbyterians and Methodists, he argues, responded differently to the new theological developments in large measure because of different conceptions of the ministry and of preparations for it. His chapter confirms the larger point of the book, namely, that theology matters.

---

1. Glenn T. Miller, *Piety and Intellect: The Aims and Purposes of Ante-Bellum Theological Education* (Atlanta: Scholars Press, 1990), 21.

The Baptist Tradition

Timothy George

From 1825, when the first Baptist seminary in America was established at Newton Centre, Massachusetts, until 1925 when fundamentalist Baptists founded Eastern Seminary in Philadelphia, Baptists in America grew from a small band of churches clustered mainly along the East Coast into a major religious body comprising the second largest grouping of Protestant Christians in America.[1] This century of advance witnessed not only the proliferation, but also the diversification of the Baptist tradition, including the influx of immigrant Baptist churches, the emergence of distinctive denominational structures among African American Baptists, and a major fissure between white Baptists of the North and South.[2] Baptists are congregationalists in polity, which means that each local church is responsible under God for establishing its own criteria for calling and training its pastoral leadership. However, despite the leveling effect of such a polity, and what might be called the fissiparous principle of Baptist history ("We multiply by dividing"), by the early twentieth century Baptists in America had entered the evangelical mainstream of Protestant church life, sharing fully the robust optimism of the age. This was due in no small measure to the development of an impressive program of theological education designed to produce a core of denominational elites equipped to further the interests of the Baptist cause in all realms of Christian activity. Yet, beneath the surface there were strains and cracks in the Baptist system, many of them related to the very structures of theological education, which could rightly be credited for much of the

1. See the collaborative volume *Baptist Advance* (Nashville: Broadman Press, 1964).
2. See Donnell R. Harris, "The Gradual Separation of Southern and Northern Baptists, 1845–1907," *Foundations* 7 (1964): 130–44. For an earlier assessment, see Robert A. Baker, *Relations Between Northern and Southern Baptists* (Nashville: Broadman Press, 1948).

Baptist success. While Southern Baptists and Northern Baptists would negotiate the minefield of modernity differently, neither would be able to escape
its impact as a defining impetus in denominational life. However, the tensions that were to disrupt Baptist life in the twentieth century were already
present in the development of a distinctive model of theological education in
the nineteenth century.

The purpose of this paper is to provide an overview of two major tensions,
each of which has important implications not only for understanding past
events, but also for forging a viable Baptist evangelicalism in theological education today. First, we shall examine the relation of pastoral calling and academic preparation for ministry; then, we shall consider the role of the seminaries as nurseries of piety or seedbeds of heresy; and, finally, we shall see
how the content of theological education has been shaped by forces and values often at odds with historic Baptist traditions.

Pastoral Calling and the Lure of the Academy

Modern historians have isolated two separable beginnings of the Baptist
movement in seventeenth-century England: The General Baptists who
evolved out of the church planted by Thomas Helwys at Spitalfields near
London in 1612, which was an offshoot of the rebaptized, exiled congregation of John Smyth; and the Particular Baptists, who arose among the underground London congregations of the 1630s.[3] The Particulars, who were Calvinistic in theology, were better educated, better organized, and more
successful than their Arminian cousins, the General Baptists, who were
drawn into the orbit of that "swarm of sectaries and sysmatics," as John Taylor put it, which included Levellers, Ranters, Seekers, Quakers, and, at the
fag end of the Puritan movement, the mysterious Family of Love.[4] In the
eighteenth century, many of the General Baptists, along with English Presbyterians, were swept into the resurgent Unitarianism of the times.[5]

For all their differences, though, both General and Particular Baptists
were nonconformists. Long after the 1689 Act of Toleration granted statu-
tory freedom of worship, Baptists, along with other dissenters, suffered ha-
rassment, discrimination, and ridicule. One critic labeled them as "miscre-

---

3. Older historians tended to blur the distinct origins of these two Baptist streams. Thus John
Marshman wrote, "They early fell into contention upon points of doctrine and split in 1611 into great
parties, called the *particular* and the *general* Baptists," *An Epitome of General Ecclesiastical History*
(New York: J. Tilden and Co., 1847), 408. A more accurate reconstruction is given in H. Leon Mc-
Beth, *The Baptist Heritage* (Nashville: Broadman, 1987), 21–63. See also the recent studies by Murray
Tolmie, *The Triumph of the Saints: The Separate Churches of London, 1616–1649* (Cambridge: Cam-
bridge University Press, 1977), and James Robert Coggins, *John Smyth's Congregation* (Scottdale,
Penn.: Herald Press, 1991).

4. Quoted, Michael Watts, *The Dissenters* (Oxford: Clarendon Press, 1978), 83.

5. See Raymond Brown, *The English Baptists of the Eighteenth Century* (London: The Baptist
Historical Society, 1986).

ants begat in rebellion, born in sedition, and nursed in faction."[6] Excluded by law from the English universities, Baptists were forced to develop informal structures for pastoral training. These included both the formation of academies, the most notable of which was the Bristol Baptist College founded in 1679, and what we might call a system of "pastoral home schooling," whereby a promising young minister would live and study as an apprentice with a seasoned pastor of repute.[7] The Baptist struggle for religious liberty continued in America where Obadiah Holmes was publicly beaten on the streets of Danvers, Massachusetts, and John Leland was clapped up in a Virginia jail.

The rise of formal institutions of theological education among Baptists in America must be seen in the context of the low esteem in which Baptist folk were generally held in the early nineteenth century. David Benedict was an alumnus of Brown University, the first college established by Baptists in America (1764); he also served as secretary of the Education Society of the Warren Baptist Association in Rhode Island. In the early nineteenth century he traveled through all seventeen states of the new nation collecting historical information and impressions about the Baptists. One person, "a very honest and candid old lady," gave Benedict the following impression she had formed of the Baptists:

> There was a company of them in the back part of our town, and an outlandish sort of people they certainly were. . . . You could hardly find one among them but what was deformed in some way or other. Some of them were hair-lipped, others were bleary-eyed, or hump-backed, or bowlegged, or clump-footed; hardly any of them looked like other people. But they were all strong for plunging, and let their poor ignorant children run wild, and never had the seal of the covenant put on them.[8]

While such a caricature may tell us more about the "candid old lady" Benedict interviewed than the Baptists she deplored, the fact is that Baptists did appeal, especially on the frontier, to those who were far removed from the benefits of education and civility. Peter Cartwright, himself a firebrand of the Methodist variety, had little use for the "proselytizing Baptist" preachers who, as he said, made so much ado about baptism by immersion that you

6. Henry Sacheverell, *The Perils of False Brethren* (London, 1709), 36.
7. On the Bristol Academy, see Norman S. Moon, *Education for Ministry: Bristol Baptist College, 1679–1979* (Bristol: Bristol Baptist College, 1979). On the tradition of "home schooling" for Baptist pastors in colonial America, see William H. Brackney, "Nurseries of Piety or the School of Christ?: Means and Models of Baptist Ministerial Education in Early America," *Faith, Life, and Witness: The Papers of the Study and Research Division of the Baptist World Alliance*, ed. William H. Brackney (Birmingham: Samford University Press, 1990). Invaluable for any study of theological education in this period is Glenn T. Miller's magisterial work, *Piety and Intellect: The Aims and Purpose of Antebellum Theological Education* (Atlanta: Scholars Press, 1990).
8. David Benedict, *Fifty Years Among the Baptists* (New York: Sheldon and Co., 1860), 93–94.

would think "that heaven was an island, and there was no way to get there but by *diving or swimming.*" Still, he admired the ability of the Baptist preachers to appeal to the masses, observing that "our Western people want a preacher that can mount a stump, a block, or old log, or stand in the bed of a wagon, and without note or manuscript, quote, expound, and apply the Word of God to the hearts and consciences of the people."[9] What formal education had to do with this kind of effectiveness was not at all apparent to many Baptists during the era of the Great Awakening. Thus, in 1795 Isaac Backus published a list of all of the Baptist ministers in New England. Of the 232 enumerated, only 13 had degrees attached to their names.[10] When the Strawberry Association in Virginia was organized in 1776, it welcomed into fellowship a minister named James Reed who was illiterate, and another, a certain Dutton Lowe, whom Robert Semple described as "not a man of much learning, but having a strong constitution, a loud voice, and a fervent spirit, [who] did great things in the name of the Holy Child Jesus."[11]

Baptist resistance to formalized structures of theological education, however, reflected not only a nonconformist legacy of political disenfranchisement and native traditions of populism and anti-intellectualism, but also a pungent theological concern. In his *Ecclesiastical Ordinances* of 1541, John Calvin had declared that no one was to enter upon the pastoral office without a calling, in order that nothing happened confusedly in the church.[12] The same sentiment had been repeated by New England Congregationalists in the *Cambridge Platform* of 1648 which declared that "no man may take the honor of a church office unto himself, but he that was called of God, as was Aaron."[13] Baptists, along with other Protestants in the Reformed tradition, believed that the pastoral calling involved both a secret, inward work of the Holy Spirit in the heart of the minister, as well as an outward, external approbation by the visible church. Gilbert Tennent's famous sermon on "The Danger of an Unconverted Ministry" had alerted many evangelicals to the problem of emphasizing the external, official call to the neglect of the personal, inner one. Baptists, along with others who were touched by the fires of awakening, resonated with Tennent's denunciation of "Pharisee–Teachers" who were "letter–learned" but unconverted, having had no experience

9. Quoted, Sidney E. Mead, "The Rise of the Evangelical Conception of the Ministry in America (1607–1850)," *The Ministry and Historical Perspectives*, eds. H. Richard Niebuhr and Daniel B. Williams (New York: Harper and Brothers, 1956), 246, 239.

10. Isaac Backus, *A History of New England With Reference to the Denomination Called Baptist* (Boston, 1781), 3:93.

11. Minutes of the Strawberry Baptist Association, 15. Quoted, Charles Allison Weed, "American Baptists and an Educated Ministry Prior to 1850" (Th.M. thesis, Crozer Theological Seminary, 1935), 58.

12. Calvin, *Theological Treatises*, ed. J. K. S. Reid (Philadelphia: Westminster Press, 1954), 58.

13. *Creeds and Platforms of Congregationalism*, ed. Williston Walker (Philadelphia: Pilgrim Press, 1969), 214.

of a special work of the Holy Ghost on their own souls." "Is a blind man fit to be a guide in a very dangerous way? Is a dead man fit to bring others to life? A mad man fit to give counsel in a matter of life and death? . . . Is an ignorant rustic, that has never been at sea in his life, fit to be a pilot, to keep vessels from being dashed to pieces upon rocks and sand-banks?"[14]

While Tennent emphasized the danger of an *unconverted* ministry, Baptists were just as wary of a converted, but *uncalled*, ministry. Thus in setting forth a plan for a literary and theological institution in New England, Jonathan Going, a leading Baptist educational strategist, emphasized evidence of "renovating grace of God" as the most basic criterion for ministerial candidacy. But beyond that, he continued, "it has ever been a distinguishing sentiment in the Baptist denomination, that a man must be divinely called to this work by the secret eternal impulse of the Holy Ghost. This sentiment should never be relinquished. Its abandonment would eventually introduce a lifeless ministry—the course and scourge of the church, the coadjutor and triumph of error and infidelity."[15]

A decade earlier Baptists of Roanoke Association in Virginia published a circular letter defending themselves against the charge of a local Presbyterian minister who was spreading the word that Baptists considered human learning of no use. While denying the charge as slanderous, these Virginia Baptists rejected as even more absurd the proposition that:

> A man of gifts and grace, who has the dispensation of the gospel committed to him, cannot be qualified for the work, until he has gone the round of academic studies—obtained a smattering of Greek and Latin—of Euclid and Algebra—navigation and surveying—then constituted a Master of Arts—and studied divinity six months or a year.

Then, with a touch of prophetic warning, they added:

> Should the period ever arrive in which Baptist churches should confine the ministry to college men only, then transmigration will be rapid, and other churches will be formed from them, as they have been built up from all others who have adopted this practice.[16]

Despite such hesitations and tensions, the Baptist educational juggernaut could not be stopped. Undaunted by the difficulties, leaders such as Richard Furman, Luther Rice, Jonathan Going, and William Staughton held before

14. M. W. Armstrong, ed., *The Presbyterian Enterprise* (Philadelphia: Westminster Press, 1956), 40–44.

15. Jonathan Going, *Outline of a Plan for Establishing a Baptist Literary and Theological Institution in a Central Situation in New England* (Boston, 1819). Reprinted in *Andover Newton Quarterly* 16 (1976): 173–87.

16. David Benedict, *A History of Baptists in America* (Philadelphia, 1813), 2:462.

Baptists the ideal of a learned ministry, which they promoted through lending libraries, educational societies, pastoral aid funds, and widow-mites societies. Staughton was a personal friend of William Carey and in his inaugural address as president of the ill-fated Columbian College in Washington, D.C., he linked the necessity of ministerial education to the worldwide missionary enterprise:

> In the present age, when missionaries are passing into almost every region of the earth, it is evident that, to enable them with greater facility to acquire new languages, and to translate the Scriptures from the original text, a sound and extensive education is not only desirable but necessary. . . .[17]

As pastor of Philadelphia's first Baptist church, Staughton had earlier summed up the sentiment which guided the Baptist educational reform movement in the first half of the nineteenth century:

> An ignorant person can no more feed the church of God with knowledge and understanding than can a shepherd his flock by leading them through a desert which has only here and there a shrub.[18]

With what Sidney Mead once called "a genius for improvisation," along with a double measure of holy grit, Staughton and his friends forged a pattern of denomination building based on the symbiosis of missions and education.[19] (Staughton's student and protégé, John Mason Peck, embodied this emphasis among the next generation of Baptist leaders.) However, the ambiguity between pastoral calling and academic training was not removed but, if anything, deepened during this period. What Glenn Miller has called "the moment of truth" came in 1853 in a famous exchange between Francis Wayland and Barnas Sears, two leading educators among Baptists of the day.

The occasion was the opening convocation of Rochester Theological Seminary. Wayland, long-time president of Brown University, delivered a three-hour message on "The Apostolic Ministry" in which he deplored the tendency of seminaries to widen the gulf between clergy and laity by training a small elite of denominational leaders rather than serving the greater, more practical needs of their vast constituency. Wayland's speech was a plea for the democratization of the church and the seminary in the interest of an aggressive evangelical renewal. Sears, a former president of Newton Seminary and, much to Wayland's dismay, his own successor as president of Brown, offered a stinging rebuttal to Wayland's position. Advanced ministerial edu-

---

17. Edward C. Starr, "William Staughton," *The Chronicle* (October, 1949). Quoted in Robert G. Torbet, "Baptist Theological Education: An Historical Survey," *Foundations* 6 (1953): 315.
18. Minutes of the Philadelphia Baptist Association, *1707–1807*, 444.
19. Mead, "The Rise of the Evangelical Conception," 210.

cation was necessary, he averred, because of the "peculiar ministerial call" which did distinguish a pastoral leader from "a private member of the church." Uneducated ministers, he warned, will not be called on to assist in the salvation of the nation. More important, the orthodox, intellectual traditions of the Reformation can only be defended by those who have been well trained in the Christian apologetic.[20] Both Wayland and Sears reflected common fears and aspirations about Baptist theological education. Significantly, both men sensed an encroaching danger from abroad. Wayland feared that the influx of Catholic immigrants, especially from Ireland, would reduce the liberties and marginalize the interests of Protestants in America. Sears, on the other hand, was one of the few Baptists who had studied in Germany at that time and warned against the increasing influence of German scholarship and Enlightenment ideology on traditional Baptist theological principles. Wayland wanted a revived and educated Baptist laity to convert or at least hold in check the papal hordes; Sears desired a cadre of pastor–theologians to ward off the German intellectual menace.

The survival and success of Baptist theological seminaries in the latter half of the nineteenth century reflects the spread of general education among Baptists, as well as the growth of denominational consciousness and an increasing need for a definite apologetic. Alexander Campbell, a sometime Baptist and lifelong opponent of theological seminaries, looked back on these developments and observed, "The Baptists too have got their schools, their colleges, and their Gamaliels too—and by the magic of these marks of the beast, they claim homage and respect, and dispute in high places with those very rabbis whose fathers were wont to grin at their fathers."[21] In decades to come, the very success of the institutions Campbell decried would place them center stage in a fierce struggle for Baptist identity in an increasingly diverse denomination.

Nurseries of Piety or Seedbeds of Heresy?

Three years after the Wayland–Sears debate at Rochester, one of Wayland's former students, James Petigru Boyce, stood to deliver his inaugural address before the board of trustees of Furman University in Greenville, South Carolina. This address became the "Magna Carta" of theological education among Southern Baptists and led to the founding of the first Baptist seminary in the South in 1859.[22] Boyce's first change was in line with Wayland's egalitarianism. He proposed that two-thirds of the student body in the theologi-

---

20. See Kenneth R. M. Short, "Baptist Training for the Ministry: The Barnas Sears Debate of 1853," *Foundations* 11 (1968): 227–34, and Miller, *Piety and Intellect*, 327–30.
21. *Millennial Harbinger*, 1:15.
22. Boyce's address is reprinted in *James Petigru Boyce: Selected Writings*, ed. Timothy George (Nashville: Broadman Press, 1989), 30–59.

cal seminary be comprised of those who had indeed been called to preach, but lacked the benefits of classical preparation. Boyce hoped that the experience of students from diverse backgrounds mingling together in a common community of learning and piety would engender mutual respect and lessen the jealousies and resentments a more elitist approach to theological education might exacerbate. Behind this change lay a fundamental principle that Baptist educators, North and South, would grapple with over the next generation: theological seminaries exist to serve the churches, and not vice versa.

If Boyce agreed with Wayland's protest against the detachment and ineffectiveness of current models of theological education, he sided with Sears in his concern for well-trained pastor-theologians who could engage the intellectual challenges of the times. Thus his second ideal was equally important: the establishment of an advanced program of theological study, which in its academic rigor would be on a par with the kind of instruction he himself had received as a student of Charles Hodge at Princeton. The seminary should prepare "a band of scholars," trained for original research, committed to accurate scholarship, capable of contributing significantly to the theological life of the church by their teaching and writing, as well as by their preaching and witness in the world. How could one institution embody the ideals of both openness and excellence? To solve this problem, Boyce's colleague, John A. Broadus, devised a curriculum based on the elective system that Thomas Jefferson had drawn up for the University of Virginia.[23]

In order to provide continuity and direction for the future, Boyce proposed yet a third change in theological education: the seminary should be established on a set of doctrinal principles to which every faculty member would conscientiously subscribe, agreeing to teach in accordance with, and not contrary to, the same. Neither Newton Theological Institute (1825), nor indeed the Southern Baptist Convention (1845), had adopted an explicit confessional standard. Many Baptists still carried painful memories of religious persecution carried out by established churches using state-imposed creeds and thus were suspicious of how such statements might be used. More recently still, Alexander Campbell had dissuaded many Baptists from their historic confessional commitments by raising the cry of "No creed but the Bible!" Over against these objections, Boyce argued that voluntary, conscientious adherence to an explicit doctrinal standard was deeply rooted in the Baptist heritage and, moreover, was necessary to protect the seminary from dangers both to the right and the left. In particular, he spoke against the "blasphemous doctrines" of Theodore Parker, who had denied that Christianity was based on a special revelation of God. At the same time, he was also concerned about populist theologies in the South, and specifically

23. For a description of this pedagogical approach, see William A. Mueller, *A History of Southern Baptist Seminary* (Nashville: Broadman Press, 1959), 112–18.

warned against the "twin errors of Campbellism and Arminianism."[24] The specific confession adopted by Southern Seminary, the Abstract of Principles, was modeled on the Philadelphia Confession of Faith which, in turn, was a Baptist adaptation of the Westminster Confession. While not as explicitly Calvinistic as these earlier documents, it nonetheless places Southern Seminary squarely within the Reformed Baptist tradition.[25]

From 1859 until 1907, when Southwestern Baptist Theological Seminary was founded in Texas, Southern Seminary remained the only theological institution supported by Baptists in the South. During these decades, Southern Seminary sustained two major controversies, one generated by an indigenous populism on the right, the other by an incipient liberalism on the left. The danger Boyce and the founders had feared from the Cambellite and Arminianian movements never materialized, those religious energies being diverted into other channels. However, among Southern Baptists themselves, a powerful grassroots reaction, known as the Landmark Movement, threatened to undermine the fragile missionary and educational structures of the young denomination. Led by a powerful orator named John R. Graves, the Landmarkers preached a gospel of Baptist exclusivism, based on the principles of radical congregationalism. In particular, they staunchly opposed alien immersion, intercommunion, and pulpit affiliation, all of which they felt weakened the claims for Baptist successionism, that is, the idea of a pure, unbroken lineage of true Baptist churches stretching back across the centuries to Jesus, John the Baptist, and the Jordan River.

The Abstract of Principles had been loudly silent on the Landmark distinctives, which were never a test of fellowship within the seminary itself. Although Boyce was personally opposed to alien immersion, he defended the right of his colleague, William Williams, to teach to the contrary, since both views were acceptable within the commonly agreed upon confessional standard.[26] The highwater mark of the Landmark attack on the seminary came near the end of the century with the pressured resignation of President William Heth Whitsitt in 1899. Whitsitt's reconstruction of Baptist history was in flat contradiction to the Landmark theory. However, in accepting his resignation, the board of trustees affirmed his loyalty to historic Baptist beliefs, leading a later historian to claim that in this controversy the seminary "lost

---

24. See Timothy George, "Systematic Theology at Southern Seminary," *Review and Expositor* 82 (1985): 33.

25. On this theme, see Mark E. Dever, "Representative Aspects of the Theologies of John L. Dagg and James P. Boyce: Reformed Theology and Southern Baptists" (Th.M. thesis, Southern Baptist Theological Seminary, 1987), and W. Wiley Richards, *Winds of Doctrine: The Origin and Development of Southern Baptist Theology* (New York: University Press of America, 1991).

26. See, for example, the following letter of James P. Boyce to John A. Broadus: "I am anxious for Williams to go to Mississippi. If they should treat him badly I shall be sorry on his account and theirs, but it will help us. Soul liberty is worth more than alien immersion, even with Landmarkers." Quoted, Mueller, *History,* 105.

its president, but did not lose its soul."[27] Shortly after this episode, many Landmarkers left the SBC to form their own separate denomination. Had the Landmarkers succeeded, Baptist educators could not have played such a prominent role in the developing evangelical interdenominational coalition of the early twentieth century. More importantly, the Landmark issue forced the seminary to make a distinction between doctrinal views that fell within the range of tolerable diversity and others which clearly undermined confidence in the essential evangelical commitment of the school.[28]

The latter issue was brought to the fore in the controversy surrounding Crawford Howell Toy, a member of the seminary's first graduating class and a distinguished professor of Old Testament there for ten years.[29] Upon joining the faculty in 1869, Toy had declared: "The Bible, its real assertions being known, is in every iota of its substance absolutely and infallibly true."[30] Over the years, however, Toy gradually moved away from this position as he came more and more under the influence of Darwinian evolutionism and the theory of pentateuchal criticism advanced by the German scholars, Kuenen and Wellhausen. Enamored by the theories of progressive scholarship he had imbibed in Germany, Toy came to deny that many of the events recorded in the Old Testament had actually occurred. Moreover, he also questioned the christological implications of many messianic prophesies including Isaiah 53. After a long and painful struggle, Toy tendered his resignation in 1879, acknowledging that it has "become apparent to me that my views of inspiration differ considerably from those of the body of my breth-

---

27. W. W. Barnes, *The Southern Baptist Convention, 1845–1953* (Nashville: Broadman Press, 1954), 138. In his farewell address as president of Southern Seminary, Whitsitt urged his colleagues to maintain "the fundamental Baptist doctrine of the universal church." See "Dr. Whitsitt's Farewell Address," *Seminary Magazine* 12 (May, 1899): 424–26. When Mullins was attacked by Landmarkers several years later, he defended Whitsitt's view as consonant with the Abstract of Principles, the Philadelphia Confession of Faith, and other historic Baptist documents. See E. Y. Mullins, "President Mullins Interviewed: About the Spiritual Church," *Baptist Argus* (Jan. 22, 1903).

28. Roger Finke and Rodney Stark have interpreted Whitsitt's disagreement with Landmark historiography as analogous to Toy's acceptance of higher critical views of Scripture. In their view, "When the Landmarkians forced Whitsitt out of Southern Seminary, they were trying to reverse a real trend toward secularization and thereby to invade the faith that overtook the Methodists and the Northern Baptists." However, this analysis ignores the fact that Landmark distinctives were never included, but rather were deliberately excluded, from the confessional commitment of the school. While the political furor over the Whitsitt matter may well have contributed to a growing suspicion and resentment by many grassroots Southern Baptists against the seminary, there is no reason to suppose that Whitsitt's views on Baptist history involved a breach with the historic commitment of the school. See Finke and Stark, *The Churching of America, 1776–1990* (New Brunswick, N.J.: Rutgers University Press, 1992), 178–87.

29. On Toy, see David C. Lyon, "Crawford Howell Toy," *Harvard Theological Review* 13 (1920): 1–2; Pope Duncan, "Crawford Howell Toy: Heresy at Louisville," *American Religious Heretics,* ed. George H. Shriver (Nashville: Abingdon Press, 1966); Billy G. Hurt, "Crawford Howell Toy as Interpreter of the Old Testament" (Ph.D. dissertation, Southern Baptist Theological Seminary, 1965).

30. Crawford H. Toy, *The Claims of Biblical Interpretation on Baptists* (New York: Lang and Hillman, 1869), 13.

ren."[31] Within a year of his resignation at Southern, Toy was appointed Hancock professor of Hebrew at Harvard Divinity School, declaring that he henceforth wished "to be known as a Theist rather than a Christian."[32] Soon thereafter he affiliated with the Unitarian denomination.

The issues which led to Toy's departure from Southern Seminary and his eventual exodus from the Baptist fold entirely were, of course, common to all Protestant denominations in the late nineteenth century. Congregationalists at Andover, Presbyterians at Union, and Methodists at Boston all came to blows over the limits of critical historical methodology in biblical interpretation. The same convulsions rocked Northern Baptists as well. Two years after Toy had departed Louisville, Ezra P. Gould, a New Testament professor with fourteen years tenure at Newton Theological Institute, was dismissed for similar reasons, despite his close friendship with President Alvah Hovey. In the next decade the same scenario was repeated at Colgate Theological Seminary with the dismissal of Nathaniel Schmidt in 1896.[33] Across the sea British Baptists were involved in a major brew ha-ha of their own known as the Down Grade Controversy. The evangelical Calvinist, Charles Haddon Spurgeon, spoke for many Baptists on both sides of the Atlantic when he observed, "The modern spirit has a tendency to dry up the Scriptures, and leave them like the skins of the grapes when all the juice has been trodden out. . . . We are improving backwards. On the table of spiritual food the joints are fine in bone and scantier in meat. There are more stones in the pie, but there is less flavor in the fruit."[34]

By the end of the nineteenth century, it was clear that a major storm was brewing among Baptists in the North. The battle focused on the theological seminaries and their role in passing on the faith intact to the rising generation of Baptist ministers. In 1897 this concern surfaced at the Baptist Congress where a fierce debate raged on the topic, "Should Denominational Beliefs Impose Limitations on Religious Teachers?"[35] Professor E. B. Hulbert of the University of Chicago Divinity School noted that "diverse views are breaking our Baptist brotherhood into parties. . . . Party names are being given or assumed. 'Conservative' and 'Progressive' are beginning to be so employed. Will they fight?" he wondered. If so, he prophesied,

31. Quoted, L. Russ Bush and Tom J. Nettles, *Baptists and the Bible* (Chicago: Moody Press, 1980), 233.

32. A. H. Newman, *A History of the Baptist Churches in the United States* (New York: Charles Scribner's Sons, 1915), 519.

33. Cf. Norman H. Maring, "Baptists and Changing Views of the Bible, 1865–1918," *Foundations* 1 (1958): 57–62.

34. Quoted, Willis B. Glover, "English Baptists at the Time of the Downgrade Controversy," *Foundations* 1 (1958): 49. See also Thomas J. Sutton, "A Comparison Between the Downgrade Controversy and Tensions Over Biblical Inerrancy in the Southern Baptist Convention" (Ph.D. dissertation, Southwestern Baptist Theological Seminary, 1982).

35. *The Baptist Congress*, 1897, 74–120.

It will be a fight all along the line, among pastors, between schools, in churches, associations, conventions, national societies. It will extend to our young people, seminaries, mission fields, religious press, to all our organized denominational activities. Many will tire of the conflict and pass over to more straight-laced or liberal communions, or will try to propulgate their views by independent movements. Old and new will wage a war of extermination, and neither will live to gain the satisfaction of having destroyed each other. If other parties are to invite and keep up a satanic spirit . . . proforce, the denomination will go to the devil.[36]

Hulbert was something of a mediating figure in the conflict, but most of his other colleagues at Chicago were eager to meet modernity on its own terms, regardless of the consequences for the denomination. Chicago was still something of a frontier town in 1892 when the original Chicago Divinity School, founded in 1866, was absorbed into the newly established university headed by William Rainey Harper and funded by John D. Rockefeller. Frederick T. Gates, secretary of the American Baptist Education Commission and one of the principal organizers of the school, expressed the high hopes many Baptists held for the university, which he declared would be "an institution wholly under Baptist control as a chartered right, loyal to Christ and his church, employing none but Christians in any department of instruction; a school not only evangelical but evangelistic, seeking to bring every student into surrender to Jesus Christ as Lord."[37] Although no confessional standard was adopted, the Articles of Incorporation required that "at all times two-thirds of the trustees, and also the president of the university and of its said college, shall be members of regular Baptist churches."[38]

Yet tensions within the Baptist constituency were evident from the founding of the university. Its president-elect, William Rainey Harper, who was subjected to something of a heresy trial arising out of allegations made against him by none other than Augustus Hopkins Strong, the denomination's leading theologian and president of Rochester Theological Seminary. The rift continued to widen until the publication of George Burnham Foster's *The Finality of the Christian Religion* in 1906 led to his expulsion from the local Baptist Pastors Association.[39] Standing firm on the principle of academic freedom, the university refused to discipline Foster, transferring him instead to the department of comparative religion. As a direct result of the Foster affair, the kind of bifurcation predicted by Hulbert began to occur. In 1907 a new state

36. Eri B. Hulbert, "The Baptist Outlook," *The English Reformation and Puritanism: With Other Lectures and Addresses* (Chicago: University of Chicago Press, 1899), 441.

37. Frederick T. Gates, quoted in *Harpers University*, 24.

38. See Thomas W. Goodspeed, *The Story of the University of Chicago* (Chicago: University of Chicago Press, 1925), 32. Cf. also Robert L. Harvey, "Baptists and the University of Chicago, 1890–1894," *Foundations* 14 (1971): 240–50.

39. George Burnham Foster, *The Finality of the Christian Religion* (Chicago: University of Chicago Press, 1906). See the helpful study by Harvey Arnold, "The Death of God-'06: George Burnham Foster and the Impact of Modernity," *Foundations* 10 (1967): 331–53.

association of Illinois Baptist churches was formed, seeking to work in friendly cooperation with the Southern Baptist Convention. By 1920 this body claimed one-half of the white Baptist associations in the state.[40] In 1913 a new theological seminary was founded in Chicago to oppose the prevailing trends at the university there. Northern Baptist Theological Seminary adopted the New Hampshire Baptist Confession as the guiding confessional standard of the school, requiring annual subscription of all faculty members.[41]

In 1853 Barnas Sears had argued for the necessity of theological seminaries, which he hoped would become nurseries of evangelical piety and bastions of Baptist orthodoxy in a world which he sensed would become increasingly hostile to historic Christian verities. By the turn of the century, it seemed to many that the seminaries themselves were in need of urgent reform. The rantings of an Illinois fundamentalist named J. J. Porter are a gauge of how a great number of grassroots Baptists viewed the situation on the eve of the fundamentalist–modernist conflict. He described a typical seminary product as

> One of these mamby-pamby, limber-back, cotton-mouth, soften-handed, apologetic baptists, spelled with a little 'b' . . . these pulpit dudes with kidded hands and velveted mouths, preaching that 'unless you repent to some extent and be converted in a measure you will be damned in all probability.'[42]

More sober and balanced, but no less telling, is the judgment of historian Norman Maring, who described the prevailing consensus in the Northern Baptist seminaries around 1920 in this way:

> Eventually, a liberal theology developed in which there was a one-sided emphasis upon immanence, a minimizing of sin, an excessive optimism about human history, and a decreasing sense of the need for redemption and of the significance of the person and work of Jesus Christ. Theology tended to become naturalistic, and preaching to become moralistic.[43]

Conclusion

From Vocation to Profession

The tension between pastoral calling and professional credentialing on the one hand, and theological integrity and academic freedom on the other, con-

---

40. Charles Chaney, "The Baptist Missionary Convention of Illinois, 1904–1919" (Th.M. thesis, Southern Baptist Theological Seminary, 1962).

41. A new statement of faith was written in the 1920s which amplified but did not lessen the orthodox theological commitment of the seminary. See Donald G. Tinder, "Fundamentalist Baptists in the Northern and Western United States, 1920–1925" (Ph.D. diss., Yale University, 1969), 265–71.

42. Minutes, Illinois Baptist General Association, 1895, 44.

43. Maring, "Baptists and Changing Views," 39.

tinued to define Baptist efforts to expand and restructure their institutions of theological education in the early twentieth century. Nowhere were the issues more clearly spelled out than in a controversial essay published in *Atlantic Monthly* in 1900. The article entitled simply, "Reform in Theological Education," was written by a Congregationalist scholar, William DeWitt Hyde, who proceeded to contrast two conceptions of theology, two types of ministers, and two philosophies of theological education, all of which, as he noted, were locked in a struggle "for supremacy in all our Protestant denominations."[44]

First he characterized two competing kinds of theology: one, based on belief in God as a "supreme being beyond the clouds," an omnipotent deity whose will had been definitively declared in a supernatural revelation, who occasionally worked miracles on behalf of his favorites, and who, at a certain moment in history, had sent his Son to rescue them from their own folly. The other type of theology envisioned God "not so much as an arbitrary authority outside the world as the spirit of love and sacrifice within it." In this system Christ effected redemption by his example, salvation is restoration to the lost life of love, and heaven is "the present experience of the joys of human love and the glory of human service and sacrifice." From these contrasting theologies, Hyde continued, derived two types of ministers. The minister of the first type warns sinners to repent, points to the sufferings of Christ as the basis of pardon, and gives assurance of "abundant entrance" into heaven. On the other hand, the minister of the other type preaches a gospel of mutual goodwill and independent self-respect; he seeks to ennoble the mind and steady the will for the tasks of shaping a more humane society based on the love of God exemplified in Jesus Christ.

Now, Hyde contended, these two conceptions of theology and two types of ministers reflected two plans of theological education. The former insisted on a curriculum based on theological content, covering the subjects of Hebrew, Greek, dogmatics, church history, and homiletics. Seminaries of this sort followed the lecture method of instruction and were based on a definite creed to which professors were asked to subscribe. Seminaries of the second, Hyde's preferred type, would look very different. While some of the same subjects would still be studied, they would be pursued with a view toward contemporary application. For example, one should study the Hebrew prophets for the light they cast on problems of taxation and labor; Luther would be held up as an example of individual courage and free thought. Most of all, students should be compelled to make their own investigations and do their own thinking, rather than being indoctrinated with a body of divinity.

Hyde was not merely a visionary but a practical reformer and he suggested several steps by which seminaries could be transferred from the old basis to

44. William DeWitt Hyde, "Reform in Theological Education," *Atlantic Monthly* 85 (1900): 16–26.

the new. The first was the removal of financial aid for students, a move that would bring the ministry into line with law and medicine and discourage "the horde of idlers and degenerates" who seemed to have a special proclivity for the ministry. Under the present conditions of subsidized theological education, he lamented, "natural selection does not get a fair chance to do its wholesome work of toning up the manhood of the ministry." Further, no prescribed creed should be employed but rather the highest standards of scientific thinking and secular learning should be encouraged. Alas, Hyde conceded, most seminaries were still in the thralldom of the older system, aiming to propulgate specific views and doctrines, rather than to investigate truths. However, "the broader conceptions of theology are stealing over the world without observation, silently and gradually, as sunlight breaks upon the sleeping world at dawn. The seminaries," he said, "hold the key to the new future."

Over the next decades, Baptist seminaries tracked the outline suggested by Hyde, as the basic model of ministry shifted from vocation to profession, and the primary community of accountability from the churches to the academy. In 1912 Shailer Mathews gave voice to this change in an article on "Vocational Efficiency and the Theological Curriculum."[45] No discussion here of the older idea of pastoral calling; no, just as medical schools, law schools, dental schools, and engineering schools produced, respectively, doctors, lawyers, dentists, and engineers, so theological schools should train students to be clergymen. To do this with "efficiency," a favorite word of the Progressive Era, required a sociological rather than a theological or dogmatic conception of relation. The minister was neither primarily prophet nor priest, but rather the leader of a church. In the curriculum Mathews proposed, there would be no requirement of Greek and Hebrew. New Testament studies would focus on the teaching and character of Jesus, as opposed to his person and work. Church history would show how Christian thought had responded to the religious needs of past generations, while systematic theology would go on to develop doctrines calculated to satisfy the religious needs of the present day. While the optimism that Mathews brought to his revision of theological education has been tempered with the passing of time, his vision of ministerial preparation soon became the reigning orthodoxy in most Protestant theological seminaries and has, with some fine tunings, remained so up to the present time.

Baptist Identity and Theological Fidelity

A second consequence of the shift from the dogmatic to the pragmatic model was the privitization of Baptist theology, a process for which the theological seminaries were the primary carriers. Traditional Baptist theology

45. Shailer Mathews, "Vocational Efficiency and the Theological Curriculum," *American Journal of Theology* 16 (1912): 165–80.

was inherently communitarian: Baptist Christians bonded together as regenerated, baptized believers in a covenanted community. They shared fellowship with other believers of like precious faith through a common confession, and they were intentional about passing on the faith to the rising generation through a shared catechism. (Baptists in both the North and South published and regularly used catechisms through the 1920s. Today "Baptist catechism" sounds like an oxymoron.) With the erosion of the orthodox Baptist consensus, however, such features of historic Baptist church life fell into disuse as a new apologetic arose. Baptist "distinctives," such as the separation of church and state, the nonsacramental character of the ordinances, and the noncreedal character of confessions appeared as a litany of negative constraints displacing any positive exposition of an essential doctrinal core. (Karl Barth's reference to the pervasive influence of infant baptism among the state churches of Europe.) The appeal to individual experience and private judgment corresponded to the shift away from biblical authority and the dogmatic consensus of historic Christianity, a consensus in which Baptists had traditionally seen themselves as full participants. Winthrop S. Hudson, one of the most perceptive interpreters of Baptist history, pointed to the impact of this development on Baptist ecclesiology.

> To the extent that Baptists were to develop an apologetic for their church life during the early decades of the twentieth century, it was to be on the basis of this highly individualistic principle. It has become increasingly apparent that this principle was derived from the general cultural and religious climate of the nineteenth century rather than from any serious study of the Bible . . . the practical effect of the stress upon "soul competency" as the cardinal doctrine of Baptists was to make every man's hat his own church.[46]

Baptists in the North consistently refused to adopt a specific confession of faith, although the new conservative seminaries they spawned (Eastern, Northern, Central, and Berkley) each required faculty members to subscribe annually to a statement of faith. The turning point in the fundamentalist struggle among Northern Baptists occurred in 1922 when the convention voted to reject the New Hampshire Confession in favor of a simple affirmation of the New Testament. Similar efforts came to naught in the 1940s, resulting in the 1946 Grand Rapids "Affirmation of Faith," a general statement affirming the inspiration of the New Testament and the lordship of Christ, a statement, as one of its critics pointed out, which could have been warmly embraced by Marcion Arius or William Ellery Channing.[47]

46. Winthrop S. Hudson, ed., _Baptist Concepts of the Church_ (Valley Forge: Judson Press, 1959), 215–16.
47. Lawrence T. Slaght, "An Appraisal of the Grand Rapids 'Affirmation of Faith,'" _Foundations_ 6 (1963): 218–32.

Evangelical vitalities in the Northern Baptist Convention were channeled into the founding of new seminaries and the spawning of new denominations. The rise of an interdenominational evangelicalism after World War II owed much to leaders who had been shaped by Northern Baptist influences. Carl Henry, Harold Lindsell, E. J. Carnell, George E. Ladd, and Bernard Ramm were all Baptist evangelicals, although in each of their cases the adjective was far less important than the noun.[48] Both Henry and Linsell had taught at Northern before becoming founding faculty members at Fuller Theological Seminary. Until 1945 the charter of Gordon Divinity School required that two-thirds of its trustees be Baptists. It was said that at one time every Baptist pastor in Boston had some affiliation with Gordon.[49] Baptist evangelicals who remained in the convention found themselves fighting an uphill battle against the increasing secularization of their denomination. As late as 1984, the American Baptist churches authorized a "blue ribbon commission on Denominational Identity" to address this concern realizing, as an American Baptist leader put it, that mere pluralism and diversity "is a lousy identity."[50]

Theological education among Southern Baptists was influenced less by the fundamentalist–modernist conflict and more by the denominational pragmatism, which provided a kind of cohesion for programmatic expansion among Southern Baptists from the thirties through the seventies. In the early decades of the century Southern Baptist leaders joined Northern Baptist conservatives in protesting against the inroads of theological liberalism and uncritical ecumenism. For example, John R. Sampey of Southern Seminary addressed the Baptist Fundamentalist Congress in 1922; also, several Southern Baptist professors, including E. Y. Mullins, contributed essays to the *Fundamentalist* pamphlets. Indeed, Mullins, like his great counterpart at Rochester, A. H. Strong, became increasingly vocal about the need to reaffirm orthodox Baptist theology in the post-World War I era. In 1925, when Shailer Mathews invoked his name in support of theistic evolution in an affidavit he had provided for the Scopes trial, Mullins fired off a brusk reply denying that he had ever been an evolutionist, preferring to call himself a developmentalist. (He did not say how a Baptist developmentalist differed from a theistic evolutionist!) More to the point, Mullins led the Southern Baptist Convention to adopt its first confession of faith, The Baptist Faith and Message of 1925, and also called for Baptist professors in all educational

---

48. See the essays on Henry, Carnell, and Ramm in *Baptist Theologians*, eds. Timothy George and David S. Dockery (Nashville; Broadman Press, 1990).

49. Tinder, "Fundamentalist Baptists," 242–44.

50. Quoted, William H. Brackney, "Commonly, (though falsely) Called . . .: Reflections on the Search for Baptist Identity," in *Perspectives in Churchmanship: Essays in Honor of Robert G. Torbet*, ed. David M. Scholer (Macon, Ga.: Mercer University Press, 1986), 81.

institutions to openly declare their adherence to fundamental doctrines of the faith or else face dismissal.[51]

Despite his indubitably orthodox convictions, it might be questioned whether Mullins' own pension for pragmatism ("efficiency" was one of his favorite words too), together with his restatement of Baptist theology in terms of an experiential model deriving from the subjectivism of Schleiermacher and the psychologism of William James, did not leave Baptists vulnerable to the very doctrinal deviations Mullins deplored. In any event, Southern Baptist churches and seminaries proceeded to develop in relative isolation from the wider evangelical community. Having rejected the separatist fundamentalism of J. Frank Norris, they felt no need to seek common links with Northern evangelicals. No more pungent evidence of this development could be given than the following reaction of an SBC agency head to the press' dubbing Jimmy Carter a Southern Baptist evangelical during the 1976 presidential campaign:

> We are *not* evangelicals. That's a yankee word. They want to claim us because we are big and successful and growing every year. But we have our own traditions, our own hymns, and more students in our seminaries than they have in all of theirs put together.[52]

When ecumenical exchange did occur, it tended to be one-way traffic to the left. While Southern Baptists could boast few heretics of the caliber of George Burnham Foster, there was over time a gradual disengagement from the evangelical Baptist consensus, a fact easily obscured by the recent obsession with the single issue of inerrancy. Yet in the end, recent denominational conflict among Southern Baptists resulted not so much from theological deviation as theological vacuity fueled by spiritual amnesia and ecclesiastical myopia.

In an age of shifting denominational identities for all evangelicals, theological educators must face again the questions that have shaped our history and heritage: the issues of pastoral calling, confessional identity, theological integrity, and ecclesial accountability. In 1906 the great British Congregationalist preacher John Henry Jowett, speaking to the context of church life in his day, made a comment that remains both an indictment and a challenge for us today, "We have toyed with the light, but we have forgotten the lightening."[53]

51. E. Y. Mullins, "Dr. Mullins Denies the Truth of Dean Mathews' Affadavit," *Western Recorder* (1925). See also Mullins' Presidential Address at the 1923 Annual Session of the Southern Baptist Convention: *Annual*, SBC (1923).

52. Foy D. Valentine, quoted by Kenneth L. Woodward, John Barnes, and Laurie Lisle, "Born Again!: The Year of the Evangelicals," *Newsweek* (October 25, 1976): 76.

53. Quoted, Willis B. Glover, "English Baptists," 47.

2

The Early Methodist Episcopal Experience

Russell E. Richey

The title, "Ministerial Education," should conjure up the recent complaint of Edward Farley and others that theological education has been collapsed into the clerical paradigm.[1] "Ministerial education" indicates that this essay considers a subset of Methodist theological education, namely, those processes, relations, and institutions that prepared persons for Methodist itinerancy. It takes that focus without conceding to Farley that Methodist theological education collapses into the clerical paradigm. Indeed, it suggests that another paradigm—the seminary paradigm—bedevils analysis and that the clerical "collapse" may have to do with how scholars have isolated and portrayed Methodist education, not how it actually behaved. For Methodists, it will be argued, ministerial education belonged to the larger pattern of education in the faith, of sanctification, of the way of holiness, and theological or seminary education constituted only one of several modalities of ministerial preparation.[2]

My argument, simply put, is that there were indeed several ways in which early Methodism prepared persons for ministry; I distinguish four. The first is termed "fraternal" to capture the largely oral apprenticeship model, which trained and educated by yoking a junior itinerant to an older, by modeling, by interaction "on the road," by practicing under supervision, by conference enquiries which assessed growth and maturity. The second might well be

1. Edward Farley, *Theologia: The Fragmentation and Unity of Theological Education* (Philadelphia: Fortress Press, 1983), chap. 2 and *The Fragility of Knowledge: Theological Education in the Church and the University* (Philadelphia: Fortress Press, 1988), part II.
2. This essay will endeavor to make that point, limiting attention to the several ways in which Methodists did undertake to prepare persons for itinerant ministry, for full membership in the Methodist connection, and for ordination as elder.

called "Wesleyan" or "connectional" to suggest how preparation through a course of study respected John Wesley's precept and example, brought somewhat more serious reading into the apprenticeship, and made conferences the agent of ministerial training. The third should properly be termed "collegiate," in recognition of the importance played by the church colleges and baccalaureate studies—education of ministers side by side with those who would remain laity—in preparing generations of persons for ministry. The fourth, "seminary" denotes not all the institutions which in the early nineteenth century bore that label, but only those postbaccalaureate endeavors that modeled themselves after Andover, Princeton, and Yale and that segregated professional studies under a theological professorate.

The progress of Methodism through these four phases is a well-told tale, often related as a triumphal pilgrimage, a pilgrim's progress. In the earliest period, from 1784 to 1820, the church failed in several valiant efforts to establish a central educational institution and had to make do with informal educational procedures. Then from 1820 till about midcentury, annual conferences proceeded on their own in a two-pronged fashion: formulating a course of study for all candidates for ministry, and establishing academies and colleges to assure that their leadership would be trained under Methodist auspices. The pilgrimage culminated, so it is suggested, around midcentury with the establishment of distinct theological schools (1839–40) at Newbury, Vermont, the predecessor to Boston, in 1854 of the Garrett Biblical Institute and in 1866 of Drew Theological Seminary.[3] Towards the seminary, then, the pilgrim, the Methodist "Christian," progresses.

This retelling draws whatever distinction it possesses not in new data on one or more phases or new insight into the dynamics of their unfolding, but rather in the simple claim that the tale should not be related as pilgrim's progress at all. The four ways of doing ministerial education—fraternal, Wesleyan (connectional or conference), collegiate, and seminary—are each legitimate, indeed, important in their own right. They may have appeared in succession. However, each needs to be examined and respected for the distinctive dimension it contributed and contributes to ministerial preparation. To interpret the first three as only phases towards fulfillment in seminary or even as preparatory stages in individual ministerial development is to miss the very different ways in which each construes and undertakes the educational process. It is also to lose sight of the fact that the first three models or patterns continued to function, indeed, continue to this day (about which more will follow). The linear, progressive schema obscures the ways the four

3. For a good illustration of this perspective, see *The Methodist Centennial Year-Book for 1884*, ed. W. H. De Puy (New York: Phillips & Hunt; Cincinnati: Walden & Stowe, 1883), 172–98. Note the recent statement, predicated on that perspective but questioning its viability, by Marjorie H. Suchocki, "A Learned Ministry?" *Quarterly Review* 13 (Summer, 1993): 3–17.

have worked readily together and construes their competition as a simple division between friend and foe of education.

Fraternal

[T]hey were like a band of brothers, having one purpose and end in view—the glory of God and the salvation of immortal souls.[4]

"Fraternal" well describes early Methodist ministry. Bound in covenant to travel, to submit to the appointive power, to accept a common wage (when it could be raised), to suffer together, to preach the Word, this fraternal order educated and trained in the same way that it worked—together on the road. William Burke, who began itinerating in the late 1780s, reported:

In the fall, at the beginning of October, brother Lowe insisted that I should accompany him round New Hope circuit. Accordingly, I arranged my business so as to make the tour of six weeks. We went on together, preaching time about, till he was taken sick and returned home, and left me to complete the round.[5]

By inviting the neophyte or prospective minister to travel along, Methodism did its theological education and preparation for ministry on the road. The individual was "on trial," learning while doing, but also under supervision and frequently traveling with an experienced itinerant, a mentor, a sage, capable of giving instruction. The pattern was well established by the first decade of the nineteenth century, linking a young person with a more experienced minister.[6] Charles Elliot described it as an apostolic plan:

4. "Autobiography of Rev. William Burke," in James B. Finley, *Sketches of Western Methodism: Biographical, Historical, and Miscellaneous,* ed. W. P. Strickland (Cincinnati: Methodist Book Concern, 1854), 58. He continued, "When the preachers met from their different and distant fields of labor, they had a feast of love and friendship; and when they parted, they wept and embraced each other as brothers beloved. Such was the spirit of primitive Methodist preachers."

5. "Autobiography of Rev. William Burke," 27. Burke registered his expectation for and value of companionship when later he lacked it: "I traveled this year alone, and had not the pleasure of seeing the face of a traveling preacher through the entire year." Finley, *Sketches,* 52. Of course, the image of the lonely itinerant drew from reality as well. Here it is captured by local preacher, Thomas S. Hinde, writing as "Theophilus Arminius" in *The Methodist Magazine* vol. V, 1822, 393:

"That the preachers suffered much in forming these new Circuits is unquestionable; having often to swim the deep and large Creeks on their horses, and to ride from twenty to thirty miles through the wilderness from one settlement to another, and not infrequently had to take up their lodgings in the woods, amidst the howling wolves and screaming panthers. It was not an uncommon occurrence for the scattered members of Society, on hearing of a preacher, to travel ten or twenty miles through the woods to invite him to come and preach at their cabin, and to mark for him a way by blazing the trees." Quoted by Wallace G. Smeltzer in *Methodism on the Headwaters of the Ohio* (Nashville: The Parthenon Press, 1951), 87.

6. "The early Methodist itinerant system functioned as a 'School of the Prophets'. Young ministers 'On Trial' were always yoked with an older and more experienced brother on one of the two-preacher, twenty-four preaching place appointments. They were required to be literate in order to be accepted, and their habits of reading, study, and personal devotions were kept under Conference oversight and

When the young or inexperienced are actually employed in preaching, under the watchcare and instruction of experienced Ministers, such as the Apostles under Christ, and Mark, Timothy, and Titus under the Apostles, we have as exact a specimen of apostolic and primitive training for the ministry as can be furnished. . . .[7]

In the traces, but in relation to other itinerants, ministers learned. The learning went on while in appointment, in riding to camp meetings and conferences, in the conferences themselves, in hearing one another preach, in counseling sessions thereafter, in coaching in spirituality—in short, in and through the operation of the Methodist connection.

The fraternal, apprenticeship style of instruction for ministry belonged to a larger pattern of Methodist teaching. Guidance, direction, counsel, discipline—the business of class and quarterly meetings—made the Methodist system a great school for growth in the Christian faith, and the life of Methodism itself an education process towards sanctification.[8] The teaching medium was Christian experience, the experienced leading the neophyte with experience being shared and experiences being related. The relational character of such learning they conveyed with familial language; they called one another brother, sister, mother, or father. Much of that sharing of experience was direct and oral. But, experience could also be conveyed in print, so realized these American sons and daughters of Wesley. Robert Roberts reported that his early tutelage in the faith involved exposure to the writings of John Fletcher and John Wesley, as well as the Bible, an instruction that preceded his formal schooling:

I had counsel, advice and prayers of the preachers, which I consider among the happiest circumstances of my early life as they took much pains with me. I began to read Fletcher's *Appeal,* Fletcher's *Checks,* and felt myself firmly established in the doctrines of the Methodists, and all that I desired to make me a Methodist was an evidence of my acceptance with God through the merits of the Redeemer.[9]

Training for ministry simply continued this process and included the reading specified as normative, Wesley's *Sermons,* his *Notes on the New Testa-*

---

guidance throughout the four years during which they qualified for Elder's ordination." Wallace Guy Smeltzer, *The History of United Methodism in Western Pennsylvania* (Nashville: Parthenon Press, 1975), 148.

7. Ibid.

8. See Glenn T. Miller, *Piety and Intellect: The Aims and Purposes of Ante-Bellum Theological Education* (Atlanta: Scholar's Press, 1990), especially 403–4. Miller portrays this period on trial in a different fashion than what is suggested here. He accents its individualistic, trial-by-error, self-knowledge, self-disciplined character and distinguishes it explicitly from genuine "apprenticeships" or from modern internships (p. 406).

9. Worth Marion Tippy, *Frontier Bishop: The Life and Times of Robert Richford Roberts* (New York: Abingdon Press, 1958), 32.

ment, the *Discipline,* which replaced Wesley's *Large Minutes* for the American church, and the hymnbook. Also important were the publications of the Methodist Book concern, in effect, the ongoing version of Wesley's *Christian Library.* Of this library, the ministers were both the students and the librarians and tutors; the dissemination of books and tracts was a central part of their business.

Illustrative of the process was the saga of James Quinn. He went as a youth of thirteen to a conference led by Asbury in Uniontown, Pennsylvania, in 1787. Several years later he was converted under two itinerants. He then apprenticed himself to, and lived with, several local preachers. He rode on his first appointment with Joseph Shane. A later assignment put him in the vicinity of several itinerants, including Enoch George (later bishop), then temporarily located, from whom he continued to learn. He says of them:

> These had all been successful and popular traveling preachers, and were considered men of first-rate talents; and, although none of them were classically educated, yet were they men of sound, well-improved mind; . . . . At the feet of these excellent men I took many useful lessons in theology; for I was more than willing to learn, and they were apt to teach.[10]

Looking back from a later day to that period before his ordination in 1803, Quinn described himself as "at that time a student of the fourth year in the Methodist theological seminary, which had its establishment in all the United States, and a few branches in the western wilds . . ."[11] He later spoke with pride of his having "had the honor of being some kind of president in Brush College for eight years, during which period I had something to do with the theological training of such men as Finley, Strange, Bigelow, Bascom, etc."[12] Quinn's editor/ biographer defended this "brush or road seminary" against midcentury detractors who favored formal theological education by comparing early Methodists to the Romans and "Washington and his brave fellows" who learned the art of war "on the toilsome march, the tented field, or battleground." "And where and how did the Methodist preachers learn to preach? By preaching." He continued and made explicit the implicit contrast of "road" training to that gained at college or seminary:

> . . . I once knew a college graduate, an A.B., thrown quite into confusion on being asked by the examining committee, "What was the object proposed by Fletcher in writing the Appeal? and what method of argument did the author

---

10. John F. Wright, *Sketches of the Life and Labors of James Quinn* (Cincinnati: Methodist Book Concern, 1851), 51, 57, 67–68.
11. Ibid., 73.
12. Ibid., 263.

pursue?" But the graduate of the Brush College could tell you very promptly almost everything about Fletcher and Wesley. The Bible, however, was their stronghold. They were at home here, and you seldom heard from them a lame or inappropriate quotation.[13]

The apparent effectiveness of such instruction led some early Methodists to disparage formal schooling altogether (so reported S. R. Beggs of Indiana Methodism around 1820). After serving as assistant class leader and receiving a license to preach, he proposed taking a couple of years of schooling. The Rev. James Armstrong dissuaded him. "He held that I could better receive my education and graduate in the 'Brush College,' as most of our preachers had done."[14] In similar terms, Joseph Trimble spoke retrospectively of his apprenticeship in the Ohio area, circa 1830:

> There were no Theological schools at that day, for the training of the young men of the church for the work of the ministry in the Methodist Church. Indeed, some of the fathers desired them not, believing that the circuit system, with a senior and junior preacher, proffered the best possible advantages for theological study and for training the young men of the Conference to be useful ministers of the Lord Jesus. This was my school.[15]

Course of Study

The perfection of theological study in the school of apprenticeship that Joseph Trimble experienced did not obtain universally. The New England Conference heard to that effect from its president protempore, George Pickering:

> The President addressed the Conference concerning the necessity of Preachers being diligent in their Studies and Labors.[16]

The 1816 General Conference discovered a number of grave problems affecting Methodist ministry, among them "the admission of improper persons into the itinerancy." The committee charged to examine the problems and propose remedies affirmed:

13. Ibid., 191–92. For similar patterns among German "Methodists," see "Life and Labors of John Dreisbach, Evangelical Minister and the First Presiding Elder in the Evangelical Association," R. Yeakel, *Jacob Albright and His Co-Laborers,* trans. from the German (Cleveland: Publishing House of the Evangelical Association, 1883), 185, 190, 283, 284–85, 294–95.

14. S. R. Beggs, *Pages from the Early History of the West and Northwest* (Cincinnati: Methodist Book Concern, 1868), 15.

15. Joseph M. Trimble, *Semi-centennial Address . . . Before the Ohio Conference of the Methodist Episcopal Church* (Columbus: Gazetter Steam Printing House, 1878), 11.

16. Minutes of the New England Conference of the Methodist Episcopal Church . . . 1766 to . . . 1845, 2 vols. (Typescript prepared by George Whitaker for New England Methodist Historical Society, 1912), 1815: 215.

Although a collegiate education is not, by your committee, deemed essential to a gospel ministry, yet it appears absolutely necessary for every minister of the gospel to study to show himself approved unto God, a workman that needeth not to be ashamed. Every one, therefore, who would be useful as a minister in the Church, should, to a sincere piety and laudable zeal for the salvation of souls, add an ardent desire for useful knowledge;—he should strive by every lawful means to imbue his mind with every science which is intimately connected with the doctrine of salvation by Jesus Christ, and which will enable him to understand and illustrate the sacred Scriptures.[17]

General Conference assigned to the bishops "or a committee which they may appoint in each annual conference" the duty of pointing out "a course of reading and study proper to be pursued by candidates for the ministry."[18] It fell, then, to annual conferences to take responsibility for theological content in ministerial preparation and to monitor the two-year reading course.[19] Conferences (with the bishops) became the educational system, setting the curriculum, enriching the apprenticeship to include explicit attention to the reading program, monitoring individuals' progress each year at the annual gathering, and certifying completion and theological adequacy.

The year after the General Conference mandate, the Baltimore Conference acted to implement the mandate. It spelled out doctrines on which the candidate must be familiar; prescribed knowledge of Scripture, geography, and history; and set forth the following program:

The art of conveying Ideas with ease, propriety and clearness is of great importance. The Candidate should understand the Articles of Religion, and the doctrines and discipline of the Church, to which he is to subscribe, and by which he is to be governed

1st On Divinity, a constant use of the Holy Scriptures. Wesley's Sermons— Notes—answer to Taylor—Saints Rest—Law's Serious Call—Benson's Sermons —Cokes Commentaries—Fletchers Checks—Appeal—Portrait of Saint Paul— Woods Dictionary—Newton on the Prophecies—and Wesleys Philosophy.

2nd Rollins' Ancient History, Josephus's Antiquities, with Wesleys Ecclesiastical History.

17. Nathan Bangs, *A History of The Methodist Episcopal Church,* 8th ed., 4 vols. (New York: Carlton & Porter, 1860), III, 43–47. Bangs reproduced the report of the "committee of *ways and means,* appointed to provide a more ample support of the ministry among us, to prevent locations, and the admission of improper persons into the itinerancy." All three factors bore, the committee indicated, on the intellectual caliber of the itinerancy. Inadequate salary led many of the most able to "locate" and thus necessitated the admission of those insufficiently gifted or prepared.

18. Ibid., 47. Bangs observed: "From that time forth a regular course of study has been prescribed by the bishops for those on trial in the annual conferences, to which the candidates must attend, and give satisfactory evidence of their attainments, especially in theological science, before they can be admitted into full membership as itinerant ministers" (p. 48).

19. See L. Dale Patterson, "The Ministerial Mind of American Methodism: The Course of Study for the Ministry of the Methodist Episcopal Church, the Methodist Episcopal Church, South and the Methodist Protestant Church, 1876–1920" (Ph.D. diss., Drew University, 1985).

3rd. The Rudiments of the English language, Alexander's Murray's or Webster's Grammar.

4th. Morse's Universal and Paines Geography.[20]

Thus came a specifically communal and theological journey into the four-year period of being on trial; thus, conferences joined the senior itinerant in traveling with the candidate into maturity in ministry. Conference examinations gave the program its rigor. Such examinations developed naturally out of the annual review of the characters of the ministers, an exacting process that had from the very first consumed much of the time of annual conferences.[21] To the review of character, now was added scrutiny of the individual's formal, but individualized, program of reading. On this reading program, annual conferences examined candidates. As early as 1819, the New England Conference was appointing a committee to give special assistance in that examination.[22] Something of the operation of the course of study can be discerned in the experience of the Rev. Jacob Lanius,[23] who was born in Virginia, moved as a child to Missouri, was licensed to preach in 1831, and accepted on trial by Missouri Annual Conference. Midway in that four-year process, specifically in mid–1833, Lanius began to note his reading, the first item being Volney's *Ruins.*[24] Over the next two years his reading drew frequent comments:

> Tues. 14th [Jan. 1834] I spent the morning in reading "Watson's Institutes and the Christian Advocate and onward. About noon I rode to Bro. Marrs where I spent the night in my usual employment of reading and conversation.[25]

20. Baltimore Conference Journal, Ms., 1817, 99–100. Quoted by William J. E. Apsley, "The Educational Concerns, 1816–1861," in *Those Incredible Methodists. A History of the Baltimore Conference of the United Methodist Church,* ed. Gordon Pratt Baker (Baltimore: Commission on Archives and History, Baltimore Conference, 1972), 132–33.

21. The examination process and review of character was carried out carefully by category, according to *Disciplinary* question. Here, for instance, were the actions of the 1832 Indiana Conference: admitting on trial, 91; examining those on trial, 91; examining the character of the deacons, 92; election of elders; examination of characters of elders, 93–94; cases heard of individuals who had withdrawn, 92–93; quasi trial of suspended preacher, 100. The numbers refer to the pages on which each process of examination begins in the republished version of that journal, William Warren Sweet, *Circuit-Rider Days in Indiana* (Indianapolis: W. K. Stewart Co., 1916).

22. "Geo. Pickering, E. Hedding, and M. Ruter appointed a Committee to examine the candidates for full connexion." Minutes of the New England Conference of the Methodist Episcopal Church . . . 1766 to . . . 1845, 2 vols. (Typescript prepared by George Whitaker for New England Methodist Historical Society, 1912), 271–72.

23. The Journal of The Reverend Jacob Lanius, an itinerant preacher of the Missouri Conference of the Methodist Episcopal Church from 1831 to 1851 a.d., ed. Elmer T. Clark., 1918 (manuscript in possession of his son, James A. Lanius, of Palmyra, Missouri).

24. Ibid., 8. The next book he read was Whepley's *Compend of Natural History* (noted Oct. 14, 1833, and Oct. 24); a grammar (noted Nov. 20, 1833); A. Campbell on the New Birth (noted Nov. 26, 1833). "I closed the examination of Paley's evidence which I very much admired and which I think is sufficient . . . to authoriticate the Holy Scripture" (Nov. 27, 1833), 10, 12, 17, and 18 respectively.

25. Ibid., 28. In Feb. 1834, confined by weather he noted: "During my confinement I was employed in reading Mr. Watson's View of the 'Deity of Jesus Christ,'" 38.

[Nov. 25, 1834] This evening I learned from Mosheim's Ecclesiasticale History that Infant Baptism was first derived by a branch of the Manichian Paulician Sect in the Eleventh Century.[26]

[Mar. 31, 1835] After dinner I took Dr. Mosheim's History of the Church and went to the grove and spent the remainder of the evening in reading, meditation, and prayer. We often find it necessary in this new and frontier country thus to retire because the people have but one room in the general and a fortune of children who surround us crying and hollering to such an extent as to render it impossible to read and understand and very often we are interrupted by a question or a statement from a good brother or sister which the rules of ministerial and Christian etiquette require us to attend to.[27]

[May 2, 1835] [P]assed the night with the family and Bro. Estes our class leader at this place in conversation on various subjects, reading the Masonic constitution which I had in my saddle bags, singing, prayer, sleep, etc.[28]

[Sept. 1836] [S]addle bags washed down stream. . . . My loss was about seven dollars worth of valuable books that I had bought in St. Louis.[29]

The reading program apparently succeeded. Lanius was ordained elder in September 1835.

Over the years the church made various improvements to the course.[30] One was lengthening it to encompass all of the trial years, that is making it

---

26. Ibid., 89. These entries followed: [Dec. 27, 1834] "I have just closed the perusal of Dr. Young's 'Night Thoughts' in which I found some sublime sentiments and Ideals," 100; [Jan. 12, 1835] "After spending the morning in conversation and reading at Father B's. . . ." 109.
The next day he employed an account of a death published in the *Christian Advocate and Journal* in a sermon. [Jan. 16, 1835] ". . . I spent the night in reading the Public Religious news, conversation and balmy sleep. . . . " 112.

27. Ibid., 143.

28. Ibid., 165.

29. Ibid., 276. On Dec. 25, 1836, he engaged in a disquisition on the dating of Christ's birth, expressed doubts on the 25th and made reference to Dr. Lightfoot. (Effectively the references to reading stop at Sept. 1835 when he was ordained elder.)

30. "As the Circuit System declined the pastoral oversight of the 'junior preacher' by the senior Circuit Rider was supplanted by a strengthening of the requirements of the Course of Study." Wallace Guy Smeltzer, *The History of United Methodism in Western Pennsylvania* (Nashville: Parthenon Press, 1975), 150.
A contemporary estimated this change as revolutionary:
"About a generation ago a great change occurred in the practical working of our ecclesiastical system. Through all the older and more settled portions of the Church the circuit system was generally abandoned. The gravity of this change has seldom, if ever, been duly estimated. Measured by its effects upon the whole Church, it is entitled to be designated a radical revolution.
The first and most serious result of this revolution was the practical paralysis of our whole system of ministerial training. The great theological seminary of Methodism was not indeed closed, but it received a blow equivalent to that which would be dealt to a college by abolishing its working faculty. . . .
It effectively deprived our candidates and junior ministry of the instruction, drill, and personal influence which they had been wont to receive from their senior associates upon the district and the circuit. It robbed them of the stimulus and profit of contact with superior minds, the advantages of living models, the blessed contagion of maturer character." William F. Warren, "Ministerial Education in Our Church," *Methodist Quarterly Review* 54 (April 1872): 246–67, 253.

a four-year program. Another change, doubtless motivated by somewhat varied success with the course from conference to conference, was greater standardization across the connection. That this was already happening, probably through the coordinating efforts by the bishops, can be seen in 1840 in the newly established North Carolina Conference. In organizing itself, it adopted a series of resolutions commending the New York Conference course of study and examination procedures and calling for the bishop to implement that program.[31]

At its organization, the Methodist Protestant Church had adopted a single, disciplinary course (in 1830). The same decision came in 1844, the year of the division of the Methodist Episcopal Church, so thereafter both the MEC and MECS had a single, national course. About the same time the German Methodists, the United Brethren, and Evangelical Association also created courses of study; later the Methodist Episcopal Church established them for the various language conferences that emerged in the nineteenth century.[32] Only during a later period, however, did the administration become centralized nationally. For the nineteenth century, this was a conference course.

And until the twentieth century the course was the way into ministry, normative for candidates who took a college degree, normative for candidates who received a seminary education. Only seminary graduates gained exemption from the course, that coming in 1900 for the Methodist Episcopal Church, in 1908 for the Methodist Protestant Church, and in 1914 for the Methodist Episcopal Church, South. When the three churches united in 1939, "more than half of all ministers who joined Annual Conferences on trial had no professional training in theological schools."[33] Seminary was made the normative route into ministry finally in 1956.

For much of its history, then, Methodism equipped for ministry through conference and through a course of study administered by conference and in a process in which judgments of satisfactory completion, preparation for ministry, and theological adequacy were made by the collegium of ministers.

Collegiate

Methodism undertook the founding of colleges out of various motives, including concern for education per se, aspirations for respectability, worries about denominational (Presbyterian especially) domination of educational

---

31. Minutes of The North Carolina Annual Conference, 1838–1885, 2 vols., xerox copy of original handwritten minutes, I (1840/41), 55b.
32. See J. Bruce Behney and Paul H. Eller, *The History of the Evangelical United Brethren Church*, ed. Kenneth W. Krueger (Nashville: Abingdon, 1979), 158–59, 192–93. See Gerald O. McCulloh, *Ministerial Education in the American Methodist Movement* (Nashville: United Methodist Board of Higher Education and Ministry, 1980), 11–15.
33. John O. Gross, "The Field of Education, 1865–1939," in *The History of American Methodism*, ed. Emory S. Bucke, 3 vols. (New York and Nashville: Abingdon Press, 1964), III, 201–49, 244.

institutions, fear of losing its own elite,[34] commitment to the unity of piety and learning, and desires to participate in the Christianization of American society. Also motivating the church were genuine concerns about preparation of persons for ministry and recognition that the system of apprenticeship had its faults.[35]

Enunciating such concerns, the general conference of 1820 added another motive, namely, its own mandate, by resolving "that it be, and is hereby, recommended to all the annual conferences to establish, as soon as practicable, literary institutions, under their own control. . . ."[36]

---

34. The 1834 Indiana Conference passed a resolution memorializing the legislature concerning Presbyterian control of the State College at Bloomington: "We look in its charter and read that the places of president, professors and tutors are open, soliciting capacity to occupy them without regard to religious professions, or doctrines. We then turn our eyes on the faculty from the organization of the institution up to this hour, and we see one common hue, one common religion characterize every member, as if capacity and fitness were confined to one church and one set of religious opinions." William Warren Sweet, *Circuit-Rider Days in Indiana* (Indianapolis: W. K. Stewart Co., 1916), 133.

Stephen Olin, an early president of Wesleyan University, appealed for support in an 1844 speech by conjuring up the specter of Methodism's losing its elite by forcing them no alternative but to attend other denominational schools: "[N]o Christian denomination can safely trust to others for the training of its sons. . . . history has too clearly demonstrated that, without colleges of our own, few of our sons are likely to be educated, and that only a small portion of that few are likely to be retained in our communion."

He estimated that three-quarters of those who had attended other denominational schools had been lost: "Many of them have gone to other denominations, many more have gone to the world. All were the legitimate children of the Church. They were her hope, and they should have become the crown of her rejoicing."

The danger he thought more likely was the loss of religious influence altogether: "It must not be forgotten that the years spent in college are those in which most conversions take place, and if the youth does not submit to obey the religious influences that surround him then, the danger is imminent that he will never become a Christian." "Christian Education," *The Works of Stephen Olin, D.D., LL.D., Late President of the Wesleyan University* (New York: Harper & Brothers, Publishers, 1852), II, 240–53, 249, 251, 252.

35. See especially Glenn T. Miller, *Piety and Intellect*; McCulloh, *Ministerial Education*; A. W. Cummings, *The Early Schools of Methodism* (New York: Phillips & Hunt; Cincinnati: Cranston & Stowe, 1886). Miller asserts in contradiction to the point being made here: "Methodist colleges did have one unusual feature: they did not self-consciously intend to educate candidates for the denomination's ministry. . . . For Calvinists, the college was a means to reform both church *and* nation; for the Methodists, the college was primarily a way to reform the nation. The church was already reformed" (421).

Miller then concedes that the college network stimulated the church's aspirations for a better trained ministry in a variety of ways.

In arguing that Methodists typically did not erect colleges for the purpose of ministerial preparation or structure curriculum to that end, Miller may well be correct. Nevertheless, as the colleges for the church, they did receive persons who would end up in ministry and so *de facto* found themselves playing that role. Appreciation for and substantiation of such a formative role for Wesleyan University is made, from close range, by James Mudge, in *History of the New England Conference of the Methodist Episcopal Church, 1796–1916* (Boston: Published by the Conference, 1910), 335–36. From his seat as long-time secretary of the New England Conference, Mudge noted that Wesleyan had trained much of the leadership, gradually conceding that role to Boston as the New England Conference focused more on the latter and Wesleyan gravitated more into the New York orbit.

36. Bangs, *History of The Methodist Episcopal Church*, III, 106. "The committee appointed to take into consideration the propriety of recommending to the annual conferences the establishment of seminaries of learning . . ." regretted that the cause had "not sooner claimed the attention of the General

General Conference's worries animated the Virginia conference in the 1820s. John Early, chair of the examining committee, noted marked deficiencies among candidates for the ministry in history, grammar, geography, and philosophy.[37] Out of that concern and with the prompting of General Conference to annual conferences, Virginia created a committee in 1825 to establish a "seminary of learning." The committee of twelve included John Early and seven laypersons. In its "Address to the Members and Friends of the Methodist Episcopal Church," the body set forth several aims, among them:

> Another great and noble object is contemplated in the establishment of this College or Seminary, and that is to afford young men, who give evidence of their being called by the Lord Jesus Christ to preach the Gospel, and that they possess the gifts and graces of the Holy Spirit, an opportunity to obtain important qualifications for the Ministry.[38]

John Early, the visionary who foresaw such purposes in the future Randolph-Macon, found himself well positioned to bring them to fruition. He served the school as president of the board of trustees from 1832 to 1868.

In fact, the colleges did not typically set up a distinctive ministerial track, structure their curricula for ministerial preparation, or feature biblical and theological studies.[39] Nevertheless, with no alternative theological programs, the colleges did serve that purpose and many of the future clergy did further their preparation at Randolph-Macon.[40]

The place of ministerial training in the founding and operation of Randolph-Macon needs to be underscored in counterpoint to recent interpretations which have minimized both church colleges' denominational and ministerial character. These interpretations have themselves corrected, indeed, overcorrected even earlier readings that made these colleges narrowly

---

Conference, considering the rapid improvement of society in almost every science, and the extension of our Church . . ." It went on to affirm: "Almost all seminaries of learning in our country, of much celebrity, are under the control of Calvinistic or of Hopkinsian principles, or otherwise are managed by men denying the fundamental doctrines of the gospel. If any of our people, therefore, wish to give their sons or daughters a finished education, they are under the necessity of resigning them to the management of those institutions which are more or less hostile to our views of the grand doctrines of Christianity.

Another capital defect in most seminaries of learning, your committee presumes to think, is, that experimental and practical godliness is considered only of secondary importance; whereas, in the opinion of your committee, this ought to form the most prominent feature in every literary institution. Religion and learning should mutually assist each other, and thus connect the happiness of both worlds together" (106–7).

37. James Edward Scanlon, *Randolph-Macon College. A Southern History, 1825–1967* (Charlottesville: University Press of Virginia, 1983), 15–22.

38. Ibid., 25.

39. Wesleyan made an overture to move to its campus the ministerial academy opened at Newbury, Vermont, but failed to carry through with an appointment and a theological department. See A. W. Cummings, *The Early Schools of Methodism,* 371–72.

40. Even as they prepared themselves through the course of study.

denominational and failed to recognize the wider views and significant local support with which they came into being.[41]

When established, Randolph-Macon understood its purposes to be communal and cosmopolitan, not narrowly sectarian (Methodist), a necessary stance in a Virginia still Jeffersonian, wary of religious establishments, and unwilling to charter institutions which could not serve the public trust. Randolph-Macon would then, like other early colleges, define its mission broadly, as in service to church and country,[42] structure its board to represent the community (as well as Methodism), open its doors to persons of all denominations, orient its training to the needs of the citizenry (not just persons who would eventually turn to ministry), and seek strong community support. James Scanlon observes,

> No denominational test was made for admittance or continuance (references to openness are seen as early as 1833), and not only was the student body diverse, but the Methodists were in the minority.[43]

However, Scanlon minimizes the Methodist imprint on the school and its service to the Methodist community, noting statistics for 1856, which put the Methodist presence in the school at 31 percent and the preministerial at only 9 percent.[44] But he also describes the role of the Methodist president, the Methodist majority of the trustees, the efforts made to hire a Methodist faculty, the support given the school by the Virginia, South Carolina, and Georgia Conferences, the special consideration given to the sons of ministers, the recurrent revivals at the school, and the significant eventual output of ministers.[45]

Scanlon's portrayal and his own statistics suggest a different conclusion—that the college was a very Methodist institution. In a counting of the occupations of the 210 early graduates by the Society of the Alumni, there were 48 teachers (13 of these professors); 43 clergy (12 also taught or served as school president); 39 lawyers (8 legislators); 31 farmers; and 29 physicians.[46]

41. See especially David B. Potts, *Wesleyan University, 1831–1910: Collegiate Enterprise in New England* (New Haven and London: Yale University Press, 1992).

42. See Potts, *Wesleyan University*, pp. 23 and following for the expansive, "Christian America" language and metaphor of motivation and intentionality.

43. *Randolph-Macon College*, 86.

44. He says, "No other official statements of the number of Methodists seem to exist. Godbold states that 'Fifty out of one hundred students at Randolph-Macon College in 1836 were members of the Methodist Church' but gives no authority for the figure. It may be taken as an upper limit." Scanlon, ibid., 86.

45. For a stronger and more persuasive case for the denominational and specifically Methodist ethos of such institutions, see Bradley J. Longfield, "'Denominational' Colleges in Antebellum America?: A Case Study of Presbyterians and Methodists in the South," *Reimagining Denominationalism*, eds. Robert Bruce Mullin and Russell E. Richey (New York and Oxford: Oxford University Press, 1994).

46. *Randolph-Macon College*, 56ff.

So Methodism educated its leadership; so it trained persons who did go into ministry alongside persons preparing for other professions; so it tutored its leadership in the evangelical liberal arts.[47]

Key to making the institution really Methodist and useful in preparation of the church's leadership was the president, typically a distinguished member of the clergy.[48] Stephen Olin played such roles at two of Methodism's important early institutions. He assumed the presidency of Randolph-Macon in 1833, after having taught at the University of Georgia. Olin taught mental and moral science, belles lettres and political philosophy, preached occasionally, delivered formal addresses, built a faculty, raised money, and cultivated conference support.[49] He led in a very clerical fashion, using the gifts and strengths of the ministerial office and relation, and building a national reputation for the school and himself.

After a period of ill health and European travel for curative purposes, Olin was elected to the presidency of Wesleyan University and continued the educational vision and legacy of the first president, Wilbur Fisk. In an 1845 statement on Wesleyan's behalf, Olin spoke of its graduates "as a class, such men as the Methodist Church most wants as instruments in the various departments of her work for fulfilling her great commission."[50] The statement would hold up. In its first half-century (1831–81), close to half its graduates entered the ministry, 90 percent into Methodist ministry. During this period, the percentage of Methodists among students, faculty, and trustees climbed, the student percentage from 50 percent in 1831 to over 80 percent in 1881, the faculty from 65 percent to 100 percent, the trustees from 65 percent to 90 percent.[51] Wesleyan became Methodism's first national educational institution. There much of its leadership received the kind of classical education that would equip them to make Methodism itself a full player in national life.

Elsewhere the pattern was similar. A good vantage from which to view it is Matthew Simpson's *Cyclopaedia of Methodism,* a boosterish volume, as its subtitle indicated: *Embracing Sketches of Its Rise, Progress and Present Condition, With Biographical Notices and Numerous Illustrations.*[52] Entries for the several Methodist colleges repeatedly cite their service in preparing

---

47. This tone to the program is well documented in Potts, *Wesleyan University,* 25–34.

48. Wesleyan's fourth (third if Nathan Bangs is not counted) president, Augustus Smith, was not a minister and Potts judges that he was as "a layman, poorly equipped to sustain the evangelical tone set for Wesleyan by his predecessors. Unable to use the pulpit he also lacked talent as a platform speaker." *Welseyan University,* 29.

49. *The Life and Letters of Stephen Olin,* 2 vols. (New York: Harper & Brothers, 1853), I, 153.

50. Ibid., II, 217.

51. Potts, *Wesleyan University,* 112, 107. Potts argues that Methodist schools became more denominationally self-conscious in the latter part of the century and the denomination more intent upon and successful in imprinting itself on collegiate affairs. Earlier he suggests colleges balanced community with denominational interest and influence.

52. Fifth Revised Edition (Philadelphia: Louis H. Everts, 1883).

persons for ministry. Of Augusta College, Bishop Simpson noted: "In its halls were educated many young men who became prominent both in the ministry and in the various professions of life." Of Wofford, "A goodly proportion of its graduates may be found in the ministry."[53] Simpson reported that by 1877 Ohio Wesleyan had graduated 683 "of whom nearly 200 have become ministers. Ten are missionaries in other lands."[54] Comparable statements about collegiate preparation of ministers occur for Madison College, Allegheny, Emory, McKendree, and, of course, Wesleyan.[55]

Methodists took collegiate education very seriously, and for good reason. The 1834 Indiana Conference, complaining that the Presbyterians controlled the state college at Bloomington and that their youth were "abandoning and renouncing the institution because the religion of their fathers (is but tolerated) and not domiciled," sought on the faculty "a due proportion from other religious denominations."[56] They also took various measures at that conference for secondary education, its staffing and financing. By the next year they had given up on transforming the state university and proposed the creation of Indiana Asbury University.[57]

The North Carolina Annual Conference came into being amid Methodism's collegiate frenzy, and its early sessions illustrate how central education and colleges became to denominational purposes. The conference met for its initial session on January 31, 1838. Various organizational activities went on. Commanding the preponderant attention, if the minutes are a reliable guide, was education. The conference "recommended the publication of Wesley's Christian Library." It took action to recommend Leasburg Academy "to the patronage of our people," appointed a committee of trustees "to cooperate with the existing board in the supervision of the School," made arrangements for nominating persons for five scholarships and "resolved 4th that the Bishop be requested [to] appoint Bro. Lorenzo Lea to the Leasburg Academy: which on motion was adopted." The next day it took action extending similar "patronage" to the Clemmonsville Academy, appointing "5 individuals to be elected as trustees by the present board," and charging the Salisbury presiding elder with the "duty of having the property of said academy properly secured to the trustees appointed from this Conference." In additional action, it instructed "the committee on the Leasburg and Clemmonsville Academies to report suitable persons to be elected as trustees of those academies."[58] The

53. Ibid., 70, 961.
54. Ibid., 676.
55. Ibid., 556, 26, 339, 576, 928.
56. William Warren Sweet, *Circuit-Rider Days in Indiana* (Indianapolis: W. K. Stewart Co., 1916), 132–34.
57. Ibid., 1835, 148–50.
58. Methodist Episcopal Church, South, N. C. Conference, Minutes of The North Carolina Annual Conference, 1838–1885, 2 vols., xerox copy of original handwritten minutes, Duke University, 7b, 8b, 9b–10a.

next report concerned a "female Collegiate Institute," appointed trustees, created a committee to pursue incorporation, authorized the acquisition of land (211 acres), addressed issues concerning staffing and operation, and requested that the bishop "appoint from this body an agent for the Greensboro Female Collegiate Institute." The next morning the conference heard a report by the agent of the flagship southern college, Randolph-Macon, set aside a time of prayer for this cause and requested an agent for it as well.[59] In the following years, the academies and colleges commanded similar extensive attention, the conference created a standing committee on academies, made provision for collections, and began to insist on reports.[60]

These efforts for education and successes with colleges came in the face of some indifference on the part of the Methodist faithful and open opposition on the part of some of its leadership.[61] Many of the colleges failed. But others survived and to their number would eventually be added universities. That topic brings us to the fourth style or phase of Methodist education for ministry.

Seminary

"I will not allow this opportunity to pass," wrote Stephen Olin, future president of Wesleyan, to Nathan Bangs, then president of Wesleyan, "without expressing my most deliberate conviction that the establishment of theological schools is indispensable to our future progress." That statement, made in 1839 to accompany a centenary donation, occurred in a long letter in which Olin summed up what Methodism had achieved in one hundred years and what it still needed to accomplish. Its future greatness, thought Olin, required greater support for education and specifically for theological education. This was a sentiment Olin had expressed at least ten years earlier.[62] Others were coming to the same conclusion, including key leaders like Randolph S. Foster, John Durbin, and John Dempster, and reformers like La Roy Sunderland,[63] and so Methodism, albeit belatedly, created institutions specifically for the preparation of persons for ministry. These initiatives came, Glenn Miller has suggested, without the great debate and the intense opposition that have been alleged.[64]

The first (organized in 1839–40) at Newbury, Vermont, lasted only a few years but brought to its faculty the person who would symbolize Methodist

59. Ibid., 12a–13a.
60. Minutes of The North Carolina Annual Conference, 1838–1885, 2 vols., xerox copy of original handwritten minutes, I (1840/41), (1844), 25a–26a.
61. Bangs, *History*, 107.
62. *The Life and Letters of Stephen Olin*, 2 vols. (New York: Harper & Brothers, 1853), I, 314, 146.
63. See La Roy Sunderland, "Essay on Theological Education," *Methodist Magazine and Quarterly Review* 16 (1834) and "Theological Education," 17 (1835): 204–21.
64. Miller, *Piety and Intellect*, 423–24.

theological education, John Dempster.[65] Appointed to teach theology, Dempster also did fund-raising and promotion for the institution and figured in its transformation into The Methodist General Biblical Institute and its removal to Concord, New Hampshire, where it reopened with three faculty (among them Dempster) and seven students. The school did not prosper and was again moved, as part of the centenary financial campaign of 1866, to become part of what would be Boston University. The same campaign launched another theological enterprise at Drew University in Madison, New Jersey. Dempster, meanwhile, had become instrumental in founding the second theological institution, Garrett Biblical Institute, which opened in 1854. Northwestern developed as an adjacent institution.[66]

In annexing seminary to university, these three set what would be an important Methodist pattern, a kind of institutionalization of Methodism's hymnic pair, knowledge and vital piety. Such a balance clearly informed the theological schools themselves. They would be institutions set in a university context, but very clearly oriented to church and ministry. Revivals and study, prayer meetings and ministerial service went hand in hand. Students came to school already active in ministry, under appointment and under supervision in the fraternal apprenticeship; continued ministerial service during their program; and left with their diploma, only to be subjected to the common regimen and hurdle of Methodist ministry: qualification under the standards of the course of study. (In 1883, the three seminaries of the MEC boasted a combined student population of 432. By contrast, the total number of preachers in the course of study was 2,550.)[67]

Conclusion

Seminary, like college, remained an option, an enhancement, an enrichment to ministry and ministerial preparation. Seminary complemented the course of study, some apprenticeship, and preparatory college work. So, because it shared its work with other agencies (or later incorporated such agencies into its own life), Methodist theological education acquired a distinctive character. David H. Kelsey recognizes this by making the Methodist pattern one of three distinctive styles of theological education. Kelsey distinguishes the kind of communities theological schools endeavor to be—the first, a Catholic pattern, aiming to be congregation or church, a doxological community; the second, a Reformed model, adjoining training to church through apprenticeship

65. Cummings, *The Early Schools of Methodism*, 369–72. See Dempster's *A Discourse on the Ministerial Call* (Concord, 1854) and *Lectures and Addresses*, ed. D. W. Clark (Cincinnati: Poe & Hitchcock, 1864).

66. A. W. Cummings, *The Early Schools of Methodism*, 375–95; McCulloh, *Ministerial Education*, 19–25.

67. *The Methodist Centennial Year-Book for 1884*, ed. W. H. De Puy (New York: Phillips & Hunt; Cincinnati: Walden & Stowe, 1883), 191, 198.

to adept ministers, in more self-consciously academic community; the third, peculiarly Methodist, and elaborated under circuit and course of study conditions, had the loosest, adjunctive or extension, relation to church and congregation (but a close relation to connection) and reached for missional community. So, for Methodists, he affirms "what constitutes the school community is its basic focus on equipping its students with professional ministerial skills and competencies."[68]

It had such a character, we would add, because it belonged within a fourfold pattern of Methodist ministerial education. Methodists, we conclude, did not succumb to Kelsey's clerical paradigm. More to the point, they did not, at least in the nineteenth century, succumb to the seminary paradigm. Instead, the fourfold pattern oriented ministerial candidates and ministerial education toward the larger universe of education (collegiate); toward the collegium of ministers, the church's theological community (the conference Course of Study); toward the Methodist people and the populace whom Methodists generally sought to reach, a people who would also be invited into a discipleship of apprenticeship (fraternal); and toward serious engagement with Scripture and with God in three persons, Father, Son and Holy Spirit (seminary). So Methodists embraced, however imperfectly, what Glenn Miller has termed the four covenants of theological education:

covenant with the educational world (collegiate);
covenant with the theological community (conference Course of Study);
covenant with the socio-cultural milieu (fraternal apprenticeship);
covenant with God and Christ (seminary).[69]

68. *To Understand God Truly: What's Theological About a Theological School* (Louisville: Westminster/John Knox Press, 1992), 50–56.
69. Comments made by Miller at the 1993 Wheaton (ISAE) Conference on Theological Education in the Evangelical Tradition.

3

Holiness Churches

Melvin E. Dieter

A persistent problem plagues all efforts to analyze movements: how, in the same instant, to portray adequately the integrating vision which creates, focuses, and energizes them, and yet be true to the diversity and pluralism inherent in the polycephalous elements which are equally essential to their life. The extensive history and the complex diversity represented in the Holiness movement of the nineteenth century and in the churches and religious agencies, which issued out of its ongoing life within and outside of the existing churches, exacerbate this difficulty. The major concern will be to focus on the tensions in educational philosophy within the movement created by the interaction of two persistent polarities: the one, its long life as a reform tradition within the established churches in pre- and post-Civil War America; and the other, the subsequent transfer of the major momentum of the movement into distinct Holiness churches and agencies around the turn of the century. To understand the development of theological education within the Holiness movement, one has to appreciate the movement's efforts to live, over its 150-year history, somewhere between the strong classical tradition of its Methodist, even Anglican roots[1] and its thorough immersion within the much more radical religious populism and biblical primitivism of American revivalism, with its separatism, premillennialism, and fundamentalism.

A Brief Historical Survey

The Holiness revival first came to visibility within the American churches in the 1830s. It has moved through at least five distinct stages in its subsequent 150-year development.

---

1. Glenn T. Miller, *Piety and Intellect: The Aims and Purposes of Ante-Bellum Theological Education* (Atlanta, Ga.: Scholars Press, 1990), 140–42.

The revival's first stage encompassed the pre-Civil War period. It located the incipient revival firmly within the existing churches and the prevailing revivalism common to most of them. The formation of two promotional centers gave focus to the developing movement—the one in New York City under the leadership of Methodist lay persons, Walter and Phoebe Palmer, and the other at Oberlin College under President Asa Mahan and theology professor, Charles G. Finney. This bipolarity roughly representing the Wesleyan/Arminian and the Calvinist/Reformed strains of evangelicalism within the revival has proven to be one of the most important identifying and defining characteristics of the movement.

The immediate post-Civil War period, in which a group of Methodist urban pastors organized the National Camp Meeting Association for the Promotion of Holiness, constituted the revival's second phase. Abetted by hundreds of interdenominational state, county, and local Holiness associations, the revival moved away from its informal, small-group base into the more public forum of large national and regional campmeetings. The existing mainstream denominations found it increasingly difficult to contain the heady wine of the growing movement in their ecclesiastical wineskins. By 1880 the first wave of "comeouters" was organizing new holiness churches across the United States, often shaped by innovative, even radical ecclesiologies.[2]

Continuing conflict between the movement and the established churches, especially within episcopal Methodism north and south, and the growing, loosely disciplined, increasingly populist movement dominated the final decades of the century—the third phase in the movement's development. Either by choice, or by force of ecclesiastical pressures of various kinds, the larger number of the revival's supporters separated from the existing denominations and regrouped in Holiness churches. The newly formed churches, in their basic historical or theological orientation, were a lot less different from themselves than their "mainline" neighbors believed them to be. The new "mainline" Holiness churches, such as the Church of the Nazarene, looked upon the revival as a further and, perhaps, even final step toward the perfection of the church, but always set within the continuum of traditional orthodoxy and church history.[3]

However, this reformist view of the mission of the movement was not shared by all elements of the revival. This third phase also gave birth to a

---

2. Such as the Church of God (Anderson), which sought the unity of all Christians around the belief that the experience of entire sanctification and the infilling of the Holy Spirit, as preached in the revival, would bring all believers together into one nonsectarian fellowship; or the Fort Scott, Kansas schism out of The Independent Holiness Churches of Missouri, who rejected observance of the ordinances; or the churches of The California and Arizona Holiness Association, who received into membership only those who testified to the experience of entire sanctification.

3. Smith, *Called unto Holiness: The Story of the Nazarenes, the Formative Years* (Kansas City, Mo.: Nazarene Publishing House, 1962), 203–4.

small, but persistent, radical element which understood and preached the revival's themes of holiness, divine healing, and the baptism of the Holy Spirit
out of quite a different historical hermeneutic. For them, the Holiness revival
was not a stage in the progression of the historical church, but rather was a
disjunctive eschatological event, born *de nova* of the Holy Spirit to usher in
a new "Age of the Spirit," to restore biblical, primitive Christianity, and prepare the world for the second coming of Christ.[4]

Most Holiness adherents, who were forced out of or voluntarily left their
mainstream churches, eventually gravitated to churches such as the Church
of the Nazarene, The Salvation Army, The Church of God (Anderson, Indiana), the Pilgrim Holiness Church, the Wesleyan Methodist Church, the Free
Methodist Church, and a whole host of smaller Wesleyan/Holiness denominations and agencies. A smaller segment of the revival's forces became the pi-
oneers of the Pentecostal movement which, in conjunction with its sibling,
the charismatic movement, has spread so profusely throughout all of contemporary Christianity. In subsequent history, pure sibling rivalry between
the two movements has constituted as great an obstacle to mutual dialogue
as the actual historical and theological differences between them.[5]

The fourth stage in the development of the Holiness movement—from
1900 to the end of the Second World War—was a time of institutionalization
and denomination building. Like other evangelical groups who had differed
with the established churches and eventually turned to their own resources
for survival and growth, the new Holiness churches organized their congregations around denominational institutions and structural patterns. It is this
period and the next that will receive particular attention as we discuss the
question of theological education within the movement.[6]

The fifth and final stage of the Holiness movement's development is the
period from the end of World War II to the present. Between the two world
wars, the general rules for the Holiness churches had grown increasingly restrictive, encouraged by the ultraism inherent in the Holiness message and
pressed to ever more radical reaction by the social and technological revolution following World War I. Many in the movement came to fear, however,
that these restrictive prudentials were smothering the vitality of both the
movement's spirituality and its outreach in evangelism and mission.

After World War II, small numbers of the more conservative elements
who stood by the traditional prudentials withdrew from the main movement
and gathered together in new Holiness denominations such as the Bible

4. Vinson Synan, *The Holiness-Pentecostal Movement in the United States* (Grand Rapids:
William B. Eerdmans Publishing Co., 1971), 95–116, 141–47.

5. Melvin E. Dieter, "Wesleyan-Holiness Aspects of Pentecostal Origins: As Mediated through the
Nineteenth-Century Holiness," in Vincent Synan, *Aspects of Pentecostal-Charismatic Origins* (Plain-
field, N.J.: Logos International, 1975), 57–80.

6. Timothy L. Smith, *Called Unto Holiness,* gives the best account of this transition, 122–204.

Methodists, The Pilgrim Holiness Church of New York, The Wesleyan
Methodist Church, Allegheny Conference, and other smaller groups organized and gathered together under the newly formed Interchurch Holiness
Convention in parallel pattern to the continuing support of the older Holiness bodies for the National Holiness Association now known as the Christian Holiness Association.[7]

Theological Education—The Early Years

During the movement's first fifty years, when membership in some Christian
denomination was required for Holiness association membership, there was
little to distinguish its philosophy and practice of theological education from
that of the denominations with which its adherents were affiliated. Because
of the dominance of Methodists in the movement, it tended to reflect the attitudes and practices of the larger Wesleyan churches.[8] Denominational
courses of study, upon which the Methodists especially relied to provide
some modicum of professional preparation for their ordinands, were the staple educational requirement for most of the pastors and evangelists who
shaped the teaching and preaching of the early movement. They became and
continue to be the basic requirement for ministerial certification in the
churches which affiliated with or rose out of the revival.[9] But the Holiness
movement not only reflected the developments in Methodist theological education; rather, from the earliest days of Methodist higher education and
throughout the nineteenth century, Holiness adherents were leaders in promoting Methodist theological education. La Roy Sunderland, Orange Scott,
Luther Lee, and other New England Methodists became active proponents
of the earliest efforts to establish formal theological education for New England Methodists a decade before they left episcopal Methodism to establish
the abolitionist Wesleyan Methodist Connection in 1843. In 1834 Sunderland wrote an "Essay on Theological Education," which stirred up an intense
debate on the topic within the New England Conference of the Methodist
Episcopal Church. The agitation eventually resulted in the founding of a conference academy, the forerunner of Boston Theological Seminary, later part

---

7. The most useful source for these new movements is *Profile of the Interchurch Holiness Convention: A Retrospect of Forty Years of IHC Ministry* (Salem, Ohio: IHC, 1992), compiled by H. E.
Schmul et al.

8. For an excellent analysis of Methodist theological education and the implications which the doctrine of holiness had for its formation, see Miller, *Piety and Intellect*, chap. 19, "The Logic of Holiness."

9. In its early years, the Church of God (Anderson) was the major exception to this rule. The
founder, Daniel S. Warner, and other leaders of this first organization of Holiness "comeouters" had
had some college training but were so committed to the "Church of God" concept that any attempt
to lay down a humanly generated course of study or man-made requirement for preaching the Word
was intolerable to them. It was God's right, not men's and women's, even those entirely sanctified, to
set the Church of God in order. See Barry L. Callen, *Preparing for Service: A History of Higher Education in the Church of God* (Anderson, Ind.: Warner Press, Inc., 1988), 12–15.

of Boston University.[10] Among the leaders of the first Methodists colleges—all leaders in the revival—were John Dempster, who founded the institutions that later became Garrett Biblical Institute and Boston University; Wilbur Fisk and Stephen Olin of Wesleyan University, the first successful school in Methodism; and Jesse Peck at Dickinson, who later became bishop. After the Civil War, there was Randolf S. Foster, later also a bishop, president of Garrett Biblical Institute and Drew University; Daniel Steele, one of the movement's strongest apologists within Methodism at century's end, who served as president of both Syracuse and Boston Universities. Phoebe and Walter Palmer, the most influential lay advocates for Christian perfection in the church, were actively involved in the founding of both Drew University and Garrett Biblical Institute.[11]

However, this level of involvement in early theological education within Methodism was not the only scene of action which determined the patterns and parameters for future theological education in the Holiness tradition. In lesser, but influential numbers, the early leadership of the revival spanned the whole range of options in ministerial preparation available within the American churches of the time. The Holiness theology, example, and educational philosophy of Congregationalists Asa Mahan, first president of Oberlin and later Adrian College, along with Oberlin's first theology professor and second president, Charles G. Finney, and Thomas Cogswell Upham, professor of mental philosophy at Bowdoin College, had enduring influence as well. Mahan challenged the classical curriculum then in vogue in American higher education. According to Madden and Hamilton, he supported the introduction or increased support of courses in Hebrew, psychology, anatomy, political economy, public speaking, Cowper's and Milton's poetry, sacred music, and English Bible—courses uncommon in most colleges of the time. Mahan was heavily influenced by Francis Wayland of Brown University and doubted the value of the classical curriculum then in vogue and was only challenged by Charles William Elliot at Harvard finally in 1869. Finney apparently supported Mahan in these moves and both agreed as well on the coeducational, dietary, and biracial reforms put in place in the early years of the college.[12] Finney's revivalistic theology, particularly as he expressed it in his *Lectures on Revivals of Religion*, had extensive influence on all sectors of the Holiness movement, becoming standard literature in its theological training pro-

10. Lee M. Haines, "Radical Reform and Piety: The Story of Earlier Wesleyan Methodism, 1843–1867," in Wayne E. Caldwell, ed., *Reformers and Revivalists: The History of the Wesleyan Church* (Indianapolis: Wesley Press, 1992), 72.

11. Timothy L. Smith, *Revivalism and Social Reform*, 121, 137; Charles Edward White, *The Beauty of Holiness: Phoebe Palmer as Theologian, Revivalist, Feminist and Humanitarian* (Grand Rapids: Zondervan Publishing House, 1986), 163.

12. *Semi-Centennial Souvenir, Adrian College: 1859–1909* (Adrian, Mich.: Adrian College, 1909), 3–4. Edward H. Madden and James E. Hamilton, *Freedom and Grace: The Life of Asa Mahan*, Studies in Evangelicalism, No. 3 (Metuchen, N.J.: The Scarecrow Press, 1982), 67–87.

grams.[13] Upham, whose wife had drawn him into the small-group Holiness meetings of Phoebe Palmer, was recognized in his time for the extensive use his works in mental philosophy enjoyed as texts in pre-Civil War American colleges. He is acknowledged today as one of the pioneer writers in abnormal psychology. He was better known in Holiness circles, however, for his application of these early principles to his understanding of the experience of entire sanctification.[14]

The effects of this involvement by leaders of the Holiness revival in a broad range of American religious traditions came to the fore immediately in the early development of theological education within the movement as it began to rally supporters for its cause. Almost as soon as the Wesleyans organized their new Methodist/abolitionist/Holiness denomination, they attempted to establish a denominational school and theological educational center of their own. A checkered pattern of successes and failures marked this and subsequent efforts of theirs, in common experience with their Methodist parent and much of expanding American Protestantism throughout the nineteenth century. Like other churches, their educational vision often proved to be greater than their financial resources. Of their earliest ventures, only Adrian, founded in 1848 as Leoni Theological Institute and Leoni Seminary, and Wheaton College, opened in December 1853 as Illinois Institute, survived. The former was nurtured to maturity by the Methodist Protestants and the latter by revivalistic Congregationalists when Wesleyan support waned.[15] Asa Mahan became the president of the Wesleyan's College at Adrian at its incorporation as Adrian in 1859.[16] His continuing influence in the Holiness revival bridged the bipolar Wesleyan/Calvinist elements of the movement, helping to make Oberlin an educational model for both Wheaton and Adrian and for the whole movement. Wheaton's influences on the Wesleyan Methodist connection continued almost to the end of the century through an agreement that allowed a Wesleyan to retain two professorships of theology at Wheaton and to provide advanced preparation for Wesleyan ministers under the auspices of the connection. In spite of this spate of college foundings and the continuing relationship with Wheaton and Adrian, how-

13. Charles G. Finney, *Lectures on Revivals of Religion* (Cambridge: Belknap Press of Harvard University Press, 1960). In addition to the influence of Finney's own writings, Aaron Merritt Hills wrote a life of Finney which circulated widely in the Holiness movement. *Life of Charles G. Finney* (Cincinnati: Office of God's Revivalist, 1902). Madden and Hamilton, *Freedom and Grace*, 90. Also see Miller, *Piety and Intellect*, 199ff.

14. Darius Salter, *Spirit and Intellect: Thomas Upham's Holiness Theology*, Studies in Evangelicalism, No. 7 (Methuchen, N.J..: The Scarecrow Press, 1986), xii–xiii. Frank Hugh Foster called Upham's *A Philosophical and Practical Treatise on the Will* (1834) "One of the first original and comprehensive contributions of American scholarship to modern psychology," and Salter says that Herbert W. Schneider recognized his *Outlines of Imperfect and Disordered Mental Action* (1840) as the "first full treatise on abnormal psychology written in the United States." Ibid.

15. Caldwell, ed., *Reformers and Revivalists*, 71–80.

16. Madden and Hamilton, *Freedom and Grace*, 154–55.

ever, the Wesleyan Methodists still relied on their conference courses of study as the main source of theological education for their ministers. The loss of denominational control over their two main collegiate centers had a distinct effect upon the Wesleyan's views on theological education. It discouraged further collegiate ventures of similar nature. With the loss of control of the colleges, they also lost much of the educational leadership of the young church, which stayed with the schools rather than the connection. This, too, made many of the membership suspicious of college-trained ministers. As the church became more and more involved in revivalism than reform after the Civil War, the fear of advanced theological education evidenced in many revival movements helped to retard further development in that area.

All of these early efforts, as well as the first educational efforts of The Free Methodist Church founded in 1860 (another new Methodist denomination which threw its fortunes in with the Holiness crusade from its beginnings), shaped the educational paradigm for the emerging Holiness tradition. Most of the founders of Free Methodism were persons with college training, and education was high on their agenda. Six years after the start of the denomination, B. T. Roberts began Chili Seminary, now Roberts Wesleyan College, near Rochester, New York. Other Free Methodist seminaries, similar to the conference secondary schools of other denominations, most with a special emphasis on pastoral and missionary preparation were established within the church.[17] Among the present Free Methodist colleges and universities, Spring Arbor and Seattle-Pacific University, in addition to Roberts, have their origins in such institutions. They served as the main centers for theological education in the church beyond the Course of Study stipulated by the denomination for ordination. The curriculum of Greenville College, begun in 1892 and incorporated as a collegiate institution in 1895, included a course leading to the Bachelor of Divinity degree in the curriculum of its theology department in 1895.

In summary then, in the earliest stages of the movement, the experience and philosophy of theological education of Holiness adherents lay within the classical denominational college and seminary tradition, which was common to the major Protestant denominations of the time, but open to innovations such as those modeled by the Oberlin experience and philosophy. The latter's emphasis on evangelism, coeducation, a greater openness to women's and Afro-American rights than was common to society in general, the value placed on work and practices, show up in subsequent structures of Holiness seminaries and colleges both in general and theological education.

---

17. One of the benefactors of Seattle Seminary stipulated that his gift was dependent upon the commitment of the trustees to make the institution a missionary training center, Wilson T. Hogue, *History of the Free Methodist Church of North America* (Chicago: The Free Methodist Publishing House, 1918), II:326.

Nevertheless, the philosophical and theological tensions, which emerged in future debates over theological education in the movement, were already surfacing. Finney's well-known aversion to Princeton's and others' accepted structures of theological education in his time and Oberlin's willingness to challenge the system were indicative of the willingness of revivalism to turn to alternative answers for theological education as the century progressed.[18] This active concern for theological education and the structures and means to promote it and even to reform it, which one sees in the Holiness revival over this period of fifty years, raise legitimate questions as to whether or not Richard Hofstadter was not too expansive in his indictment of Finney and others in the evangelical establishment of this period for a lack of intellectualism. He fails to see that the Holiness revival and revivalism as a whole was not only a midwestern phenomenon, but had roots as deep in the urban centers of eastern America as it did at Oberlin or other centers on the western frontier.[19]

Theological Education in the Campmeeting Churches

As the hundreds of Holiness associations began to separate or be separated from the existing churches in the final quarter of the nineteenth century, the influences of the more classical, more culturally centrist ethos of many of the denominations in which Holiness Association members had held their membership increasingly gave way to the movement's formation by the more conservative, populist, even anticultural forces inherent in late-century revivalism. But as we shall see, the adoption of the ethos, which later issued in twentieth-century fundamentalism, was never complete. The strongly conservative, traditional, Bible-centered doctrinal stance of the movement made it very sympathetic to the fundamentalist's concerns. But the ambiance of the Wesleyan-Arminian theology and practice within which its dominant elements had developed and were now largely ensconced always deterred their wholesale acceptance. Its inclination to give greater weight to the testimony of experience, rather than the test of creed to authenticate one's claims to Biblical Christianity, tended to keep the movement positioned in a mediate point of tension somewhere along the continuum between the liberal and fundamentalist polarities of the ongoing contest in the American churches.

This mediate position of the Holiness forces living between mainline and revivalistic religion, and later, as a more irenic conservatism, somewhere be-

18. Garth M. Rosell and Richard A. G. Dupuis, eds., *The Memoirs of Charles G. Finney: The Complete Restored Text* (Grand Rapids: Zondervan Publishing House, 1989) 45, 272–74; Haines, "Radical Reform and Living Piety," 73; Donald W. Dayton, *Discovering an Evangelical Heritage* (New York: Harper and Row Publishers, 1976), 39–43.

19. Hofstadter develops his thesis in his classic work, *Anti-Intellectualism in American Life* (New York: Alfred A. Knopf, 1962).

tween fighting fundamentalism and mainline liberalism, constitutes, I believe, one of the most critical interpretive factors for understanding the tradition within American religion, and especially within evangelicalism. It is particularly relevant to an understanding of the continuing underlying tensions over theological education within Holiness churches created at the turn of the century. These tensions produced a growing preference among a significant number of their constituents for alternate structures of theological education, rather than that offered by the liberal arts and graduate professional theological studies.

The rise of the Bible institute movement within revivalistic evangelicalism after 1880 set up this struggle between competing educational philosophies among Holiness people. It continues to agitate the movement to this day. With its advent, the Bible institute (or missionary institute) became the structure of choice for early theological education among the newly organized Holiness denominations, although never the exclusive choice.[20] Given its mediate position in American evangelicalism, it was almost inevitable that the Holiness movement should become a major field of contest in the long rivalry between the more focused, abbreviated, practical preparation promised by the Bible institute and the broader, more extended, curriculum of the traditional liberal arts tradition. In fact, it is a little recognized fact in the history of the Bible institute/college movement that it was Holiness movement agencies that pioneered the first Bible and missionary training institutes in America. During this period, at the same time that the movement continued to found traditional seminaries and colleges, it started and supported two of the first three Bible or missionary training institutes founded in the United States—A. B. Simpson's Missionary Training Institute in New York City (later in Nyack, N.Y.),[21] and Lucy Osborne's Union Missionary Training Institute at Niagara, N.Y. (later in Brooklyn, N.Y.).[22] Even the third and most famous of them all—Moody, in Chicago—was strongly tied to the Holiness revival. A student who was at Moody in 1900 remembered that "much was said about the 'second blessing' . . . ." He noted that all night prayer meetings were held for those who wanted to seek the experience and many claimed it.[23]

20. Virginia Lieson Brereton's *Training God's Army: The American Bible School, 1880–1940* (Bloomington, Ind.: Indiana University Press, 1990) is the only major work in print on the philosophy and history of the Bible school movement. Also, see Larry James McKinney, "An Historical Analysis of the Bible College Movement During Its Formative Years, 1882–1920" (D.Ed. diss., Temple University, 1985) and Safara Witmer, *The Bible College Story: Education with Dimension* (Manhasset, N.Y.: Channel Press, 1962).

21. Brereton, *God's Army,* xvii, 6, 79, 82. McKinney, "Bible College Movement," 115ff.

22. Lucy D. Osborne, *Heavenly Pearls Set in a Life: A Record of Experiences and Labors in America, India and Australia* (New York: Fleming H. Revell Company, 1893), 271–86. Brereton, *God's Army,* 71.

23. Brereton, *God's Army,* 5, 21–22. Brereton, "Fundamentalist Bible School," 53, quotes the memoir.

A complex of factors contributed to the readiness of many in the later nineteenth century movement to forsake the traditional patterns for theological education, which, up to the time of the formation of the first distinctively Holiness churches, had been the common experience of the revival's adherents. After 1900, at some point or other in developing its programs of theological education, every Holiness church utilized the Bible school model to establish most of its new schools. The basic issues for theological education inherent in the rise of the Bible institute/college movement cannot be limited to those commonly offered in explanation of the phenomenon. The claims that the widespread preference by revival and missionary movements for the Bible institute over the classical tradition for theological education mainly represented a basic anti-intellectual disposition among their advocates are much too superficial. Most of our discussion to this point should give some caution to pushing such arguments too far. It is true that at times, and for some among the revival's supporters, the debates between the supporters of the liberal arts and those of the Bible institute centered on those categories. John Wesley's commitments to attempt to hold together true knowledge and vital piety did not take with all his namesakes.[24] The rapid changes taking place in church-related seminaries and colleges, especially in Methodism, in the last decades of the century reinforced the latent suspicions of many pious Christians that too much learning was a threat to Christian spirituality and evangelistic zeal. Once considered bulwarks of orthodoxy and schools of piety, changing educational philosophies seemed to them to be taking these institutions closer to the world and further away from the church. Robert Chiles, the premier historian of theological transition in American Methodism notes that the years following 1890 saw "an extensive reconstruction of theology according to 'liberal' criteria. The shift signaled the end of one theological era and the beginning another. 'Liberal evangelicalism' had prevailed."[25] That all this was happening in institutions sponsored by the same churches with whom Holiness supporters were in increasing conflict fed the fires of their distrust for such educational centers and helped them turn to alternate forms of ministerial education.

The majority of Holiness adherents, then, were not expressing an anti-intellectualism in their growing rejection of the traditional patterns of theological education; rather, it was just that! They were critical of the ability of the established educational structures to service the needs of an extremely focused evangelistic/missionary movement whose revivalism increasingly

24. The writer's own father noted that the greatest regret of his life was that in 1925, as a young United Brethren pastor, he joined the Pilgrim Holiness Church, and listened too long to some of his peers who advised him that there was little value in formal education. He eventually learned differently, completed some college work, and became president of Beulah Park Bible School, one of the early schools of the Pilgrim Holiness Church. Harold D. Dieter, "Papers," in possession of the writer.

25. *Theological Transition in American Methodism: 1790–1935* (New York: Abingdon Press, 1965), 186.

failed to command their interest or respect. The Bible institute provided a more promising and pragmatic answer to the evangelistic focus and needs of the Holiness community. The earliest Holiness Bible institutes were begun to provide some modicum of education and preparation for the first missionaries for the international expansion of the Holiness tradition through the Christian and Missionary Alliance and the Holiness movement within Methodism respectively. The precedents established by A. B. Simpson and William and Lucy Osborne soon established the patterns and potential for other such structures within the movement as it began to separate from the older churches and build its own institutional life. The new educational centers quickly became essential elements in sustaining the mission and very existence of the movement. J. O. McClurkan, founder of the Bible school in Nashville, Tennessee which now is Trevecca Nazarene College wrote

The urgency of the case demands "short cut" methods in preparing for the work. Training schools, Bible institutes, etc., are springing up all over the country. Notwithstanding the criticisms hurled at these schools, they have come to stay.[26]

Another dynamic inherent in the life of the movement, which encouraged the Bible institute alternative for theological education over the classical liberal arts track, was the intense involvement of a large number of committed lay persons in the evangelistic activity of the Holiness associations. There was little opportunity for such persons to receive any further preparation for ministry in the traditional theological schools of the period.[27] The Pentecost-oriented theology which permeated every nook and cranny of the Holiness tradition in the latter half of the nineteenth century was taken seriously. The movement helped to foster increasing expectations and opportunities for lay ministry in the churches. A theology of personal vocation for every Christian had been part of Protestant theology since Luther; but a Pentecost-centered theology, closely tied to a rising commitment to a premillennial view of history within the perfectionist context of the movement, brought the divine call to a prophetic ministry to "all flesh" with an unusual intensity. Everyone was a potential recruit for evangelism and ministry. Lay men and women experienced the same sense of call and responsibility for the gospel and its promulgation which had long been the province of the ordained ministry of the denominations. Isaiah Reid, professor at one of the Nazarene's earliest schools, Deets Bible College, said that

We are at a period when there is a manifest coming of self-consciousness among the "unordained" democracy of the common people. Their sense of

---

26. J. O. McClurkan, *Chosen Vessels* (Louisville, Ky.: Pickett Publishing Company, 1901), 193.
27. Brereton makes an interesting comparison between the educational philosophy of the Bible college and that of the normal schools which were developing at the same time. *God's Army,* 56–58.

ownership instead of being owned pervades their thought. . . . The dominating of officialism has served its time and is a cast-off bearskin of the other life which the church world once lived. Holiness liberates from the Sanhedrin. It breathes the air of freedom. It can build its own house.

And it could build its own schools![28]

This broadening of the definition of ministry especially encouraged the ministry of women long before mainline Christianity accepted it after World War II. Like their mentor, Wesley, they had learned that the Holy Spirit sang in soprano, as well as in base. McClurkan noted, "We have seen uneducated, frail women, filled with the Spirit, more powerful in winning souls than half a dozen cultured doctors of divinity."[29] Regardless of what they thought about educational philosophy in general, there was little doubt in the minds of many Holiness leaders that the developing liberal tradition in ministerial education in the established denominations was part and parcel of the old, lifeless, religious wineskins which had not been able to contain the new wine of the revival.

It is not surprising that a movement which had at its core religious convictions such as those outlined above had little hope that the educational or religious culture that reigned in the established theological departments and schools of that time could prepare its young men and women for holy living and urgent evangelism. The supportive community life frequently experienced in closely-knit, family-like relationships, a common focus on the preparation for service in a clearly defined mission, and a sense of immediacy and active involvement in ministry all made for a context and ambiance of community and commitment, which had the potential for transforming life and learning in the Bible institute. At their best, they promised the personal and group reinforcements, rewards, and intense experience of education in community, which Dietrich Bonhoeffer described in his *Life Together*. For these and other more pragmatic reasons, such as the more modest resources required for their creation and support and less restrictive regulation by governmental educational agencies, the Bible school became the early school of preference for theological education among the Holiness groups who were organizing new churches at the turn of the century.

One of the most influential of the first Holiness Bible schools was God's Bible School in Cincinnati, Ohio.[30] Its founder, Martin Wells Knapp, a Methodist pastor who had cast his lot with the emerging Holiness associations, was an ardent champion of the sector of the movement, which viewed the life and mission of the church through the icon of the Pentecost event.

28. "Under the Palms," *Nazarene Messenger* (February 27, 1908): 10.
29. McClurkan, *Chosen Vessels*, 194.
30. Lloyd Raymond Day, "A History of God's Bible School in Cincinnati, 1900–1949" (unpublished M.Ed. thesis, University of Cincinnati, 1949).

Graduates were enthusiastic revivalists "on the holiness line" and "on the faith line,"[31] who started Holiness churches, schools, and mission stations across the United States and around the world. It especially influenced the development of the Pilgrim Holiness Church, the second largest of the camp-meeting churches to emerge at the end of the century. The church actually was nurtured by the constituency which Knapp had attracted through his *God's Revivalist*, the periodical which publicized his multifaceted ministries. By 1913 school and church parted institutionally, but the Bible college ethos continued to dominate the educational development of the church. A system of regional Bible schools modeled after God's Bible School became the basic theological educational centers for the Pilgrims.

But the older liberal arts tradition still persisted, even in this Holiness church which was as strongly evangelistic and missionary minded as any in the movement. Two efforts to establish liberal arts colleges, which of course also served as ministerial training centers, had hard going. Early in the church's history, the general church purchased Kingswood Holiness College in Kingswood, Kentucky to provide theological education in a broader curriculum of liberal studies than that offered in the Bible institutes already serving and supported by various sectional interests in the church. Competition from already existing Bible schools and the financial stringencies of the Great Depression finally ended the venture. Only after World War II did the church try again to rally support for a denominationally supported liberal arts institution with its potential for encouraging an alternate, more classical, seminary-oriented, ministerial education model to complement its Bible college track.[32]

To understand why the Bible school/college has largely passed from the scene in Holiness theological education today is to pick up again on the other side of the experience of the movement introduced at the beginning of this paper. In the formation of their theologies of the church and ministry, inherent tensions within the tradition, created both by historical incidence and philosophical commitments, came to the fore. The differences between those who favored a training institute over college as the better setting for theological education and those who did not were not limited to those in the movement who had left the older churches for the new Holiness denominations. Both Iva Vennard's Chicago Evangelistic Institute and John Wesley Hughes' Asbury College were supported by Holiness Methodists who had continued as a movement within the church after the separation of large numbers into

---

31. Persons "on the faith line" not only went to mission fields in response to a personal call from God, but went believing that God would supply their support by guiding spiritually sensitive Christians to help them as needed. George Mueller of Bristol orphanage fame was the model for such ministries. See A. T. Pierson, *George Mueller of Bristol* (London: Pickering and Inglis Ltd., [1899]).
32. Lee M. Haines and Paul William Thomas, *An Outline History of the Wesleyan Church*, 3d rev. ed. (Marion, Ind.: The Wesley Press, 1985), 131, 147–48.

the Holiness churches. In combination with the more radical, often anticultural thrusts of the movement as most of its adherents moved out of the regular religious establishment and into new revivalist churches, there remained a strong latent attachment to historic Methodism and other more culturally centrist traditions.

But the continuing differences of opinion on these issues is illustrated best in the institutionalizing experience of the Church of the Nazarene. Phineas Bresee and other founders of the church, which dates to the founding of the First Church of the Nazarene in 1895 in Los Angeles, were more successful in bringing together a larger number of Holiness movement leaders and adherents than anyone else. Their strong organizational thrust and aggressive evangelism quickly made them the largest of the Holiness churches. They also had attracted the largest number of mainline pastors and people into their denomination. Consequently, they enjoyed considerably more diversity in their ranks than many of the smaller Holiness churches. They turned to the Bible school model in some of their earliest educational ventures. But not all! Mainly under the leadership of Rev. A. M. Hills, a graduate of Oberlin and Yale, as well as a student of Finney, others of their early colleges were founded around the classical college, even university model. In the course of institutional amalgamation and educational development within the church, both the former and the latter eventually evolved into the regional liberal arts colleges with strong Bible departments under the control of local districts. These constituted the main centers for theological education for the church until the establishment of a general, church-controlled seminary in 1945 to join Asbury Theological Seminary, which in 1923 had become the first theological seminary to serve the movement. In addition, Anderson School of Theology, Western Evangelical Seminary, The Evangelical School of Theology and Wesley Biblical Seminary—all accredited institutions—now serve the movement.

These later developments and the general history of the movement would seem to indicate that the Holiness churches following well-established patterns for the socialization and acculturation of movements were rapidly coming full circle back into becoming mainstream, middle-class religious institutions. As the holiness movement had less need for peripatetic evangelists, such as those who created and shaped the tradition, and a greater need for pastors and administrators to serve established full-service churches in America's middle-class communities, there was less and less need for the mission-centered, movement-oriented community and curriculum of the Bible college. The broader, more culturally centrist offerings of the liberal arts tradition became more attractive.

A series of decisions concerning the ministerial educational institutions in the recent history of The Wesleyan Church demonstrate the validity of this scenario at work within a major Holiness denomination. Before the merger of the Pilgrim Holiness Church and the Wesleyan Methodist Churches, which formed the new Wesleyan Church in 1968, the Pilgrim Holiness Church had had four Bible colleges and one liberal arts institution. The Wesleyan Methodists had had four liberal arts colleges—some of which had been begun as Bible institutes or colleges—and a Canadian Bible college. Following earlier similar action by the Free Methodist Church, they also had established a Wesleyan Seminary Foundation related to Asbury Theological Seminary to encourage graduate theological education for their ministry. The educational policy of the new denomination retained the Asbury Seminary relationship and recommended the completion of the Master of Divinity curriculum as the preferred, but not required, track for readiness for ministry. At the undergraduate level it continued the two alternate tracks for theological education, which had become rooted in the history of both traditions. Through a series of mergers among the existing educational institutions, the new denomination retained four liberal arts colleges, one Bible college in the United States, and one in Canada. Subsequently, those institutions that had not been accredited with appropriate regional and professional agencies all achieved accreditation.

But in the twenty-five years since then, various factors legislated against the continuing support for the Bible college track. Setting aside problems presented by the context of trying circumstances, which plague all smaller private colleges and especially church-related institutions, much more basic forces were at work. The changing nature of the Bible college movement itself pushed it further and further toward the liberal arts in its drive for accreditation and a better position in the fierce competition for undergraduate students. On the other hand, all Wesleyan liberal arts colleges had always been required to provide strong undergraduate programs in their religion departments, which would meet the denomination's requirements for ordination. This tended to make them serve their related church as more efficient undergraduate theological centers than is common to other church-related institutions. The changing ethos within the church and its continued melding into middle-American culture added to the trends. In 1990, with all of its educational institutions under heavy financial pressures, the General Board of the church decided to close United Wesleyan College, which had been created by the merged church out of three of the former Bible colleges of the Pilgrim Holiness Church. Only one small Bible college remains in the church, Bethany Bible College, mainly serving the church in Canada. In effect, the Wesleyans had turned to the patterns which the Wesleyan Methodist arm of the merged church had begun at Wheaton and Adrian 140 years before.

Just when the story of this ambivalence in the theological education of the movement seems to have come to a rather logical end, however, the history of theological education in the Church of the Nazarene, the largest of the American Holiness churches, during the same period in the sixties and subsequently, indicates that the trends in the movement are by no means set in concrete. After having capped its years of development of policies and programs for theological education with the establishment of an accredited denominational theological seminary in 1945, almost twenty years later, against strong opposition from within its established educational and ecclesiastical structures, the general assembly of the church decided it was necessary to create again a denominational Bible college to provide an adequate supply of the kind of ministers demanded by the district superintendents, who worked most directly in providing ministers. The new Nazarene Bible College at Colorado Springs, Colorado quickly became one of the larger Bible colleges in the United States. It is now one of the major sources of pastoral and missionary candidates for the ministry of the denomination.[33]

The tensions between being a church and being a revivalistic movement obviously continue. For the Holiness movement, the classic questions of the historian of theological education as to who was to be taught, what they were to be taught, and why they were to be taught must be answered with full awareness of those tensions.

33. B. Edgar Johnson and J. H. Mayfield, eds., *Journal of the Sixteenth General Assembly of the Church of the Nazarene* (Meetings held in Memorial Coliseum, Portland, Oregon; June 21 to 26, 1964), 189. Many of these issues are addressed in William C. Miller, "The Nazarene Colleges and Transition in American Higher Education, 1900–1920" (unpublished paper, Library, Nazarene Theological Seminary).

4

Presbyterian and Methodist Education

Gary Scott Smith

"What precisely must be taught in a theological seminary," wrote B. B. Warfield in 1917, depended upon what conception of the nature of the church and of the ministry and its functions an institution held. Because the primary task of the church was to preach the gospel, "the real purpose of the seminary," Warfield insisted, was to help students know the Bible "in all its details, and in all its power."[1] The curriculum at Princeton Theological Seminary was designed, he maintained, to produce "sound biblical critic[s]," "defender[s] of the Christian faith," "able and sound divine[s], useful preacher[s], faithful pastor[s]," and "scholar-saints" who could guide their parishioners in spiritual things.[2] In a lecture delivered at Drew Theological Seminary in 1907, Herbert Welch, president of Ohio Wesleyan University, argued, by contrast, that the task of seminaries was to produce Christian workers, not theological scholars, to graduate gardeners, not botanists. "[B]y example and practice as well as by precept," he declared, seminary students must "actually learn how to address children, to preach in the open air, to conduct an after-meeting, to deal with inquirers, [and] to organize a church for evangelism and a community for reform."[3] Summarizing the recent trends in theological education at Methodist's Garrett Biblical Institute, Frederick Eiselen declared in his 1925 presidential inaugural address that the "ultimate aim of the theological seminary" was to train prospective ministers to "build up the kingdom of God" and to lead or at least inspire "all movements and agencies for social betterment of the community."[4]

1. B. B. Warfield, "The Purpose of the Seminary," *The Presbyterian* (Nov. 22, 1917): 8–9.
2. B. B. Warfield, "Our Seminary Curriculum," *The Presbyterian* (Sept. 15, 1909): 7–8.
3. Herbert Welch, "Elements of Power in Theological Education," *Christian Advocate* (hereafter CA), 82 (Dec. 19, 1907): 2063–65, quotation from 2064.
4. Frederick Eiselen, "The Theological School To-day, Inaugural Address," in *The Theological School To-day* (Evanston, Ill.: Garrett Biblical Institute, 1926), 21.

As these quotations suggest, during the early twentieth century Presbyterians and Methodists developed rather different conceptions of the purposes of seminary education. During these years the seminaries of the Presbyterian Church in the United States of America (PCUSA) generally emphasized the intellectual and theological content they wanted future ministers to understand, embrace, and defend. Before 1920, most PCUSA seminaries, led by Princeton, adhered faithfully to and proclaimed fervently the basic theological tenets of evangelical Christianity as much or more than other theological schools. Prior to 1920, the seminaries of the Methodist Episcopal Church, led by Garrett, Drew, and Boston University School of Theology, promoted earlier evangelical emphasis on revivalism and social reform more zealously than did Presbyterian seminaries or those of almost all other Protestant bodies.

During the years from 1890 to 1920, the curricular focus of America's Protestant theological seminaries shifted from exegetical and historical theology to practical theology, as evident in increased course offerings in sociology, psychology, religious education, ethics, missions, rural and urban ministry, and other subjects. During this period the number and variety of courses the seminaries offered increased substantially, the amount of electives rose, and more opportunities for specialization and field work were developed. In most American seminaries, between 1890 and 1920, Greek and Hebrew became electives, practical theology came to include ethical and social issues, as well as the care and cure of souls, and homiletics courses increasingly emphasized how to transform study of the Bible into suitable preaching material. All seminaries were affected by a shift from a paradigm which made the "acquisition of scholarly knowledge of theological disciplines" (biblical studies, church history, systematic theology, and practical theology) the focus of ministerial training to one which prepared students for the "designated tasks or activities" of a parish or a specialized ministry (a "professional model" of education).[5] In general, however, the curriculum was altered by adding new courses "which were either subdivisions of the four-fold pattern (ethics) or new fields of practical theology."[6] While modifying its curriculum to include new disciplines and courses, Princeton and, to a lesser extent, other Presbyterian seminaries sought to

5. Edward Farley, *Theologia: The Fragmentation and Unity of Theological Education* (Philadelphia: Fortress Press, 1983), 11.
6. Ibid., 124. See Robert A. Kelly, *Theological Education in America: A Study of 161 Theological Seminaries in the United States and Canada* (New York: George H. Doran Co., 1924), 61–151. Robert Lynn argues that four forces prompted the multiplication of seminary courses: the adoption of an elective system, the "proliferation of programs for specialized ministries," the desire of increasingly better educated and more research-oriented faculty to teach courses related to the areas of their expertise, and sufficient capital funds to finance this growth. See "Notes Toward a History: Theological Encyclopedia and the Evolution of the Protestant Seminary Curriculum, 1808–1868," *Theological Education* (spring 1981): 131.

preserve the old paradigm. Most Methodist, Lutheran, Baptist, Congregational, and interdenominational seminaries, by contrast, embraced the
task-oriented model and began to redesign their curricula to insure that
each discipline (and the courses required for graduation) contributed directly to providing the knowledge and skills they deemed necessary for effective ministry.

This modification of the goals, resources, programs, curricula, and, in
some cases, the underlying theological standards and commitments of the nation's seminaries was a response to new social and economic challenges, the
influence of the social sciences, new perspectives and methods in education,
the expanding role of government in society, and the changing needs of the
church. In the thirty years after 1890, Protestant seminaries grappled with in-
suring academic freedom, developing programs for field education, and in-
corporating new courses on sociology, Christian education, evangelism, missions, the psychology of religion, comparative religions, ethics, and music
into the curriculum. They also worked to improve their standards for admission and the quality of their instruction, to standardize their curricula and requirements, and to prepare graduates for lifelong learning. Many seminaries
struggled to raise money and debated how to recruit students, how much aid
to give them, and how to best promote their spiritual life. At the same time,
these institutions faced the challenges arising from higher criticism, new biblical studies, and modernist theology which sought to adapt the message of
the gospel to contemporary culture and sometimes even questioned the foundations of Christian faith.

During the late nineteenth and early twentieth centuries, evangelical
Protestant seminaries strove to maintain their distinctive theologies, heri-
tages, and missions while restructuring their education in order to better
equip men and women to serve the church as pastors, teachers, lay workers,
evangelists, administrators, Christian education directors, and ministers of
music. While evangelical Protestants provided theological education
through a variety of means—seminaries, colleges, training schools, and correspondence courses—this study will focus on theological seminaries.
Moreover, this essay will primarily analyze the programs and practices of
PCUSA and Methodist Episcopal seminaries during the years between 1890
and 1920.[7] It will examine Princeton Theological Seminary and Garrett Biblical Institute as the most representative and influential models of the theological perspectives, goals, and curricula of these two denominations. As
Robert L. Kelly declared in his much acclaimed and debated *Theological
Education in America: A Study of 161 Theological Seminaries in the United
States and Canada* (1924), "Princeton Theological Seminary and Garrett

7. For an overview of the history and emphases of America's Protestant seminaries, see "Theological Seminaries," *The New Schaff-Herzog Encyclopedia of Religious Knowledge*, vol. XI, 343–94.

Biblical Institute as types of denominational seminaries represent opposite poles in structure and purpose of programs of study. Each of these schools has a profound influence in shaping the thought and practice of other schools of its denomination."[8]

No seminary had more impact upon the theological perspective, the curricula, and the institutional design and practices of evangelical seminaries during the years from 1890 to 1920 than Princeton Theological Seminary.[9] By its centennial celebration in 1912, the nation's second oldest seminary had enrolled 5,742 students, 1,200 more than any other American seminary. From 1890 to 1920 the enrollment at PTS averaged about 200 students, most of whom were Presbyterians. During this period the seminary educated about 25 percent of the PCUSA's theological students. Its graduates played major roles in the PCUSA, in other Protestant denominations, and in many other aspects of the nation's life. By the seminary's centennial, 56 of its graduates had served as moderators of the PCUSA General Assembly and five as bishops of the Episcopal Church.[10] By one estimate, more than one-half of the leaders of the PCUSA's missionary and benevolent work in the century preceding 1912 had studied at Princeton.[11]

Despite the repeated claims of Charles Hodge, Francis Patton, and others that no new theological ideas had originated at Princeton and that the seminary simply taught historic Reformed orthodoxy, its professors developed a "Princeton Theology," based upon a high view of biblical inspiration and authority, "consistent advocacy of Reformed faith," Scottish Common Sense Realism, and the importance of religious experience, which profoundly shaped the thought and life of evangelical seminaries, pastors, and lay people during the period under consideration.[12] From the pens of Princeton Seminary professors came a torrent of books, pamphlets, addresses, and articles published in periodicals and Bible dictionaries. Equally important was the *Princeton Theological Review* and its predecessors, edited and largely written by Princeton professors, which from 1841 to 1929 was the leading organ of the Reformed faith. Admired by most conservatives and respected by many liberals, these publications helped to shape evangelicals' views of bib-

8. Kelly, *Theological Education in America*, 88.

9. Kelly argued in *Theological Education in America* that Princeton Theological Seminary had "a wide influence among other denominations," 88.

10. William H. Johnson, "Princeton in Theological Education and Religious Thought," in *The Centennial Celebration of The Theological Seminary of the Presbyterian Church of the United States of America at Princeton, N.J.* (Princeton, N.J.: Princeton Theological Seminary, 1912), 445–46.

11. William H. Roberts, "From the Presbyterian Church in the United States of America," in *The Centennial Celebration*, 532.

12. See Mark A. Noll, *The Princeton Theology, 1812–1921: Scripture, Science, and Theological Method from Archibald Alexander to Benjamin Breckinridge Warfield* (Grand Rapids: Baker Book House, 1983), 25–34. See, for example, Francis Patton, "Princeton Seminary and the Faith," in *The Centennial Celebration*, 349–50.

lical authority, higher criticism, and doctrinal theology. The writings of the Princeton faculty, wrote three University of Chicago Divinity School professors in 1912, were "the best case" which could be made for orthodoxy and exemplified the "best conservative scholarship of the country."[13] Mark Noll argues that the theological perspective developed at Princeton "was always Calvinistic," faithfully upheld "the Bible as a repository of divine truth," expressed "great confidence in the capacities of evidence, reason, and logic," and consistently asserted that "proper science and biblical faith were compatible."[14] The seminary's exposition of biblical orthodoxy strongly affected the theological position of the PCUSA as a whole and contributed significantly to the matrix of beliefs which came to characterize fundamentalism in the years after 1920.[15]

During the years before 1920 Princeton also powerfully influenced the theological perspective and educational program of other PCUSA seminaries. It set high academic standards for its sister institutions. Lane in Cincinnati, Louisville, Dubuque, San Francisco, and Omaha Seminaries closely followed Princeton's model both in theological orientation and curricular structure. While Auburn in New York, Western in Pittsburgh, and McCormick in Chicago developed curricula which differed somewhat from that of Princeton, all of the PCUSA's eleven other seminaries shared Princeton's concern for academic rigor and solid intellectual preparation for ministry.[16] One major reason for Princeton's influence upon other Presbyterian seminaries was that its graduates had founded or had been among the earliest faculty at most PCUSA seminaries. By 1912, 108 of Princeton's graduates had taught at the denomination's other seminaries and almost one-third of the present faculty at these seminaries were graduates of the New Jersey institution.[17]

During the years from 1890 to 1920, Princeton professors increasingly used military metaphors to describe the mission of their institution. Princeton Theological Seminary was, in the words of Francis Patton, its president

13. Gerald Smith, Shirley J. Case, and D. D. Luckenbill, "Theological Scholarship at Princeton," a review of *Biblical and Theological Studies* (New York, 1912) by members of the PTS faculty, *American Journal of Theology* (hereafter *AJT*) 17 (Jan. 1913): 94–102, quotations from 94–95.

14. Noll, *The Princeton Theology*, 40.

15. See Ernest Sandeen, *The Roots of Fundamentalism, British and American Millenarianism, 1800–1930* (Chicago: University of Chicago Press, 1970) and George Marsden, *Fundamentalism and American Culture* (New York: Oxford University Press, 1980).

16. Kelly, *Theological Education in America*, 90. See also Lefferts Loetscher, *The Broadening Church: A Study of Theological Issues in the Presbyterian Church Since 1869* (Philadelphia: University of Pennsylvania Press, 1957), 74–82; John Q. Adams, *A History of Auburn Theological Seminary, 1818–1918* (Auburn, N.Y.: Auburn Seminary Press, 1918); James McClure, *The Story of the Life and Work of the Presbyterian Theological Seminary* (Chicago, 1929), esp. 82–98; James Walther, *Ever a Frontier: The Bicentennial History of the Pittsburgh Theological Seminary* (Grand Rapids: Eerdmans, 1994).

17. Johnson, "Princeton in Theological Education," 440.

from 1902 to 1913, a "fortress" of orthodoxy and a "training camp for sol-diers of the cross."[18] The citadel of divine truth, the seminary's professors de-clared, must be protected at all costs from the increasingly fierce assaults of both modern culture and modernist theology. Through their teaching and publications they sought to strengthen the evangelical stronghold so that it could better resist these attacks. Not content, however, with a merely defen-sive posture, the men who taught at Princeton also insisted that they were preparing soldiers (primarily pastors and professors) to wage a counteroffen-sive against the enemies of the gospel. The principal weapons they hoped to give these combatants were intellectual rigor, a biblically grounded theology, an understanding of the original biblical languages and the principles of sound exegesis, a proper hermeneutic, a commitment to Calvinism, and the ability to preach well-reasoned, constructed, and delivered sermons.[19] Patton insisted that the seminary could render "no more important service" than "the defense of historic Christianity."[20] Princeton prepared men, declared William Henry Roberts, stated clerk of the PCUSA general assembly, who could "defend her faith against infidels and heretics" by aggressively pro-claiming "the Calvinistic and biblical system of truth."[21]

These military metaphors produced a definitive conception of ministry, which demanded a particular type of curriculum. After 1890 most Protestant seminaries revised their curricula in response to modern intellectual and social currents. The growing importance of the natural and social sciences, the ex-pansion of elective courses in colleges, the application of candidates for the ministry who were not trained in the classics, and the growing interest in social, political, and economic issues all compelled seminaries to reexamine the theory underlying and the arrangement of courses in their curricula. Moreover, changes in theological interpretation and new views of the Bible raised ques-tions about how to teach courses in theology and about the relative importance of exegesis, biblical languages, and instruction in English Bible.[22] In the midst of this ferment over curricula and theology, Princeton, however, continued to adhere strongly to the traditional fourfold pattern of exegetical theology, sys-tematic theology, church history, and practical theology.[23] While recognizing that the task of ministers changes over time and that faculty must continually

18. Francis Patton, "A Theological Seminary," *Princeton Theological Review* (hereafter *PTR*) 14 (Jan. 1916): 74.
19. Roberts, "From the PCUSA," 529–30. Cf. Johnson "Princeton in Theological Education," 452; J. Ritchie Smith, "The Place of Homiletics in the Training of the Minister," *PTR* 14 (Jan. 1916): 106.
20. Patton, "A Theological Seminary," 81, 80.
21. Roberts, "From the PCUSA," 530. Cf. Patton, "Princeton Seminary and the Faith," 367; Min-utes of the General Assembly of the PCUSA (hereafter Minutes), 1908, 187.
22. Johnson, "Princeton in Theological Education," 445–46; Carl Patton, "The American Theo-logical Scene; Fifty Years in Retrospect," *JR* 16 (Oct. 1936): 445–62.
23. On the development and use of the fourfold pattern, see Glenn Miller, *Piety and Intellect: The Aims and Purpose of Ante-Bellum Theological Education* (Atlanta: Scholars Press, 1990).

respond in their teaching and publications to new theories, discoveries, and cultural currents, the seminary sought to proclaim "a permanent gospel."[24] In his 1915 inaugural address as the seminary's new president, J. Ross Stevenson declared that many Americans were demanding "a complete readjustment, if not a sweeping revolution" of seminary education. Reformers wanted to replace "the conventional Seminary curriculum" which they denounced as futile and inept with "an up-to-date system" based on "pedagogical experiments" and tentative sociological theories.[25] While constantly striving to make the seminary's education more practical and culturally relevant, the Princeton faculty sharply resisted what they considered to be educational fads.

As other evangelical seminaries began to reduce their language requirements and increase the offerings of the new disciplines, and liberal seminaries shifted the foundation of biblical studies from exegesis to historical analysis, and substituted philosophy of religion for dogmatics and apologetics, professors at Princeton and most other PCUSA seminaries continued to stress exegetical and scriptural theology.[26] Exegetical theology included subjects which focused directly upon the Bible: archaeology, Greek and Hebrew, and biblical interpretation, including critical methods and exegesis. Many urged seminaries to "dispense with the dead languages and the dry bones of scholastic theology and study the living problems of the day."[27] Princeton, however, retained required courses in Greek and Hebrew exegesis, as well as its concentration on scriptural theology.[28] Pastors did not need to be philologists, but they did need to have the tools to "search the scriptures" for themselves. This emphasis on biblical languages and exegesis was closely connected with Princeton's commitment to defending a high view of the authority and inspiration of the Bible.[29] Biblical theology, which was made a new department at Princeton in 1894, dealt with the chronological unfolding of the covenant of grace.[30] The Princeton faculty claimed that they had

24. J. Ross Stevenson, "Theological Education in the Light of Present Day Demands," *PTR* 14 (Jan. 1916): 82.

25. Ibid., 83.

26. See G. F. Moore, "Modern Theological Education," *Independent* 55 (Sept. 17, 1903): 2211–14.

27. Johnson, "Princeton in Theological Education," 446.

28. Francis Patton, "Theological Encyclopedia," *PTR* 2 (Jan. 1904): 118. Cf. William B. Greene, "The Elective System in Our Colleges and the Curriculum of Our Theological Seminaries," *Presbyterian and Reformed Review* 11 (Jan. 1900): 80. The question of whether or not to require Hebrew and Greek for the B. D. degree was heavily and hotly debated in the years between 1895 and 1920.

29. See Johnson, "Princeton in Theological Education," 446–47, quotation from 447. Presbyterian seminary professors objected to the proposal made by the Religious Education Association in 1910 that Greek and Hebrew not be required for graduation on the grounds that this would send out large numbers of pastors who lacked the ability to use the tools of modern biblical scholarship. See James Kelso, "New Ideals in Theological Education," *Bulletin of the Western Theological Seminary* (hereafter *BWTS*) 2 (Oct. 1910): 25–26.

30. See Geerhardus Vos, "The Idea of Biblical Theology as a Science and as a Theological Discipline" in *Inauguration of the Rev. Geerhardus Vos as Professor of Biblical Theology* (New York: Anson D. F. Randolph Co., 1894), 3–40.

always examined the best available evidence from tradition, philology, ar-chaeology, and comparative religion.[31] The seminary's professors, J. Ross Stevenson explained, did not ignore or simply condemn modern theological currents and destructive criticism but rather faced them head-on with "un-flinching honesty and courage."[32]

Princeton and other PCUSA seminaries served a confessional church, which guarded its strong historic commitment to Reformed theology by re-quiring all of its ministers to subscribe to the Westminster Confession of Faith, pass thorough ordination examinations, and ordinarily to complete a graduate theological education. As a result, the denomination's seminar-ies made the study of systematic theology central in their curricula. In 1909, for example, the General Assembly urged its presbyteries to examine all li-centiates carefully to see if they had been "well instructed and indoctrinated in the principles, doctrines, and polity of the Presbyterian Church" and to verify that these candidates were "in hearty accord with these principles and doctrines, and loyal to evangelical Christianity."[33] Under the direction of Charles Hodge, then A. A. Hodge, and finally B. B. Warfield, all out-standing defenders of Reformed orthodoxy and authors of important works on systematic theology, the study of this discipline flourished at Prin-ceton in the second half of the nineteenth century and the first two decades of the twentieth century. Using the building blocks provided by all the other parts of the curriculum, the systematic theologian constructed an explana-tion and defense of biblical truth. Systematic theology arranged scriptural truth in a "series of articulated propositions," in "a logically correlated form."[34] As the "crown and head" of the theological disciplines, B. B. Warfield wrote, it utilized the truths of other disciplines to "systematize and defend revealed truth."[35] In the years from 1890 to 1920 systematic theology continued to be the most important discipline in PCUSA seminar-ies and the subject most diligently studied by the communion's ministers after graduation.[36] John DeWitt, professor of church history at Princeton, argued that Presbyterian clergy, more than ministers in other denomina-tions, felt "obliged to have a theology," which they could state and defend. Presbyterian ministers, he concluded, were better versed in systematic the-ology than in any other subject and tended to preach theologically based sermons.[37]

31. Johnson, "Princeton in Theological Education," 451.
32. Stevenson, "Theological Education," 88. Cf. William Farmer, "New Testament Interpretation in the Light of Certain Modern Conditions," *BWTS* 4 (July 1912): 13–21.
33. Minutes (1909): 165. Cf. Minutes (1915): 286.
34. John DeWitt, "Relations of Church History to Preaching," *PTR* 5 (Jan. 1907): 100.
35. B. B. Warfield, "The Idea of Systematic Theology," *Presbyterian and Reformed Review* 7 (April 1896): 254, 255.
36. DeWitt, "Church History," 101.
37. Ibid. Cf. James Snowden, "Theology and Life," *BWTS* 5 (July 1913): 16–23.

The study of church history was also important at Princeton and other PCUSA seminaries. Courses in this discipline helped future ministers understand that Christianity was a powerful historical force which had influenced all facets of life.[38] Through the study of this subject, seminarians could gain a larger vision, more respect for other theological traditions, and greater openness to change.[39] Knowledge of the past provided a basis for evaluating the present. As "a record of victories," church history inspired optimism and continued efforts to change the world.[40]

Because the curriculum at Princeton so strongly emphasized exegetical, historical, and systematic theology, practical theology was less important during the years under consideration than at many other Protestant seminaries. While Princeton had historically taught various aspects of practical theology—preaching, worship, polity, pastoral care, catechetics, evangelism, missions, and organized Christian work—the institution did not establish a chair in practical theology until 1906, much later than most other seminaries.[41] By this time, the directors and faculty at Princeton, like those at many other Protestant seminaries, had become convinced that a more "practical, spiritual, and Evangelistic interpretation of the Bible" was necessary to "directly equip the preacher for his pulpit and the pastor for his personal work."[42]

Of the subjects taught in connection with practical theology, homiletics occupied the most important place in curriculum of Princeton and other PCUSA seminaries.[43] As Francis Patton put it in 1903, Princeton was "first of all, a school for training men to preach the Gospel."[44] Students must be taught the proper way to construct and deliver sermons. Evangelical Presbyterians and Methodists both believed that the purpose of preaching was to convert sinners and inspire Christians to lead a life of holiness and service, but their students learned how to preach different types of sermons in seminary homiletics classes. Both groups insisted that sermons should be "vivid, striking, [and] picturesque"[45] and taught students how to deliver

---

38. DeWitt, "Church History," 104.
39. Robert H. Nichols, "Church History and the Minister," *Auburn Seminary Review* (hereafter *ASR*) 9 (Nov. 10, 1913): 380–82.
40. Ibid., 386.
41. For an analysis of the seminary curricula in this area of study, see Gerald B. Smith, *Practical Theology: A Neglected Field in Theological Education* (n. p. [1905]), 16–21.
42. Charles Erdman, "Modern Practical Theology," *PTR* 5 (Jan. 1907): 88. McCormick Seminary was more advanced than other PCUSA seminaries in the area of field work, as its students were all assigned to work in missions, settlement houses, or institutional churches in Chicago. See Edgar P. Hill, "City Missions and Theological Students: An Experiment in Ministerial Training," *The Missionary Review of the World* 35 (Aug. 1912): 601–5.
43. On the increased importance of preaching during the late nineteenth century, see Winthrop Hudson, *The Great Tradition of the American Churches* (New York: Harper & Row, 1953), 157–94.
44. Patton, "Theological Encyclopedia," 110.
45. Ritchie, "The Place of Homiletics," 111.

sermons with passion, power, and conviction. Presbyterians, however, put much more emphasis on the construction of sermons. A good Presbyterian sermon contained a logically developed argument, apt illustrations, and scriptural doctrines.[46] According to J. Ritchie Smith, who taught homiletics at PTS, each text should be "studied minutely, word by word," in order to discover its precise meaning, its historical or doctrinal setting, and its "relation to the whole scheme of Scripture [sic] truth." The preacher must then "marshall his thoughts in logical order, with cumulative power, so as to drive home a single impression." Only then would the sermon be clear, forceful, and effective.[47]

The many criticisms of Protestant seminaries and the growing pressure to reconstruct their curricula in the early twentieth century prompted the PCUSA General Assembly to appoint a committee of ministers and elders in 1909 to investigate how the denomination could better prepare clergy to combat urgent social problems, increase missionary efforts at home and abroad, and utilize sound business methods in church administration.[48] More than 70 percent of the nearly three hundred PCUSA pastors who replied to a questionnaire the committee devised complained that their seminary education had not adequately prepared them for the practical aspects of the pastorate and insisted that more courses in sociology, methods of church work, English Bible, and Christian education were especially needed. Almost 60 percent of the approximately two hundred laymen who responded to the committee's survey judged the preaching of recent seminary graduates to be inadequate to win people to Christ, lacking in spiritual power, or too indirect and impractical.[49] The committee's 1910 report pointed out that many PCUSA seminaries, in an attempt to improve the ability of their graduates to pastor effectively, had recently added or required courses in English Bible, missions, methods of Christian work, sociology, evangelism, Christian education, and ethics. Nevertheless, the committee concluded that seminarians

46. Ibid., 107. See also William Stevenson, "Ministerial Efficiency," *BWTS* 6 (July 1914): 281–82.

47. Ibid., 109–10. See also James Kelso, "The Importance of Preaching," *BWTS* 5 (Oct. 1912): 49–53; "Our Intellectual Ideals," *ASR* 1 (Nov. 10, 1905): 283–84. At Princeton, the core of the homiletics curriculum was a preaching clinic where the professor and classmates critiqued the content, form, and delivery of student sermons. PTS students also studied the sermons of such masters as Phillips Brooks, Charles Spurgeon, and Dwight Moody. See Frederick Loetscher, "Homiletics as a Theological Discipline," in *Biblical and Theological Studies*, 418–21; Smith, "The Place of Homiletics," 112; Herrick Johnson, *The Ideal Ministry: A Comprehensive Handbook on Homiletics* (New York: Fleming H. Revell, 1908); David Breed, *Preparing to Preach* (New York: Doran, 1911). Loetscher and Smith taught homiletics at Princeton, Johnson at McCormick, and Breed at Western Theological Seminary.

48. Minutes, 1909, 165. See, for example, Thomas Day, "Theological Seminaries and Their Critics," *Presbyterian and Reformed Review* 11 (April 1900): 298–308; A. A. Berle, "The Rout of the Theological Schools," *Bibliotheca Sacra* 64 (July 1907): 566–87.

49. Minutes, 1910, 215–18. The committee's report concluded that two factors were primarily responsible for the defects of PCUSA seminaries: the college elective system inadequately prepared many students for seminary and the seminaries lacked adequate funding.

still needed to have more training in four areas: spirituality, knowledge of the Bible, understanding of the world, and elocution.[50]

Despite proposing these changes, however, the committee reasserted that exegesis and biblical, systematic, and pastoral theology, especially homiletics, were of "primary importance." Other subjects, while very useful, must remain secondary.[51] Moreover, the committee firmly stated that the denomination would not "lower the standard of ministerial education."[52] Its members urged PCUSA seminaries to continue to teach Hebrew and Greek and the "principles and methods of scientific exegesis" so that students could independently study the Bible.[53]

During the years between 1890 and 1920 Presbyterians were convinced that their seminaries were loyal to the principles of the Reformed faith and to evangelical Christianity, were based upon standards of academic rigor and scholarship equal to or greater than other American seminaries, and were graduating ministers whose character, conviction, and training enabled them to serve God faithfully and his people energetically.[54] Summarizing Princeton's mission, its president J. Ross Stevenson declared in 1915 that the institution sought to produce ministers who had a deep piety and a "definite, consistent, and compelling message." The seminary strove to be a "nursery of vital piety," a center of scholarship, a defender of biblical ortho-

50. Committee members urged the denomination's seminaries to foster the spiritual life of their students by developing a course in spiritual dynamics, by assigning professors pastoral responsibility over groups of students, and by enlisting and directing students in more forms of Christian service. To promote spiritual formation, PTS held daily prayer in the morning and evening which all students were expected to attend, Sunday morning chapel services, Sunday afternoon "conferences" led by professors, and missionary meetings on Sunday evening. See B. B. Warfield, "The Religious Life of Theological Students," in *Selected Shorter Writings of Benjamin B. Warfield*, ed. John Meeter (Nutley, N.J.: Presbyterian and Reformed, 1970), vol. 1, 411–25; William K. Selden, *Princeton Theological Seminary: A Narrative History, 1812–1992* (Princeton: Princeton University Press, 1992), 70. The committee also advised Presbyterian seminaries to give the study of the English Bible a preeminent place in the curriculum. See Minutes, 1910, 223. See also James Kelso, "The Study of the English Bible in the Theological Seminary," *BTWS* 5 (Jan. 1913): 73–84; "Presbyterian Theological Seminaries and the Bible," *BTWS* 5 (Jan. 1913): 85–114. The committee also urged PCUSA seminaries to teach more about the history, polity, policies, and practical methods of the work of the church. In addition, its members recommended that all students study social conditions and problems either through specific courses or as part of their work in practical theology. See Minutes, 1910, 224–27. Even after the pleas of the committee in 1910, the study of sociological issues or social problems remained meager at the denomination's seminaries, except Auburn and Western. See Riley Little, "The Theological Seminary and the Social Problem," *BWTS* 2 (April 1910): 22–24; Minutes, 1915, 286. Finally, committee members counseled seminaries to provide more frequent practice in elocution so that all future ministers would be "trained to speak clearly and impressively" (Minutes, 1910, 225).

51. Minutes, 1910, 221.

52. Ibid., 220.

53. Ibid., 220.

54. In 1900, 80 percent of PTS's students were college graduates as compared with 60 percent of students at New York's General (Episcopal) Seminary, 20 percent of students at Rochester Theological Seminary (Baptist), and 12 percent of students at Drew Theological Seminary (Methodist). See S. D. McConnell, "The Education of Preachers," *World's Work* 2 (June 1901): 839.

doxy, a friend of revival, a champion of social reform, and an advocate of missions.[55]

Since the founding of their denomination in America in 1706, Presbyterians had insisted upon an educated ministry. As the twentieth century dawned, they acknowledged that some men had powerfully preached the gospel without any special preparation, but they insisted that the ministry of these men would have been even more effective if "they had enjoyed the advantages of theological education."[56] They responded to charges that graduates of theological seminaries were not being adequately prepared for the practical tasks of ministry and were being outstripped by those educated at lay training schools or in the school of experience by insisting that the most effective preparation for the pastorate was a solid grounding in the theological sciences.[57] Presbyterians argued that it was impossible to prepare students for all the problems they would encounter in their practical work in the ministry. Therefore, no matter how urgent and intense the demand might become to introduce new subjects of practical theology into the curriculum, the seminary must not deemphasize "the great and masterful branches of the theological encyclopaedia."[58]

In the years between 1890 and 1920 Princeton and other PCUSA seminaries were more conservative than innovative. They continued to emphasize biblical and theological studies, to require Hebrew and Greek, to offer a minimal number of electives, and to teach relatively few courses in the new disciplines of Christian education, psychology of religion, Christian sociology, and missions.[59] Auburn, Western, and McCormick increasingly added courses in these newer areas, but Princeton, while revising its offerings somewhat, retained its long-standing concentration on the fourfold curriculum.[60] To critics, Princeton's "highly cerebral theological tradition often resulted in an intellectualism unrelated to vital religion, the currents of secular and scientific thought, and the practical life of the Church."[61] Some objected that seminaries like Princeton devoted too much time to systematic theology and biblical languages, resulting in the study of "much irrelevant material" and "microscopic" examination of only small portions

55. Stevenson, "Theological Education," 83–94, quotations from 87, 84.

56. Russell Cecil, "The Making of a Minister," in *The Centennial Celebration*, 396.

57. Ibid., 400; Patton, "A Theological Seminary," 74–75.

58. Patton, "A Theological Seminary," 76.

59. It is striking that PCUSA seminaries did not offer more specific courses to prepare missionaries as concern for missions was frequently raised at General Assemblies and PCUSA seminaries sent many graduates to the mission field. See, for example, Minutes, 1904, 151; 1919, 218.

60. Beginning in 1914 the number of electives offered at PTS increased substantially. By 1921 the seminary catalogue listed 86 courses offered in eight departments: Old Testament, New Testament, Semitic Philology, Church History, Apologetics, Systematic Theology, Practical Theology, and Christian Ethics.

61. Hugh T. Kerr, Jr., ed., *Sons of the Prophets: Leaders in Protestantism from Princeton Seminary* (Princeton, N.J..: Princeton University Press, 1963), xii.

of the Bible.[62] Princeton focused more on what seminarians needed to know to be theologically orthodox, biblically literate, and historically grounded than on the specific skills they needed to minister effectively to church members and the larger community. Supporters insisted, however, that Princeton zealously guarded the faith and produced ministers who were well equipped to serve the Lord. More than any other group, the Princeton faculty preserved "the vitality and integrity of evangelical theology in the face of great changes in American life."[63] The seminary strove to maintain a proper balance between general theological learning and professional training for the ministry, between sound scholarship and practical preparation for service.[64] Nevertheless, PTS and its sister seminaries tended to make academic study and the cultivation of the mind more important than practical preparation for future pastoral responsibilities.[65]

In contrast to Presbyterians, Methodists did not expect all their ministers to earn a seminary degree or to affirm belief in a set of specific doctrines. Presbyterians had already founded eight seminaries by the time the Methodist Episcopal Church established its first seminary in 1847, which eventually became Boston University School of Theology. Two of the denomination's other important seminaries between 1890 to 1920 were Garrett Biblical Institute, which opened in Evanston, Illinois in 1854, and Drew Theological Seminary, which was founded in 1867 at Madison, New Jersey. From 1816 until the mid-twentieth century, however, most Methodist pastors were educated not in theological seminaries, but only through the denomination's approved Course of Study.[66]

62. See "The Question of Theological Education," *Reformed Church Review* 4 (April 1900): 256–57.

63. John Woodbridge, Mark Noll, and Nathan Hatch, *The Gospel in America: Themes in the Story of America's Evangelicals* (Grand Rapids: Zondervan, 1979), 54. This phrase is from Woodbridge, Noll, and Hatch; the argument is mine, not theirs.

64. See Kelly, *Theological Education in America*, 235, for a discussion of the deficiencies of seminaries as "centers of scholarly pursuits."

65. In *Theological Education in America* Kelly urged seminaries to rely on empirical investigation rather than "tradition . . . imagination . . . [or] guesswork" in shaping their programs, 223.

66. Initially, each annual conference devised a list of books upon which candidates for the ministry were examined in order to be admitted to conference membership. In 1848 the Methodist Episcopal Church established a denomination-wide program with a formal list of readings, and in 1878 the Methodist Episcopal Church, South did the same. By 1893 the MEC's program was supervising the work of 3,545 students in a four-year correspondence course. See John Vincent, "Our Largest School of Theology," *Methodist Review* (hereafter *MR*) 53 (1893): 190–205. The Course of Study included "biblical introduction and exegesis; encyclopedia and methodology; natural, biblical, historical, comparative, and practical theology; homiletics; and ecclesiastical law . . . [world] history; rhetoric; logic; psychology; and political economy," 190. In their 1896 quadrennial address, the Methodist bishops urged the denomination to accept certificates from Methodist seminaries in place of the Course of Study. This change was not made, however, until 1928. See *Journal of the General Conference of the Methodist Episcopal Church* (hereafter *Journal*), 1896: 402. In 1896 the General Conference did decide to permit the substitution of credits earned in college and seminary for equivalent parts of the Course of Study. See also, L. Dale Patterson, "Improvement in Methodist Ministerial Education at the

During the late nineteenth and early twentieth centuries, some Methodists, unlike Presbyterians, questioned the value of a seminary education.[67] In 1886 Daniel Curry, the editor of the *Methodist Review*, listed the liabilities of theological schools. They tended, he claimed, to put too much emphasis on scholarship and too little on practical preparation for ministry. Seminaries produced many ministers who were out of touch with ordinary people. Their graduates had to "disuse and practically unlearn a large proportion" of their seminary training because it was either unnecessary or counterproductive.[68] In 1900 *The Christian Advocate* reported that the 441 souls won to Christ by 56 students from Garrett Biblical Institute during the Christmas recess refuted the heedless and hurtful criticism that a theological education diminished the "evangelistic fervor and efficiency" of ministers.[69] While admitting that many Methodists had been "suspicious of theological schools as tending to breed 'lazy, self-opinionated, hair-splitting divines,'" the editors of *The Christian Advocate* in 1903 denied the charge of *The Congregationalist* that Methodist ministers had been instructed "not to study but to exhort."[70]

Nevertheless, by the late nineteenth century, as Methodists became more educated and prosperous, many of them demanded better-trained ministers. As a result, many Methodist colleges and universities were founded to help prepare ministers, efforts were made to improve the content and the administration of the Course of Study, and more seminary graduates began work as Methodist ministers each year.[71] In 1896 the editors of the *Methodist Review* complained that young ministers did not fully appreciate the advantages of a seminary education. Deterred from attending by the cost in time and money, they did not receive the beneficial knowledge and the useful training in the work of the ministry that seminaries provided. Ministers could not properly understand and use higher criticism without "the serious and careful training of the theological school." Private study of the new methods of exegesis and biblical criticism, the editors insisted, would "mislead or bewilder" ministers; these new developments must not be ignored because they could enable preachers to "present biblical fact and truth with greater accuracy and, therefore, with more force."[72]

End of the Nineteenth Century," *Methodist History*, 23 (Jan. 1985): 68–78; Gerald O. McCulloh, *Ministerial Education in the American Methodist Movement* (Nashville: United Methodist Board of Higher Education, 1980), 11–15.

67. See Frederick Norwood, *The Story of American Methodism* (Nashville: Abingdon Press, 1974), 306–8.

68. Daniel Curry, "Ministerial Education," *MR* 68 (July 1886): 586–90, quotations from 589, 586.

69. "Theological Students and Evangelistic Services," *CA* 75 (Feb. 8, 1900): 235.

70. "A Fearful Nod in Boston," *CA* 78 (Dec. 3, 1903): 1953. Cf. Bryon H. Stauffer, "Comments on the Article on 'The Average Sermon,'" *MR* 87 (July 1905): 638.

71. "Education for the Ministry," *MR* 67 (July 1885): 598.

72. "Our Schools of Theology," *MR* 78 (July 1896): 613–20; quotations from 619.

By 1900 most Methodists did not regard theological schools as unnecessary or as impediments, but many still took more pride in the Course of Study, and a seminary education remained the exception rather than the rule.[73] In 1903 the editors of *The Christian Advocate* reported that the denomination's seminaries were graduating less than 25 percent of the one thousand new ministers the MEC needed each year.[74] Fears persisted that a seminary education might undermine the faith of their students and produce ministers who could not understand or preach effectively to the average church member.[75] Many Garrett students testified in 1906 that they had been advised against attending a seminary lest it destroy their faith.[76] A 1911 editorial in the *Christian Advocate* acknowledged that there "were many debatable questions as to the best place and method of training" ministers, a statement no Presbyterian periodical made during this period.[77]

It is difficult to determine which seminary had the most influence on the Methodist Episcopal Church during the years from 1890 to 1920, especially on behalf of evangelicalism. During this period Boston University School of Theology, Garrett Biblical Institute, and Drew Theological Seminary were by far the most important Methodist seminaries in terms of numbers of students and quality of professors, program, and facilities. Of the three, Boston was clearly the most liberal in theology, while at both Garrett and Drew evangelical liberalism generally prevailed. Because *Theological Education in America,* as previously noted, judged Garrett to be the most prominent, influential, and representative Methodist seminary, it has been chosen for closer examination.

Along with many other seminaries in the 1890s, Garrett offered both degree and diploma programs. After 1892 it awarded the B. D. only to students who had also graduated from college. In the 1890s the seminary made both Hebrew and Greek optional and created a department of English Exegesis and Sacred Rhetoric. During the decade, Garrett's curriculum stressed both

---

73. See Norwood, *The Story,* 308.

74. "Additional Editorials," *CA* 78 (Aug. 27, 1903): 1392. George Mains estimated in "Book Concern Dividends for the Younger Minister," *MR* 98 (March 1916) that only 25 percent of Conference members were graduates of both a college and a seminary (200). Cf. "Some Values of a Seminary Education," *MR* 98 (Jan. 1916): 124. By comparison, the 1926 U.S. religious census figures reveal that more than 40 percent of the ministers of the nation's seventeen largest white Protestant denominations had not graduated from either a college or a seminary and that only 33 percent of them had graduated from both. See C. Luther Fry, *The U.S. Looks at Its Churches* (New York, 1930), 63, 144.

75. See, for example, Stauffer, "Comments," 636–38.

76. O. F. Merrill, "Within the Seminary," *Semi-Centennial Celebration of Garrett Biblical Institute* (Evanston, Ill., 1906), 201.

77. "Leveling an Obstacle," *CA* 86 (Sept. 7, 1911): 1204. In 1912 the MEC General Conference legislated that no men be admitted "on trial" to the ministry unless they could meet college entrance requirements. As late as 1939 more than 50 percent of ministers who joined MEC Annual Conferences on trial had not attended seminary, and not until 1956 did the General Conference make graduation from seminary the regular qualification for Conference membership. See "Theological Education in the Methodist Churches," in Emory S. Bucke, ed., *The History of American Methodism,* vol. III (New York: Abingdon Press, 1964), 243.

exegetical and practical theology.[78] At the turn of the century the original missionary motive of the seminary remained powerful. Garrett fostered interest in missions through special classes, the distribution of literature, and lectures given by missionaries on furlough.[79] The YMCA played a vital role at the seminary, especially in promoting spiritual formation and evangelism. In the early twentieth century, by one estimate, the average Garrett student spent seventeen hours per week in class and forty-two hours studying outside of class. Since many seminarians were employed three days a week in student pastorates, they had to spend fifteen hours a day the remaining four days each week to complete their academic work.[80]

As the old century closed and the new one began, both the Methodist leaders assigned to investigate Garrett each year and many alumni professed great delight with the seminary's program. The 1899 Conference visitors were impressed with the progressiveness of the curriculum, especially the study of the English Bible and the social sciences, which enabled the "great truths of theology" to be examined in relation to efforts to realize the kingdom of God on earth. The visitors insisted that Garrett neither undermined Christian piety nor promoted "doctrinal demoralization," accusations hurled at theological seminaries by irresponsible, ill-informed critics. Many graduates testified instead that their seminary experience had significantly strengthened their spiritual life and their commitment to orthodox Christianity.[81] The Conference visitors of 1900 lauded the seminary's "progressive conservatism"[82] and its "combination of comprehensive and exact scholarship with aggressive spirituality." They commended the faculty for emphasizing the "formation of Christly character and the spirit of evangelicalism" more than "the exact formulation of dogma" and were gratified that students unanimously testified to having developed "deepened devotion, increased faith," and "broader intellectual vision."[83] The 1907 visitors concluded that students were "being safely and thoroughly trained in the practical use of the Old and New Testaments" and in an understanding of the era's social and spiritual problems.[84]

In 1912 Garrett created two totally separate schools—the Graduate School of Theology, offering the B. D. degree, and the Diploma School of

78. In 1985 graduation requirements at Garrett included 34 hours in exegetical theology, 32 hours in practical theology, 17 hours in systematic theology, and 11 hours in historical theology. By this date courses in missions and Christian sociology were being offered. See Kelly, *Theological Education in America*, 68–69.

79. *Catalogue of Garrett Biblical Institute, 1911–1912*, 20; Frederick Norwood, *From Dawn to Midday at Garrett* (Evanston, Ill.: Garrett-Evangelical Theological Seminary, 1978), 57.

80. Merrill, "Within the Seminary," 199–203.

81. "Chicago," *CA* 74 (June 8, 1899): 912.

82. John Faulkner used this same phrase to describe the attitude and approach of Drew. See John Faulkner, "Theological Seminary Orthodoxy," *MR* 86 (July 1904): 632.

83. "Commencement at GBI," *CA* 75 (May 24, 1900): 859.

84. "Garrett Biblical Institute," *CA* 82 (July 25, 1907): 1184.

Theology.[85] While sharing facilities and some faculty, each program had its own catalog. The next year the seminary's enrollment reached a record high of 219, and Garrett established a new curricular structure. Twenty-three of the forty-five hours needed for the B. D. degree were elective courses. Students specialized in one department among the biblical, historical doctrine, pastoral and social service, foreign missions, and religious education divisions, and then spread their remaining courses over the four other areas.[86]

During the years from 1890 to 1920 the seminary's task of preparing ministers became more difficult because the role of the clergy became more complex. President Ezra Tipple told the 1906 graduating class at Drew Theological Seminary that a minister was expected to be "a shepherd of the flock, a man of affairs with administrative abilities, [a] bookkeeper, committeeman, counselor, teacher, [and] miracle-worker."[87] Like other seminaries during these years, Garrett existed to train ministers who could use the Bible in a scholarly and disciplined manner, carefully and soundly exegete the Scriptures, work to remedy social and economic problems, and serve as models of "culture united with evangelistic fervor."[88] With Presbyterians, Methodists believed that pastors who combined deep spirituality with intellectual culture would have the most powerful and effective ministries.[89] Unlike Princeton, however, Garrett saw its primary role as preparing pastors who could care for people with a wide variety of spiritual, social, psychological, and physical needs, rather than as producing minister-theologians who could defend biblical orthodoxy. Consequently, Garrett's curriculum placed significantly less emphasis on theology and much more stress on practical preparation for ministry.[90] For several years Garrett's catalog stated that the aim of the seminary was to furnish the church "with scholarly and efficient pastors"

85. "The Theological Schools," *CA* 87 (Nov. 28, 1912): 1686. This same division existed at Boston University School of Theology. GBI's Diploma School was closed in 1930.

86. The 1913–14 catalogue states that GBI recognized the tendency toward "diversified and specialized forms of ministerial service—prophetic, pastoral, educational, and institutional," but declared the institution's primary aim was training pastors. The Bible was "the heart of the theological curriculum"; the seminary had continuously "fostered a study of the Scriptures at once devout and scholarly." The biblical department guaranteed "the diligent student a reading knowledge" of Greek and Hebrew and "a working knowledge of the contents of Scripture." The historical doctrine division sought to help students formulate for themselves "the doctrines of the Christian faith into a clear and comprehensive system." The pastoral and social service group focused on the art of preaching, firsthand study of actual conditions of ministry, and analysis of the principles and methods of church administration. See *Catalogue, Graduate School of Theology, Garrett, Biblical Institute, 1913–1914*, 8, 15, 16, 17.

87. Ezra S. Tipple, "The Chief Work of the Minister of God," *MR* 89 (Jan. 1907): 31–49, quotation from 31.

88. J. Harvey Walker, "Beyond the Seminary," in *Semi-Centennial Celebration*, 206–7.

89. See Mains, "Book Concern Dividends," 203, 216.

90. This was also true of the Boston University School of Theology. By 1896 its curriculum was divided into eight areas, including practical theology, comparative study of religions, and sociological studies (including missions). Richard Cameron argues in *Boston University School of Theology, 1839–1968* (Boston: Boston University School of Theology, 1968) that "practical Christianity" dominated the curriculum at the seminary from 1911 until 1926 (33–35, 45–51).

who "by their persuasive speech and pastoral skill" could "lead many to Christ."[91] In 1905 Garrett's president Charles Little proclaimed that ministers should study "with the one great aim"—to learn how "to save the lost and redeem the world."[92] Another Garrett president, Charles Stuart, argued in 1913 that recent modifications in the study of the Old and New Testaments, systematic theology, and church history, as well as new courses in the psychological and sociological study of religion emphasized the need for pastors to work for social betterment.[93] By 1921 Garrett's graduation requirements included twelve hours in exegetical theology, six hours in historical theology, six hours in systematic theology, and forty hours in practical theology.[94] By this date all six major MEC seminaries stressed religious education and social service more than exegetical and historical theology.[95] More than the seminaries of other denominations, Methodist theological schools featured required and elective courses in practical theology, religious education, and psychology of religion.[96]

Although all Protestant seminaries were offering and requiring many more courses in practical and pastoral theology in 1920 than they had in 1890, by the latter date most of them still provided little clinical training for their students. Instruction in pastoral methods and practices was usually academic and theoretical. Students were rarely trained in actual parish work; few had the opportunity to serve as assistants to experienced ministers. Moreover, most seminaries did not closely supervise student field work. Garrett's provision and supervision of city clinical work was an exception to this rule. Its program consisted of three aspects: observation of social service and human welfare agencies; service as pastors of "student churches" or as pastoral assistants in large urban congregations; and open air preaching, often

91. See, for example, Catalogue of GBI, 1907–1908, 13.

92. Charles Little, "The Seminary and the Schools of Research," Catalogue of GBI, 1904–1905, Magazine Supplement, 48–53, quotations from 49, 51.

93. See Charles Stuart, "The Seminary and Social Leadership," The Bulletin, Garrett Biblical Institute 1 (Jan. 1913): 11–28, quotation from 23.

94. Kelly, Theological Education in America, 69. Cf. John A. Faulkner, "Theological Education in America in the Light of Recent Discussion," MR 85 (Jan. 1903): 59–60; Herbert Welch, "Elements of Power in Theological Education," 2064; J. F. Heisse, "The Pulpit as the Chief Factor in Social Reform," MR 90 (March 1908): 247–57.

95. By 1921 PCUSA seminaries required an average of eleven hours of Hebrew and eleven hours of Greek for graduation; MEC seminaries required two hours of Hebrew and seven hours of Greek. Methodist seminaries required fewer hours of exegetical and systematic theology for graduation than did either Presbyterian or Episcopal seminaries. See Kelly, Theological Education in America, 99–100. The three other significant MEC seminaries during these years were Maclay College of Theology founded in 1887 and moved to the campus of USC in Los Angeles in 1894, Iliff School of Theology established in Denver in 1892, and Kimball School of Theology opened in 1907 in Salem, Oregon.

96. Kelly observed that the greatest differences among Methodist, Presbyterian, and Episcopal seminaries were in the field of practical theology, as Methodist institutions taught courses covering "the whole realm of social service and applied Christianity," which allowed students to specialize in these areas (Theological Education in America, 100).

in conjunction with rescue missions, ministry to immigrants, or service in courts and correctional institutions. Seminary professors closely monitored the work of student interns through frequent on-site visits and regular conferences at Garrett.[97]

Methodist seminaries, like their Presbyterian counterparts, sought to prepare pastors to preach persuasively and powerfully. The primary task of a Methodist minister, Ezra Tipple declared in 1906, was not to pastor, advise, or administer but rather to preach.[98] Methodists placed much more importance on stirring emotions and saving souls through Sunday sermons than did Presbyterians. Lewis Brastow of Yale Seminary contended in *The Modern Pulpit* (1906) that Methodism's chief contribution to American preaching had been in its emphasis on personal piety and experiential religion.[99] Every great Methodist preacher, argued C. E. Cline, had the power to make people feel. Through their preaching they aroused deep emotions in the hearts of sinners which convicted them to repent.[100] Brastow contended that Methodism "more fully than any other Protestant church" was "committed to the evangelistic type of preaching."[101] As part of Drew Theological Seminary's homiletics curriculum, students took a four-hour course in pastoral evangelism, which included a practicum.[102] Methodism's commitment to evangelism also led its seminary homiletics classes to stress the importance of fluency, freedom, and forcefulness in preaching.[103] Despite Methodist ministers' widespread use of extemporaneous preaching designed to evoke an emotional response and to save souls, the communion's seminaries, like those of other denominations, increasingly emphasized the theory, construction, and delivery of sermons, the history of preaching, and practicums that involved speaking before a class and receiving student and instructor criticism.[104]

The Methodist emphasis on the practical also affected the way that church history was taught at the denomination's seminaries. In his book, *On the Value of Church History* (1920), John Faulkner described the benefits many Methodist seminary professors believed the subject had for their students. The study of church history was valuable, he argued, because it analyzed historic theological debates, shed light on Christian doctrine, and explained

97. Boston University School of Theology also developed an extensive program of field work. See Kelly, *Theological Education in America,* 145–51.
98. Tipple, "The Chief Work of the Minister of God," quotations from 32, 34, 41. Cf. Richard Gilbert, "The Ministerial Vocation," *MR* 98 (Nov. 1916): 916–23.
99. See the *MR* 89 (July 1907): 624.
100. C. E. Cline, "What of the Revival?" *MR* 86 (March 1904): 298–99.
101. Quoted in "Modern Methodist Preaching," *MR* 89 (July 1907): 625.
102. Only about 25 percent of the 161 institutions Kelly studied offered courses in evangelism by 1920. Baptist and Methodist seminaries taught more of these courses than the seminaries of other denominations. See *Theological Education in America,* 141.
103. "Modern Methodist Preaching," 626.
104. Kelly, *Theological Education in America,* 136.

how Christian institutions and practices developed. It also promoted tolerance, understanding, and broad-mindedness, delineated "the vital, evangelizing currents of history," examined the forces that had "Christianized nations and civilization," illuminated the Bible and religious truth, and provided interesting illustrations for sermons.[105]

While Methodists did not stress the study of biblical languages as much as Presbyterians did, some Methodists did extol the virtues of Greek and Hebrew. In 1904 the editors of the *Methodist Review* chided ministers who had "not opened their Hebrew Bible[s] since they left seminary."[106] The next year the editors rebuked ministers who told seminary students that the knowledge of biblical languages had "been of absolutely no use to them." The study of Greek and Hebrew, the editors maintained, was valuable because it enabled ministers to use the critical commentaries and to prepare better sermons.[107]

Garrett and other MEC seminaries diligently strove to promote Christian piety among their students. One reason many students came to seminary, GBI's president, Frederick Eiselen, explained, was to deepen their own spiritual life through Christian fellowship, the development of their spiritual gifts, and the practice of personal devotions. This was accomplished by the example and spiritual direction of the faculty, classroom instruction and interaction, prayer meetings, the reading of devotional literature, and chapel services.[108]

In the years from 1890 to 1920 Methodist theology underwent much more of a transition than did Presbyterian theology. During the 1890s, evangelical Arminianism and liberal evangelicalism gave way to the evangelical liberalism of Milton Terry, Olin Curtis, Henry Sheldon, Harris Rall, and Albert Knudson.[109] Professors in Methodist seminaries increasingly studied in European (especially German) universities where they were heavily influenced by rationalism, philosophical idealism, and biblical criticism. The rise of the social gospel, with its emphases on the social teachings of Jesus, the kingdom of God, and reformation of American society, also profoundly affected Methodist theology. Their concern about social ethics led Methodists to both theological reformulation and practical action.[110]

Opposition to the efforts of MEC seminary professors to accommodate the denomination's theology to the new critical studies of the Bible and intellectual currents was evident in many articles published in the *Methodist Review* and

105. John Faulkner, *On the Value of Church History* (New York: The Methodist Book Concern, 1920).
106. "Seasonable Advice to Theological Students," *MR* 86 (Nov. 1904): 973.
107. See "The Relation of Greek to a Theological Course," *MR* 87 (Nov. 1905): 975–77, quotation from 977. Cf. "The Value of Hebrew and Greek to the Minister," *MR* 96 (March 1914): 307–11.
108. Eiselen, "The Theological School To-Day," 25–28.
109. See Robert Chiles, *Theological Transition in American Methodism: 1790–1935* (New York: Abingdon, 1965), 65.
110. See Gerald McCulloh, "The Changing Theological Emphases," in *The History of Methodism*, vol. II (New York: Abingdon Press, 1964), 595–96.

in various books, especially those of John Faulkner, professor of church history at Drew Theological Seminary, and Harold Paul Sloan, professor of systematic theology at Temple University.[111] During the early twentieth century, evangelical Methodists pressured their denomination to include only those books in the Course of Study that they considered to be in harmony with Methodist doctrinal standards.[112] The efforts of evangelicals were unsuccessful, however, as extensive changes in the Course of Study in the MEC in 1916 and the MEC, South in 1918 added even more works by theological liberals.[113]

While the PCUSA clearly affirmed its theological beliefs in the Westminster Confession of Faith, adopted by the denomination in 1729 and revised in 1903, the Methodist Episcopal Church did not have such a clearly defined or binding doctrinal standard. As a contemporary Methodist scholar argues, Methodism evolved "with a minimal *theological* self-consciousness." Its leaders have usually emphasized particular themes such as "religious experience," "assurance," and "holiness," but they have "stopped short of claiming that the Methodist position amounted to a peculiar *configuration* of common Christian doctrine."[114] This contention can be clearly seen in the years from 1890 to 1920. In their Episcopal Address of 1900 the Methodist bishops identified the denomination's cardinal tenets as belief in "one living and personal God" who sustained and ruled the world, in the deity, lordship, atonement, and resurrection of Jesus Christ, in ministry of the Holy Spirit, in God's "impartial love" for "the whole human family," and in surrender to Christ as the only means of salvation. "Beyond the limits of these central and constitutive verities of the Christian faith," the bishops declared, "Methodism has never insisted on uniformity of thought or statement. It has allowed freedom of reverent inquiry. . . . In its Christocentric theology and its spirit of aggressive evangelism it has found sufficient safeguards against individual eccentricities of thought."[115] The bishops insisted in their 1904 address that their denomination had "always been strenuously insistent as to the doctrines essential to Christianity and exceedingly tolerant as to nonessentials."[116] Notably absent

111. See, for example, John Faulkner, *Modernism and the Christian Faith* (1921); Harold Paul Sloan, *Historic Christianity and the New Theology* (1922).
112. See William W. Sweet, *Methodism in American History* (Nashville: Abingdon Press, 1953), 392.
113. See John Faulkner, "One Hundred Years of Episcopal Methodism," *CA* 101 (Sept. 9, 1926): 1124.
114. Albert Outler, "Methodism's Theological Heritage," in Thomas C. Oden and Leicester R. Longden, eds., *The Wesleyan Theological Heritage* (Grand Rapids: Zondervan, 1991), 193. Cf. Thomas A. Langford, *Practical Divinity: Theology in the Wesleyan Tradition* (Nashville: Abingdon Press, 1983), 79, 87, 110ff., 126, 170, 193, 261–71.
115. *Journal*, 1900, 58–59, quotation from 59. An expanded statement of these convictions is reprinted in the 1908 Episcopal Address as a "full, complete, and true" account of the faith of the denomination. See *Journal*, 1908, 128–29.
116. *Journal*, 1904, 121. Cf. John A. Faulkner, "Theological Seminary Orthodoxy: A Statement in History," *MR* 86 (July 1904): 631.

from this list of essentials is any statement about the authority and infallibility of the Bible or the virgin birth and miracles of Christ, doctrines which were crucial to evangelical Presbyterians like those at Princeton.[117]

The same passion for revivalism, social reform, and personal holiness that helped to make the nineteenth century the "Methodist age" informed its seminary education in the years from 1890 to 1920. Concentration on these elements, coupled with its seminaries' practical preparation for ministry, played a major role in the denomination's growth during the first half of the twentieth century. The failure of its theological seminaries to articulate clearly, teach, or defend a theological system (beyond key essentials), or its clergy and laity to agree upon one, however, eventually contributed to Methodism's theological confusion, lack of direction, diminished spirituality, and loss of membership in the years after 1965.

Evangelism, social reform, spiritual formation, biblical theology, and the defense of orthodoxy are all important components of the evangelical tradition. Today's evangelical seminaries probably find it no easier to give these five important aspects of the gospel a proper and prominent place in their curricula than did their predecessors in the early twentieth century. Today's evangelical pastors have an even more diverse set of roles to perform than clergy did during the Progressive era. Their congregations expect them to be persuasive preachers, wise teachers, competent counselors, efficient administrators, compassionate visitors, sensitive spiritual guides, community leaders, and much more. As a result, evangelical seminaries continue to struggle with how to balance the academic and the practical in their programs with how to prepare prospective pastors for these varied roles which require different gifts and training. To serve the church and the world effectively, today's evangelical seminaries must help students to develop a personal, biblically based theology and to learn how to defend the faith (Princeton's specialties). They must also train students to evangelize the unsaved, to model and promote personal spiritual development, and to encourage efforts to remedy social ills (Garrett's strengths). The experience of Princeton Theological Seminary and Garrett Biblical Institute during the years from 1890 to 1920 highlight the difficulties involved in trying to prepare future ministers to fulfill these diverse responsibilities. Their histories, as well as those of their sister seminaries during this thirty year period, demonstrate that arranging the program of theological education to emphasize some important aspects of the evangelical tradition can easily lead to giving insufficient attention to others.

---

117. Methodists did believe that communions had the right to expect professors in their seminaries to represent truly them by teaching and promoting their central beliefs and practices. See "Theological Schools and the Church," *MR* 77 (July 1895): 641; "Boston University School of Theology," *CA* 75 (March 1, 1900): 328.

Part 2

Spiritual Formation and Theological Education

A recent article in *Christianity Today,* entitled "Re-Engineering the Seminary," examined several aspects of the problems confronting evangelical seminaries, both from within these schools and from the churches that they serve. One of the greatest concerns, according to the article, is that of the spiritual formation of seminary students. While evangelical theological education appears to do well in preparing students for the intellectual aspects of ministry, such as biblical interpretation, theological understanding, and historical awareness, many church leaders and seminary administrators worry that seminarians graduate with insufficient spiritual awareness or vitality.

As the chapters in the second section demonstrate, this concern about the spiritual formation of students preparing for ministry is in many respects a variation on an old evangelical theme. From the training of ministers during the era of Protestant scholasticism, to evangelical pastors in the eighteenth and nineteenth centuries, to the desire today for godly ministers, the spiritual vitality of students training for the ministry has been a paramount concern. Usually this desire for godly ministers has taken shape in the fear that intellectual sophistication undermines spiritual vitality. What has mattered most to evangelicals historically is not what ministers know, but whether they have had an authentic experience of God's grace.

The chapters in this part of the book illustrate this point well. Richard A. Muller begins with the training of ministers in the era of Protestant scholasticism, the time when, according to many evangelicals of later periods, concerns for theological rigor triumphed over interest in vital or heartfelt religion. What Muller shows, however, contrary to many of the caricatures, is that Protestant scholastics stressed the need for spiritual zeal and Christian character as much as their later detractors. In the next chapter, David Kling examines the tradition of theological education in eighteenth-century New England before the rise of seminaries. This essay not only provides some insight into the workings of an older apprentice-model of theological education for which some contemporary faculty and administrators long, but it also encourages some reflection upon the structures and forms of education necessary for spiritual formation of a genuine kind. Finally, James E. Bradley offers a provocative study of changing conceptions of pastoral theology in nineteenth-century Anglo-American Protestantism and uses his findings to make insightful comments on the reasons for the separation of theological knowledge and spiritual formation, which has constantly dogged the history of evangelical seminaries. The history that follows will certainly not resolve the dilemmas facing contemporary evangelical seminaries, but may provide a helpful perspective for pastors, faculty, administrators, and students who wrestle with the relationship between correct theology and genuine piety.

5

The Era of Protestant Orthodoxy

Richard A. Muller

It can easily be argued that one of the primary roots of the Reformation was curricular reform in the university, specifically the reform of the theological curriculum.[1] Of the early Reformers, Luther, in particular, was an academician. As Gordon Rupp commented,

> We shall never understand Luther unless we remember that he was by trade a Theological Professor, that year in, year out (the exceptions can be counted on the fingers), twice a week at the appointed hour, he walked into the lecture-room and addressed successive generations of students, and this for thirty years until he was old and feeble and could only croak his last lecture.[2]

Luther's insistence on the study of Scripture in the original languages, his attacks on late medieval scholastic theology, and his demand for the liberation of theology from Aristotle rested, of course, on theological premises, but their most immediate impact was on the reshaping of the theological curriculum at Wittenberg. So, too, were the efforts of Luther's close associate, Philip Melanchthon, in the areas of logic, rhetoric, and ethics, attempts to reframe the curriculum under the pressure of new theological and philosophical assumptions. This reframing of the theological curriculum, first, to meet the needs of the early Reformation protest and, subsequently, to meet the needs of an institutionally, as well as theologically, successful Protestantism occupied the minds of teachers of theology throughout the sixteenth and the seventeenth centuries. In the following essay, we will briefly

1. Cf. E. G. Schwiebert, *Luther and His Times: The Reformation From a New Perspective* (St. Louis: Concordia, 1950), 293–302 with Heinrich Boehmer, *Martin Luther: Road to Reformation*, trans. J. W. Doberstein and T. G. Tappert (Philadelphia: Muhlenberg, 1946), 157–63.
2. Gordon Rupp, *Luther's Progress to the Diet of Worms* (New York: Harper & Row, 1964), 24–25.

trace out the earlier development of methods and rules for the study of theology, emphasizing the Reformed side of the development, and then focus our attention on the completed form of Protestant theological education offered in the works of the seventeenth-century Reformed writers, Voetius and Witsius.[3]

From Reformation to Orthodoxy: The Trajectory of Protestant Theological Education

The crisis of the Reformation brought new questioning of the grounds for theology and of the proper methods of study. Already at the beginning of the sixteenth century, Erasmus had put his humanist sensibilities to work on these questions and, in the preface on theological study affixed to the 1519 edition of his Greek New Testament, he strongly encouraged the study of biblical languages, and collateral disciplines like logic and rhetoric.[4] Erasmus counseled that Aristotelian and scholastic philosophy be studied, but not overemphasized: doctrinal theology ought to be constructed by the orderly, topical collation of texts from the Scriptures and the fathers. He also emphasized, quite strongly, the relationships between study of the materials of theology and the development of personal piety. Prayerful study should transform life and ultimately issue forth in public morality and piety.

Influenced both by Erasmus's humanistic piety and by the Reformation battle cry of *sola Scriptura,* Melanchthon on the Lutheran side and Bullinger on the Reformed wrote treatises on the spirituality and methodology of theological study. Melanchthon's *Brevis ratio discendi theologiae* is only a few pages long. It emphasizes the centrality of faith and justification not only to theology, but also to the shaping of the curriculum. The New Testament, Melanchthon asserts, ought to be studied before the Old Testament and the exegesis of Romans and the Gospel of John should frame the study as beginning and end in order to establish the doctrinal foundation. The Old Testament ought to be read in sequence, beginning with Genesis and concluding with the Psalms and the Prophets.[5] Melanchthon also of-

---

3. Discussion of the Lutheran development can be found in Robert D. Preus, *The Theology of Post-Reformation Lutheranism,* 2 vols. (St. Louis: Concordia, 1970–1972).

4. On Erasmus, see, e.g., Carl S. Meyer, "Erasmus on the Study of the Scriptures," in *Concordia Theological Monthly* 40 (1969): 734–46; Albert Rabil, Jr., *Erasmus and the New Testament: The Mind of a Christian Humanist* (San Antonio: Trinity University Press, 1972); Heinze Holeczek, *Humanistische Bibelphilologie als Reformproblem bei Erasmus von Rotterdam, Thomas More, und William Tyndale* (Leiden: Brill, 1975); Marjorie O'Rourke Boyle, *Erasmus on Language and Method in Theology* (Toronto: University of Toronto Press, 1977); W. van 't Spijker, "Gereformeerde Scholastiek II: Scholastiek, Erasmus, Luther, Melanchthon," *Theologia Reformata* 29 (1986): 7–27.

5. Melanchthon, *Brevis discendae theologiae ratio,* in *Philippi Melanchthonis opera quae supersunt omnia,* eds. C. G. Bretschneider and H. E. Bindseil, 28 vols. (Halle/Braunschweig, 1844–), vol. 2, cols. 455–62.

fered his students a series of brief works on the method of Christian preaching, notably, the section *De sacris concionibus* in his *De Rhetorica libri tres* (1519), *De officiis concionatoris* (1529), and *De modo et arte concionandi* (1540).[6] Beyond this, the prefaces to various editions of his *Loci communes*, offered suggestions on the pattern and method of theological system. Here, Melanchthon emphasized the identification and arrangement of the fundamental theological topics and recommended a model in which causes preceded effects and in which the "historical series" of events in the plan of redemption be observed. Thus, discussion of God precedes the doctrine of creation, sin precedes redemption, law precedes gospel.[7] What we do not find in Melanchthon's work is an integrative approach to the study of theology as a whole or a discussion of the life and character of theological students, although Melanchthon did recommend study of the church fathers, particularly of Augustine, of the Greek and Latin classics, and of philosophy. Melanchthon warned of the dangers of worldly wisdom, but nonetheless insisted, like Erasmus, that philosophy could not be ignored.

A more thoroughly integrative approach, written from a very practical standpoint and including both curricular and attitudinal insight was, however, forthcoming from Heinrich Bullinger. His *Ratio studiorum* (1527) offered a basic approach to study followed by a presentation of philosophical and theological *loci communes* and a brief, axiomatic statement of Christian doctrine—in short, it provided a general approach to study followed by a basic pattern of instruction focused on theology.[8] Bullinger recommends a disciplined structuring of the hours of the day to avoid waste of time, particularly in the morning, and indicates that the day's study ought

6. Philip Melanchthon, *De Rhetroica libri tres* [later, *Elementa rhetorices*], in *Opera quae supersunt omnia*, vol. 13, cols. 413–506; *De officiis concionatoris*, in *Suppelmenta Melanchthonia*, V. Abteilung, Teil II, *Homiletische Schriften*, eds. P. Drews and F. Cohrs (Leipzig, 1929), 5–14; and *De modo et arte concionandi*, in ibid., 33–55; also see Uwe Schnell, *Die homiletische Theorie Philipp Melanchthons* (Hamburg: Lutherisches Verlagshaus, 1968), 54–57 for a discussion of these treatises plus Melanchthon's two unpublished works on the subject, *Quomodo concionator novitus concionem suam informare debet* (ca. 1532–36) and *De ratioine concionandi* (1552); both treatises are edited in *Homiletische Schriften* (17–19 and 59–79 respectively).

7. Philip Melanchthon, *Loci communes* (1533) in *Opera quae supersunt omnia*, vol. 21, col. 253–54. The definitive study of Melanchthon's concept of historical or scriptural series is Peter Fraenkel, *Testimonia Patrum: The Function of Patristic Argument in the Theology of Philip Melanchthon* (Geneva, 1961), 52–109; also see the discussions of Melanchthon's contribution to theological method in Robert D. Preus, *The Theology of Post-Reformation Lutheranism*, 2 vols. (St. Louis: Concordia, 1970–1972), I, 77–82; and Richard A. Muller, *Post-Reformation Reformed Dogmatics* (Grand Rapids: Baker Book House, 1987–), vol. I, 66–67; and also see Robert Kolb, "Teaching the Text: The Commonplace Method in Sixteenth Century Lutheran Biblical Commentary," in *Bibliothèque d'Humanisme et Renaissance* 49 (1987): 571–85.

8. Heinrich Bullinger, *Ratio studiorum, sive de institutione eorum, qui studia literarum sequuntur, libellus aureus. Accessit eodem dispositio locorum communium, tam philosophicorum, quam theologicorum. Item, Christianae fidei perspicue & breviter proposita quaedam axiomata. . . .* (Zürich, 1594).

to begin with prayer. There can be no success in study unless God instills it *(nisi Deus aspiret)*: Bullinger's prayer requests the ability to serve God in purity of life with wisdom, intelligence, and memory, under the law of God, with genuine reverence and erudition.[9] After further counsel about the conduct of the day, including comments about meals and the importance of evening study, Bullinger proposes a course of readings, beginning with "profane letters." Pagan authors, he notes, were read and used by the apostle Paul and by fathers like Basil the Great; so too, Quadratus, Aristides, Justin, Irenaeus, Tertullian, Clement of Alexandria, and Origen. Even so, the various divisions of philosophy—verbal, moral, and natural—ought to be studied and the works of the poets, orators, and ancient historians carefully perused.[10]

Bullinger introduces his discussion of the study of sacred letters with a citation from the Wisdom of Solomon: "The spirit of wisdom will not be sent into a wicked mind."[11] Here, especially, must iniquity be set aside and a love of God be fostered through prayer. In order for a right understanding, Bullinger notes, there must be sound belief, true worship, piety, and reverence to the end that all good results are dedicated to the glory of God.[12] Study in the ancient languages is necessary, Bullinger notes; for a right understanding of the text, he recommends Conrad Pellican's work on the Hebrew language, Sebastian Munster's and Elias Levita's Hebrew grammars; for Greek, the works of Rellicanus, Melanchthon, and Ceporinus.[13] Commentators, too, are to be consulted for the sake of understanding more clearly the "truth" of the Greek and Hebrew texts. He recommends Zwingli, Erasmus, Pellican, Oecolampadius, Melanchthon, Capito, and Munster.

Further, the basic linguistic techniques necessary to the understanding of Scripture do not differ from those necessary to the reading of classical literature.[14] But the student of Scripture must also be aware of its unique center or *scopus* of meaning to which all the books of Scripture point, the covenant of God in which "God first binds himself to us . . . and then prescribes what is required of us." It is, then, in the light of this broader understanding that the tropes, analogies, and symbols in the text are to be understood. Bullinger concludes his discussion of Scripture with a lengthy examination of forms and patterns of interpretation.[15]

9. Bullinger, *Ratio studiorum*, 2v–3r.
10. Ibid., 7v–9v. Bullinger devotes several successive chapters to the various types of profane letters that ought to be studied and mastered: 10r–22r.
11. Ibid., 22v, citing Wisdom 1:4.
12. Ibid., 22v–23r.
13. Ibid., 27v–28v.
14. Ibid., 26v.
15. Ibid., 30r–32r. On the "scope" of Scripture, see Boyle, *Erasmus on Language and Method*, 75–79 and Muller, *Post-Reformation Reformed Dogmatics*, II, 211–30.

If the emphasis of Bullinger's treatise fell on the exposition of Scripture and on the identification of the theological topics or *loci communes* to be elicited from Scripture, he also clearly assumed both a breadth of general learning and a consistent exercise of piety on the part of the theological student—indeed, he viewed both as prerequisites to theological study. In addition, Bullinger's own experience of teaching in a Cistercian monastery surely appears in the treatise, in the form of the ordering of the hours of the day, the planning of meals, and the intentional right ordering of the inward self through preparatory prayer.[16] This is a point of continuity in theological education that connects the later Middle Ages (and, in fact, the greater part of the Christian tradition) with the Reformation and, as will be evident in the discussion of Voetius, with post-Reformation Protestant orthodoxy as well.

The propaedeutic essays of Melanchthon and Bullinger were soon followed by lengthier essays on theological study by less-famous writers like David Chytraeus (a pupil of Melanchthon),[17] and Andreas Hyperius.[18] Chytraeus and Hyperius do not identify a strictly defined model for theological study, such as the gathering of all subdisciplines into biblical, historical, systematic, and practical fields, but they do enumerate various aspects or elements of theological study that resemble this later and more elaborate "theological encyclopedia." Chytraeus presents ten rules for theological study, beginning with prayer and concluding with "cross and affliction." Nothing in theology, he argues, can be learned apart from a right relationship with God and none of the subject matter can be divorced from personal piety. With these two rules of spiritual discipline framing his entire program, Chytraeus can go on to place the careful and continual study of Scripture second, the gathering of theological topics *(loci)* and the practice of logic and rhetoric in third, fourth, fifth place, and the study of languages, the reading of biblical commentaries and patristic study, history, and philosophy rounding out the list.[19]

Hyperius's far more detailed work, the *De theologo, seu de ratione studii theologiae,* may well be the most extended Protestant essay on the basic study of theology written in the sixteenth century.[20] In addition to this larger

16. On Bullinger's life, career, and basic thought, see David C. Steinmetz, *Reformers in the Wings* (Philadelphia: Fortress, 1971), 133–42; also note the major study by Fritz Blanke, *Der junge Bullinger, 1504–1531* (Zürich, 1942).
17. David Chytraeus, *De Studio theologiae* (Wittenberg, 1562); cf. the discussion in Preus, *Theology of Post-Reformation Lutheranism,* I, 104–7.
18. Cf. the survey of propaedeutic works in Hagenbach, 121–23 with Muller, *Post-Reformation Reformed Dogmatics,* I, 67–72; and Preus, *The Theology of Post-Reformation Lutheranism,* I, 82–88.
19. Preus, *Theology of Post-Reformation Lutheranism,* I, 105–6.
20. Andreas Hyperius, *De Theologo, seu de ratione studii theologici, libri IIII* (Basel, 1559); cf. W. van 't Spijker, *Principe, methode en functie van de theologie bij Andreas Hyperius,* Apeldoornse Studies, 26 (Kampen: J. H. Kok, 1990).

curricular essay, Hyperius also produced two treatises on preaching, *De formandis concionibus sacris* and *opica theologica*,[21] and a treatise on the right method of reading and meditating on Scripture.[22] Quite characteristic of older Protestantism, Hyperius's works viewed theological study as an aid to piety and directed his readers to work prayerfully with due respect to their sources. He also very clearly draws on the medieval background of Protestantism in his identification of theology as a form of *sapientia* or wisdom, as well as a form of knowledge or intellective discipline, a *scientia*. Indeed, the apostle Paul himself, Hyperius argues, defines theology as "a wisdom not of this world . . . wisdom in a mystery . . . that was ordained by God before all words and revealed by his spirit."[23] This identification, moreover, provides him with the foundational assumption of his treatise, perhaps drawn from Bullinger, that the study of theology must be guided by the sapiential writings of the Old Testament: "The fear of God," he wrote, citing Proverbs 1:7, "is the beginning of knowledge *(scientia)*." The student of theology must, therefore, "prepare [his] soul for the diligent reading of sacred letters" by calling on God in prayer to purge him of "wicked affections," illuminate his darkness and render his soul calm, gentle, benevolent, and humble, to the exclusion of vanity and contentiousness.[24] Theological study, therefore, is not merely the learning of certain materials but the spiritual formation of the person. Again Hyperius has recourse to Proverbs: "he who walks with wisdom, is wise."[25]

Beyond piety and spiritual formation, Hyperius also assumes a rigorous course of study in various disciplines that are "necessary" to theological knowing: philosophy in its subdisciplines of grammar, logic, and rhetoric, as taught by the classical pagan writers and by the fathers of the church;[26] the mathematical arts of arithmetic, geometry, music, and astronomy;[27] physics;[28] ethics, politics, economics, and metaphysics, again all resting on the classical models;[29] history, architecture, and agriculture;[30] and above all the

21. Andreas Gerardus Hyperius, *De formandis concoinibus sacris seu de interpretatione scripturarum populari libri II* (Marburg, 1553); also printed at Dortmund (1555), Marburg (1562), Basel (1563, 1579), and Halle (1781); the treatise is available in a modern German translation with an introduction by Ernst Christian Achelis and Eugen Sachsse in *Die Homiletik und die Katechetik des Andreas Hyperius* (Berlin: Reuther & Reichard, 1901).

22. Andreas Hyperius, *De sacrae scripturae lectione ac mediatatione quotidiana, omnibus omnium ordinum hominibus Christianis perquam necessaria, libri II* (Basel, 1561); translated as *The Course of Christianitie: or, As touching the Dayly Reading and Meditation of the Holy Scriptures*, trans. John Ludham (London, 1579).

23. Hyperius, *De theologo*, 40, citing 1 Cor. 1 (cf. 1 Cor. 1:28–31, 2:7).

24. Ibid., 34.

25. Ibid., 36, citing Prov. 13:20.

26. Ibid., 45–52 (lib. I, cap. 4).

27. Ibid., 52–55 (lib. I, cap. 5).

28. Ibid., 55–57 (lib. I, cap. 6).

29. Ibid., 57–64 (lib. I, cap. 7).

30. Ibid., 64–65 (lib. I, cap. 8).

classical languages, especially Hebrew and Greek.[31] In what is certainly a reflection both of the Melanchthonian roots of his thought and of the needs of curriculum in a time of the institutionalization of Protestantism, Hyperius argues the relevance and suitability of philosophical study on the ground that the "human" discipline of philosophy is a gift of God.[32] All of these subjects of study are, of course, recommended by way of preparation for theology—and reflect a humanistic revision of the medieval university curriculum that still respects the trivium and quadrivium, but has broadened study particularly in the direction of languages and has insisted on the reading of sources in their original tongues.

Hyperius next divides the course of theological study into three general topical areas that adumbrate the eventual division of theological study into a "fourfold encyclopedia"—Scripture and its interpretation,[33] doctrinal theology or the *loci communes*,[34] and practical, consisting in the history and governance of the church, including polity, ritual, worship, and preaching.[35] The text of Hyperius's *De theologo*, extending to more than seven hundred pages, is far too detailed to examine here. Suffice it to say that, like Melanchthon, Hyperius understood doctrinal topics as following from exegesis, but he does not sever the study of the Old Testament from the study of the New Testament, and he recognizes that theological works of the past, particularly the works of the fathers, contribute to the identification of *loci*. It is also noteworthy that historical study, if not clearly distinguished from polemics as in the eighteenth- and nineteenth-century fourfold encyclopedia, is, nonetheless, understood by Hyperius as consisting in more than polemics.[36] His massive essay also continues to emphasize the importance of piety and prayer as it develops its curriculum and, in much the same spirit as Bullinger's *Ratio studiorum*, assumes a vast bibliography of biblical texts and tools, patristic texts, classical works in the various areas of philosophy, theological works of the Reformers and, in Hyperius's case, a knowledge of the major scholastic theologians as well. As Van 't Spijker has argued, the unifying characteristic of Hyperius's approach lies in its consistent union of learning and with religious life—of *ratio* and *oratio, eloquentia* and *pietas*—its stress on *pietas literata* and *literatura pia*.[37]

The orthodox or scholastic era of Protestantism was a time of further codification and institutionalization in the churches of the Reformation, in which

31. Ibid., 65–80 (lib. I, cap. 9).
32. Ibid., 47; and cf. the discussion in Van 't Spijker, *Principe, methode en functie*, 25–29.
33. Hyperius, *De theologo*, 80–425 (lib. II, cap. 1–38).
34. Ibid., 425–562 (lib. III, cap. 1–8).
35. Ibid., 562–756 (lib. IV, cap. 1–10).
36. Modifying the arguments of Edward Farley, *Theologia: The Fragmentation and Unity of Theological Education* (Philadelphia: Fortress, 1983), 78–79.
37. Van 't Spijker, *Principe, methode en functie*, 29.

the initial efforts of Bullinger, Hyperius, and others in defining the shape of Protestant theology and at the same time of Protestant theological study were refined, elaborated, and adapted to new circumstances on the grand scale typical of the age of the baroque.[38] It is also one of the periods in the history of the church most subject to adverse comment and negative assessment in works of history and theology. The strict application of scholastic method by the Protestant thinkers of the period that has so often drawn anachronistic and theologically motivated critique from historians and theologians of the nineteenth and twentieth centuries not only aided this process of codification, it also provided one of the several crucial links between developing Protestantism and the ongoing Western intellectual and academic tradition. Indeed, the scholasticism of the late sixteenth and early seventeenth centuries ought not to be understood as a simple return to medieval methods; rather, it was the result of a developing tradition of logic, rhetoric, and learning that altered the patterns of scholastic education even as it preserved them.[39] Thus, also, the drive to enunciate and to maintain a churchly and confessional orthodoxy or "right teaching" that was characteristic of the era both reinforced the relationship of Protestantism to the great tradition of Christianity and encouraged Protestant teachers to examine theological training as one aspect of the ongoing codification and institutionalization of reform.[40]

Even so, powerful continuities in doctrine, biblical interpretation, and the method and approach of theological study can be identified between the Protestantism of the sixteenth and that of the seventeenth century.[41] The in-

38. For further discussion and definition of Protestant scholasticism, see: Muller, *Post-Reformation Reformed Dogmatics*, vol. I, 30–36, 730–74, 307–11; and idem, "Orthodoxy, Protestant" s.v., in *Encyclopedia of the Reformed Faith*, ed. Donald McKim (Louisville, Ky.: Westminster/John Knox Press, 1992). The best histories of the theology of the period remain Wilhelm Gass, *Geschichte der protestantischen Dogmatik in ihrem Zusammenhange mit der Theologie*, 4 vols. (Berlin, 1854–1867); Isaac A. Dorner, *History of Protestant Theology Particularly in Germany*, trans. Robson and Taylor, 2 vols. (Edinburgh: T. & T. Clark, 1871); and Otto Ritschl, *Dogmengeschichte des Protestantismus: Grundlagen und Grundzüge der theologischen Gedanken—und Lehrbildung in den protestantischen Kirchen*, 4 vols. (Leipzig: J.C. Hinrichs, 1908–1912; Göttingen: Vandenhoeck & Ruprecht, 1926–1927).

39. For further discussion of the impact of the scholastic revival on Protestant thought, see: Hans Emil Weber, *Die philosophische Scholastik des deutschen Protestantismus in Zeitalter der Orthodoxie* (Leipzig, 1907); idem, *Der Einfluss der protestantischen Schulphilosophie auf die orthodox-lutherische Dogmatik* (Leipzig, 1908); Ernst Lewalter, *Spanisch-jesuitisch und deutsch-lutherische Metaphysik des 17. Jahrhunderts* (Hamburg, 1935; repr. Darmstadt, 1968); Paul Dibon, *L'Enseignement philosophique dans les Universités neerlandaises à l'epoque précartesienne* (Amsterdam, 1954); and Richard A. Muller, *God, Creation and Providence in the Thought of Jacob Arminius: Sources and Directions of Scholastic Protestantism in the Era of Early Orthodoxy* (Grand Rapids: Baker Book House, 1991).

40. See further, Richard A. Muller, "*Vera Philosphia cum sacra Theologia nusquam pugnat*: Keckermann on Philosophy, Theology and the Problem of Double Truth," *The Sixteenth Century Journal* vol. XV, no. 3 (fall, 1984): 341–65; and idem, "Scholasticism Protestant and Catholic: Francis Turretin on the Object and Principles of Theology" in *Church History* vol. 55, no. 2 (June 1986): 193–205.

41. I have traced some of these issues of continuity and discontinuity in *Christ and the Decree: Christology and Predestination in Reformed Theology from Calvin to Perkins* (Durham, N.C.: Labyrinth Press, 1986; Grand Rapids: Baker Book House, 1988); and *Post-Reformation Reformed Dogmatics*, I, 112–21, 167–93, 308–11; II, 86–97, 159–68, 182–97, 243–61 et passim.

stitutionalization and codification of church and doctrine associated with scholastic orthodoxy entailed, in no small part, the institutionalization and codification of doctrinal and educational principles and concerns enunciated by the Reformers. In the seventeenth and early eighteenth century, even Hyperius's lengthy treatise was dwarfed by the introductory descriptions of theological study by Johannes Gerhard, Abraham Calovius, and Johannes Buddaeus among the Lutherans, and Johannes Alsted and Gisbert Voetius among the Reformed.[42] In all of these works, the *sola Scriptura* of the Reformation is maintained while the exegetical study of Scripture is reinforced by intense study of ancient languages. The seventeenth century was the age of the great Protestant Hebraists and Orientalists—Buxtorf, Lightfoot, Walton—and of the great London Polyglott Bible. From exegesis, the authors move to doctrinal or systematic theology. Gerhard describes a five-year course of study, beginning with three years of biblical and doctrinal study. In the third year students would study the great debated questions in polemic with Roman Catholics, Reformed, and Anabaptist writers. In the fourth year preaching would be added to the course and in the fifth year, church history.[43] Voetius presents a similar model, as do the other authors noted.[44] Here, too, as we noted in the work of Hyperius, the fourfold model of encyclopedia continues to emerge in the movement of the curriculum from biblical to dogmatic study and in understanding of ecclesiastical discussion as concerned with the history, but also with the present practice of the church.[45]

The Theological Task: Gisbert Voetius's Paradigm for Theological Education

Gisbert Voetius's *Exercitia et bibliotheca studiosi theologiae* or *Exercises and Library for the Student of Theology* (1651) is one of the academic and spiritual landmarks of the era of Reformed orthodoxy. Voetius himself was, by all testimony, one of the most adept of the Protestant scholastic theologians—adept at biblical languages and theological exegesis, adept at catechetical theology and intricate dogmatic argumentation, and adept, above

---

42. Cf. Hagenbach, 123–25 with Muller, *Post-Reformation Reformed Dogmatics*, I, 267–76; and Preus, *Theology of Post-Reformation Lutheranism*, I, 120–28.

43. Johann Gerhard, *Methodus studii theologiae* (Jena, 1620); note also the prolegomena to his *Loci Theologici*, 9 vols., ed. Preuss (Berlin, 1863–75); cf. Preus, *Theology of Post-Reformation Lutheranism*, I, 120–21.

44. Gisbert Voetius, *Exercitia et bibliotheca studiosi theologiae* (Utrecht, 1651).

45. Cf. Farley, *Theologia*, 62–80. Farley quite correctly argues that much of the unity of pre-Enlightenment theological study arose out of the stress on theology as a *praxis* or *scientia practica* and on the cultivation of a theological disposition or *habitus* combining in students learning and piety. Farley does, however, overemphasize the modern, post-Schleiermacherian character of the fourfold encyclopedia and, in his interpretation of the older theology, he overestimates the weight of the subjective disposition in relation to the objective content of theology. For an appreciation and critique of Farley, see Richard A. Muller, *The Study of Theology* (Grand Rapids: Zondervan, 1991), 28–37, 45–50.

all, at disputation and polemic. The greater part of his published output took the form of theological disputations on virtually all of the topics in dogmatics and against nearly all of the doctrinal adversaries of the Reformed faith.[46] He was not a specialist in polemics, like his colleague Johannes Hoornbeeck,[47] but he brought to the polemical task not only a mastery of style, but also a mastery of materials that made him a dread opponent. Granting that his reputation rests largely on these disputations, it is hardly surprising that he, together with the greater number of his scholastic contemporaries, is thought of as an unremitting logician rather than as a warm-hearted pietist and that historians have generally seen fit to remember with kindness not the sometimes stringent scholastic argumentation of Voetius, but the covenantal biblicism of his chief adversary, Johannes Cocceius, the inherent problems and idiosyncrasies of Cocceius's exegesis and dogmatics notwithstanding.[48]

If Voetius was a scholastic and a logician, however, he was also a theologian who emphasized the covenantal theme of Reformed theology, and stressed the need for personal character and piety—indeed, of spiritual exercise—among his students. His teaching produced such lights of the later seventeenth century as the covenant theologian, Herman Witsius, and the leading teacher of the Dutch pietist movement known as the *Nadere Reformatie*, Wilhelmus à Brakel.[49] This other side of Voetius's teaching was presented at the very beginning of his academic career in his inaugural address at Utrecht, *De pietate cum scientia coniungenda* (On the Conjunction of Piety With Learning), developed in his *Exercitia pietatis in usum juventutis academicae* (Exercises in Piety for Young Scholars),[50] and subsequently documented on a grand scale in his *Exercises and Library for the Student of Theology.*

46. Gisbert Voetius, *Selectae disputationes theologicae*, 5 vols. (Utrecht, 1648–1669). The standard work on Voetius remains Arnoldus Cornelis Duker, *Gisbertus Voetius*, 3 vols. (Leiden: Brill, 1897–1914); also see Jan Anthony Cramer, *De theologische faculteit de Utrecht ten tijde van Voetius* (Utrecht: Kemink, 1932) and C. Graffland, "Gereformeerde scholastiek VI: De invloed van de scholastiek op de Nadere Reformatie" in *Theologia Reformata* 30 (1987): 109–31, 313–40 (118–28 deal specifically with Voetius).

47. Cf. Johannes Hoornbeeck, *Socinianismus confutatus*, 3 vols. (Utrecht, 1650–64) and idem, *Summa controversiarum religionis, cum infidelibus, haereticis, schismaticis* (Utrecht, 1653).

48. Cf. Charles S. McCoy, "The Covenant Theology of Johannes Cocceius" (Ph.D. diss., Yale University, 1956) and idem, "Johannes Cocceius: Federal Theologian," in *Scottish Journal of Theology* 16 (1963): 352–70 with the alternative view in Muller, *Post-Reformation Reformed Dogmatics*, II, 119–22.

49. See Wilhelmus à Brakel, *The Christian's Reasonable Service in which Divine Truths concerning the Covenant of Grace are Expounded, Defended against Opposing Parties, and their Practice Advocated*, trans. Bartel Elshout, with a biographical sketch by W. Fieret and an essay on the "Dutch Second Reformation" by Joel Beeke (Ligonier, Penn.: Soli Deo Gloria Publications, 1992).

50. Gisbert Voetius, *Ta asketica sive Exercitia pietatis in usum juventutis academicae nunc edita. Addita est, ob materiam affinitatem, Oratio de pietate cum scientia conjungenda habita anno 1634* (Gorinchem, 1664); also Gisbert Voetius, *Inaugurele rede over Godzaligheid te verbinden met de wetenschap: Latijnse tekst opnieuw uitgegeven met Nederlandse vertaling, inleiding en toelichtingen door Dr. Aart De Groot* (Kampen: J. J.. Kok, 1978).

The *Exercises* begin with that perennial question of the church and its of-fices—how does one identify naturally gifted individuals who will, in Voetius's terms, be capable of the demanding course of "higher study" necessary for the understanding of theology? Such individuals, Voetius begins, are to be identi-fied by professors in the university, by pastors, elders, and catechists of the church, in short, by those already chosen within the community to exercise such judgments. Gifted individuals may be identified either from among the uneducated or the educated—the former, he notes, will be, as yet, devoid of error and delusion, the latter will at least have been able to demonstrate their ability and erudition. Also required are personal character traits such as "pi-ety, zeal, natural gifts, a capacity for remembering," a high theological elo-quence, and a willingness to serve the cause of the gospel.[51] Although he does not want to delimit unnecessarily the age of candidates, Voetius suggests that they be no younger than eighteen or twenty years and that they have com-pleted their basic education in elementary Latin, philosophy, catechetical the-ology, and the lower curriculum or trivium.

It is an unfortunate error, he adds, to secure candidates with promises of stipends before fully assessing their gifts. Even more problematic is the fail-ure to identify the truly best candidates because of assumptions concerning social class; it is just as likely, Voetius indicates, for natural abilities to be found among the general populace as among the nobility. Natural abilities, piety, zeal, eloquence, modesty in behavior, prudence, serious demeanor, courtesy, and generosity, are to be preferred to social rank![52] Beyond this, "it is a most grave error of epidemic proportion" to assume that an adolescent deemed studious and moral will necessarily retain and enrich these traits dur-ing his education with careful supervision of parents and mentors and to fall into the trap of equating the inception of theological study with "repentance and conversion from sin."[53]

This clear emphasis on piety and personal religion over social status and prior training in no way leads Voetius to deemphasize learning. After making the case for character and religiosity, he devotes three detailed chapters to the educational preparation for theological study, developing a curriculum and a discipline designed to bring mastery in languages, rhetoric, logic, phi-losophy, general knowledge of such diverse fields as history, geography, pol-itics, and astronomy and, above all, a well-honed technique for and ap-proach to the discipline of study. Thus, Voetius recommends a sevenfold pattern for study consisting in *lectio, meditatio, auditio, scriptio, collatio, collegia,* and *enotatio,* correlated with formal instruction in the various dis-ciplines *(institutio)* and training in various lexical and linguistic tools *(appa-*

51. Voetius, *Exercitia et bibliotheca,* 1–2.
52. Ibid., 3–4.
53. Ibid., 5.

ratus).[54] By *lectio,* or reading, Voetius means a threefold pattern of studying basic disciplines: first, the student examines "synoptic or systematic" works that survey a field; second, he should read the foremost authors whose works both comment on all the significant topics and eludicate the relevant debates; and, third, the student ought to study carefully the classic authors—"Aristotle, Euclid, Ptolemy and so forth." This effort should be followed by a time of *meditatio,* during which "definitions, distinctions, theorems, solutions related to necessary issues, especially to theology are inwardly grasped and committed to memory."[55] In addition to reading and meditation, there is also listening, or hearing *(auditio),* consisting in the "delivery of expositions of Scripture and of the theological topics and in theological and philosophical disputation."[56]

As a fourth element in study, Voetius recommends *scriptio,* or written composition, guided and organized according to the traditional categories of predication, on the basic themes of study, particularly those relevant to theology. Thus a student ought to be able to formulate his thoughts in writing on the category of "substance" with specific attention to created substances such as human beings, animals, and things in the inanimate order, especially those identified in Scripture. "Quality" also ought to be discussed—with reference to such issues as physical, intellectual, or volitional qualities. In the category of "disposition" the student ought to be prepared to discourse on the intellectual dispositions of wisdom, prudence, art, superstition, and virtue, while under the rubric of "action," such issues as creation, conservation, generation, action and reaction, and so forth. These and other categorical presentations should be accomplished with due attention to examples— again, often drawn from Scripture.[57] In support of his written exercises in the disciplines, a student must engage in *collatio* and *collegia,* the gathering and recapitulation of materials. Reading, meditation, hearing, composition, gathering, and recapitulation are finally sharpened by "enotation," by which Voetius understands a mental survey of the studied and memorized materials with a view to the inward systematization and summation of a discipline according to its "problems, arguments, objections, assumptions, distinctions, [and] examples."[58] *Enotatio,* thus, is the internalization of a scholastic method. Taken together in the context of a detailed curriculum, these seven aspects of disciplined study point toward a highly structured, but also a care-

---

54. Following the order of Voetius, *Exercitia et bibliotheca,* 37–41, 48–56, 60–66 where the series is given, in direct relation to the theological curriculum, as *lectio, meditatio, auditio, scriptio, collatio, collegia, enotatio, institutio,* and *apparatus;* but cf. ibid., 22–28, where Voetius offers his general definitions in terms of preparatory study and arranges the series as *lectio, meditatio, enotatio, scriptio, collatio, collegia, auditio, institutio,* and *apparatus.*

55. Ibid., 22–23, cf. 39.

56. Ibid., 40.

57. Ibid., 23–25, 40.

58. Ibid., 22–23, cf. 40–42.

fully integrated pattern of education, designed with a view toward mastery of the field both in theory and in practice. This full course of instruction *(institutio)*, Voetius adds, ought moreover to embrace not only the life of intellect, but also works of Christian love *(caritas)*.[59]

The latter point—the connection between study and *caritas*—becomes the subject of an entire chapter in Voetius's *Exercises*. He indicates a series of "general adjuncts and special efforts and exercises" belonging to theological study. The "general adjuncts" that must accompany study are "the practice of piety," "academic devotion *(cura)* and scrutiny *(inspectio)*," and "examination." The "practice of piety," Voetius insists, ought to be "instilled and enriched" so that the student comes ever "closer to God through continual meditation on sacred things." This may be accomplished through "the frequent hearing of sermons, catechization, reading and meditating on Scripture" followed by "private prayer," the "examination of one's conscience," renewals of faith and repentance—all under the care of church and school as represented by parents, mentors, counselors, and professors. Externally, piety ought to be further reinforced by regular evaluation by and conversation with professors in order that "deceit and spiritual cancers" *(fucos and carcinomata)* be cast out and that "by degrees" the student will advance in "piety, modesty, diligence, and gifts."[60] The piety and devotion of the faculty, all of whom should have passed through a similar training, is assumed by Voetius. Professors in the theological faculty serve, thus, as pastors within the institution and consistently engage in the spiritual formation and correction of their students. The second adjunct to formal study, "academic devotion and scrutiny" or, one might say, "management and inspection," takes place both privately and publicly, the former through the work of "ephors" or tutors, and the latter through the oversight of classes and synods, as well as that of the faculty. The third adjunct, examination, ought never to be perfunctory, but ought to be conducted with some gravity at the conclusion of semesters during the interval or period of theological study and at the end of the year during the second and third intervals.[61]

Having presented his basic pattern of discipline and piety, Voetius next describes the recommended three-part course of study in preparation for the ministry. In the first interval of study there are two basic tasks, a primary and a secondary. The primary task is the introduction to theological study, and the secondary is the review and supplementation for the sake of theological learning of the student's previous studies in philosophy, language, and the arts.[62] Voetius divides the primary educational task into three parts: textual

59. Ibid., 27–28.
60. Ibid., 31–33.
61. Ibid., 33–34.
62. Ibid., 35, 43.

or biblical, systematic or dogmatic, and disputative *(elenctica)* and problematic theology. The first interval's biblical study stresses what Voetius, in accord with the Reformers and with his orthodox Protestant contemporaries, viewed as the books most central to the theological understanding of Scripture as a whole (Genesis, Isaiah, Psalms, Matthew, John, Romans, and Hebrews) and then takes up crucial texts in Scripture that are "the grounds *(sedes)* of the [theological] topics *(locorum communium)* . . . for example, Romans 3 and 4 on justification, Romans 9 and Ephesians 1 on predestination, Genesis 3 and Romans 5 on the first sin of Adam, 1 Corinthians 11 on the Lord's Supper, 1 Timothy 3 on the office of ministry, and 1 Corinthians 5 on excommunication."[63] At the same time, the beginning student will be introduced to "systematic theology," not, Voetius adds, in the form of an epitome or summary, but thoroughly and fully examined with a view to moral and ascetic theology and to ecclesiastical polity, as well as to the more strictly dogmatic topics. And finally, the student will be exposed to "disputative and problematic" theology with specific focus on "the controversies of the present day between the orthodox [Reformed faith] and the Socinians, Remonstrants, Papists, Anabaptists, Enthusiasts, Libertines, Jews, Epicureans, [and] Atheists."[64] In this curriculum, Voetius indicates, it should be emphasized that the proper order of learning and of argument proceeds from the study of Scripture and of exegetically elaborated *loci communes* to "positive or systematic theology" and then, only on that foundation, to polemical topics. Also to be emphasized throughout this curriculum is the overarching identification of theology as the discipline concerned with "faith and practice," the latter term indicating both piety and the administration of the church.[65]

Study of each of the three portions of the curriculum ought to proceed according to the pattern of *lectio, meditatio, auditio, scriptio, collatio, collegia,* and *enotatio.* Thus Scripture ought to be read using the original languages supplemented by Mercer's and Drusius's annotations on the Old Testament and by Beza's and Piscator's annotations on the New Testament. In the systematic field, students ought to engage in the "repeated reading" of Ames' *Medulla* and Maccovius's disputations, enriched, for good measure, by a reading of Gomarius's disputations as well. Problematic or polemical theology should survey Ames' refutation of Bellarmine, Hoornbeeck's exposition of the errors of Socinianism, and the relevant sections of the major dogmatic works of Polanus, Wendelin, and Alsted—and a host of other authors.[66] As for their meditation, students ought to study and memorize "select themes

63. Ibid., 35–36.
64. Ibid., 36.
65. Ibid., 36–37.
66. Ibid., 37–38.

and sayings of Scripture" together with their analysis and exposition in the original languages. Similarly, the basic theological topics should be committed to memory following the outlines of Ames or Maccovius, with close attention to definitions and distinctions. Listening to and participating in disputations and the composition of suitable topical analysis will follow, succeeded by the final efforts of gathering, recapitulating, and annotating mentally the entire course of study.[67]

As their secondary task in their first part of theological study, future pastors and teachers review the course in philosophy with a view to engaging in disputation. They also study chronology, the history of the Old and New Testaments, review Latin by reading various church fathers like Lactantius, Tertullian, Arnobius, and Prudentius, and refresh their Greek through Plotinus, Proclus, Epictetus, and such fathers as Athenagoras, Justin, Clement of Alexandria, Origen, and Athanasius. Voetius recommends specifically Origen's *Contra Celsum* and Athanasius's *Contra Arianos*.[68] He concludes his discussion of the secondary areas of study by noting important editions of Scripture and commentators to be consulted in attaining proficiency in Hebrew and by recommending the study of Aramaic, Syriac, and Arabic.[69]

In the second stage of their study, theological students move forward from the basic exercises in their primary work of theological study and secondary work in the study of philosophical and ancillary disciplines to patterns of study more directly related to the work of the pastor. Voetius recommends that the secondary emphasis of study be medicine, jurisprudence, and their cognate disciplines, plus studies in history, antiquities, and the more practical areas of cases of conscience and counsel. At the same time, the primary theological work takes on a practical aspect and becomes considerably more diverse, now divided into textual or biblical study, the "practice of preaching," church polity, disputative or scholastic theology, patristics, and the later history of the church. In other words, the fundamental work of biblical study continues, systematic and polemical theology moves forward into the more technical areas of scholastic disputation, the historical concentration of earlier secondary study now passes over into the examination of church history, and what today would be called the more practical or pastoral disciplines appear both at the primary level in preaching and at the secondary in the areas of conscience and counsel.[70] As noted, moreover, in the discussion of Hyperius's *De theologo,* polemical and historical theology are not identical—indeed, in Voetius's model of study they are quite distinct.

67. Ibid., 39–41.
68. Ibid., 43–44.
69. Ibid., 44–45.
70. Ibid., 47–48, cf. 49–50 for clearer indication of historical emphases.

Here, too, study proceeds according to the model of *lectio, meditatio, auditio, scriptio, collatio, collegia,* and *enotatio,* correlated with *institutio* and the relevant *apparatus.* And, once again, the recommended bibliography is imposing. Scripture continues to be approached by way of the original languages and scholarly annotations with the pattern of reading emphasizing both central themes and the study of entire books from beginning to end with careful attention to annotations and marginalia. Theological reading, in view of the practical turn of the curriculum, now includes Calvin's *Institutes,* various works of English Puritan theology—notably by Perkins, Bolton, Baynes, Downham, Sibbes, and Reynolds—and the writings of Taffin, Teelinck, and Udemanns, associated with the *Nadere Reformatie.* Such works, comments Voetius, serve "as supplements to practical theology and to the development of sermons."[71] Polemical or disputative theology now also shifts its emphasis, including not only works directed against the sects and heretics of the seventeenth century, but also against Mohammedans. Voetius indicates that students ought to examine the Koran and he recommends Aquinas's *Summa contra gentiles* with the annotations of Francis de Sylvestris (Ferrariensis). Among the historical works added to the reading list are Scultetus's *Historia Reformationis* and the compendia of church history by Paraeus, Osiander, and Baronius. Voetius also recommends the reading of martyrologies—again because they provide both indications of style and content suitable to sermons.[72] The recommended time of meditation ought to concentrate, as before, on Scripture and theological themes, the latter specifically identified as "ascetic," "patristic," and "casuistic," as well as "natural and scholastic." "Hearing" in this phase of study consists in the public presentation of various didactic, historical, biblical, and philosophical topics.[73]

Voetius's fourth element of study, *scriptio* is worked out in vast detail for this second phase of study: the work of writing annotations on difficult places, basic themes, and, indeed, the chapters of Scripture must be supplemented by analysis of the more "difficult problems related to the sacred history" and by "disquisitions concerning various literal and philological interpretations of Scripture." Here the student's use of grammatical and lexical tools and his ability to work in the cognate languages comes to bear. In addition, the student must begin to prepare sermons with attention to substance and form, as well as to apparatus, at all times supported by practice in elocution and memory. Exercises in composition should also address issues of morality and conscience, as well as current theological debate with Jews, pagans, Mohammedans, and enthusiasts. The subsequent exercises of *collatio* and *collegia* call for further topical reading and the careful study of issues through the bibliography—which, for Voetius, must range from bibli-

---

71. Ibid., 48.
72. Ibid., 49–50.
73. Ibid., 50.

cal and lexical apparatus, to compendia and systems of theology written by medieval teachers, Protestant theologians, and recent Roman Catholic thinkers.[74] Through meditation and composition, the student integrates theological learning with personal piety and draws both inwardly to create a proper disposition for ministry. And, in addition to this more private pattern of study, Voetius details at length academic exercises in public disputation, preaching, and lecturing intended to solidify learning and churchly skills.[75]

The third interval or phase of theological study continues the patterns of the previous two parts, but in greater detail and, Voetius indicates, extends into the several years of parish ministry.[76] No new subjects are presented at this point. Instead, Voetius's version of what might be called seventeenth-century Reformed "extended education" consists in the repetition and supplementation of what has already been learned. The burden placed on *lectio* becomes quite intense—students and new ministers are called on to read heavily in the theological and controversial literature of the day, with continued attention to the basic theological *loci*. Various works dealing with "the more sound *(sanior)* theology from the tenth century to the time of the Reformation" are recommended—including both the theology of those who "separated from popery," such as the Waldenses, Wycliffites, and Hussites, and the theology of those faithful who remained, as catalogued by Flacius Illyricus and Plessaeus. Here, Voetius specifically recommends the study of Aquinas's *Summa theologiae*.[77]

Meditatio during the third phase of theological education ought to be "occupied primarily with particular chapters and places in Scripture, both those [that] give the greatest difficulty either in the controversies of the present day or that appear to contradict one another, and to those [that] most properly and fully support practical and homiletical theology."[78] Voetius here recommends strongly the works of authors like Perkins, Bolton, Baynes, Preston, and Hooker as supportive of piety and practice. Similarly, the continuing work of personal composition ought to emphasize the writing of sermons and the examination of the text of Scripture. The subsequent work of gathering, recapitulation, and final notation reflects the earlier efforts to learn and reinforce materials, while the work of *institutio* or instruction now focuses on the process of preparation for "scholarly and ecclesiastical" examinations, both public and private—in short, for the final examination preparatory to full admission to ministry. Here again, Voetius offers rather daunting bibliographical advice.[79]

74. Ibid., 50–58.
75. Ibid., 69–100.
76. Ibid., 69.
77. Ibid., 60–61.
78. Ibid., 62.
79. Ibid., 62–67.

Throughout this course of theology, with its integration of piety and learning, Voetius insisted on the importance of piety in the life of Christians in general and on the ongoing relationship of piety to theology. To this issue he also devoted a separate treatise, his *Ta asketika, sive exercitia pietatis*, in which he emphasized the disciplined character of piety necessary to ministerial study—in his terms, the substance and subject of the discipline called *ascetica,* "ascetics." "Ascetics," he wrote, "is the theological teaching *(doctrina)* or division of theology that contains the method and description of exercises in piety." These exercises consist, specifically, in "the *praxis* of meditation, petition *(praecatio),* the renewal of repentance, faith, [and in] preparation for and participation in the Lord's Supper, . . . the right ordering of thoughts, the *praxis* of the Sabbath day, spiritual warfare, inward trials, the control of the tongue . . . [and] the excitement of love for the divine."[80] The fundamental relationship between this work of inward formation of spirituality and character and the study of theology proper lies in the fact, Voetius argues, that "theology is a practical science or discipline" and that practical uses can and must be "subjoined" to the various doctrinal topics. It is, of course, true, Voetius continues, that meditation on Scripture is sufficient for the formation and reinforcement of the piety of the unlearned—but training in piety in the academic context, specifically for "theological students and ministerial candidates" is another matter. Here a variety of authors ought to be read: Voetius notes Daniel Tossanus's *L'exercice de l'ame fidele,* Johannes Gerhard's *Exercitium pietatis quotidianum quadripartitum,* and the Dutch translation of Lewis Bayly's *The Practice of Pietie,* both for the sake of refining one's personal disciplines along well-tried paths and for the sake of avoiding the errors of "pseudoexercises" like those of the papists.[81] Understood rightly, the entire study of theology will be directed toward "the art [or technique] of applying theology to use and practice, to the edification of conscience, and to the direction of the will and its affections." In short, "saving doctrine" is always to be directed toward "the practice of piety, the art of worshiping God, affective theology, and the imitation of Christ."[82]

80. Voetius, *Ta Asketika sive de exercitiis pietatis,* 1–2. The term *militia spiritualis* or spiritual warfare reflects Voetius's strong ties to the Puritan tradition of conscience with its militant language of inward conflict against temptation: cf. John Downham, *The Christian Warfare, wherein is first generally shewed the malice, power, and politike strategems of the spiritual enemies of our salvation, Satan and his assistants the world and our flesh* (London, 1604; 2d edition, 1608). A second part was published in 1611 and the third edition, enlarged to four parts, in 1612. The language of warfare is also found in Thomas Brooks, *Precious Remedies Against Satan's Devices* (London, 1652), idem, *Heaven on Earth: A Treatise of Christian Assurance* (London, 1654) and in John Bunyan, *The Pilgrim's Progress From This World to That Which is to Come* (London, 1687) and idem, *The Holy War made by Shaddai upon Diabolus for the Regaining of the Metropolis of the World; or, the Losing and Taking Again of the Town of Mansoul* (London, 1682).
81. Voetius, *Ta Asketika sive de exercitiis pietatis,* 3–6.
82. Ibid., 12.

The Goal:
Herman Witsius on the Character of a Theologian

Witsius's oration on the character of a theologian not only consciously
bridges the gap between the study and the practice of theology, it also and
more specifically provides an index to the goal and the real result of Voetius's teaching, inasmuch as Witsius had studied at Utrecht under Voetius.[83]
His oration, moreover, was delivered as his inaugural address at the University of Franecker, as he prepared to assume the role of professor of theology
for the first time. The oration is both retrospective and prospective. It looks
back on Witsius's own theological education, clearly reflecting the model of
Voetius's *Exercises* with its balance of personal, spiritual, and intellectual
formation, and it looks forward toward Witsius's own appropriation of this
educational approach in his career as a teacher.

For all Witsius's training in technical theology and incredible expertise in
Hebrew, Greek, and Latin, the initial and certainly the strongest voice in his
inaugural address is that of the *Nadere Reformatie*. He frames his discourse
with three biblical texts, the Song of Hannah (1 Sam. 2:7–8), David's response to God's promise of an everlasting kingdom (2 Sam. 7:18, 20), and
the Lord's promise of assistance to Joshua (Josh. 1:9). From the first text,
Witsius draws a personal lesson of the divine providence that "makes poor
and makes rich," that "brings low" and "also exalts," that "raises the poor
from the dust . . . to make them sit with princes and inherit a seat of honor."
It was the astonishing work of God, he writes, that first elicited this hymn
from a "pious mother" and that now similarly presses him to review "the
whole course of his life" and especially the divine assistance given to him
throughout his work in the "sacred office" of Christian ministry. Reflecting
surely on the history of Samuel, Witsius indicates that his "pious parents" devoted him to the church at an early age and "took care to have [his] mind
instilled with such doctrinal and practical teachings" as would train him up
to do "no dishonor to the house of God." Granting all this, neither his parents nor he could have predicted his promotion to the professorship at Franecker—this "seat of honor."[84]

His reaction is both one of joy and amazement and one of fear. Like
David, he is constrained to ask himself, "Who am I, O Lord God, and what

---

83. Herman Witsius, *On the Character of the True Divine: An Inaugural Oration, Delivered at
Franecker, April 16, 1675,* trans. John Donaldson, preface by William Cunningham (Edinburgh:
James Wood, 1855). Some two decades later, on his inauguration as professor of theology at Leiden,
Witsius's views had changed but little. At that time he offered as an address his *Theologus modestus,
delineatus. Oratione inaugurali, qua publicam theologiae professionem in Adademia Lugduno-Batava
auspicatus est, die sexto decimo Octobris 1698* (Leiden, 1698). On Witsius's life and thought, see
J. van Genderen, *Herman Witsius: bijdrage tot de kennis der gereformeerde theologie* (s'Gravenhage:
Guido de Bres, 1953).

84. Witsius, *Character,* 8.

is my house that thou hast brought me thus far?" He has been brought from the daily task of catechizing and prayer and from the work of preaching a simple word of sound instruction "to the Christian common people" to be "a new teacher in this venerable seat of learning," a new participant in a "circle of erudite men." His consolation and his strength come not from himself, but from the Lord, who said to Joshua, "Have I not commanded thee? Be strong and of good courage . . . for the LORD thy God is with thee wherever thou goest."[85]

Once he has established his view of God's providential guidance over all life and, particularly, over his own, Witsius moves on to the main body of his discourse in which he proposes to examine the true theologian "as a student, as a teacher, and as a human being," because, he notes, "no one teaches well unless he has first learned well; and no one learns well unless he learns in order to teach; and both learning and teaching are in vain and unprofitable, unless accompanied by practice." Schooling, therefore, is important, but so also is personal manner and method, and beyond that, at the human level, "the habits of soul and outward walk" by which a teacher "may adorn his doctrine."[86]

As a first level of training, Witsius recommends "the lower school of nature," in which the student should examine not only "the wonders of divine providence" but also "the monuments of ancient as well as modern history," "the shrines of all the arts," and "the beauties of various tongues." Careful study ought to be made of grammar, logic, and rhetoric so that the student can learn "rules for definition, division, and arrangement" of his knowledge and also "the art of discoursing" about the topics learned "not only with purity and precision, but also with elegance and effect." So, too, should "moral precepts" be learned from the great philosophers, and moral examples from "the monuments of history."[87] All these things ought to be recognized as divine gifts and be memorized and treasured as a foundation for further learning. And if grammar, logic, and rhetoric are not immediately understood as divine, comments Witsius in a biblical echo of the scholastic identification of philosophy and its subdisciplines as the *ancilla theologiae*, they can surely be taken up into the service of religion and theology—and used "as the Israelites of old did the Gibeonites, whose work it was to cleave wood and to draw water for the use of the Sanctuary."[88]

What is significant here—as was also the case with Voetius—is the expectation of a breadth of culture and learning in the clergy. Indeed, this rather learned student, habituated to the reverent observation of nature, learned in

85. Ibid., 9–10.
86. Ibid., 13–14.
87. Ibid., 14, 16.
88. Ibid., 16.

history and languages, well versed in the arts and the skills of communication, is only a beginner. Witsius comments that these studies cannot absorb all of the time of the student, who must devote the greater part of his intellectual energies to the study of Scripture; these initial studies were merely the prerequisite for theological education. Biblical study, moreover, while assuming the obvious attainments of the one who engages in it, ought nevertheless to bring humility. "Sitting humbly before God," Witsius continues, the theological student ought "to learn from [God's] mouth the hidden mysteries of salvation, which eye hath not seen, nor ear heard . . . which no power of reason, however well trained, could discover."[89]

Witsius quite clearly regards this course of study as a spiritual exercise conducive to building and cultivating personal character. Spiritual discipline is not something to be added to the curriculum, so much as it is a fundamental aspect of the student's approach to the life of study and to the life of ministry for which it prepares him. The theologian or minister ought to so imbibe the teaching of Scripture as truly to meditate on it "day and night" and continually to "draw wisdom" from it. In words that reflect the earlier tradition of Protestant theological education, notably the sapiential approach of Hyperius, Witsius insists that the goal of this meditation is not a human, but a "divine faith" that rests "in God alone" and draws its strength from the "power" of God's Word.[90]

There is one character trait necessary to attaining such a goal. In a highly rhetorical style, Witsius asks "What will render the soul teachable and obedient when speaking of God?" His answer, "respect" or "propriety"—*modestia.* What, similarly, will enable a theologian to study the deep mysteries of religion without rashness? Again, "respect" or "obedience"—*modestia.* Or again, what is required for a mind to be persuaded of the truth of the holiest teachings of the Christian religion? Again, he answers, "respect" or moderation of life—*modestia.*[91] No matter how learned the theologian or minister, he must retain the humility and modesty suitable both to the task of ministry and to the divine truths that he serves.

Even so, the true theologian is a "humble disciple of the Scriptures," who does not speak on his own authority and who recognizes that those who enter the study of theology enter into a knowledge of things hidden to the unaided human reason. This divinely given knowledge depends not merely on the reading of Scripture, but also on attention to the inward witness of the Spirit. Spiritual things are not understood by "the blind eyes of nature"; "In order to understand spiritual things, we must have a spiritual mind," a mind conformed by God's gracious work to the mind of Christ. Witsius thus in-

89. Ibid., 17–18.
90. Ibid., 18–19.
91. Witsius, *Theologus modestus*, 29.

sists, as his teacher Voetius had argued so pointedly more than two decades earlier, that learning of a curriculum, and graduation with a degree is not enough. "He who is a student in this heavenly school," Witsius writes, "not only knows and believes, but also has a sensible experience of the forgiveness of sins, the privilege of adoption and gracious communion with God, the grace of the indwelling Spirit . . . and the sweet love of Christ."[92]

So, too, will the theologian or minister acquire, by the grace of God's Spirit, skills in the "art of teaching" and a profound desire to communicate what he has learned to others. Witsuis, for all his mastery of the various theological disciplines and, in that time, his nearly unequaled skills in the ancient languages, scorns the "pedant from the schools" who has memorized a host of facts and is able to state them with facility, but who is not genuinely schooled in his mind and heart. Such teachers can discourse on doctrine and even on "the Christian warfare" without ever reflecting on their own experience. The true theologian will teach out of the experience of a living faith and, Witsius adds, in a spirit of unfeigned love for God and God's children. His theology will consistently be placed in the service of the gospel, both to impart its truths and to fill its hearers with the Spirit of Christ.[93] Even so, the theologian or minister, guided by the love of God, will never act out of greed or covetousness, and will never seek his own glory, but only the glory of God. He will teach only "what is certain, sound, solid, and fitted to cherish faith, excite hope, promote piety, and preserve unity and peace." He will not "itch after innovation" but will rest on the deposit of biblical truth held within the Reformed churches and work to defend that truth against its adversaries.[94] Piety, for Witsius, excludes neither learning nor polemic! This portrait of the "true theologian," Witsius acknowledges in conclusion, is an ideal and a standard to which he himself has not attained—but he holds it forth, nonetheless, as the goal for all who train for the ministry. He asks for the aid of his colleagues, notably his elder colleague, Nicholas Arnold, renowned for his refutation of the *Racovian Catechism* of the Socinians, in leading him toward the consistent vindication of God's truth, the defeat of heresy, and the inculcation of piety as he attempts to lead his own students toward that goal.[95]

Concluding Reflection

The Reformed pastor of the sixteenth and seventeenth centuries was, by all accounts, a learned person. Even if the curricula set out by Hyperius and Voetius were ideals to be striven for, rather than goals to be reached by all

92. Witsius, *Character,* 24–25.
93. Ibid., 28, 30.
94. Ibid., 31–33.
95. Ibid., 40.

students, the standards they present were very high—and, given the presence of other disciplines like study of the classics, medicine, and jurisprudence at the edges of the curriculum, very broad indeed. Given also the high standards of character and piety set forth by Voetius and Witsius, there is little wonder that the clergy of the sixteenth and seventeenth centuries had such status in and impact on society. The model, if not classist—Voetius had held forth against this—was surely somewhat elitist. They excelled both in learning and in character, and they had a sense of purpose guided by an assumption of the unity and the unified goal of their knowledge and their ministerial task. Their education, whether in the academic pattern of *lectio, meditatio, auditio, scriptio, collatio, collegia,* and *enotatio,* or in the equally structured exercises in piety, was designed as a form of inward or spiritual discipline that balanced the issue of objective content with the concern for subjective reception and appropriation.

All of the writers noted, moreover, from the Reformers to the post-Reformation Protestant orthodox, despite the increasing identification of subdisciplines characteristic of the latter, viewed theology as a single united discipline. Whatever the tools and categories or modes of approach to the materials of theology, theological study was viewed as having a single object, God and the works of God, and as having a single goal, the glory of God in the salvation of believers; or, from another perspective, as having a single foundational source, the revelation of God in Scripture, and a single earthly purpose, the renewal of the life of human beings by God's grace in the church. Nonetheless, as we have seen, the basic structure that would become the fourfold encyclopedia was present—as, arguably, was the problem identified by Farley as the "diversified encyclopedia." The distinction between the canon of Scripture in the Old and New Testaments and churchly theology served to distinguish biblical or exegetical from dogmatic, polemical, and historical study. In addition, in Voetius's model, biblical studies were conjoined with their own ancillary linguistic fields and their own distinct apparatus, while dogmatic and polemical theology were quite naturally placed together. Historical study was distinguished from polemics, albeit placed as one discipline among others in a somewhat eclectic category. And the more pastoral studies, such as preaching, counsel, piety, and church polity, if not a precise grouping, were, nonetheless, associated by Voetius. Given both the detail and the technical character of the various disciplines, the issue of specialization and of diversification was also present in the seventeenth-century curriculum—indeed, the intellectual demands placed on students were arguably more intense than in the present and the burden of integrating the various subject areas into a functional whole as heavy or heavier, even granting the greater incentive to conceiving the large discipline of theology as a spiritual unity.

Perhaps the archetypal products of this understanding of the unity of theological study are Wilhelmus à Brakel's *Redelijke Godsdienst* or *Christian's*

Reasonable Service (1700)[96] and Petrus van Mastricht's *Theoretico-practica theologia* (1714)[97] in which exegetical, dogmatic, polemical, and practical elements are combined into single systematic expositions of the Christian faith. In Mastricht's work, the organization of each doctrinal topic manifests this precise fourfold division, whereas in à Brakel's treatise, the exegetical and dogmatic discussions are blended together, the polemic treated as "objections" to doctrinal formulation, and the practical application offered as a concluding pastoral reflection on the texts and doctrine.[98] It is important to recognize that in these, as in all of the works noted, "practical" does not indicate a tendency toward technique or the study of technique; instead it indicates, as it did in the curricular projects of Bullinger, Hyperius, Voetius, and Witsius, knowledge oriented toward a goal, specifically, the goal of salvation. Technique, of course, had been instilled in the exercises in writing, meditation, speaking, and so forth, but it was viewed as a necessary adjunct, not as the central discipline. Homiletics, or "Christian rhetoric," then, is a practical form of theology, not because it is a technique, but because it is learned for the sake of a goal external to it, the goal of the salvation of believers. Even so, à Brakel's and Mastricht's practical discussions deal primarily with the personal appropriation or application of doctrine.

According to the older model for the study of theology, the distinction between theory and praxis was not a distinction between a set of theoretical disciplines and a set of practical disciplines. More specifically, biblical, historical, and doctrinal or systematic studies were not viewed as purely theoretical—and homiletical, ministerial study was not viewed as practical in the modern sense of the term. Theology, as a whole, was understood, particularly by the medieval Thomists and Augustinians and by later Roman Catholic and Reformed Protestant writers, to be a theoretical and a practical study in all of its aspects: theoretical because its contents deserve to be known as a goal of knowing, and practical because its contents direct the human spirit toward its goal of eternal salvation. The modern loss of this understanding of theory and praxis has created problems for theology, not the least of which is a confusion over the character and use of the subdisciplines of theology and, because of this confusion, a failure to recognize the relationship of what today are called theoretical disciplines to the practice of Chris-

---

96. Wilhelmus à Brakel, *Logike Latreia, dat is Redelijke Godsdienst in welken de goddelijke Waarheden van het Genade-Verbond worden verklaard* (Dordrecht, 1700), trans. as *The Christian's Reasonable Service in which Divine Truths concerning the Covenant of Grace are Expounded, Defended against Opposing Parties, and their Practice Advocated*, 4 vols., translated by Bartel Elshout, with a biographical sketch by W. Fieret and an essay on the "Dutch Second Reformation" by Joel Beeke (Ligonier, Penn.: Soli Deo Gloria Publications, 1992).

97. Petrus van Mastricht, *Theoretico-practica theologia*, editio mova (Utrecht, 1724).

98. For an appreciation of Mastricht's method, see Richard A. Muller, "Giving Direction to Theology: The Scholastic Dimension," in *Journal of the Evangelical Theological Society* 28/2 (June 1985): 183–93.

tianity. The older Protestant educational model inculcated both a rigorous engagement with the technical disciplines and a rigorous cultivation of personal and corporate piety—and, what is more, it assumed that each of these aspects of theological study reinforced the other and led to the spiritual formation of the whole person. At the beginning and at the end of the educational process, Witsius reminded his hearers that "humility is the mother, and the root, and the nourisher, and the foundation, and the bond of all good: without it we are profane and detestable creatures."[99]

The beginning of this change of perspective concerning theory and praxis were evident toward the very end of the era of orthodoxy in the pietist critique of Protestant scholasticism.[100] A significant distinction must be made, however, between the German Lutheran pietism of Spener, with its sometimes pointed critique of scholastic orthodoxy, and the Reformed "pietism" of the *Nadere Reformatie*, in which Voetius and many of the Reformed scholastics participated. On the Reformed side, there was far less tension between dogmatics and piety and pietism did not press so pointedly against Protestant orthodox theology. It was, in fact, the model of the Reformed pastor as set forth by the English Puritans and the theologians of the *Nadere Reformatie* that framed much of the pietist critique of German Lutheran ministry. The German pietists drew a line between the academic study of theology and the cultivation of the religion of the heart. Not that they either abandoned academics or failed to understand that academic study demanded inward, spiritual discipline; the pietists were far more academic and, indeed, scholastic than contemporary evangelical critics of academic theology.[101] Rather the pietists made a sharp distinction between the theology of the regenerate and the theology of the unregenerate, potentially identical in intellectual content and distinguished only by the piety of the individual. At the same time, they emphasized not only the inward renewal of the individual, but also its outward manifestation in personal lifestyle and in social programs. The effect of these two perspectives, taken together, was to disengage doctrinal theology, despite its traditionally practical thrust, from the various manifestations of Christian practice. This particular form of the pietist critique, moreover, has had a greater impact on modern theology than the model presented by Re-

---

99. Witsius, *Theologus modestus*, 35, citing Chrysostom, *Homily XXX on Acts*.

100. On pietism and its relation to orthodoxy, see F. Ernest Stoeffler, *The Rise of Evangelical Pietism* (Leiden: Brill, 1965); idem, *German Pietism During the Eighteenth Century* (Leiden: Brill, 1973); I. A. Dorner, *History of Protestant Theology*, trans. George Robson and Sophia Taylor, 2 vols. (Edinburgh, 1871); Hans Leuba, *Orthodoxie und Pietismus: Gesammelte Studien* (Bielefeld: Luther-Verlag, 1975).

101. Cf. Richard A. Muller, "J. J. Rambach and the Dogmatics of Scholastic Pietism," in *Consensus: A Canadian Lutheran Journal of Theology* 16/2 (1990): 7–27 with Preus, *Theology of Post-Reformation Lutheranism*, I, 219–22, 232, 405, 412; Friedrich Kalb, *Theology of Worship in 17th Century Lutheranism*, trans. Harry Hamann (St. Louis: Concordia, 1965), x–xi, 157–71; and Leuba, *Orthodoxie und Pietismus*, 50–59.

formed orthodoxy in association with the *Nadere Reformatie* because of the rootage of much of Schleiermacher's thought in German pietism. As Farley has pointed out, in the wake of Schleiermacher's reinterpretation of religion, theology, and the curriculum, the practical emphasis, coupled with religion, can exist independently of theology as an exercise in ministerial practice while the classical disciplines of theology can become increasingly purely theoretical enterprises.[102] In contrast to this bifurcation, the approach of the Reformers and, perhaps even more so, that of their orthodox or scholastic successors, points toward a unity of theory and practice, of learning and piety, and potentially toward a way out of our contemporary dilemma.

102. Farley, *Theologia,* 80–81.

6

New Divinity Schools of the Prophets

David W. Kling

In 1976 Henry May observed that the New Divinity men—that cadre of orthodox Calvinist clergy who drew inspiration from Jonathan Edwards— "have long since been almost forgotten." Nearly two decades later, a growing body of scholarship assures us that these "great men of their day" will not be forgotten.[1] Indeed, scholars have engaged the New Divinity as a major reclamation project. Undoubtedly, heightened interest in the New Divinity men and the movement they created was initially quickened by the revival of interest in Jonathan Edwards, for to study the Edwardsean legacy was, in large measure, to study the New Divinity. As well, graduate students, always in search of subjects "almost forgotten," found in the New Divinity fresh fodder for dissertations. Whatever the stimulus—the renewed attention to Edwards or the comments of May himself—the New Divinity has emerged as a subject of sustained inquiry.[2]

---

1. Henry F. May, *The Enlightenment in America* (New York: Oxford University Press, 1976), 59.
2. The following either focus exclusively on or give substantial space to the New Divinity: William Breitenbach, "Unregenerate Doings: Selflessness and Selfishness in New Divinity Theology," *American Quarterly* 34 (winter 1982): 479–502; idem, "The Consistent Calvinism of the New Divinity Movement" *William and Mary Quarterly*, 3d ser., 41 (April 1984): 241–64; idem, "Piety and Moralism: Edwards and the New Divinity," in *Jonathan Edwards and the American Experience*, eds. Nathan O. Hatch and Harry S. Stout (New York: Oxford University Press, 1989), 177–204; Joseph Conforti, "Samuel Hopkins and the New Divinity: Theology, Ethics, and Social Reform in Eighteenth-Century New England," *William and Mary Quarterly* 34 (Oct. 1977): 572–89; idem, "The Rise of the New Divinity in Western New England, 1740–1800," *Historical Journal of Western Massachusetts* 8 (January 1980): 37–47; idem, *Samuel Hopkins and the New Divinity Movement: Calvinism, the Congregational Ministry, and Reform in New England between the Great Awakenings* (Grand Rapids, Mich.: Christian University Press, 1981); idem, "Joseph Bellamy and the New Divinity Movement," *New England Historical and Genealogical Register* 137 (1983):126–38; idem, "Edwardsians, Unitarians, and the Memory of the Great Awakening," in *American Unitarianism, 1805–1865*, ed. Conrad Edick Wright (Boston: Northeastern University Press, 1989), 31–50; idem, "The Invention of the Great

Because nearly all of these studies focus on a single person, theme, or event, none comprehensively addresses the form of association which sustained the New Divinity movement for three-quarters of a century. Movements arise through collective action based upon shared convictions and goals, and they endure through informal or formal organizational structures.[3] The instance of the New Divinity movement is no exception. While no established hierarchy emerged within the New Divinity, its informal "schools of the prophets" provided the infrastructure for the growth and longevity of a movement. For three generations, these schools transmitted New Divinity theological precepts and ministerial models.

Despite monopolizing theological training for well over a half century, the schools of the prophets have not been sufficiently appreciated. Thirty years ago, C. C. Goen recognized the schools as "a phenomenon of major magnitude in ministerial training"; more recently, Glenn Miller noted that the New Divinity theologians "made 'reading divinity' an art"; and other historians have devoted significant space to these schools.[4] But the influence of New Divinity schools of the prophets on the religious and social life of New England—even the world, if one considers their impact on the modern missionary movement—has been vastly understated.

Numbers alone are impressive. Between 1750 and 1825, over five hundred clerical aspirants studied in New Divinity schools of the prophets. Long-term

Awakening, 1795–1842," *Early American Literature* 26 (1991): 99–118; Robert L. Ferm, *Jonathan Edwards the Younger: 1745–1801* (Grand Rapids, Mich.: Eerdmans, 1976); James Dale German, "The Preacher and the New Light Revolution in Connecticut: The Pulpit Theology of Benjamin Trumbull, 1760–1800" (Ph.D. diss., Univ. of California, Riverside, 1989); Allen C. Guelzo, *Edwards on the Will: A Century of American Theological Debate* (Middletown, Conn.: Wesleyan University Press, 1989); James Hoopes, "Calvinism and Consciousness from Edwards to Beecher," in *Jonathan Edwards and the American Experience*, 205–25; idem, *Consciousness in New England: From Puritanism and Ideas to Psychoanalysis and Semiotics* (Baltimore: The Johns Hopkins University Press, 1989); David W. Kling, *A Field of Divine Wonders: The New Divinity and Village Revivals in Northwestern Connecticut, 1792–1822* (University Park, Penn.: Penn State University Press, 1993); Richard Rabinowitz, *The Spiritual Self in Everyday Life: The Transformation of Personal Religious Experience in Nineteenth-Century New England* (Boston: Northeastern University Press, 1989); Richard D. Shiels, "The Connecticut Clergy in the Second Great Awakening" (Ph.D. diss., Boston Univ., 1976); idem, "The Second Great Awakening in Connecticut: Critique of the Traditional Interpretation," *Church History* 49 (Dec. 1980): 401–15; Mark Valeri, "Joseph Bellamy: Conversion, Social Ethics, and Politics in the Thought of an Eighteenth Century Calvinist" (Ph.D. diss., Princeton Univ., 1985); idem, "The New Divinity and the American Revolution," *William and Mary Quarterly*, 3d ser., 46 (Oct. 1989): 741–69.

3. For a historical discussion of the way elites organize, see Peter Dobkin Hall, *The Organization of American Culture, 1700–1900: Private Institutions, Elites, and the Origins of American Nationality* (New York: New York University Press, 1982).

4. Clarence C. Goen, "Changing Conceptions of Protestant Theological Education in America," *Foundations* 6 (1963): 297; Glenn T. Miller, *Piety and Intellect: The Aims and Purposes of Ante-Bellum Theological Education* (Atlanta: Scholars Press, 1990), 55; Mary Latimer Gambrell, *Ministerial Training in Eighteenth-Century New England* (New York: Columbia University Press, 1937), chaps. 6–7; Roland Bainton, *Yale and the Ministry: A History of Education for the Christian Ministry at Yale from the Founding in 1701* (New York: Harper, 1957), chap. 5; Conforti, *Samuel Hopkins*, chap. 2.

influences are more impressive. These schools transmitted the piety, theology, and legacy of the Great Awakening through several generations, and hus profoundly contributed to a "Second" Great Awakening.[5] Moreover, Yale College is often cited for producing the many provincial college presidents of northern antebellum New England, when, in fact, the schools of the prophets played an important mediating role by stamping these sons of Yale with the peculiar New Divinity imprimatur.[6] A similar claim can be made for New Divinity influence in the training of clergy for home and foreign missionary service. Some of the earliest missionary organizations in America (e.g., the Connecticut Missionary Society, the Massachusetts Missionary Society, and the American Board of Commissioners for Foreign Missions) owe their origins largely to the inspiration of the New Divinity men and their schools.[7] Not until the rise of the professional seminary, beginning with Andover in 1808, did the hegemony of schools of the prophets among New England Calvinists weaken, although in some quarters New Divinity mentoring practices persisted well into the 1820s. For nearly three-quarters of a century schools of the prophets proliferated, reproducing the teaching, preaching, and mentoring practices of the New Divinity in a remarkably consistent fashion. The New Divinity theology—the first and perhaps the most enduring of indigenous theologies in America—owed its sustaining power to these schools.[8] Moreover, the medium was an indispensable part of the message, for in the environment of personal interaction students imbibed not only a theology, but a way of life. In these household seminaries, the light of the gospel and the heat of heartfelt religion passed through three and sometimes four generations of ministers.

This essay traces the origin and development of the schools of the prophets. I argue that their profound and widespread influence not only enabled the New Divinity movement to prosper, but distinguished these schools as America's single most important source of ministerial training from the mid-eighteenth century to the establishment of seminaries in the early nineteenth century. At the risk of homogenizing the turns and twists of a complex and dynamic movement, I emphasize its continuities. For some ministerial aspirants, New Divinity theology had its own intrinsic appeal; for others, it was simply the theology of the day. In either case, the schools of the prophets provided the medium for the transmission of New Divinity theology.

5. Conforti, *Samuel Hopkins*, chap. 11, and esp. Kling, *Field of Divine Wonders*.
6. The following Yale alumni who became college presidents received theological instruction in the schools of the prophets: Azel Backus (Hamilton), Henry Davis (Middlebury, Hamilton), Edward Dorr Griffin (Williams), Heman Humphrey (Amhurst). Other New Divinity trained ministers who became college presidents included Jonathan Edwards Jr. (Union), Zephaniah Swift Moore (Williams, Amherst), and Stephen Chapin (Columbian).
7. Conforti, *Samuel Hopkins*, 157–58.
8. For a terse summary of New Divinity theological views, see Breitenbach, "Piety and Moralism," 191.

Origins of Schools of the Prophets

Throughout the colonial period and well into the nineteenth century, preparation for the Congregational ministry followed a pattern indebted to sixteenth and seventeenth-century English Puritanism. Puritans viewed the university as representing an essential element in the preparation of a preacher,
but not the sole element. Beyond formal instruction at Oxford or Cambridge,
the major influence of a mentor—be he a tutor, a preacher, or a pastor—was
often decisive in "equipping the ministry." Training at the university was
often followed by an apprenticeship under a respected minister. This pattern
of supervision, developed early within the Puritan movement, became widespread in England, was transported to America in the seventeenth century,
and continued throughout the eighteenth and into the early nineteenth centuries.[9] Thus, training for the ministry followed a two-step process of formal
education and brief apprenticeship. In her study of ministerial training in
eighteenth-century New England, Mary Gambrell calculated that of the
more than eight hundred ministers ordained between 1740 and 1810, fewer
than twenty were not definitely known to have been awarded a college degree.[10] At both Harvard and Yale, a classical liberal arts education, permeated with the study of Protestant theology ("theoretical divinity"), informed
the college curriculum.

A college education may have provided training *for* the ministry, but a settled clergyman provided training *in* the ministry.[11] Under the tutelage of an
experienced practitioner, clerical candidates received the rudiments of professional preparation. Despite the high value placed upon a learned ministry
within the Calvinist tradition, Congregationalists in New England and Presbyterians in the middle colonies—the two largest religious bodies in colonial
America—imposed no formal, uniform training upon their ministers beyond
a college education. Typically, a ministerial candidate "read divinity" or
"studied theology" with another pastor—be he a relative, a local pastor, a
well-known theologian—or with the president or professor of divinity at
Harvard or Yale.[12]

    9. Gerald R. Cragg, "Training in the Ministry—The Older Tradition," *Andover Newton Quar-
terly* 8 (March 1968): 226–29. For examples of the continuity of these tutorial practices in America,
see William O. Shewmaker, "The Training of the Protestant Ministry in the United States of America,
Before the Establishment of Theological Seminaries," *Papers of the American Society of Church History,* 2d ser., 6 (1921): 150–52.
    10. Gambrell, *Ministerial Training in Eighteenth-Century New England,* 52. The realization of
the educational ideal for ministers represented a continuation of past practices. Gambrell calculated
that between 1640 and 1740, of 250 ministers known to have been ordained, only 25 were not definitely known to have held a college degree (pp. 21–22).
    11. Sidney E. Mead, "The Rise of the Evangelical Conception of the Ministry," eds. H. Richard Nie-
buhr and Daniel D. Williams, *The Ministry in Historical Perspectives* (New York: Harper, 1956), 242.
    12. Harvard established the Hollis chair in divinity in 1721; Yale, its chair in 1756.

Apprenticeship practices were not confined to the Congregationalists or Presbyterians, nor were such practices limited to ministerial education, for aspiring lawyers and physicians prepared for their careers in much the same way. The antecedents for apprenticeship training are found, of course, in the distant past of the medieval guild system and more directly in English nonconformist practices. In addition, the peculiar demands and conditions of the New World created first, by distance, and then exacerbated by the sundering of European ties following the Revolution, encouraged apprenticeship practices. Lacking their own universities or official credentialing agencies in America, and often faced with critical shortages, such groups as Lutherans, Episcopalians, and a number of Reformed bodies (Presbyterians, Dutch Reformed, Associate, Associate Reformed, and Reformed Presbyterian) supplied an educated ministry through "household seminaries."[13] In some cases, private teachers or academies were denominationally appointed, created, and regulated; in others, they emerged spontaneously as a means of addressing the need of an educated ministry. Depending upon a student's prior preparation, as well as the educational demands of a particular religious group, the length and nature of study ranged from several months of informal reading to a prescribed four-year curriculum. Following this "seminary" training, such as it was, a student became eligible for ordination into the work of the ministry.

As long as stability and general unity characterized New England Puritanism, decisions regarding study with a settled minister followed the path of expediency. That is, the personal knowledge of a minister or the proximity of a minister to where the candidate resided largely determined the pairing of candidate and teacher. The Great Awakening, however, fractured Puritanism and, in so doing, challenged long-standing practices of ministerial education. Indeed, as scholars have reiterated, the Awakening proved to be a wa-

---

13. On general educational efforts prior to the advent of formal seminaries, see Samuel Simpson, "Early Ministerial Training in America," *Papers of the American Society of Church History,* 2d ser. 2 (1910): 117–29; Shewmaker, "Training of the Protestant Ministry," 71–197; and Frank Dixon McCloy, "The History of Theological Education in America," *Church History* 31 (1962): 449–53. On Lutheran ministerial training, see B. Stadtler, "The Education of Ministers by Private Tutors, Before the Establishment of Theological Seminaries," *Lutheran Church Review* 12 (April 1894): 167–83; Frederick G. Gotwald, "Theological Education in the Lutheran Church in the United States Prior to the Founding of Wittenberg College and Seminary in 1845," *The Lutheran Quarterly* 46 (Jan. 1916): 82–100. On Dutch Reformed ministerial training, see biographical sketches of Dirck Romeyn, John H. Livingston, Philip Milledoler, Andrew Yates, and Solomon Freligh in William B. Sprague, *Annals of the American Pulpit* (New York: Carter and Brothers, 1857–69), v. 9 ("Reformed Dutch"). For the Associate Church, see biographical sketch of John Anderson in Sprague, *Annals* 9 ("Associate"): 17–31; and Jesse Johnson, "Early Theological Education West of the Alleghanies [sic]," *Papers of the American Society of Church History,* 2d ser. 5 (1917): 119–30. On Associate Reformed ministerial training, see sketch of John Mason in Sprague, *Annals* 9 ("Associate Reformed"). On Reformed Presbyterian training practices, see sketches of James McKinney, Alexander McLeod, and Samuel Brown Wylie in Sprague, *Annals* 9 ("Reformed Presbyterian").

tershed not only in theological training, but an important moment in the history of American higher education.

The stinging criticisms of Gilbert Tennent, George Whitefield, Jonathan Edwards, and others, who contended that colonial colleges offered "light but no heat," knowledge but no piety, resulted in a profound reordering of ministerial education throughout the colonies. The fragmentation of Puritanism in New England, and Presbyterianism in the middle colonies into New Light-Old Light, New Side-Old Side parties (and the subsequent splintering within these groups) bred competition and a struggle for power. Whose churches, schools, colleges, and form of religiosity would ultimately prevail? The result was aggressive attempts by "new" evangelical parties to advance their convictions on the relationship between religion and learning, between experiential knowledge of Christ and education.

Pro-revivalists made efforts to institutionalize the Awakening with the founding of the College of New Jersey (Princeton) in 1746, and the colleges of Rhode Island (Brown), Dartmouth, and Queens (Rutgers) in the 1760s and 1770s. However much these colleges succeeded in furthering the goals and aspirations of New Light and New Side parties (and some question whether they did),[14] other more immediate forces were at work to sustain the evangelical Calvinists' goal of coupling piety with learning.

For Scots-Irish Presbyterians, this goal was advanced first, by William Tennent's Log College (founded 1727), and then, following the Old Side-New Side split in 1741, by New Side academies established by Tennent's students.[15] To the north, New Light Edwardseans sought to maintain evangelical piety and learning by working within the well-established structures of ministerial education, yet bending those structures to their own purposes.

Although New Side Presbyterians largely succeeded in creating their own alternative educational institutions, New Lights were stymied by the heavy hand of Old Light rule at Yale. (Actually, New Sides themselves had experienced Old Light policies, for Yale had been a viable educational alternative for Presbyterians prior to the Awakening.) Under the imperious President Thomas Clap, Yale instituted measures to snuff out any threat of New Light enthusiasm or censoriousness. And so David Brainerd and the brothers John and Ebenezer Cleaveland became martyrs to the New Light cause and further

14. Richard Hofstadter, *American at 1750: A Social Portrait* (New York: Vintage Books, 1973), 285–86.

15. On the Log College and New Side Presbyterian academies, see Archibald Alexander, *The Log College: Biographical Sketches of William Tennent and His Students. . . .* (1851, reprint, London: Banner of Truth, 1968); Thomas Murphy, *The Presbytery of the Log College; or the Cradle of the Presbyterian Church in America* (Philadelphia: Presbyterian Board of Publications, 1889); and esp. Douglas Sloan, *The Scottish Enlightenment and the American College Ideal* (New York: Teachers College Press, 1971), chap. 2.

heightened controversy over Yale's fitness to train evangelical ministers of the gospel.[16]

Edwards and other friends of the Awakening, realizing that their interests were not shared by officials at either Yale or Harvard, sought alternative means to perpetuate vital piety in ministerial training. For the more radical Separatists, it meant complete repudiation of the spiritually corrupt colleges and the erection of the short-lived "Shepherd's Tent" (1742–43) in New London, Connecticut. The brainchild of Timothy Allen and James Davenport, the "Tent"—no more than the second floor of a house—functioned as a school to aid and abet the most radical of religious enthusiasts. It was at New London, by the instigation of Davenport and the hearty support of students, that in March of 1743, citizens burned heretical books and worldly clothing. To Old Lights, such actions were bad enough, but when these radicals claimed a direct inspiration of the Holy Ghost for their actions, even New Lights, such as Edwards and Joseph Bellamy, repudiated them and the Shepherd's Tent folded. Criticizing existing colleges was one thing; creating an institution based on divine revelation was quite another.[17]

In the wake of the Shepherd's Tent debacle, modern New Lights continued to bemoan spiritual decay in the colleges, but their dismay did not result in a wholesale rejection of existing institutions. Yale was valued and respected, for it provided the rudiments of ministerial education, especially instruction in languages and literature. But Yale was not enough, nor was just *any* pastor an appropriate theological guide. There emerged, then, a self-conscious desire among New Light clerical aspirants to complete their ministerial preparation under sympathetic ministers. Indeed, the ousted John Cleaveland so admired Philemon Robbins's evangelical preaching that he chose this New Light pastor as his theological mentor.[18] As the moderate New Light party evolved into the New Divinity in the 1760s, the schools of the prophets were born both out of protest and by default. Because Yale failed as a nursery of piety, the burden now fell upon New Divinity men to ensure that the theology and vital piety of the Awakening were transmitted to the rising generation of ministers. Consequently, while Yale was led by Old (or moderate) Calvinist presidents for the remainder of the century, increasing numbers of graduates completed their ministerial preparation in New Divinity schools of the prophets. Rather than study with the familiar

16. For a general treatment of Yale's response to the Great Awakening, see Richard Hofstader and Walter P. Metzger, *The Development of Academic Freedom in the United States* (New York: Columbia University Press, 1955), 163–77; Brooks Mather Kelley, *Yale: A History* (New Haven: Yale University Press, 1974), 49–55.

17. On this episode, see Richard Warch, "The Shepherd's Tent: Education and Enthusiasm in the Great Awakening," *American Quarterly* 30 (summer 1978): 177–98.

18. Christopher M. Jedrey, *The World of John Cleaveland: Family and Community in Eighteenth-Century New England* (New York: Oxford University Press, 1979), 40.

neighborhood pastor or a reverend uncle, ministerial candidates consciously sought out those of proven New Divinity theological credentials and evangelical piety. Within the broad pattern of Congregational ministerial training, then, an intentionally directed form of apprenticeship arose in the years following the Awakening.

The New Divinity and Schools of the Prophets

With the emergence of New Divinity schools of the prophets a movement was born. And as more New Divinity pastor-teachers opened their homes to prospective ministers, the movement increased in number and expanded its local and translocal ties. By 1800, the Edwardseans secured footholds along the eastern seaboard, in Vermont and New Hampshire, and could claim northwestern Connecticut and western Massachusetts as their own territory.[19] Samuel Hopkins, one of the patriarchs of the New Divinity movement, calculated that the number of New Divinity clergy grew from a handful in 1756 to nearly fifty in 1773 and by 1797 topped the one hundred mark.[20] By President Stiles' reckoning in 1792, over one-third of the Connecticut Congregational pulpits ("58 or 60 out of 168") were filled with New Divinity men and numbers were increasing.[21] In 1813, the Rev. William Bentley, the proto-Unitarian from Salem, Massachusetts, preferred grudging tribute to the New Divinity, recording that it was "the basis of the popular theology in New England."[22] From 1750 to 1825, over five hundred men passed through the schools of the prophets, imbibed Edwardsean theology, and thus collectively established the most powerful theological movement in New England.[23]

Several dozen New Divinity pastors trained clerical candidates, but a few eminent divines tutored significant numbers over the course of their ministerial careers. Jonathan Edwards took in students such as Samuel Hopkins and Joseph Bellamy, who, in turn, trained a generation of New Divinity men. Bellamy was the first to establish a school for the training of New Divinity

19. Conforti, "The Rise of the New Divinity in Western New England," Kling, *Field of Divine Wonders*.

20. Samuel Hopkins, *Sketches of the Life of the Late Rev. Samuel Hopkins, D.D.*, ed. Stephen West (Hartford, Conn.: Stephen West, 1805), 102–3.

21. Ezra Stiles, *The Literary Diary of Ezra Stiles*, ed. Franklin B. Dexter (New York, 1901), 3: 463–64.

22. William Bentley, *The Diary of William Bentley, D.D., Pastor of the East Church, Salem, Massachusetts* (1905–14; repr., Gloucester, Mass.: Peter Smith, 1963), 4:302.

23. This figure was calculated by identifying New Divinity pastor-teachers and then identifying their students. Sources: Sprague, *Annals of the American Pulpit*, vols. 1–4; Franklin B. Dexter, *Biographical Sketches of the Graduates of Yale College with Annals of the College History* (New York: H. Holt, 1885–1912), vols. 1–5; Joseph Vaill, "Theological Education in Connecticut, Seventy Years Ago," *The Congregational Quarterly* 6 (1864): 137–42; Calvin Durfee, *Williams Biographical Annals* (Boston: Lee and Shepherd, 1871). See also appendices of New Divinity men in Conrad Wright, *The Beginnings of Unitarianism in America* (Boston: Beacon Press, 1955), 288–91; Conforti, *Samuel Hopkins*, 227–32; and Kling, *Field of Divine Wonders*, 245–50.

pastors at his parsonage in Bethlehem, Connecticut, and over the course of his career he trained some sixty ministers. His fame as a revivalist preacher, coupled with the publication of *True Religion Delineated (1750)*, established him as a leading proponent of the New Divinity. Consequently, students began showing up at Bellamy's "log college" to study with "the pope of Litchfield County." Near the end of Bellamy's career, Nathanael Emmons of Franklin, Massachusetts, emerged as Herr Professor Doktor of the New Divinity. For over fifty years he put over ninety students through the rigors of his brand of New Divinity theology.[24] Other leading educators included Charles Backus of Somers, Connecticut, who trained thirty students.[25] Other Connecticut New Divinity men such as Benjamin Trumbull of North Haven, John Smalley of Berlin, Levi Hart of Preston, Jonathan Edwards Jr. of New Haven, Nathan Perkins of West Hartford, and Ebenezer Porter of Washington educated about ninety students, ranging between ten and twenty each. In western Massachusetts, a hotbed of New Divinity sentiment from 1775 to 1825, Stephen West, Ephraim Judson, Jacob Catlin, Theophilus Packard, Alvan Hyde, and Edward Dorr Griffin trained over seventy-five students.

A detailed genealogy of New Divinity men can be reconstructed by tracing three and sometimes four generations of education in schools of the prophets. Jonathan Edwards mentored Bellamy and Hopkins, who established their own schools; John Smalley, a student of Bellamy, continued the tradition by training twenty students, including Nathanael Emmons. And so it went. By 1800 hundreds of New Divinity men could trace their pedigree back through several teachers to Edwards himself.[26] Unraveling this complex web of New Divinity relations reveals that Congregationalists who played major roles in the outpouring of the early nineteenth-century revivals, as well as in the formation of and participation in the modern missionary movement, received their instruction, direction, and inspiration in New Divinity schools of the prophets.[27] For example, Hopkins trained Edwards' son, Jonathan Jr.,

24. Edwards A. Park, "Memoir of Nathanael Emmons," in *The Works of Nathanael Emmons, D.D.* (Boston: Crocker and Brewster, 1861), 1: 221–63; John T. Dahlquist, "Nathanael Emmons: His Life and Work" (Ph.D. diss., Boston University, 1963), 203–4.

25. On Backus, see Sprague, *Annals,* 2:61–68; Vaill, "Theological Education," 139; on Burton, see Asa Burton, *The Life of Asa Burton Written by Himself,* ed. Charles Latham Jr. (Thetford, Vt.: First Congregational Church, 1973); Sprague, *Annals,* 2:140–47.

26. For example, see the "genealogical tree" in Kling, *Field of Divine Wonders,* 31.

27. This informal web of connections characterizes purposive movements in general, both in the past and present. The New Divinity movement closely followed bonding patterns of the English Puritan movement. As David D. Hall notes, "Family intermarriage, familial patterns of recruitment, and a complex set of spiritual relationships were other bonds among the members of the [Puritan] brotherhood." Thus, "John Cotton, who owed his conversion to the preaching of William Perkins and Richard Sibbes, was the spiritual father of John Preston, who in turn converted Thomas Shepard." As with the New Divinity, these Puritans did not agree on all theological issues, "yet the brotherhood functioned as a real association, a group that had a purpose to accomplish." See Hall, *The Faithful Shepherd: A History of the New England Ministry in the Seventeenth Century* (1972; New York: Norton, 1974), 50.

who, in turn, trained Edward Dorr Griffin, a leading revivalist, seminary professor, and college president. In the early 1820s, during the first years of his presidency at Williams College, Griffin continued the tradition of New Divinity mentoring by instructing recent graduates.

From Bellamy's rustic school there issued a number of influential New Divinity leaders, including Levi Hart, who trained Charles Backus and Asa Burton—two men whose prodigious teaching efforts have already been cited. Backus, in turn, mentored three college presidents—his nephew, Azel Backus of Hamilton; Zephaniah Swift Moore of Williams and later Amherst; and Henry Davis of Middlebury and later Hamilton. Included among Backus's students who initiated their own parlor seminaries were Alvan Hyde and Jacob Catlin, colleagues in Berkshire County, Massachusetts. To cite a final example, John Smalley, a student of Bellamy's, tutored Ebenezer Porter, a leading pastor-revivalist in Washington, Connecticut, and later professor of homiletics and president of Andover. During his pastorate in Washington, Porter trained both Gordon Hall and Harvey Loomis, Williams College graduates (1807) who, at the famous 1806 Haystack Prayer Meeting at Williams, were among those who dedicated their lives to overseas missionary service.

Like other social groupings, the schools of the prophets created a discrete group identity. Indeed, they functioned not only as parlor seminaries and ministerial placement centers, but furnished the social matrix for marriage and associational bonds. In some cases, students married the daughter or relative of their mentor; in others, a spouse was discovered within the larger New Divinity social network. Levi Hart not only listened to the words of Bellamy, but found a wife in his mentor's daughter. Jeremiah Hallock tapped into the New Divinity extended family by marrying the sister to the wife of his mentor, Abraham Fowler.

The schools of the prophets also created a sense of social cohesiveness that enabled the movement to flourish. With college acquaintances renewed, friendships made, values shared, and piety enhanced, teacher and students set about their common task. Moreover, prospective pastors were initiated into the private, as well as the public, side of ministerial life. Their mentor not only imparted theology in the study and preached the Word in the meetinghouse, but he also proferred pastoral advice and provided a model of godly living. In his deportment at home with his wife and children, and in his pastoral relations, the teacher transmitted attitudes and values that his students carried with them into their own ministerial careers. Herman Humphrey, an 1805 graduate of Yale, and later president of Amherst College, recalled his tenure of instruction with Asahel Hooker: "Living in his family, observing how he went out and came in, how he walked before his flock . . . enjoying his daily conversations, sitting under his ministry, and getting insensibly as it were, initiated into the duties of the pastoral office, by the light of his example, were among the most important benefits enjoyed in his school."[28]

Instruction in Schools of the Prophets

The course of study, as well as the demands placed upon students in schools of the prophets, varied from instructor to instructor. Accounts of actual instruction are fragmentary, but piecing them together yields a remarkably consistent pattern of training practices for three-quarters of a century. Students were presented with a series of theological questions in a fashion reminiscent of catechetical instruction. With questions before them—and primarily by independent study—they wrote "dissertations." A student covered the standard topics in Protestant scholastic theology in a kind of "short course" which, at a seminary today, might constitute a year-long survey in dogmatic theology.

This New Divinity penchant for the scholastic pattern of education included directed reading, personal instruction, and answering questions in "polemical" (systematic) or didactic theology. Theological study was foremost, as is attested by the long hours (thirteen to eighteen hours a day) some New Divinity instructors spent wrestling with post-Great Awakening theological issues. The other three areas of the traditional fourfold pattern of theological education (church history, practical theology, Bible) were subordinated to the study of theology. As one might expect, instructors ignored the church fathers, paid scant attention to scriptural exegesis or linguistics, and slighted the notion of doctrinal development other than to relate the usual tale of medieval corruptions and Reformation correctives.[29] In the charged atmosphere of theological debate and emerging Protestant pluralism during the last half of the eighteenth century, polemical theology was *de rigueur* for the New Divinity.

The informal nature of the schools of the prophets dictated against standardized educational procedures. A degree of coherence was maintained through constant interaction among New Divinity men or by teachers simply duplicating the methods and questions of their New Divinity predecessors. Bellamy and Hopkins exchanged correspondence over a common core of theological questions, and in 1756 Bellamy went so far as to suggest that they coauthor a text of questions to be used in the schools.[30] Because Bellamy's school was one of the earliest and the most popular of the day, his system of teaching became the New Divinity *modus operandi*. John Smalley followed Bellamy's pedagogical lead, as did his student, Nathanael Emmons.[31] Other

---

28. Sprague, *Annals*, 2:321; see also Vaill, "Theological Education," 141–42.
29. Gambrell, *Ministerial Training in Eighteenth-Century New England*, 135.
30. Conforti, *Samuel Hopkins*, 37.
31. "Memoir of Nathanael Emmons, D.D.," in *The Works of Nathanael Emmons, D.D.*, ed. Jacob Ide (Boston, 1842), 1:xxiv.

instructors, such as Charles Backus, Jonathan Edwards Jr., Stephen West, and Asahel Hooker, supplied questions and required students to write "dissertations" on standard theological topics.[32]

To answer theological questions, students consulted Scripture and read a variety of theological treatises—both orthodox and heterodox. They then discussed their dissertations and assigned readings with their teacher for an hour or two in the afternoon or evening. A rather revealing indicator of the growing theological contentiousness during the last half of the eighteenth century (or perhaps a testimony to a more comprehensive approach to theology) was the increasing number of questions added to the instructor's list. Jonathan Edwards, for example, compiled a list of ninety questions for his students; a generation later, his son's list ran to over three hundred.[33] Jonathan the Younger's questions ranged from the standard catechetical queries ("For what purposes was revelation necessary?" and "Was Christ a son from eternity?") to specific New Divinity concerns ("What is the difference between natural and moral necessity?" "What do you mean by disinterested love?" "Do the unregenerate grow better in the use of means?"). Maltby Gelston, a student of the younger Edwards, kept a notebook in which he recorded the answers to some five hundred questions covering the basics of didactic theology. Presumably, all of his answers were committed to memory.[34]

A severe handicap to training in the schools of the prophets was the country parson's library. Because the books available to students were often meagre and uneven in quality (with the exception of Nathanael Emmon's holdings), priority was placed upon depth of understanding, not breadth of knowledge. A student of Stephen West recalled that "the books to be read were few, among them were Hopkin's *System of Divinity* and a few other important works such as might be expected in the library of a country minister."[35] For three-quarters of a century, the New Divinity canon built upon the writings of Edwards and Bellamy and then, as they came available, expanded to include the works of other New Divinity authors—Hopkin's *System of Divinity* (1793), and selected theological treatises by Stephen West and John Smalley.[36]

---

32. On West, see Sprague, *Annals*, 1:553; on Hooker, see Sprague, *Annals*, 2:320–21; on Backus, see Vaill, "Theological Education," 141.

33. See "The Theological Questions of President Edwards, Senior, and Dr. Edwards, His Son" (Providence, R.I., 1822).

34. Gambrell, *Ministerial Training*, 134.

35. Sprague, *Annals* 1:553.

36. For an extended discussion of New Divinity library holdings, see Gambrell, *Ministerial Training*, 108–24; on Emmon's holdings, see John T. Dahlquist, "Nathanael Emmons: His Life and Work" (Ph.D. diss., Boston University, 1963), 102–10. For other references to New Divinity "reading lists," see Robbins, *Diary*, 1:36–50; Park, "Memoir of Emmons," 218–19.

The Faithful New Divinity Master

After studying with a New Divinity teacher for as little as three months or with several teachers intermittently for three years, after reading and learning New Divinity dogmatics, and after living with a pastor, his family, and a few other students, what expectations did an aspiring pastor take with him into the ministry? What goals did New Divinity teachers have for their students? Indeed, who was the ideal New Divinity minister? In many ways, the model of a faithful New Divinity minister mirrored the general Protestant conception of the evangelical minister as one who preached the Word of God for the salvation and edification of his hearers. Richard Baxter's *The Reformed Pastor* (1655) remained a popular handbook for Congregational ministers throughout the colonial era and well into the nineteenth century. This classic of pastoral theology emphasized the primacy of theological study, but subordinated its study to practical ends.[37] Perhaps for this reason—for its utilitarian bent—the New Divinity never found the pastoral Baxter as compelling as the more speculative Edwards.

New Divinity ordination sermons, published during the last half of the eighteenth century, reiterated the evangelical view of the ideal pastor. At the same time, the New Divinity uplifted prominent themes in Edwards that emphasized the role of the minister as a theologian. Edwards' 1744 ordination sermon, "The True Excellency of a Gospel Minister," served as a paradigm for the New Divinity conception of the ministry. Taking his text from John 5:35 (where Christ observed that John "was a bright and shining light"), Edwards averred that "light and heat must be united in a minister of the gospel."[38] By "light" he meant that ministers must possess correct doctrinal knowledge, or "great speculative knowledge." In order to reveal the mind and will of God, the gospel minister knew the things of God. Light, however, was not sufficient. As Edwards had noted some years before, the people of Northampton did not so much need their heads stored as their hearts touched. To be able to touch the heart, the gospel minister needed "heat," consisting of a "holy zeal," an "ardour in his heart," or a "heart warmed and inflamed with a great love to Christ."[39]

Ordination sermons elaborated Edwards' twofold model. The overarching goal of the ministry remained consistent: to advance the kingdom of Christ through the promotion of salvation and piety.[40] To that end, a faithful

37. See James E. Bradley's chapter below.
38. Jonathan Edwards, "The True Excellency of a Gospel Minister" (1744), in *The Works of President Edwards* (1847; repr., New York: B. Franklin, 1968), 10:506.
39. Ibid.
40. Nathan Perkins (a sermon preached at the installation of the Rev. Solomon Wolcott, Hartford, Conn., May 24, 1786), 23; Charles Backus, "The Faithful Ministers of Jesus Christ Rewarded" (a sermon delivered at the ordination of the Rev. Azel Backus, Litchfield, Conn., April 6, 1791), 7; Asa Burton (a sermon preached at the ordination of the Rev. Timothy Clark, Windsor, Vt., January 1, 1800), 16.

New Divinity minister of the gospel met three qualifications. First, he himself was regenerate, having an "experiential acquaintance with Christianity."[41] Second, he was knowledgeable. Thoroughly grounded in the ancient languages, Scripture, and doctrine, he was a "workman" engaged in "deep thought," "hard study," "mighty in Scriptures, and expert in reasoning upon divine subjects."[42] During the last decades of the eighteenth century, a period which increasingly emphasized the ability of humans to take control of their personal and political destinies, the New Divinity considered the defence of the Calvinist faith as a primary qualification to the ministry.[43] A godly minister, then, was a "watchman," ever vigilant in defence of the faith against corrupting influences, whether in the form of spiritual apathy among parishioners or of outright challenges posed by "deists" and "infidels."[44]

Piety, the final qualification for the ministry, outwardly expressed an inwardly changed heart. True virtue or self-giving love was a fruit of salvation, the result of the work of Christ in one's heart. A man of piety, or "a real good man" as the New Divinity called him, exhibited a love to Christ and relished "the moral beauty of scripture doctrines."[45] A godly minister thus gave evidence of the work of grace in his life.

Having met these prerequisites for ministry, the New Divinity pastor fulfilled his duty in the ministry by preaching the gospel. Speaking the Word of God—primarily in Sabbath sermons, but also in midweek lectures, conferences, and house visitations—was the God-ordained means of bringing sinners to salvation, and saints to edification. The New Divinity repeatedly emphasized that evangelical preaching embraced "the whole counsel of God," "all the doctrines of Christianity," or "the full gospel plan."[46] This,

41. Levi Hart, "The Christian Minister, or Faithful Preacher of the Gospel Described" (a sermon delivered at the ordination of the Rev. Joel Benedict, New London, Conn., February 21, 1771), 8–9.

42. Benjamin Trumbull (a sermon delivered at the ordination of the Rev. Lemuel Tyler, New Haven, Conn., May 7, 1789), 7; Charles Backus, "Qualifications and Duties of the Christian Pastor" (a sermon delivered at the ordination of the Rev. Freegrace Reynolds (Boston, October 29, 1795), 10–12; Jonathan Edwards Jr., "The Duty of Ministers of the Gospel to Preach the Truth" (a sermon delivered at the ordination of the Rev. Edward Dorr Griffin, Hartford, Conn., June 4, 1795), 13; Perkins (a sermon preached at the installation of Wolcott), 16; Nathanael Emmons (a sermon delivered at the ordination of the Rev. John Smith, Concord, N.H., January 4, 1797), 22.

43. Backus, "Faithful Ministers," 24; Trumbull (a sermon delivered at ordination of Tyler), 8; Charles Backus, "Ministers Serving God in the Gospel of His Son" (a sermon delivered at the ordination of the Rev. Timothy Mather Cooley, West Springfield, Mass., February 3, 1796), 11.

44. Backus, "Faithful Ministers," 22; Asahel Hooker, "The Immoral and Pernicious Tendency of Error" (a sermon delivered at the ordination of the Rev. James Beach (Hartford, January 1, 1806), 23.

45. Perkins (a sermon preached at installation of Wolcott), 8; Jonathan Edwards Jr., "All Divine Truth Profitable" (a sermon preached at the ordination of the Rev. Dan Bradley, New Haven, Conn., January 11, 1792), 37; Nathanael Emmons (a discourse preached at the ordination of the Rev. Eli Smith, Worcester, Mass., November 27, 1793), 14; Charles Backus, "The High Importance of Love to Jesus Christ in the Minister of the Gospel" (a sermon delivered at the ordination of the Rev. John Hubbard Church, Amherst, N.H., October 31, 1799), 9.

46. Hart, "The Christian Minister," 16; Perkins (a sermon preached at the installation of Wolcott), 26; Charles Backus, "The Benevolent Spirit of Christianity Illustrated" (a sermon delivered at the ordination of the Rev. Thomas Snell, Worcester, Mass., June 27, 1798), 25; Nathan Perkins (a

of course, meant preaching the unpopular doctrines of the New Divinity, and uplifting the "hard sayings" of Calvinism: human depravity and accountability, the curse of the law, God's electing degrees, and the demand for immediate repentance. As Christianity in the new republic became increasingly audience oriented and lay driven, New Divinity teachers reminded their students that however offensive the message may be to some, they were, nevertheless, obliged to preach unvarnished New Divinity truths.[47] To be sure, these pastors had mixed success as preachers—some like Samuel Hopkins stupefied, others like Edward Dorr Griffin stunned—but they all enjoined a manner of preaching congruent with Edwards' teaching on the head and the heart.[48] For the Edwardseans, knowing religion and being religious constituted inseparable aspects of a single reality, and the preached sermon was the most appropriate God-ordained vehicle for apprehending this reality.

Finally, New Divinity ministers counseled the display of "distinguishing marks of conversion." These marks included self-sacrifice in placing the cause of Christ before personal pleasure, zealousness in the work of God, and devotion to the spiritual life. Edwards' advice became the constant refrain through the years: "As to the things of the world, you are not to expect outward ease, pleasure, and plenty; nor are you to depend on the friendship and respect of men, but should prepare to endure hardness, as one that is going forth as a soldier to war."[49] New Divinity teachers urged their students to practice constant self-examination in order to know the true condition of their corrupt hearts, so as to affirm their dependence upon a sovereign, yet merciful, God. Moreover, what mentors demanded of themselves they enjoined upon their students: rigorous study, disciplined habits, and single-minded devotion to the ministry. Criticizing "indolence" as "inexcusable" and a form of "worldliness," they fulfilled the divine calling with a self-denying holy zeal.[50] Wary of unprofitable conversation (even with parishioners!),[51] ever mindful of the need for vigilance against the powers of darkness (whether real or imagined infidelity), and captured (at times enraptured) by a vision of God's glory, the New Divinity viewed the calling to the ministry as an either/or proposition. "There can be no neuters in the cause of Christ," warned Nathanael Emmons, "he that is not

---

discourse delivered at the ordination of the Rev. William F. Miller, Hartford, November 30, 1791), 12; Backus, "Ministers Serving God in the Gospel," 11.

47. Perkins (a sermon preached at installation of Wolcott), 29; Nathan Perkins (a sermon delivered at the ordination of Rev. Hezekiah N. Woodruff, New London, Conn., July 2, 1789), 7.

48. For the varying approaches, attitudes, and successes of New Divinity preaching, see Kling, *Field of Divine Wonders*, chap. 4.

49. Edwards, "True Excellency of a Gospel Minister," 509.

50. Perkins (a sermon preached at the installation of Wolcott), 16; Edwards Jr., "Duty of Ministers," 15.

51. Backus, "Qualifications and Duties," 9; Emmons (a sermon delivered at ordination of Smith), 8.

for him, must be against him. You must be conformed either to Christ or to the world."[52]

Perpetuating the Schools of the Prophets: Rural New England Colleges as Feeders

According to the standard histories of theological education in New England, the story of the New Divinity schools of the prophets concludes with the opening of Andover Seminary in 1808.[53] This first seminary, after all, had New Divinity men among its founders and first professors, and thus siphoned off potential students from schools of the prophets.[54] The professional seminary filled the obvious need of training the growing number of male converts from the Second Great Awakening who felt called into full-time Christian service. And so the overworked New Divinity pastor-teacher with his meagre collection of books and desultory educational requirements happily yielded to seminary professors, well-stocked theological libraries, and formal curricula. Coincident with the professions of law and medicine, the study of divinity went the way of general professionalization.[55] Together, these developments betokened the final chapter in the history of the schools of the prophets.

There is, however, an epilogue to the story, for just as the professional study of law and medicine did not immediately displace traditional apprenticeship practices, so the opening of Andover did not lead to an abrupt closing of the schools of the prophets. Even with the founding of additional seminaries (Princeton in 1812, Harvard in 1815, Bangor in 1816, Auburn in 1818, General in 1819, and Yale in 1822), the schools of the prophets, albeit in considerably reduced numbers, persisted. We may view the years from 1808 until the mid–1820s as a transitional phase during which several options lay before clerical aspirants. Some continued to receive all of their postgraduate theological training with a New Divinity "prophet"; others studied with a pastor and at a seminary; still others made the transition complete by preparing exclusively at one of the newly established divinity schools.

A vital component in the continued influence of schools of the prophets was the New England provincial college. Whereas Yale had served as the primary feeder to schools of the prophets throughout the eighteenth century, rural New England colleges emerged as the primary feeders during the first quarter of the nineteenth century. Just as many church-related colleges today

52. Emmons (a sermon delivered at ordination of Smith), 29.

53. See Gambrell, *Ministerial Training in Eighteenth-Century New England*, chap. 8; Bainton, *Yale and the Ministry*, chap. 7.

54. See Leonard Woods, *History of Andover Theological Seminary* (Boston, 1885).

55. On the rise of these professions, see Samuel Haber, *The Quest for Authority and Honor in the American Professions, 1750–1900* (Chicago: University of Chicago Press, 1991).

function as feeder schools to denominational seminaries, so in the early republic a number of newly formed colleges funneled aspiring ministers to
New Divinity finishing schools. The reason for this development is apparent:
New Divinity men filled leadership posts in these colleges and thus strongly
influenced the choice of a graduate's theological training. Presidents and professors at Dartmouth, Williams, and to a lesser extent Hamilton and Union,
channeled graduates to established New Divinity teachers such as Charles
Backus, Nathanael Emmons, Ephraim Judson, Alvan Hyde, and Asa Burton.

The early history of Williams College, from 1793 to 1836, provides an instructive example of how New Divinity influence at an undergraduate institution was parlayed into continued New Divinity mentoring practices. The
New Divinity presence at Williams also illustrates the primary strength of the
movement in backcountry, rural areas, and away from the pluralistic setting
of urban areas. Williams' first institutional leaders were all men of New Divinity stripe, with connections to the schools of the prophets. They served as
the college's first three presidents (1793–1836), the first five vice presidents,
and as members of the board of trustees.[56] Though not always successful in
imposing New Divinity views upon Williams, these men influenced the institution theologically and nurtured men of piety and evangelical zeal who min-
istered at home and abroad.

Because of its strong New Divinity identity, Williams attracted students
from New Divinity strongholds. Griffin exulted that from New Divinity-
soaked Litchfield County, Connecticut, "the spirit of a new era" of revivals
and missionary outreach "crept upon the college."[57] Through the influence
of New Divinity ministers in northwestern Connecticut and western Massachusetts, many young men from rural New England entered Williams, including Samuel Mills Jr., the oft-cited "father of the modern missionary
movement." Imbued with the New Divinity principle of a "selflessness" exhibited for the greater glory of God, Williams students supplied the largest
number of missionaries to the American Board of Commissioners for Foreign
Missions before 1840.[58] Some of the nation's earliest foreign missionaries,
including those associated with the Haystack Prayer Meeting of 1806, followed graduation from Williams with theological study in schools of the
prophets. Historians of missions concur that the primary theological impetus
for American foreign missions in the early republic originated with Edwards,

---

56. The college's presidents were Ebenezer Fitch, 1793–1815; Zephaniah Smith Moore, 1815–21;
and Edward Dorr Griffin, 1821–36; the first five vice presidents were Stephen West, Alan Hyde, Samuel Shepard, Timothy Mather Cooley, and Emerson Davis; New Divinity members of the board included the Reverends Daniel Collins, Seth Swift, Job Swift, Ammi Robbins, and Jacob Catlin.

57. Edward D. Griffin, "A Letter to the Rev. Dr. William B. Sprague"; published in the appendix
to his volume of lectures on revivals (Albany, 1832), 6.

58. Clifton Jackson Phillips, *Protestant America and the Pagan World: The First Half Century of
the American Board of Commissioners for Foreign Missions, 1810–1860* (Cambridge, Mass.: Harvard
University Press, 1969), chap. 1.

whose beatific concept of "disinterested benevolence" was modified by Samuel Hopkins into an evangelical activism.[59] Thus, Williams became the principal breeding ground for America's modern missionary movement.

With a potent New Divinity presence at Williams, professors, presidents, and board members influenced the choice of theological education of graduates who intended to serve the cause of Christ as pastors or missionaries. Prior to Andover's establishment, 70 percent (38 of 55) of Williams' alumni who entered the ministry apprenticed with a New Divinity pastor-teacher.[60] Beginning with the graduating class of 1807, ministerial and missionary candidates sought opportunities for professional theological education at Andover, and then at Princeton after 1812. Nevertheless, the schools of the prophets continued to draw their fair share. Between 1807 and 1822, of the 120 alumni seeking theological education, 35 studied with a New Divinity pastor, 42 studied at Andover, and 11 at Princeton.

After 1822 only a handful of students preferred the schools of the prophets, but New Divinity connections persisted and remained crucial during Griffin's presidency from 1821 to 1836. These alliances are illustrated in personal relationships, which translated into institutional ties between Williams and Auburn Theological Seminary. Griffin persuaded Williams graduates to pursue theological training at Auburn, where his longtime friend, James Richards, taught Edwardsean theology from 1823 to 1842.[61] Between 1824 and 1837, forty-five Williams graduates attended Auburn, the second highest number among feeder institutions to the seminary.[62]

During this same interval, no Williams graduates studied in schools of the prophets. For all intents and purposes, by the mid–1820s the apprenticeship form of theological education had become a thing of the past. For good *and* for ill, theological training had become a professional enterprise. For good, because educational standards rose. Students now received well-rounded instruction according to the fourfold pattern of theological educa-

59. On the influence of the New Divinity generally, and Hopkins in particular on the American foreign missionary movement, see Oliver W. Elsbree, *The Rise of the Missionary Spirit in America, 1790–1815* (Williamsport, Penn., 1928); William Warren Sweet, *Religion in the Development of American Culture, 1765–1840* (New York: Scribner's, 1952), 231; R. Pierce Beaver, "Missionary Motivation Through Three Centuries," in *Reinterpretation in American Church History*, ed. Jerald Brauer (Chicago: University of Chicago Press, 1970), 121–26; Phillips, *Protestant American and Pagan World*, chap. 1; Charles L. Chaney, "God's Glorious Work: The Theological Foundations of the Early Missionary Societies in America, 1787–1817" (Ph.D. diss., University of Chicago, 1973), Conforti, *Samuel Hopkins*, 157–8.

60. These and subsequent calculations on Williams graduates (unless otherwise noted) are based upon Durfee, *Williams Biographical Annals*.

61. For the Edwardsean views of Griffin, see Kling, *Field of Divine Wonders*; for Richards, see Sprague, *Annals* 4:99–112; John Quincy Adams, *A History of Auburn Theological Seminary, 1818–1918* (Auburn, N.Y.: Auburn Seminary Press, 1918), 73; Samuel Gridley, "Biographical Sketch," in James Richards, *Lectures on Mental Philosophy and Theology* (New York, 1846), 86–87; and Richards, *Lectures*, 97–153, 476–501.

62. Adams, *History of Auburn Theological Seminary*, 94.

tion. They also received a more thorough and exacting education from skilled professors.

But there were flaws. The close personal ties between teacher and students, the effective mentoring practices, the living model of pastoral commitment, the practical experiences—these were casualties to the modern theological seminary. Perhaps we would do well to ponder whether modern evangelical theological education—with its specialized programs, satellite seminaries, and plethora of correspondence courses—has properly served ministerial students. Has the spiritual formation of pastors suffered due to institutionalization and concomitant bureaucratization? The answer given by some evangelical seminaries is "yes." The preliminary findings of a long-range study recently completed by one of the country's premier evangelical seminaries identified as a major issue the institution's role in spiritual formation. "We generally agree that spiritual development of the pastor is extremely important," noted the report's author. "But we have been unable or unwilling to give to the development of the character and spirituality of [our] students nearly the time and attention that we have given to the intellectual skills necessary for careful handling of Scriptures.[63] The New Divinity schools of the prophets are a pertinent reminder that the message cannot be separated from the medium.

---

63. Quoted in Roger Bryant, "Decade of Transformation at TEDS," *Trinity Wellspring* 5 (fall 1993): 11.

7

The Nineteenth Century

James E. Bradley

Previous accounts of the growing rift between piety and learning in late nine-teenth-century evangelicalism have emphasized such conditions and causes as the American penchant for pragmatism, the influence of Scottish Common Sense philosophy, the anti-intellectual legacy of revivalism on the one hand, and the challenges of higher criticism, science, and the rise of the universities, on the other.[1] Alternatively, Edward Farley has laid great stress on the im-portance of the fourfold division of the theological curriculum for the trans-formation of theological education.[2] Several provocative studies of American Protestant thought have recently relocated the so-called critical period for theology and the church from the last quarter of the century to the late 1840s and early 1850s.[3] Further insight into the nature and timing of this crisis in American Evangelicalism may be gained by turning attention to the English tradition of practical theology. Part of the problem of the widening gulf be-tween piety and learning appears to be related to the pervasive influence of this English Evangelical tradition in America. The sources of English practi-cal theology that Edward Farley and Thomas Oden first drew attention to

---

1. For the traditional viewpoint, see Arthur M. Schlesinger Sr., "A Critical Period in American Protestantism, 1875–1900," *Massachusetts Historical Society Proceedings* 64 (1932): 523–48; Robert T. Handy, "Fundamentalism and Modernism in Perspective," *Religion in Life*, 24 (1955): 381–94; George M. Marsden, *Fundamentalism and American Culture: The Shaping of Twentieth-Century Evangelicalism: 1870–1925* (New York: Oxford University Press, 1980); and Ferenc Morton Szasz, *The Divided Mind of Protestant America, 1880–1930* (University: University of Alabama Press, 1982).

2. Edward Farley, *Theologia* (Philadelphia: Fortress Press, 1983).

3. Bruce Kuklick, *Churchmen and Philosophers: From Jonathan Edwards to John Dewey* (New Haven, 1985), 209–14; D. G. Hart, "Divided Between Heart and Mind: The Critical Period for Prot-estant Thought in America," *Journal of Ecclesiastical History* 38 (1987): 254–70; James Turner, "Sec-ularization and Sacralization: Speculations on Some Religious Origins of the Secular Humanities Cur-riculum, 1850–1900," 76, 93, n. 12, in *The Secularization of the Academy*, eds. George M. Marsden and Bradley J. Longfield (New York: Oxford University Press, 1992).

may thus provide fresh insights into one neglected root of the growing conflict in mid to late nineteenth-century American evangelicalism.[4]

I

The most influential authors of English pastoral theology were George Herbert, Richard Baxter, Gilbert Burnet, Thomas Secker, Philip Doddridge, Isaac Watts, John Mason, and a number of authors of shorter letters of advice.[5] George Herbert and his late seventeenth-century counterpart, Anglican Bishop Gilbert Burnet, were to the Anglican tradition what Richard Baxter and his mid-eighteenth-century counterpart, Philip Doddridge, were to the Dissenters: exemplars that had enormous influence on their respective traditions, and indeed, far beyond them. Each of the authors were themselves pastors; they were at one and the same time highly gifted scholars and well-experienced shepherds who wrote when advanced in years. The character of their writings was sermonic and hortatory and they should be placed squarely in the center of a broader tradition of English devotional or practical divinity. The interdependence of these texts upon each other is quite remarkable in itself. Watts, Doddridge, and Mason relied explicitly on Baxter's *Reformed Pastor,* but this was to be expected, since they all belonged to the Dissenting tradition.[6] Mason, the Congregationalist, however, was also heavily indebted to Bishop Burnet, citing him over and over again.[7] The numerous editions of these works attest to their popularity, and probably to their influence. Herbert's pastoral, *A Priest to the Temple,* had gone to the fourth English edition by 1701, and it was often republished in England in the nineteenth century.[8] Baxter was reprinted too often to record. Burnet was published regularly in England in the eighteenth century, and his discourse had reached the fourteenth edition by 1821.[9] Watts' work, first published in 1731, came out in a third London edition in 1742. Portions of these texts were frequently anthol-

---

4. Farley, *Theologia,* 8–9; Thomas C. Oden, *Care of Souls in the Classic Tradition* (Philadelphia: Fortress Press, 1984), 27. This study thereby departs from the recent institutional approach of Glenn Miller, *Piety and Intellect: The Aims and Purposes of Ante-Bellum Theological Education* (Atlanta: Scholars Press, 1990), and the focus on higher education in Louise L. Stevenson's *Scholarly Means to Evangelical Ends: The New Haven Scholars and the Transformation of Higher Learning in America, 1830–1890* (Baltimore: Johns Hopkins University Press, 1986).

5. A much fuller treatment of pastoral and practical theology will appear in my book entitled "Spiritual Formation in the Study of Theology and Ministry: The Protestant Tradition of Practical Theology, 1640–1925."

6. Isaac Watts, *An Humble Attempt Towards the Revival of Practical Religion Among Christians, by a Serious Address to Ministers and People* (London, 1742), 73, 79; Philip Doddridge, *Lectures on Preaching, and the Several Branches of the Ministerial Office* (London, 1821), 19; John Mason, *The Student and Pastor: Or, Directions How to Attain to Eminence and Usefulness in Those Respective Characters* (London, 1760), 33.

7. John Mason, *The Student and Pastor,* 8, 45, 54, 63–65, 110, 127, 143, 160.

8. In 1807, 1832, 1842, 1898, and 1916 the work was anthologized or found in new editions of his collected works in 1807, 1834, 1836, 1845, 1846, 1905, and 1961.

9. In 1713, 1736, 1766, 1777, 1805, 1818, and 1821.

ogized in the nineteenth century, and, in addition, there were several important abridgments. Henry Owen's abridgment of Burnet, first published in 1766, had gone through a fifth edition by 1807, and Samuel Palmer's abridgment of Baxter, first produced in 1766, came to a second edition in 1808.[10] These classic texts provided the theological substratum for many of the letters of advice to students of theology and young ministers.

The most noteworthy characteristic of the English tradition of practical theology is its theological coherence. From 1650 to 1850, a comparison of the authors of pastoral theology and the letters of advice to young ministers in a wide variety of denominations failed to reveal significant theological discrepancies between them. Differences of taste and conflicting estimates of the worth of certain writers persisted, but the commonality of the desired goal for the prospective minister is convincingly shown by the fact that Nonconformists often recommended that their students read the practical divinity of Anglican authors, and Anglicans, in turn, saw the value of the books and sermons of the Nonconformists. Doddridge, for example, recommended almost as many Anglican writers of practical divinity as he did Nonconformist.

The English tradition of pastoral theology put great stress on the inward preparation of the soul for the tasks of ministry. The person's soul and affections must be turned to God, and this piety, especially among prospective ministers of the gospel, was to be eminent to an unusual degree and combined with a studious temperament. The emphasis on piety meant that from the very outset there was a built-in distinction in practical theology between piety and intellect. The very means George Herbert used for understanding the Bible were ordered by the priority of piety, namely, a holy life, prayer, comparing text with text, and, finally, commentators and Fathers.[11] Holiness itself was gained, first, said Herbert, "by choosing texts of devotion, not controversy; moving and ravishing texts, whereof the Scriptures are full."[12] The ministerial temper, including felt love for God and compassion for our fellow human beings, in which all the duties of ministry ought to be performed, constituted a large part of the sapiential aspect of the inner life that Edward Farley brought to light. The young minister was thus to manifest an "evident tincture" of piety and zeal, and it was generally believed that the office itself "promotes, not one virtue, but a temper, which disposes the mind to the culture of every virtue."[13]

10. Henry Owen, *Directions for Young Students in Divinity, with Regard to Those Attainments, Which Are Necessary to Qualifying Them for Holy Orders,* 5th ed. (London, 1807).

11. George Herbert, *A Priest to the Temple, or the Country Parson, His Character, and Rule of Holy Life* (London, 1671), 9.

12. Herbert, in Edwards A. Park, *The Preacher and Pastor, by Fenelon, Herbert, Baxter, Campbell* (Andover, 1845), 173.

13. *The Faithful and Unfaithful Minister Contrasted,* 4th ed. (Bath, 1769), 7. As with most of the shorter letters of advice, this treatise was anonymous.

This felt piety was cultivated by a variety of means, including studying Scripture, especially, as Herbert put it, "moving and ravishing" texts, and by attending to the exhortations and examples of those with great pastoral experience. Many moving biblical passages stand behind the language of Isaac Watts, when he asked how he might "press these momentous concerns on all our heart?" and again, "What pathetic language shall I choose, what words of awful efficacy and divine fervour, which may first melt our spirits into softness, and then imprint these duties upon them with lasting power?"[14] "If you hear the prayers of gifted me," said Doddridge, "as often as you can, you will naturally slide into their method; and if they be men of deep piety, you will enter deeply into the same spirit."[15]

Learning, of course, was highly prized, albeit of a particular kind. The scholarly status of the clergy remained a strong ideal throughout the seventeenth and eighteenth centuries, and even for those who might not aspire to the more elevated ranks of a scholar, the study of the Bible, biblical languages, theology, and the classics was expected. It was thus widely assumed that the "character" of a clergyman necessitated diligent study, especially of the Bible.[16] Study procured a cleric's reverence as a person of knowledge; it also enabled one to teach sound doctrine, vindicate the truth, and answer false teaching.[17] Felt piety, affection for God, actually clarified and strengthened one's thinking. General studies were necessary, according to Isaac Watts, in order to improve the reasoning faculty, and they also helped young people to think more accurately, and speak more clearly on a variety of topics.[18]

What has not heretofore been sufficiently recognized, however, is that the dominant theme in the English literature of pastoral and practical theology was the utility of learning; learning must serve piety and the ministry and serve them directly. Because the value of study was tied so closely to the development of character, learning was always viewed as instrumental, and to the extent that it was not conducive to piety, it was suspect. From Baxter forward, practical theology was valued more highly than systematic theology, and a fateful rift began to develop early in the tradition, not through the formal distinction explicated by Edward Farley,[19] but through what in time became an undue criticism of any theological reflection whose imme-

---

14. Watts, *An Humble Attempt,* 93.

15. Doddridge, *Lectures,* 12–13; for other exhortations to model one's preaching style on great preachers, see Mason, *Student and Pastor,* 62, 64–65.

16. John Ryland, *An Essay on the Dignity and Usefulness of Human Learning, Addressed to the Youth of the British Empire in Europe and America* (London, 1769), 4. This, of course, is true of both Nonconformist and Anglican contexts. I deal with the topic in much greater length, especially the use of the classics, in chapter 4 of "Spiritual Formation in the Study of Theology and Ministry."

17. Thomas Secker, *Eight Charges Delivered to the Clergy of the Dioceses of Oxford and Canterbury,* 2d ed. (London, 1771), 275, 277, 290.

18. Watts, *An Humble Attempt,* 12–13.

19. Farley, *Theologia,* 39–44.

diate relevance was not evident. In large measure, this tendency can be attributed to the urgency of evangelical ministerial piety and the demands of gospel duties.[20]

This weighting of the tradition on the practical side can be found in many of the major documents. Burnet wrote, "I confess I look upon this [that is, learning] as so much inferior to the other [piety and a good soul], and have been convinced by so much Experience, that a great Measure of Piety, with a very small Proportion of Learning, will carry one a great Way, that I may perhaps be thought to come as far short in this, as I might seem to exceed in the other."[21] Watts' treatise included a subsection entitled "Of a Minister's Private Studies" in which he said, "Let us take heed that none of these studies carry our thought away too far from our chief and glorious design, that is, the ministry and gospel of Christ." In this, as in all of their studies, students were exhorted to remember that they were consecrated, set apart, to "the service of the sanctuary" and that all study must serve this end.[22]

It is true that the manuals of pastoral theology recommended a range of books on theological topics. But even here there was an undercurrent of what can only be called suspicion of learning for its own sake. Of systems, Burnet recommended that two be read "with Exactness," because, he added, "they are almost all alike." It would be ideal, he opines, to read two of opposing views, since "the swallowing down whole Systems by the Lump, has help'd to possess Peoples Minds too early with Prejudices. . . ."[23] By the mid-eighteenth century, John Mason recommended making oneself a master of one short system of divinity.[24] Several Anglican letters of advice went so far as to say that the study of sermons, which included copying out or transcribing them for the purpose of developing both manner and substance, was more formative for the minister than a body of divinity.[25] Thomas Secker compared the study of doctrines and controversies unfavorably to the more needful study of practical, devotional literature.[26]

Not only was practical theology prized above the rest, polemical theology in particular was often considered detrimental to piety. We have found hints of this in Baxter, but other formative influences in the early history of devotional and pastoral theology added their authority to the notion. Jeremy Taylor, for example, encouraged ministers to read good books of "learned, pious, obedient and disinterested" authors. But controversy in divinity, said

20. Richard Baxter, *The Reformed Pastor* (London: James Nisbet, 1860), 150–51.
21. Gilbert Burnet, *A Discourse of the Pastoral Care*, 4th ed. (London, 1736), 145–46.
22. Watts, *An Humble Attempt*, 17–18.
23. Burnet, *Discourse*, 148.
24. Mason, *Student and Pastor*, 25.
25. *Advice to a Young Student*, 2d ed. (1730) 13–14; *Advice from a Bishop* (1759), 86; James D. Coleridge, *Practical Advice to the Young Parish Priest* (London: J. G. & F. Rivington, 1834), 30.
26. Secker, *Eight Charges*, 20.

Taylor, was to be avoided.[27] Watts, as well, recognized the importance of doctrine, but felt that religious controversies tend "to hurt the spirit of true godliness."[28] At midcentury, Mason recommended reading books on only the most important controversies against the Deists and the Catholics. Other controversies and debates in divinity were to be avoided; "Tis scarce to be imagined what harm these theological subtleties do us." In Mason's judgment, "Debates in divinity are like rocks not only steep and craggy, but barren and fruitless, and not worth the pains of climbing to the top."[29] This is an emphasis that seems to increase with time, at least among the Methodists and Anglican evangelicals. At the end of the eighteenth century, Adam Clarke, the Methodist commentator (and no mean scholar in his own right), admonished young pastors to meddle as little as possible in controversial writings in theology, for they "seldom tend to improve the mind and *sweeten the Temper.*"[30] In some pastors, the emphasis degenerated into a criticism of other forms of literature; the Anglican evangelical Richard Cecil said, and this in the context of advice to young ministers, "I used to study Commentators and Systems; but I am come almost wholly, at length, to the Bible."[31]

With an emphasis on tender piety and devotion on the one hand, and an avoidance of controversial writings on the other, writers of practical theology in the English tradition adopted a fundamentally ambivalent attitude toward scholarship and learning. This ambivalence is entirely explicable within the context of the nature and urgent duties of the ministry, and it appears to have contributed to a valuable irenicism within the Protestant pastorate. Many of the authors of pastoral theology were persons of theological latitude and moderation. Baxter, for example, pled for peace among Christians of different denominations[32] and Gilbert Burnet's Low Church comprehensive outlook and moderation toward the Dissenters is equally well known. Watts' *Orthodoxy and Charity United,* published in 1745, dealt with the need for tolerance toward persons of different opinions and practices in religion. The letters of advice to theology students and young ministers, whether Anglican or Nonconformist, endlessly reiterated the same kind of emphasis on subjective piety and a corresponding moderation.[33] Additional threads of

27. Jeremy Taylor, *Rules and Advices to the Clergy of the Diocese of Down and Connor,* 2d ed. (London, 1663), 29.
28. Watts, *An Humble Attempt,* 43.
29. Mason, *Student and Pastor,* 66.
30. Adam Clarke, *A Letter to a Preacher, on His Entrance Into the Work of the Ministry,* 3rd ed. (London, 1812), 39.
31. Richard Cecil, *The Works of the Rev. Richard Cecil,* ed. Josiah Pratt, 2d ed. [London, 1816], III, 448.
32. See "The Reformed Pastor" in Park's anthology, *The Preacher and Pastor,* 332–33, 335.
33. *Advice to a Young Clergyman, How to Conduct Himself* (1741), 14. *The Faithful and Unfaithful Minister,* p. 9. See also, *Advice to a Son at the University* (1725), 79, 81, 84, and Mason, *Student and Pastor,* 25–26.

this characteristic irenicism may be traced to the English evangelicals' sympathy for revivalism, but to give too much emphasis to the broadening tendencies of romanticism or the universalistic overtones of Scottish Common Sense philosophy is to multiply sources beyond necessity.

II

Did this tradition of English practical divinity influence theological education in America in the first half of the nineteenth century, and if so, how? First, the availability of the major manuals of English pastoral theology in nineteenth-century America is easily established. George Herbert's *A Priest to the Temple* was reprinted at least eight times in the United States before 1860.[34] Similarly, if the anthologies of pastoral theologies are included, Richard Baxter's *Reformed Pastor* went through eight or more printings in America between 1800 and the Civil War.[35] Doddridge's *Lectures* were reprinted twice (1808 and 1833), but Burnet, as an Anglican who wrote in the same tradition as Herbert, and Mason, the Nonconformist, were less popular with only one American edition each (1813 and 1794, respectively).[36] Despite the availability of this literature, historians have almost completely overlooked it in attempting to account for nineteenth-century intellectual and theological developments among the clergy.

Recent studies by Bruce Kuklick and D. G. Hart located the first seeds of the rancorous divisions between late nineteenth-century liberals and conservatives much earlier than expected, tracing them to the celebrated debates over religious epistemology between Horace Bushnell, Charles Hodge, Henry B. Smith, and Edwards A. Park.[37] To this point, however, scholars have accounted for the changing conceptions of epistemology, primarily on the grounds of German and English romanticism and Scottish Common Sense philosophy. An earlier study utilized the works of Edwards A. Park as a trial balloon to examine the impact of the English materials on one prominent educator.[38] Here it was shown that the entire substance of Park's famous sermon of 1850 on "The Theology of the Intellect and that of the Feelings" was found five years earlier in his anthology of predominantly English pastoral theology. Already in 1845 Park drew upon Richard Baxter to illustrate the

34. Repr. 1837, 1842, 1843, 1845, 1849, 1851, 1855, and 1857.
35. Repr. 1810, 1811, 1821, 1825, 1829, 1837, 1850, and 1860.
36. Though Watts was well known for his hymnody and practical divinity, his treatise was not reprinted, and neither, apparently, was Secker's.
37. Kuklick, *Churchmen and Philosopher,* 209–14; D. G. Hart, "Divided between Heart and Mind," 254–70. According to James Turner, "Secularization and Sacralization," 76, 93 n. 12, the coherence of the college curriculum that was grounded in theological considerations concerning the connection between all knowledge and the Creator rapidly unraveled after 1850.
38. A much fuller treatment of Park's theology is available in my paper "English Practical Theology and the 'Divided Mind' of American Protestant Thought" presented at the 1993 spring meeting of the American Society of Church History, Williamsburg, Virginia.

importance of subordinating all our activities, including philosophy, to the supreme duty of preaching. Park concluded his essay with a long, passionate appeal by Baxter, in which Baxter lists all of the intellectual and literary attainments of his forty years in ministry, citing some thirty-one learned philosophers and divines, only to say, "But how loath should I be to take such sauce for my food, and such recreations for my business. The jingling of too much and false philosophy among them often drowns the noise of Aaron's bells. *I feel myself much better in Herbert's temple.*" The fine ambiguity of Baxter toward human learning, clearly reflected in Park, is revealed in Baxter's phrase, "I have read almost all of the physics and metaphysics I could hear of. I have wasted much of my time among loads of historians, chronologers and antiquaries. I despise none of their learning; all truth is useful."[39] Wasted, but not despised! Truthful, but because useful! This is the pragmatic spirit, if it may be so said, that animates much of Park's writing, and it is the same spirit that animates the writings of many other evangelical theological educators in antebellum America. It is the thesis of this chapter that this emphasis is traceable directly to the English tradition of pastoral theology.

Since the test case of Park allowed us to trace clear lines of influence to the English tradition, it seemed desirable to attempt to draw out further connections of influence over a longer period of time. Four overlapping groups of American literature were examined in this investigation. The first body of published literature was comprised of letters of advice to American students of theology and young ministers. The second category includes the lectures and sermons of theological educators in other fields of study, such as systematic theology and church history, and draws particularly on inaugural lectures for seminary and departmental chairs. The third group of pamphlets includes the seminary chapel addresses of theological educators.[40] Finally, I sampled the vast literature of articles on "Ministerial Qualifications" in a variety of denominational quarterly reviews (Lutheran, Congregational, Methodist and many others).[41] Currently, more than twenty authors affiliated with some twelve American theological seminaries have been examined, including four Presbyterian seminaries, two Episcopalian, a Baptist, Congrega-

---

39. Quoted in Park, *The Preacher and Pastor,* 46.

40. A subset of materials that may be useful in this regard is found in the college inaugural addresses and chapel sermons; I have located those of Ashbel Green (1802, 1821, 1822), Edward Dorr Griffin (1828), Beriah Green (1832), George E. Pierce (1836), and Benjamin Hale (1837). Altogether addresses from eight colleges have been examined, including ones from Harvard, Yale, Princeton, Williams, Dickinson, Middlebury, Western Reserve, and Oglethorpe. The chapel addresses in these colleges revealed many references to the formation of men for ministry, since many of the graduates became ministers. In fact, at Williams it was claimed that more than a third of the graduates had become preachers of the gospel. I have also looked at several sermons preached before the Society for Promoting Theological Education, including those of A. D. Mayo (1857) and John G. Palfrey (1831).

41. I have located such articles for the following years: 1821, 1833, 1837, 1838, 1850, 1854, 1865, 1867, 1875, 1879, 1884, 1885, 1887, 1893.

tional, Dutch Reformed, German Reformed, Associate Reformed Synod, and Evangelical Lutheran, and there are a handful of additional sermons and addresses that do not have any specific institutional location.[42] All four varieties of published treatises in America refer occasionally to the English authors of practical theology, and they commonly do so with high praise and strong recommendations that these authors be read. Baxter is often referred to,[43] and so is Bunyan, Doddridge, Cecil, and a host of lesser known authors of practical theology.[44] Students were exhorted to meditate on the English authors of devotional and practical theology so that they might learn the art of holy living. These classics of devotion and pastoral theology were often enlisted in support of the very distinctions between piety and learning that this literature everywhere defends, and they were occasionally quoted directly.[45] The continuity in the tradition is thus clearly suggested

42. Presbyterian: Auburn, Theological Seminary in New York City, Western Theological Seminary, and Princeton; Episcopal: Seminary of the Protestant Episcopal Church in the Diocese of Kentucky, and Berkeley Divinity School; Baptist: Newton Theological Seminary; Congregational: Andover; Dutch Reformed (Reformed Church in America): New Brunswick Theological Seminary, Theological Seminary of the German Reformed Church, Associate Reformed Theological Seminary, Gettysburg Evangelical Lutheran Seminary.

43. See, Samuel H. Cox, *The Ministry We Need: Three Inaugural Addresses delivered at Auburn, June 18, 1835* (New York, 1835), charge by J. W. Adams, 29; Cox was Professor of Sacred Rhetoric and Pastoral Theology at Auburn; Samuel F. How, *The Necessity of Eminent Piety in the Gospel Ministry: A Sermon Preached in the Reformed Dutch Church at New Brunswick, N.J.* (New Brunswick, 1838), 10; How was Pastor of the church; William G. Schauffler, "Advice to a Theological Student," *New Englander* 5 (1847): 511; Schauffler was a missionary to Constantinople; Nicholas Murray, *The Ministry We Need: A Discourse at the Inauguration of the Rev. Alexander T. McGill, D.D. as Professor of Pastoral Theology Princeton* (Philadelphia, 1854), 21; Murray was a Presbyterian minister at Elizabethtown, N.J.

44. On Bunyan, John T. Pressly, *An Address at the Opening of the Session of the Theological Seminary of the First A [ssociate] R [eformed] Synod of the West, Nov. 20, 1856* (Pittsburgh, 1856), 19; Pressly was professor of theology—didactic, polemic, and pastoral; A. Essick, *Counsel to Young Men: A Sermon Preached to the Students of Pennsylvania College and the Theological Seminary at Gettysburg, Feb. 27, 1862* (Gettysburg, 1862), 5,7; Essick was pastor of St. James Evangelical Lutheran Church; on Doddridge, Murray, *The Ministry We Need*, 10; on Cecil, B. B. Smith, *An Address Delivered on the Occasion of the 3rd Commencement, October 26, 1836, of the Theological Seminary of the Protestant Episcopal Church in the Diocese of Kentucky* (Lexington, 1837), 13; also such well-known authors as Owen, Flavel, and Charnrock, on Alexander Proudfit, *An Address, Delivered to the Students of Theology, at the Seminary, in the City of New York, at the close of the Session, in 1821* (Salem, N.Y., 1822), 36; on a variety of other figures, including some Scots authors, such as Robert Leighton, see Cox, *The Ministry We Need*, 40; Alonzo Potter, *The Proper Method, Matter and Object of Ministerial Study. A Charge to the Clergy of the Protestant Episcopal Church in Penn.*, (Philadelphia, 1850), 19; Potter, D. D. was bishop of the diocese of Pennsylvania; Proudfit, *Address*, 36; on John Scott, see Samuel Simon Schmucker, *An Inaugural Address, Delivered Before the Directors of the Theological Seminary of the General Synod of the Evangelical Lutheran Church*, (Carlisle, Penn., 1826), 33; Schmucker was Professor of Christian Theology at the Lutheran Seminary at Gettysburg; Schauffler, "Advice," 511; How, *The Necessity of Eminent Piety*, 6; on Robert Hall, see Pressly, *An Address*, (1856), 14; Pressly, *Annual Address to the Students of the Associate Reformed Theological Seminary, Allegheny City Pa., Nov. 9, 1853* (Pittsburgh, 1853), 14–15, and yet others, as Campbell, Blair, Martyn, and Richmond (Schauffler, "Advice," 508, 511).

45. Baxter by How, *The Necessity of Eminent Piety*, 10; Leighton by Potter, *The Proper Method*, 19–20.

by the explicit dependence of the later authors on earlier sources and by the preservation of many of the subtler arguments concerning the nature and influence of ministerial piety. At the same time, the emphases of these sources are combined with frequent allusions to the religious awakenings, a characteristic penchant for activism, and the odd reference to Scottish philosophy.[46] Revivalistic, missionary fervor is evident in many of these writings, and occasionally one finds explicit dependence on Baconian induction and Common Sense philosophy; combined, these influences undoubtedly served to reinforce the main contours of English practical theology.

What, precisely, were the dynamic relationships between piety and learning in this literature? First, as one would naturally expect, theological educators uniformly expressed the ideal that genuine piety should be wed to sound scholarship. The promotional literature of early Princeton stated the matter forcefully and Andover expressed the same ideal. Andover provided institutional structures to support the desired outcome; indeed, it was precisely the desire to better support both piety and learning in the ministry that gave rise to the seminary movement.[47] Presbyterians and Congregationalists, however, were not alone in expressing the centrality of this ideal; across the denominational and theological spectrum, the goal was the same. Episcopal, Lutheran, and even theologically liberal educators agreed that in the preparation of students for the Christian ministry, great erudition should go hand in glove with fervent piety.[48]

It was widely assumed, then, that intellectual improvement and the advance of Christian piety were necessarily united, and especially this was so in the preparation of ministers.[49] The bare statement of the desirability of uniting piety and learning, however, does not take us very far into the heart of the matter; we must inquire further concerning the nature of the two and the

46. Jonathan Miller, *The Holy Scriptures the only Instruction to the Christian Preacher, Concio ad Clerum: A Sermon Delivered in the Chapel of Yale College* (New Haven, 1812), 21–22; Miller was pastor of the church in Burlington, Conn.; Edward Dorr Griffin, *Sermon at the Dedication of the New Chapel of Williams College* (Williamstown, 1828), 33; Cox, *The Ministry We Need*, 88; and on Lord Bacon and also Common Sense realism, Lewis Green, *Inaugural Address, Delivered Before the Synod of Pittsburgh . . . in 1840* (Pittsburgh, 1843), 8–10; Green was professor of biblical literature in Western Theological Seminary.

47. *A Brief History of the Theological Seminary of the Presbyterian Church, at Princeton . . . with its Constitution, Bye-laws etc* (Princeton, 1838), 3; *Laws of the Theological Institution in Andover* (Andover, 1817), 5–6; Ashbel Green, *An Address to the Students and Faculty of the College of New Jersey,* (Princeton, 1802), 9; *History of Princeton,* 11. Schmucker, Inaugural Address, 6, 34. The same principle, of course, is found in the college movement. Samuel B. How, an address delivered at his inauguration as principal of Dickinson College in Carlisle, Penn. (Carlisle, 1830), 19.

48. B. B. Smith, An Address, 16, Episcopal; S. S. Schmucker, Inaugural Address, 5, Lutheran; John G. Palfrey, an address delivered before the Society for Promoting Theological Education (Boston, 1831), 15, liberal.

49. References could easily be multiplied. See, for example, Cox, *The Ministry We Need,* 159–60; David Elliott, an introductory address delivered to the students of the Western Theological Seminary (Pittsburgh, 1842), 3; Schauffler, "Advice," 506, 508, 511; How, An Address, 4.

relationship between them. Since the formal curriculum of study at seminary was rigorous, sometimes complaints were heard that study detracted from piety. But the underlying assumption that study was conducive to piety and holy affections was far more prevalent. The very fact that occasionally reassurances that learning was not hurtful to piety were needed suggests an inherent tension; true learning, according to the Presbyterian, Philip Milledoler, has "never injured the church and never will. Such is the harmony existing between the works and word of God, that discoveries in the former will never cease to promote our regard for the latter."[50] S. S. Schmucker, the great leader of Lutheranism, observed that some people held that we may take learning so far, but not beyond a point, without danger to our faith. Grounding his response, like Milledoler, in the goodness of creation, he believed that "a religion that is from God, will not shrink from investigation, nor tremble before the intellectual altitude of friends or foes."[51] But it was precisely the affective nature of piety in the English tradition and its relationship to learning that led to serious problems for theological education in the 1820s and 1830s.

How then did the evangelical English tradition of practical theology inform "the reciprocal influence of knowledge and religion?"[52] English practical theology had taught that regeneration was the basis for the ministerial office, and that piety, engendered by the Holy Spirit, enjoyed a priority from whence everything essential to the office of ministry flowed. According to the English tradition, true piety involved first the affections and a special temper of soul; second, piety was connected to intellectual development, but also distinguished from it; and third, piety was the principal motive to ministerial practice. Each of these themes figured prominently in the early literature of seminary education in America.

First, American educators, construing Christian ministry in the tradition of Baxter and Burnet, argued that one who was indifferent to his own salvation could not be concerned for the salvation of others. Moreover, a vivid sense of spiritual reality was required to understand the worth of souls, what awaits us in the life to come, and God's character. Therefore, a felt and fixed resolution "to live for God and for the spiritual welfare of our fellow men" was the very foundation of Christian ministry. This foundation made everything else relative, for "without this, learning, genius and eloquence will be of no avail."[53] When the Right Reverend B. B. Smith, bishop of the Protes-

50. Milledoler, *Charge to the Professor and Students of Divinity* (n.p., n.d.), 108. Milledoler was president of Rutgers College and professor of didactic and polemic theology.

51. Schmucker, Inaugural Address, 24.

52. The phrase is Nathan S. S. Beman's, an oration pronounced at Middlebury before the associated alumni of the college, on the evening of commencement, August 17th, 1825 (Troy, 1825), 24.

53. How, *The Necessity of Eminent Piety*, 4, 10. This kind of emphasis, uniting piety and feeling, is absolutely pervasive, says Proudfit, "The love of Jesus 'shed abroad in the soul by the Holy Ghost,' correcting your motives, regulating your desires, sanctifying your aims, and animating to unwearied

tant Episcopal Church in Kentucky and professor of the Theological Seminary in Lexington, sought to describe the "tone and type" of piety needed in ministers in "our age" and in "our country" in 1837, he described this piety in the identical terms of a two-hundred-year-old tradition. To minister in holy things, ministers must possess "the most deep and heartfelt personal piety" for "piety is the very breath of the living ministry;—mental power, erudition, tact, influence, are the mere members, which it sets at work in its divine pursuits."[54]

A strong emphasis was thus placed upon the religious affections and the practical theology that nurtured these feelings. The call to heartfelt piety was necessary both for the minister's own spiritual formation and the ability to counsel and preach, in a word, to function effectively as a minister. In addition, as one might expect, the spiritual disciplines that nurtured the devotional life—prayer, fasting, meditation, solitude, and self-examination—were the same as the earlier English literature.[55] With no evident difference between the denominations, American theological educators linked piety with "elevated" affections, "excited," "absorbing," or "enlivened" feelings, or the "sensibilities of the heart" in general, to the essential nature and fruitful performance of Christian ministry.[56]

From the writings of Timothy Dwight in the first decade of the century to the eve of the Civil War, the old distinction reiterated endlessly in English pastoral theology was reiterated in America: The preacher "should *feel the truth,* which he knows, and believes." By an unseen economy in the moral

---

diligence in the performance of every duty, may be pronounced the radical qualification of the minister of the cross. This is the vivifying principle which will diffuse life, and warmth, and energy through all your administrations, both private and public" An Address, 30. H. J. Ripley writes "There can be but one opinion as to the importance of eminent piety in ministers. Their own happiness, both in public and in private, depends materially upon their religious feeling." *Hints on the Promotion of Piety in Ministers of the Gospel; Read before the Conference of Baptist Ministers in Massachusetts at their Annual Meeting in Boston* (Boston, 1832), 5; Ripley was professor of biblical literature and pastoral duties in the Newton Theological Seminary. Schauffler concurs: The minister's whole framework and constitution require "the cherishing and cultivation of pious affections." This is obviously essential for the profession, but "his own eternal interests require it also; for there exists no heaven for mere *intellectual* beings, to which he may go when his pious sensibilities are dead." *Advice,* 509. Milledoler asks pointedly, "How shall they sympathize in the sufferings of God's people, who have no spiritual feeling?" *Charge,* 115.

54. Smith, *An Address,* 12. As another Episcopalian put it: "A devout and conscientious spirit is infinitely more important than any knowledge. . . ." Potter, *The Proper Method,* 4–5.

55. See, for example, Ripley, *Hints,* 6–7; James Richards, *Lectures on the Prayer of Faith* (read before the theological students at Auburn N.Y., and published at their request, New York, 1832), 6; Richards was pastor of the First Presbyterian Church of Newark, and apparently also professor of Christian theology at Auburn, 1823–1843.

56. Lewis Mayer, inaugural address delivered by Rev. Lewis Mayer at his inauguration as principal in the Theological Seminary of the German Reformed Church (Carlisle, Penn., 1825), 11; Mayer was the first professor of theology in the Seminary; Schmucker, Inaugural Address, 34; Ripley, *Hints,* 8; Richards, *Lectures,* 11; J. W. Adams, in Cox, *The Ministry We Need,* 12, 39–40; Murray, *The Ministry We Need,* 21.

and intellectual order, it was believed that only those truths that were felt would make a lasting impression on others. The converse was equally true: "A cold preacher naturally makes a frozen audience."[57] As one put it, "*Without feeling,* good speaking is playing the actor on the stage; and if the subject of the speech is a sacred one, it is strange fire upon the Lord's alter." Preachers were to "stir the hearts of others by the great truths which fill their own."[58] In these connections between holy affections and effective preaching, the dependence of the Americans on the English literature is most obvious and the two form, in fact, one continuous tradition.

Second, from the beginning of study to the actual attainment of knowledge, Christian piety and its attendant affections were active. Clearly, attachment of the affections to the object of study was viewed positively, and while in some authors the connection was made explicit, in all, it seems to have been assumed.[59] As God is the God of all creation, the most extensive freedom in intellectual enquiry is compatible with the deepest reverence.[60] Implicit in this argument, however, is the crucial and highly problematic corollary that free inquiry requires reverence. These assumptions pertained as well to the study of the Bible and to the study of theology. The connection between intellect and piety was ultimately traced to the educator's understanding of the perceptive faculties.[61] In his inaugural address for the professorship of biblical literature at Western Theological Seminary, Lewis Green put forth the same idea of exegesis of the Bible as Edwards A. Park; the best exegesis should stir our feelings, and the more intense the emotion, the better.[62] The corollary to the unity between God and God's good creation was the connection between good and holy affections, understanding moral and religious truth, and intellectual acumen. The literature is uniform on the corollary between the purity of the will and the penetration and clarity of the understanding. Episcopalian Alonzo Potter wrote: "We all can form ourselves to habits of mind more just and active than they have yet attained. All can

57. Timothy Dwight, a sermon preached at the opening of the Theological Institution in Andover; and at the ordination of Eliphalet Pearson (Boston, 1808), 19.

58. Schauffler, *Advice,* 508; Murray, *The Ministry We Need,* 31. The connection is made in many, if not most of the writers. See Smith, An Address, 13; Pressly, An Address, 15; the same principle of "sensibility of every kind" being perfected by "exercise on its appropriate objects" is found in the study of pious examples in church history. Alexander T. McGill, an inaugural address delivered before the board of directors at their meeting in November, 1842 (Pittsburgh, 1843), 11;

59. Griffin, Sermon, 32; Potter, *The Proper Method,* 6.

60. Potter, *The Proper Method,* 18.

61. "Religious and moral truth, and loveliness, to be understood, must be felt; and to him who knows them not, by an inward experience, words can convey no clearer conception of their nature, than they can give, of sight, to one born blind from birth" Lewis Green, Inaugural Address, 16. Arguing the same case, S. S. Schmucker drew out the subtle connections to Lockean philosophy. Inaugural Address, 17.

62. "Then enter, if you can, into the feelings of the despised and persecuted One . . . [for] this is the perfection of Exegesis. . . ." Green, Inaugural Address, 15.

cultivate those moral dispositions, which predispose us to love the truth, and aid us in understanding it."[63]

The conviction that piety contributed directly to the clarity of one's thought and the power of one's reason was widespread; that "the state of the affections has a strong bearing on the mutual proportions and relations, in which things may be presented to the mind," was a commonplace assumption clearly related to Scottish Common Sense realism, but also derived, in no little measure, from English practical theology.[64] Bela Bates Edwards, Park's colleague at Andover, developed these widely held views at length in an essay on the "Influence of Eminent Piety on the Human Mind." In 1834 Edwards argued that true piety leads to intellectual advancement "by the serenity and purity which it spreads over the affections." He proceeded to offer us some insight into the theory of human nature behind this view. "The cultivation of the social affections is necessary to the highest intellectual progress. The connection between all the parts of the human constitution is intimate, and is not to be trifled with. Destroy the affections, and as a general thing you cripple the intellect."[65] In this, his thinking is indistinguishable from that of Edwards A. Park.

The devotion of the soul to God was, therefore, thought conducive to intellectual activity since both practices were inward and contemplative in nature, and this leads us to the third point—that piety was also closely connected to outward action and the practice of ministry. A strong activist strain was very evident in all of the writings of antebellum theological educators. Besides theology, wrote Alonzo Potter (later founder of the Episcopal Philadelphia Divinity School), we need education in letters and "even science," but let these be subordinate to our proper goal in ministry.[66] Milledoler observed in similar terms that superficial reading will not do; rather, "the whole circle of the sciences" must be pressed into duty in service of Christ.[67] Devotion, thus, must stimulate ministers "to constant exertion for the good of others," and without it "piety becomes stagnant, melan-

63. Potter, *The Proper Method*, 5. Not surprisingly, in this view a humble, holy minister of Christ will be saved from error because truth follows holiness, correct doctrine follows piety. Proudfit, *An Address*, 30.

64. Beriah Green, *Four Sermons, Preached in the Chapel of the Western Reserve College* (Cleveland, 1833), 35; Green explores the "bearing of benevolence or selfishness on the attention requisite to understand any given case of practical concern," thereby connecting affections of the heart, rights, justice, and intellectual acuity (p. 34). McGill makes virtually the same argument; we understand the state of another person's mind by reproducing the inward spirit of the person in our own understanding and this requires "depth and delicacy" in our own religious feelings. McGill, inaugural address, 10–11. J. W. Adams observes the same connection between the perception of truth and the affections. Adams in Cox *The Ministry We Need* (p. 29), reflecting on Baxter and other heroes of the faith.

65. Bela Bates Edwards, "Influence of Eminent Piety on the Human Mind" *American Quarterly Register* 7 (August 1834): 9–10, 12.

66. Potter, *The Proper Method*, 10.

67. Milledoler, *Charge*, 119.

cholic, profitless."[68] Exhortations to vigorous action on the basis of benevolent or social affections abound in the American literature of ministerial
formation, and it is widely assumed that practical theology leads appropriately to effective practice.[69] Our "spiritual cadets," wrote one educator,
"pant for action and victory in the field militia. And this passion for work
is not to be regretted."[70] Much of this emphasis can be traced simply to the
well-known revivalistic, activistic character of American Christianity, and it
is generally indistinguishable from the American evangelical ethos and idiom. The features that are, at a minimum, reinforced by the English tradition include the emphasis on holy affections, the subordination of scholarship and reading to piety in the formation of the minister, and the strong
emphasis on practice.

The integration of intellect, will, and affections, and the way that piety
was construed as influencing the intellect, meant that educators also delineated a reciprocal influence of intellect on piety. On the whole, this reciprocal
influence was understood positively, and, of course, the study of practical
theology was viewed as particularly conducive to forming a pious temper.
But, if pious study could enlarge the soul, then evidently some aspects of
study could also contract it. If theological learning did not support piety, it
was, in the tradition of English practical theology and the American literature that follows it, highly suspect. Some educators argued that theological
students needed more rigorous study than they were obtaining, and others
argued for less, but most educators consistently placed piety as a priority
over learning, and they believed that if study failed to be conducive to piety,
it should be foresworn.[71] In this sense, as well as in the matter of the goal of
study, the intellect was clearly subordinate to the heart. Because the religious
affections were tender, and precisely because they were susceptible to influence, they had to be guarded and protected. Simon S. Schmucker, in his inaugural lecture at Gettysburg, reassured his hearers that "intellectual altitude" was not dangerous to faith, but drew the line at the point of
jeopardizing subjective piety. Describing the characteristics of the new Lutheran Seminary at Gettysburg, Schmucker observed:

"*Again, the mode of recitation should be less rigid than in Colleges. . . .* Now,
it is evident that too great rigour of recitation, would force the student of hum-
bler talents to subtract from the hours of devotion, that he may add to those of
study: or, at least, excessive application to study, would induce a lassitude of

68. Alfred Brunson, "Ministerial Qualifications," *Northwest Christian Advocate* 2 (May 17,
1854): 77; Smith, An Address, 13.
69. Ashbel Green, *Doing Good in Imitation of Christ: A Discourse Delivered in the College of
New Jersey* (1822), 24; Schauffler, "Advice," 511; Pressly, Annual Address, (1853), 16–17.
70. Cox, *The Ministry We Need*, 159.
71. Evidently this was especially the case among Methodists. Brunson, "Ministerial Qualifications," 77.

mind unfavourable to the duties and enjoyments of devotion. Such intellectual pressure, long continued, would impair the spirituality of his religious exercises, and ultimately rob him of 'those soul-refreshing views of Jesus and his word,' which were the delight of his soul, the evidence of his filiation, and his strongest stimulus to industry and usefulness. A student, therefore, ought never to prosecute study to the detriment of devotion; and if his soul becomes enveloped in doubts and fears, it may, on some occasions, not be amiss to devote whole days to practical reading and exercises, until he regain a preponderance of spiritual feeling, and satisfactory evidence of acceptance with God."[72]

Bela Bates Edwards adopted precisely the same structure of argument as Schmucker, arguing that there is an intimate connection between religious feelings and intellectuality, but he drew the conclusion that this was a problem only for the unregenerate student.[73]

This orientation to the importance and tenderness of religious affections meant, in concrete practice, a discrediting of technical biblical and theological scholarship, both in history and with contemporary, especially German, theology. Offhand remarks, like Nicholas Murray's in 1854, betray the common suspicion. Said Murray, "We owe the glorious Reformation far more to the piety, than to the policy or talents of the reformers." Then, appealing to such men as Baxter, Doddridge, Edwards, and other eminent preachers, he observed that "we find that decided, warm-hearted piety was the great element of their success."[74] Polemical or systematic theology was a standard part of the American seminary curriculum, but these authors typically valued practical theology more.[75] Cox had reassured his hearers that he had a proper respect for learning: "We object not to *science*, any quantity of it; if it be not falsely so called and dotting on its *oppositions* to the Father of lights."[76] Following explicitly the British tradition of practical theology, Alonzo Potter quoted approvingly those who belittled students who would spend days "pouring upon casuists and schoolmen, and such like." Potter, the Episcopalian, found scholars even in his own denomination, who spent their talents on "elaborate trifling," "verbal disputations," and "childish criticisms,"—people who labor over "insoluble enigmas" in "metaphysical and sacramental theology." "We should beware of study, divorced from action," he admonished, "as carefully as we should beware of action unenlightened by study."[77] In every reference to study, however, it must be remembered that for the evangelical this was study of a particular kind. Generally

72. Schmucker, Inaugural Address, 36–37.
73. Edwards, "Influence of Piety," 12.
74. Murray, *The Ministry We Need*, 10.
75. Said Schmucker, "To the subject of Pastoral Theology he must therefore lend his most devout attention" Inaugural Address, 30. See Lewis Green, Inaugural Address, 5, for a similar emphasis.
76. Cox, *The Ministry We Need*, 101–102, 113.
77. Potter, *The Proper Method*, 19–20, 11–12.

speaking, little patience was felt for "speculative points," even less for "controversial subjects," because the doctrines of the Bible are not speculative, "but of a practical nature, adopted to inform the mind, to improve the heart, and to regulate the life."[78] The values inculcated here are the values of experimental religion; in this, God's Word is all, and in this, the Christian theologian finds his sole business.[79]

Because of the tenderness of pious feelings and because of the urgency of ministerial practice, the critique of speculation in theology was pervasive. Practical earnestness will guard us, said one educator, even in our theological studies, for it will save us from books too frivolous on the one hand, or "too purely speculative on the other."[80] Precisely as in the English literature of practical theology, opposition to speculative or controversial themes was connected with a piety of feeling. The Episcopalian, B. B. Smith, argued much like Edwards Park when he said that we need a piety that is "steady and pervading, not fitful or partial."[81] The pervading influence of piety was thus the *sine qua non* of sound theological education, and this piety was incompatible with controversy and hair-splitting theological distinctions.

This general orientation of American theological education created an atmosphere that was predictably hostile to the newer German theological and historical scholarship. The new scholarship seemed on the surface to be inimical to the pious spirit of the fledgling seminaries. While practical theology with its understanding of emotion was wonderfully well suited to the Awakenings in an expansive American context, it was ill adapted to prepare the minister-scholar for the new science of critical biblical scholarship. The reaction to German scholarship was strong and uniform, for here were doctrines that were not "in order to holiness" nor were they "practical." The idea of a biblical and theological scholarship that did not conduce directly to piety and Christian practice seemed to be strange fire indeed. The problem of German scholarship, moreover, was tied explicitly by these authors to the issues of piety and practice. In an address of 1838 to the theological seminary at New Brunswick, Samuel F. How alluded to the "venerable and holy men of God who lived and wrote before them [these modern German authors], and who were distinguished for the elevation of their piety and learning, and for the extent of their labours and usefulness. . . ." He then added, with a note of sarcasm, that these were "mere babes in theological knowledge, compared with these famous modern neological Germans." These latter professors of theology, these doctors of divinity, are "rank infidels and enemies to the gospel." "This disposition to undervalue the writings of those who were emi-

78. Proudfit, Address, 29; Pressly, Annual Address, (1853), 8.
79. Ashbel Green, *Doing Good,* 21. See also, Lewis Green, Inaugural Address, 5.
80. Schauffler, "Advice," 510; Potter, *The Proper Method,* 11.
81. Smith, An Address, 14.

nently pious, and learned; nay who were giants in theological knowledge, and to substitute for theirs the works of neologists and infidels, is a sure mark of the decay of piety in the ministry, and is fraught with mischief to the church and to the interests of true godliness." How continued, "I hesitate not to assert, that in all that is calculated to form the useful pastor, and the exemplary christian, the superiority is decidedly with the old divines."[82]

The method, as well as the tone of the new scholarship, seemed foreign. On the grounds of disinterested and impartial science, Cox asked in his Auburn Address if the professors of their seminaries should leave the practical conclusions of their lectures to be drawn out by each student himself. This provided Cox with the opportunity to criticize "the high places of theological light in Europe." We must state the reasons for our position, but offer our own "conviction of the truth and duty of the matter." The detached way of teaching theology is "favorable to skepticism or infidel indifference; and has resulted by fatal experiment in this and kindred evils, in Germany and other places where it has been speciously adopted."[83] Congregationalist Leverett Griggs expressed, in his words, the "deep and painful conviction" that American theology had been "greatly injured" by German theology. "And what is there in German theology so much superior to works in our own language?" he wondered. The student of the ministry is to "shut up the gate-way against this and every other path that may lead you from the pure fountain of divine truth."[84] Lewis Green, professor of biblical literature at Western Theological Seminary, expressed similar concerns. He launched a nearly violent polemic against "our foreign Exegetical scholars," in his inaugural lecture at Western in 1840. He called for a "native Exegesis" "using the results of German investigation, yet independent of German authority, founded upon the solid basis of a pure devotion, a sound orthodoxy, and a sober, solid Anglo-Saxon common sense." Here we find explicitly that the basis of biblical scholarship was to be devotion and the mental approach characterized by English common sense. Green continued, German theologians are "literary scavengers" without "talent or life"; they are, in a word, infidels "with all the characteristic defects of a nation, who have no word in their language for 'common sense'; because there is, among them, no corresponding idea."[85]

Even German Lutheran scholars in this country, who generally praised German research and writing on other topics, were sometimes antagonistic to German biblical criticism and theology. William Schauffler, for example, who applauded and recommended German works on eloquence and moral philos-

---

82. How, *The Necessity of Eminent Piety,* 16–17. Others clearly felt the same and were even more dismissive: McGill observed in 1843 that the "New Theology is but the sickly spawn of robust old heresies." McGill, An Inaugural Address, 9; and Brunson, "Ministerial Qualifications," 77.
83. Cox, *The Ministry We Need,* 141.
84. Leverett Griggs, *Letters to a Theological Student* (Boston, 1863), 40–42.
85. Lewis Green, Inaugural Address, 17–18.

ophy, insisted that students make a proper selection in theology, "leaving out neological trash, which never exhibits much of real learning or depth. . . ." Here, as elsewhere, the connection with piety was explicitly drawn. Schauffler writes that in religion, "external means are valuable helps, but private prayer and meditation, are the living breath of a Christian's spiritual existence and of his influence" and it is for this reason, that "if you consult German commentators, ask first whether they were pious men: if they were not, use them with *great caution.*"[86] S. S. Schmucker, like Schauffler, expressed little or no fear of the extension of learning in the physical, or even the moral sciences.[87] But neither author could imagine that detached biblical studies could offer much in the realm of theological education for ministry. In the literature of American theological education, ministerial piety and effective preaching had become the standard by which all theological learning was judged.

The earlier emphasis in English practical theology on doctrinal moderation and irenicism could still be found, but now, in the context of the new critical studies, it was muted. It does appear, however, that practical theology reinforced the breadth of perspective on doctrinal and denominational distinctives that was already characteristic of the unitive evangelicalism of the United Front. The idea that religious controversy hurt the spirit of true devotion, here, as in England, probably had a beneficial effect. Since a Christian leader, according to Cox, "ought to be large and noble in his feelings, conciliatory and slow to censure," one finds a real impatience with the "lynx-eyed detectors of heresy." Creeds and symbols have been wrongly used by the "superficial, the lovers of logomachy, and the charged conductors of discord among brethren." Instead, a "catholic spirit" is recommended.[88] Eliakim Phelps, who gave the charge at the installation of Cox, also recognized the necessity of conflict with unbelief, but recommended "a catholic spirit" divested of the spirit of sectarianism and bigotry.[89] Other authors used the same language; when exhorting students to study comprehensively, they were to do so "in a large and catholic spirit." Of course, denominational identity remained a desideratum. One educator observed, "We want not our young brethren to be bigots; but we charge you to make them thorough Presbyterians."[90]

Conclusion

This chapter has examined traits that were characteristic of nineteenth-century American evangelical educators in a variety of denominations, includ-

---

86. Schauffler, "Advice," 506, 512, 413. Schauffler's advice is identical to the English authors: "Believe no philosopher who has not the countenance of the Bible (p. 507).

87. Schmucker, Inaugural Address, 24.

88. Cox, *The Ministry We Need*, 6–7, 118–119.

89. Eliakim Phelps, *Charge*, in Cox, *The Ministry We Need*, 56.

90. Potter, *The Proper Method*, 13; Murray, *The Ministry We Need*, in his address to McGill, 30.

ing Episcopalian, Lutheran, Baptist, Methodist, Dutch Reformed, German Reformed, and Presbyterian. I have argued that the seeds of division between piety and intellect may have originated in part from an unexpected, and on the surface, apparently benign source, intrinsic to the evangelical tradition. By the mid-nineteenth century, the tradition of English practical theology had, for more than two hundred years, repeatedly set forth a crucial distinction between the intellect and the feelings, and this distinction was thus well developed and readily available long before the rise of Common Sense philosophy or romanticism. The understandable interest scholars have expressed in tracing the impact of influential thinkers like Dugald Steward, Coleridge, and Schleiermacher, combined with Edwards A. Park's pivotal role in introducing German theology to America through the pages of *Bibliotheca Sacra*, appear to have distracted us from an examination of the more obvious sources of influence. Modern scholarship seems to have given insufficient attention to the fact that in the first half of the nineteenth century American theologians were first preachers and pastors. We have tended, perhaps, to observe them through a twentieth-century lens that has detached theology from the pulpit, rather than through an eighteenth-century lens that typically combined preaching, the ministerial office, and the teaching of theology.

Since, in this context, the preparation of the minister was almost always chronologically prior to the development of the scholar, the arguments concerning the importance of piety in relation to learning set forth by eminent, even legendary pastors and scholars, may have been especially persuasive; these views were, after all, commonly adopted early in one's career. In addition, the distinctions outlined here were framed in the context of impassioned pleas that bore directly on ministerial identity. It seems plausible, then, that the literature shaped the outlook of several generations of professional clergy-scholars, possibly more so than the new philosophies arising from Scotland and Germany. Structural considerations also, undoubtedly, played a role. Early seminaries in this country often possessed only a single professor who attempted to cover all of the disciplines, as was the case with Simon Schmucker at Gettysburg. Even as the institutions grew, professors commonly bridged several disciplines at one time, and they readily moved from one area of work to another. For example, Alexander T. McGill taught both pastoral theology and church history, first at Western, and subsequently at Princeton and H. J. Ripley was professor of biblical literature and pastoral duties at Newton. This breadth seems to have contributed to the preoccupation of these educators with practical theology, and it may have contributed to the sway of practical theology and its attendant piety over the other disciplines.

This study of the assumptions of early nineteenth-century American evangelical educators suggests that when we examine their emphasis on study and learning closely, it is learning of a particular kind with distinctive and limited purposes. We need to make a clear distinction between the ideal of a piety united to general theological study on the one hand (an ideal that was every where championed), and the challenge of the newer critical studies and technical research, on the other. To say that piety and intellect were united in the evangelical ideal is not enough because the study that theological educators envisioned was always dominated by the practical goal of directly serving evangelical piety and ministry. It was, in fact, the dynamic interplay of piety and theological study that turned out to be the leading problem for nineteenth-century evangelical theological education.

Theological study in the antebellum American context informed, if not controlled, by the English tradition of practical theology, was born in devotion to God and it was to end in service to God and the church. But the emphasis on tender affections and ministerial effectiveness was so emphatic that critical scholarship was neglected, and the newer historical studies were viewed as intrinsically at odds with the aims and purposes of theological education. Hence, as the newer criticism began to make itself felt in the 1820s and 1830s, it was rejected with a holy aversion. If, as James Turner has argued, the unraveling of the connection between all knowledge and the Creator contributed to a crisis after 1850, the growing rift between affective piety and technical theological knowledge at about the same time compounded the problem of religion's relationship to science.

On the other hand, we cannot criticize the educators of the day for not envisioning a bolder role for theological education. The very idea that the college professor should also become a researcher was just at this moment appearing, and it was a long ways from becoming fully developed.[91] Moreover, when this ideal became influenced by the notion of pure research later in the century, the earlier fears of evangelical educators seem to have been fully justified. What we can conclude is that in the long run, the English tradition of practical theology did not serve evangelicals well, in so far as it failed to prepare them for the onslaught of critical and scientific thought. Moreover, this tradition seems to have hastened the demise of the pastor as the best-trained and most-gifted intellectual in the community.

For evangelicals, Edward Farley's enthusiasm for the English tradition of theological education, with its central organizing principle of a theological *habitus* centered in piety, needs to be moderated. His critique and rejection of the fourfold curriculum with its inherent centripetal tendencies may be appropriately applied to liberal theological institutions, but should his criticisms be applied to evangelical institutions? To this day, evangelicals have not lost their experiential core, and yet it was a particular expression of this core that contributed to an unhealthy bifurcation between the things of the

91. Stevenson, *Scholarly Means*, 66.

mind and those of the heart. Farley's analysis does not fully appreciate this reality, and his critique thus should not be applied uncritically to evangelical institutions.

To suppose that the English tradition of practical theology ought to be resurrected and applied today is to make a serious miscalculation concerning its inherent weaknesses. The characteristic longing for spiritual formation that is found today in evangelical institutions is unlikely to be effectively addressed by looking to the ministry departments of our schools, to courses in the spiritual disciplines, or even to entire programs in formation. If this survey of the widening gulf between piety and intellect in the early nineteenth century has any lessons to teach, then it is that ministerial formation is not something that can be developed by adding on to an intellectually disciplined curriculum. Rather, the entire intellectual regimen of those preparing for ministry must be construed as Christian formation and spiritual discipline. Especially in a day when the complexity of ethical decisions demands that a heart of Christian compassion be closely integrated with the toughest and most precise thinking imaginable, we must not allow ourselves to separate the genuine love of God from clear and informed thinking, whether in our separate departments, our programs, or our curricula.

If we ask the broader question of the long-term influence of the tradition of English practical theology, it appears from this review that the influence of these neglected sources was neither straightforward nor free from contradiction. The emphasis on the utility of knowledge and the subservience of all knowledge to the end of piety seems to have ill prepared students and scholars alike for coping with the full range of critical thought emerging in the new German scholarship.[92] If such connections as those examined here were indeed widespread, they might help account for the embittered response to new scholarship in the very last decades of the century. In its characteristic subordination of all learning to the goal of piety and the mission of the church, practical theology seems to have contributed to a built-in tendency for evangelical pastors to overreact to critical scholarship that dealt in a scientific way with the Bible; the critical, detached understanding of God's Word was apparently understood as sharply antithetical to preconceived notions of the true purposes of knowledge. It may be that this longer prehistory of anti-intellectualism in American theological education will shed new light on the origins of the fundamentalist-modernist controversy.

But if the English tradition of pastoral theology contributed in the long run to the origins of fundamentalism, and if the tradition was a protean, as

---

92. The study of English pastoral theology does help account for what, according to Carl Diehl and Glenn Miller, remains perplexing, namely, the American scholars' (and in the case of Miller, Lutheran) inability to come to terms with German scholarship. See *American and German Scholarship, 1770–1870* (New Haven: Yale University Press, 1978), 94–96; and *Piety and Intellect*, 381–82.

it appears to have been, it may have contributed to the opposite tendency as well. At the same time that they emphasized the spiritual utility of knowledge, the manuals and letters of English practical theology encouraged a piety of feeling, and this appeared, especially in the thought of the Andover "liberals" like Park and Edwards, congruent with some aspects of the new thought in the nineteenth century. The characteristic irenicism and broad-mindedness of a Baxter, a Doddridge, and a Watts was translated by some American educators into an emphasis on the importance of maintaining a catholic spirit. And hence, the knowledge of the heart that we have observed in both the English and the American traditions of practical theology may have contributed indirectly to the Christocentric liberals' remarkable capacity to adapt to the new currents of critical and scientific thought.

Part 3

Women and Theological Education

One of the most significant developments within theological education in recent years concerns the changing student population. No longer are students coming straight from undergraduate degrees to seminary. And no longer are seminarians only single, white men fresh from college. To respond to the diversity of the student body, and in some cases to attract these new students, seminaries have instituted a variety of new degrees and programs. These efforts are not only designed to address needs of the students themselves, but also the constituencies they represent.

An important factor in these changes is the increasing enrollment of women at seminary. The third section of this book addresses the presence of women in evangelical theological education explicitly. The first chapter by Karin Gedge examines the presence of women in theological education not as students, but as the predominate group in the churches that seminary graduates served. It shows how the question of gender may affect theological education even before women show up at seminaries as students. In the particular case of nineteenth-century evangelical pastoral theology, the goal of training pastors who could minister effectively to women occupied the minds of theological educators well before the recent advent of female seminarians. The failure of evangelical theological education to tackle of significant component of pastoral duties and, as Gedge shows, the move to shore up the masculine status of the minister through professionalism offer a lesson that seminary and church leaders today will want to consider.

The question of women in evangelical theological education also raises important considerations about the kind of education that nonseminarians

171

may receive through other informal means. As the chapter by Virginia Brereton makes clear, women may not have received theological training in the formal sense, but they did obtain theological education in a variety of innovative, even if separate, ways. Though such education did not result in a degree, it still may be possible to consider such nonseminary methods of instruction as theological education proper. Such a phenomenon testifies to the strength and adaptability of the evangelical tradition. In other words, the theological education of women outside the seminary classroom testifies to the unwillingness of evangelicals to be bound by any particular institution or form in the pursuit of proclaiming the gospel and calling upon believers to lead holy lives. It also points to the important ways that all believers receive theological education even if not enrolled at a seminary or divinity school. Brereton's chapter suggests, furthermore, that the enrollment of women and other "nontraditional" students at evangelical seminaries may bring an end to older, informal means of theological instruction, stifle the vigor and entrepreneurial spirit that has marked the evangelical tradition, and cause seminaries to monopolize the enterprise of theological education.

8

Ministry to Women in the Antebellum Seminaries

Karen E. Gedge

Sometime during the last decades of the nineteenth century, Professor James H. Fairchild addressed a lecture to the seminarians of Oberlin Theological Department on an issue he felt had been ignored for far too long. His subject for the day was "the relations of the pastor to the women of his church and congregation." Fairchild, who looked back over a teaching career of six decades or more, could not recall ever receiving "enlightenment" on the subject of women during his own education at Oberlin between 1838 and 1841 when he sat in the pastoral theology lectures of Charles Finney. But the now aged professor was convinced of the importance of the subject and confident that as "patriarch" of the faculty he could assume the "delicate responsibility" without apology. In the first draft of the lecture he prepared on the sensitive topic, he referred to the problem of women in the pastoral relationship as "forbidden territory," but later he crossed out the proscriptive adjective and replaced it with "forgotten." Fairchild's confusion over the source of the neglect—a strong social taboo or collective amnesia—accurately reflected the attitude of nineteenth-century theological educators toward the issue. The seminary curriculum consistently avoided and ignored pastoral work in general, but the pastoral relation with women in particular was truly hazardous "territory," a dangerous and uncharted province for the seminary student and novice pastor.[1]

Fairchild's identification of women in the pastoral relationship as both a neglected and problematic subject seems to contradict many contemporary

1. James Harris Fairchild, "The Relations of the Pastor to the Women of his Church and Congregation" (typescript with manuscript corrections, undated, Fairchild Papers, Oberlin College Archives). Fairchild taught at Oberlin until his death in 1903.

and historical views of early nineteenth-century American religion that have posited a strong alliance between clergy and women. Frances Trollope, an Englishwoman who wrote the widely read *Domestic Manners of the Americans* in 1835, pointed to the ardent and potent bond between women and their ministers as a significant characteristic of American religion. "The influence which the ministers . . . have on the females of their respective congregations," Trollope observed, "approaches very nearly to what we read of in Spain, or in other strictly Roman Catholic countries." Conversely, she noted women held an "influential importance" with the clergy and in return women "seem to give their hearts and souls into [the clergy's] keeping." Historians have generally supported this contention. E. Brooks Holifield, in his *History of Pastoral Care,* asserted that nineteenth-century pastoral theologians showed a "special interest in the spirituality of women" and agreed that pastors needed to understand and work with women in order to be successful in their mission. Richard Shiels, Harry Stout, and Catherine Brekus have provided some of the statistical evidence to support the long-recognized fact of women's majority in the pews. Barbara Welter argued that women's enormous influence on Protestant religion softened orthodox Calvinism. Ann Douglass claimed that an alliance between ministers and women writers sentimentalized not only American Protestantism, but American culture in general. Finally, dozens of historians have documented women's participation in nineteenth-century revivalism, benevolent organizations, mission societies, and reform movements, and argued that religion empowered women and offered them the opportunity to widen their sphere of influence.[2]

Historians also have noted a backlash against this "feminization" of the church that occurred in the decades after the Civil War. More recently, some historians have argued that the backlash occurred much earlier, in the antebellum period. Catherine Brekus has noted that female preachers met increased opposition in the 1840s. Terry Bilhartz has suggested that the Second Great Awakening of the first four decades should be considered an "ambitious but unsuccessful" attempt to "masculinize" American churches and halt the ebbing tide of male declension. The professionalization of the ministry that developed during the antebellum period—the founding of seminaries, national religious organizations, denominational structures, and profes-

2. Frances Trollope, *Domestic Manners of the Americans,* ed. Donald Smalley (New York: Knopf, 1949), 75; E. Brooks Holifield, *A History of Pastoral Care in America: From Salvation to Self-Realization* (Nashville: Abingdon, 1983), 122; Richard D. Shiels, "The Feminization of American Congregationalism, 1730–1835," *American Quarterly* XXXIII (1981): 46–62; Harry Stout and Catherine Brekus, "Declension, Gender, and the New Religious History," in Philip R. Vandermeer and Robert P. Swierenga, eds., *Belief and Behavior: Essays in the New Religious History* (New Brunswick, N.J.: Rutgers University Press, 1991), 15–37; Barbara Welter, "The Feminization of American Religion," in *Dimity Convictions: The American Woman in the Nineteenth Century* (Athens, Ohio: University of Ohio Press, 1976), 83–102; Ann Douglas, *The Feminization of American Culture* (New York: Knopf, 1977).

sional journals that historian Donald Scott described in his book *From Office to Profession*—should also be considered a reaction to male declension and "feminization." Professionalization was an attempt to redefine the ministry as a masculine endeavor amid shifting notions of gender roles.[3]

Historians of gender have described the significant change in culturally defined models of gender roles that took place against the background of industrialization and urbanization in the first half of the nineteenth century. In the colonial period, the patriarch of the preindustrial family had long served as a model for masculinity in general. He also served as a powerful paradigm for the pastor. The traditional masculine role was the father, the head of a hierarchical family. His domain was the household where both production and child care were located under his supervision. Indeed, colonial child rearing literature was addressed to the male head of the family. Likewise, the colonial pastor was the patriarchal head of his hierarchical parish family. His work, too, was located in his own and others' households and consisted of the education and care—the "feeding" of his flock. Even ministerial education during this period took place in the parsonage. A few young men lived with a clergyman's family, read theology, and made pastoral rounds under their mentor's close supervision until they were licensed to preach or ordained. In short, familial ideology served as a powerful organizing principle for colonial society, church, and state.[4]

The patriarchal model began to lose its power during the American Revolution, however, and quietly faded with the growth of urbanization and industrialization after the turn of the nineteenth century. For the growing middle class, at least, an ideology of separate and gendered spheres replaced it. Production moved out of the home into the workshop, factory, or office—spaces that were now designated as the public or masculine sphere. Men participated in a commercial and political world of competition and contention, while women were confined to a domestic sphere of harmony and sentiment. Child rearing became the central function of the household and primarily the responsibility of women in the private or feminine sphere. Religion occupied an ambiguous position somewhere between the two spheres. Often the

3. Catherine Brekus, "'Let Your Women Keep Silence in the Churches': Female Preaching and Evangelical Religion in America, 1740–1845" (unpub. Ph.D. diss., Yale University, 1993); Terry D. Bilhartz, "Sex and the Second Great Awakening: The Feminization of American Religion Reconsidered," in *Belief and Behavior*, 117–35.
4. For the definition of shifting masculine roles see Mark C. Carnes and Clyde Griffen, eds., *Meanings for Manhood: Constructions of Masculinity in Victorian America* (Chicago: University of Chicago Press, 1990); Elizabeth H. Pleck and Joseph H. Pleck, eds., *The American Man* (Englewood Cliffs, N.J.: Prentice-Hall, 1980); E. Anthony Rotundo, *American Manhood: Transformations in Masculinity from the Revolution to the Modern Era* (New York: Basic Books, 1993). For the method of educating ministers in the colonial period see David Allmendinger, *Paupers and Scholars: The Transformation of Student Life in Nineteenth Century New England* (New York, 1975); Gerald Cragg, "Training the Ministry—The Older Tradition" *Andover Newton Quarterly* 8 (March 1968): 223–34; Mary L. Gambrill, *Ministerial Education in Eighteenth-Century New England* (New York, 1937).

church appeared to be the province of women in the domestic sphere, and clergymen to be their special allies in moral guardianship.[5]

When Professor Fairchild contended that the topic of women in the pastoral relationship was neglected and avoided by seminaries throughout the nineteenth century, his assertion seemed to contradict accepted interpretations of nineteenth-century religion, gender, and culture. But, in fact, the seminaries served to distance the clergy from the domestic sphere and from women in order to assert the masculinity of the profession. Clergy calling for a professionalized ministry invoked not the old patriarchal model, but the new competitive model of masculinity. In 1845 George Ide argued for the foundation of a new Baptist seminary by summoning military and entrepreneurial models and demanding a ministry of "such vigour and such resources, that it can grapple with the most astute and polished minds, and become by its lofty standing and its masterly power, the object of veneration instead of scorn or pity." He likened the theological seminary to the military academy, an institution that would provide the church with "commanders" who would "arrange and concentrate her forces, and conduct them on, conquering and to conquer, to her ultimate and universal dominion." The minister, he insisted, "must show qualities of business, energy, [and] performance" in order to be effective.[6]

The new theological seminaries were quite unlike the familial parsonage school that combined scholarship with a practical apprenticeship in pastoral work. The all-male institutions emphasized the "masculine" intellectual subjects of biblical scholarship, systematic (or better, controversial and polemical) theology, and rhetoric and dissertation, all at the expense of pastoral theology and the practical but "feminine" skills of care, nurture, and personal instruction. The best and brightest graduates of these institutions sought professional positions in prestigious urban pulpits, in powerful national religious organizations, in exotic foreign missions, in religious publishing, or in the seminaries themselves. As historian Donald Scott noted, pastoral work was "subtly downgraded" by this professionalization of the ministry. However, the fact that the work was primarily a service to women in the domestic sphere was also a significant cause of its deteriorating status.[7]

5. For the definition of separate spheres, see Nancy Cott, *Bonds of Womanhood: Women's Sphere in New England, 1780–1835* (New Haven, 1977); Barbara Welter, "The Cult of True Womanhood," in *Dimity Convictions*.

6. George B. Ide, *The Ministry Demanded by the Present Crisis* (Philadelphia: American Baptist Publication Society, 1845), 31, 66, 92–93.

7. For discussions of the professionalization of the ministry, see Burton J. Bledstein, *The Culture of Professionalism: The Middle Class and the Development of Higher Education in America* (New York: Norton, 1976), esp. 173–76; Daniel Calhoun, *Professional Lives in America, 1750–1850*; Donald M. Scott, *From Office to Profession: The New England Ministry, 1750–1850* (Philadelphia, 1978), 66. Professionalization as a "masculinization" process has long been documented by feminist historians of medicine. See Ruth J. Abram, ed., *Send Us a Lady Physician: Women Doctors in America,*

Pastoral theology was the stepchild of the nineteenth-century seminary curriculum. Appended to the end of the three-year course, it was devoted primarily to preaching, ecclesiastical history, and church polity. Many young men were ordained before completing the entire seminary curriculum. Personal pastoral work—the face-to-face dialogues between pastor and parishioner—was largely neglected. The causes and consequences of the problem of women in the pastoral relationship can be found in the profound paradoxes that marked the teaching and practice of pastoral theology in general in the antebellum seminaries. When pastoral work was addressed in short lecture courses or in pastoral texts and manuals, it was frequently depicted as a necessary but awful, onerous, and perilous duty. The parish was a kind of social minefield, full of hazards for even a conscientious pastor. Survival required the mastery of a vague curriculum in manners and a "knowledge of men and things" that was not covered in the academic seminary course work. But despite its perils, pastoral work must not be avoided. Evangelical pastors, in particular, labored under an imperative that required them to fashion an individualized message tailored to a wide variety of social and spiritual estates. They were urged to develop an intimate and personal relationship with parishioners in order to give each his "due portion"—rich and poor, old and young, anxious and skeptical, complacent and pious.[8]

The instructions to young pastors in pastoral manuals and lectures were characterized by defensive tactics, contradictory advice, and veiled warnings. Successful pastors somehow negotiated a narrow path between unacceptable extremes. The minister was dignified, but not aloof; he condescended without patronizing. With the growth of what Sydney Ahlstrom termed "demo-

---

1835–1920 (New York: Norton, 1985); Jane B. Donegan, *Women and Men Midwives: Medicine, Morality, and Misogyny in Early America* (Westport, Conn.: Greenwood Press, 1978); Regina Markel Morantz-Sanchez, *Sympathy and Science: Women Physicians in American Medicine* (New York: Oxford University Press, 1985). For the early seminary curriculum, see Robert Wood Lynn, "Notes Toward a History: Theological Encyclopedia and the Evolution of Protestant Seminary Curriculum, 1808–1868," *Theological Education* (spring 1981): 118–144; Glenn T. Miller, *Piety and Intellect: The Aims and Purposes of Antebellum Theological Education* (Atlanta: Scholars Press, 1990); Natalie Naylor, "Raising a Learned Ministry: The American Education Society: Indigent Students and the New Charity" (unpub. Ed.D. diss., Columbia University, 1971), and "The Theological Seminary in the Configuration of American Higher Education in the Antebellum Years," *History of Education Quarterly* 17 (spring 1977): 17–30. See also the general catalogues of various nineteenth-century seminaries in the Yale Divinity School Archives. Theological education in the seminaries not only deprived the pastor of his practical training, it deprived some women of the chance for a theological education. Ronald W. Hogeland, in "Charles Hodge, The Association of Gentlemen and Ornamental Womanhood: 1825–1855," *Presbyterian History* 53 (1975): 239–55, noted that the switch from parsonage schools to seminaries robbed the pastor's daughter of a theological education, a privilege she sometimes obtained by sitting in on theological "classes" and discussions with her father's students (250).

8. The manuals' emphasis on manners places them in the genre of etiquette and advice manuals so popular in the nineteenth century. For the obsession with manners and appearance in Victorian America, see Karen Halttunen, *Confidence Men and Painted Ladies: A Study of Middle-Class Culture in America, 1830–1870* (New Haven: Yale University Press, 1982); John F. Kasson, *Rudeness and Civility: Manners in Nineteenth-Century Urban America* (New York: Hill and Wang, 1990).

cratic evangelicalism," the clergy no longer enjoyed the deference and respect, born of fear and awe, that was granted to the traditional patriarchal pastor. Instead, clergy were compelled to live "on terms of intimacy and equality" with their parishioners. But this new egalitarian ideal of the pastoral relationship was elusive. It was achieved not with the masculine faculties of argument and dissertation, but with the feminine arts of influence and persuasion. Professor Heman Humphrey's manual insisted that "in this familiar intercourse between minister and people, a great deal, I was going to say almost everything, depends on the *manner.*" Religious topics presented in a "formal, stiff and awkward" manner would "chill the heart." But a pastor with a warm personal manner would find especially receptive listeners. "When your own heart is full, you will be at no loss for words and thoughts," Humphrey assured his readers. "They will spontaneously gush out warm and sparkling as from an overflowing fountain, and will excite a sympathetic response in every bosom." The spontaneity of the ideal discussion implied that there was little the young man could do to prepare himself for successful dialogues with parishioners. The ideal pastoral discussion utilized none of the scholarly and rhetorical skills the young man had honed in the seminary. Instead, the implicit eroticism of such language reflected the intense emotionalism and intimacy that characterized the ideal evangelical pastoral relationship.[9]

The difficulty of achieving this ideal is evident in the pastoral journals of young seminarians and graduates. The paradoxical and equivocal nature of the advice left novice pastors feeling inadequate, insufficient, and ill at ease in their pastoral work. One year into his first pastorate, Jonathan Lee recorded his feelings of "unworthiness & insufficiency." Before delivering his first sermon as a student at Rochester Theological Seminary, Edward Gurney was confident of his intellectual preparation, but not of his piety and manner. "My head may with study prepare sermons but they will want soul and pungency," he lamented, "I am yet in spiritual babyhood." Charles Hodge, an early student and protege of Samuel Miller and Archibald Alexander at Princeton Seminary, chastised himself for a number of faults in his early pastoral work. Hodge worried about the effectiveness of his preaching and was dismayed

---

9. Enoch Pond, *The Young Pastor's Guide* (Bangor, Maine: E. F. Duren, 1848), 67, 323; Heman Humphrey, *Thirty-four Letters to a Son in the Ministry* (Amherst, Mass.: J. S. & C. Adams, 1842), 206. For the influence of democratic ideology in the Jacksonian era on American religion, see Sydney E. Ahlstrom, *A Religious History of the American People* (New Haven, Conn.: Yale University Press, 1972), part IV; and Nathan O. Hatch, *The Democratization of American Christianity* (New Haven, Conn.: Yale University Press, 1989). Holifield's *History of Pastoral Care,* Chapter 4, stresses the ideal balance that nineteenth-century pastors sought between piety and intellect, sentiment and reason, but does not discuss the practical consequences of trying to achieve that elusive ideal. The eroticism of evangelical rhetoric has been examined by many historians. See, for example, Henry Abelove, *The Evangelist of Desire: John Wesley and the Methodists* (Stanford, Calif.: Stanford University Press, 1990); Charles Lloyd Cohen, *God's Caress: The Psychology of Puritan Religious Experience* (New York: Oxford University Press, 1986); George Rawlyk, *Ravished by the Spirit: Religious Revivals, Baptists, and Henry Alline* (Kingston, Ontario: McGill-Queen's University Press, 1984); and Barbara Welter, *Dimity Convictions.*

that after five months of preaching, he had seen "no visible fruit resulting from my labours." "It is painful to preach Sabbath after Sabbath & I see no solitary instance of seriousness & conversation," he complained. But most of all, Hodge found personal conversation distressing. While supplying two separate pulpits on the same day, he was forced to spend several hours dining and riding with one of the parishioners. "This method of spending the Sabbath I find very unprofitable[.] I have neither talent nor piety to give a spiritual & devout character to conversation & hence other subjects than piety become the matters of discussion." Perhaps Hodge's uncomfortable experiences as a fledgling pastor convinced him to turn his career to teaching, where his intellect compensated for his deficient pastoral skills. He soon joined the faculty at Princeton Seminary and enjoyed a long and distinguished tenure there.[10]

The inherent paradoxes of pastoral theology confused and troubled young men. Isaac Bird fretted constantly over his manner and effectiveness. Striving to develop a proper ministerial demeanor, Bird rebuked himself for his sinful levity, his "want of solemnity" and sobriety. However, when a fellow classmate chided him for being too serious, he realized he had "acquired habits of reserved gloominess & melancholy to a degree of which I am told I am not conscious," and concluded that "[a]n alteration must be made, or I shall never have influence half so extensive in society." Significantly, Bird also worried about the masculinity of his vocation. One of his brothers, a hardened skeptic, insulted him by saying that religion "unmans" a person. Bird found comfort and reassurance that the ministry was a masculine endeavor in the remarks of his fellow seminarians who compared their urgent mission to a military campaign. "The simile of Br. L—was very striking," admired Bird. "He compared us to a collection of rulers in time of war met to reproach themselves & each other for failure in duty when the enemy were in the very act of sacking the city & house in which they were holding consultation." Martial imagery also structured Bird's vision of God's kingdom. On observing an impressive militia muster one day, Bird wrote that the "grand performance" reminded him of the "order in heaven." Military metaphors offered an anxious clerical profession reassurance of its essential manliness.[11]

---

10. Edward F. Gurney diary, July 13, 1851, American Baptist Historical Society; Jonathan Lee diary, July 9, 1816, p. 190, Yale Manuscripts and Archives; Isaac Bird journal, March 6, 10, 18, 26, 30, April 10, 1813, Isaac Bird papers, Yale Manuscripts and Archives; Charles Hodge diary, Oct. 31, 1819, March 12 and May 7, 1820, Charles Hodge papers, Firestone Library, Princeton University.

11. Isaac Bird diary, May 15, 1814; March 5, 1817; Sept. 30, 1819. Erving Goffman identified the paradoxical problem in *The Presentation of the Self in Everyday Life* (Garden City, N.J.: Doubleday, 1959). Though he did not cite the clergy as an example, Goffman understood that those without a tangible product to sell were at a disadvantage. "[T]he more the individual is concerned with the reality that is not available to perception, the more must he concentrate his attention on appearances." Individuals dwell in a moral world because they are concerned with maintaining the impression that they are living up to community moral standards. "But [as] performers, individuals are concerned not with the moral issue of realizing these standards, but with the amoral issue of engineering a convincing impression that these standards are being realized" (pp. 249–51).

The troubled status of pastoral theology in the seminary curriculum and the anxiety of novice pastors embarking upon the work owed much to its domestic and feminine character. The pastor was unlikely to find many men on his pastoral rounds unless he sought them in the public workplace, which was not very conducive to religious conversation. In contrast to preindustrial times when men labored at home, the nineteenth-century pastor encountered mostly women, children, and servants on his visits. The fact that pastoral work was more and more a service to women was rarely acknowledged, however. Instead the pastoral relation with women was ignored and avoided because it embodied all the tensions and paradoxes inherent in pastoral theology. Of more than a dozen manuals published during the nineteenth century, only one major text, Samuel Miller's *Clerical Manners and Habits,* addressed at any length the pastor's largest constituency.[12]

Caution, ambivalence, and contradiction marked the few references to women. Aware of the tendency to devalue the female portion of the congregation, Miller advised young men not to "adopt those contemptuous expressions concerning the female sex. . . ." To do so was "to depreciate, in the view of many, a most precious part of the church of Christ. . . ." He acknowledged that "[t]he female part of every congregation have, in general, an influence, which, while it cannot be defined, cannot, at the same time, be resisted." "[F]or the most part," he temporized, "this influence, I believe, is as just in its ultimate award [sic], as it is sovereign in its sway."[13]

Miller's counsel on treating the "female portion" was more detailed and positive than comparable literature in this genre, yet it displayed the same contradictory qualities of pastoral advice in general. For example, Miller warned his readers not to underestimate the rational capabilities of women. They possessed as much "native intellectual *soundness* and *justice* of mind" as men, and could converse on all serious and religious subjects. A young pastor performed a major disservice to his female parishioners if he thought

---

12. Samuel Miller, *Letters on Clerical Manners and Habits: Addressed to a Student in the Theological Seminary, at Princeton, N.J.,* 2d ed. (Princeton: Moore Baker, 1835). Heman Humphrey's only advice on the subject of women was to suggest that though both sexes might meet together in Bible classes, there were advantages to meeting separately, *Thirty-four Letters,* 188. The following manuals contained little or no specific mention of women: Richard Baxter, *The Reformed Pastor; A Discourse on the Pastoral Office. Designed principally to explain and recommend the duty of personal instruction and Catechising, to which is added an appendix, containing some hints of advice to students for the ministry, and to tutors, abridged and reduced to a new method by Samuel Palmer,* (London: J. Buckland, MDCCLVXI, 1766, first written in 1655); Theodore L. Cuyler, *How to be a Pastor* (New York: The Baker and Taylor Co., 1890); James M. Hoppin, *The Office and Work of the Christian Ministry* (New York: Sheldon and Co., 1870); Cotton Mather, *Manuductio and Ministerium: Directions for a Candidate of the Ministry,* (New York: Columbia University Press, 1938, repr. of 1726 edition); Edwards A. Park, ed., *The Preacher and Pastor, by Fenelon, Herbert, Baxter, Campbell* (Andover, Mass.: Allen, Morrill and Wardwell, 1845); Joseph Parker, *Ad Clerum: Advices to a Young Preacher* (Boston: Roberts Brothers, 1871); William G. T. Shedd, *Homiletics, and Pastoral Theology* (New York: Charles Scribner & Co., 1867).

13. Miller, 346, 317.

them capable only of trivial and light-hearted talk. Yet Miller seemed to contradict himself when he cautioned the young pastor to avoid all controversy with women, for his own self-protection. "In acuteness, wit, sprightliness, and delicate raillery," Miller wrote, "[women] often prove very powerful opponents; while the hands of a male adversary are, in a great measure, tied, so that he cannot wield with unrestrained freedom many of those weapons which he might properly, and with great effect, employ against an adversary of his own sex." Thus, the seminary-trained minister was warned not to engage in serious religious discourse with women since he was deprived of much of the intellectual arsenal he had assembled for use in theological debate. His knowledge of controversial or polemical theology—the cornerstone of the seminary education—was inappropriate for women, the pastor's largest constituency. Instead, he must rely on piety and proper manners to guide him in his relations with them.[14]

Such paradoxes pervaded this literature. At times the young man was urged to seek women's company for his own benefit. "[Women's] presence has a tendency to restrain from improprieties of conduct, to soften the manners and to promote good moral sentiments and feelings," asserted William Cogswell in his *Letters to Young Men Preparing for the Ministry*. "Their delicacy and refinement are adapted to check the boisterous passions and to tame the brutal." In other words, an awkward, inexperienced pastor had little to offer women, but he might profit from exposure to their piety, virtue, and refined manners. On the other hand, writers often cautioned pastors to avoid women and not to waste time at ladies' tea parties or allow women to impose on their kindness by requesting protection when traveling. Methodist writers were terse and blunt. "Speak sparingly, and cautiously, with women," they advised. More reasonable, but still inhibiting, was the counsel that urged pastors to "exercise great delicacy," "scrupulous delicacy," or even "perfect delicacy," in conversation with women.[15]

Women could be rational, refined, and virtuous and at the same time trivial, tiresome, and treacherous. Their influence was powerful and benign if the young man had the social skills to maintain their support. But women also posed what most writers considered to be the most serious threat to a minister in his pastoral work. Even the appearance of indiscretion was as serious as any actual offence. "[M]ore than all," warned Professor Enoch

14. Miller, 90, 346.
15. *The Clerical Life: A Series of Letters to Ministers* (New York: Dodd, Mead, and Company, 1898), 120–25; Miller, 388, 327, 344; Methodist Episcopal Church, *The Methodist Discipline of 1798, including the annotations of Thomas Coke and Francis Asbury* (facsimile ed., Academy Books, Rutland, Vt., 1979), 59–62; Adam Clarke, LL.D.F.A.S. *The Preacher's Manual: including Clavis Biblica, and A Letter to a Methodist Preacher*; Also, Thomas Coke, LL.D, *Four Discourses on the Duties of a Minister of the Gospel* (New York: T. Mason and G. Lane, for the Methodist Episcopal Church, 1837), 79; Williams Cogswell, D.D., *Letters to Young Men Preparing for the Christian Ministry* (New York: Saxton & Miles, 1842), 166.

Pond, "let [the pastor] indulge in too great liberties with the other sex, so that respectable females shall be afraid of him, and others shall laugh at him" and his character will be destroyed. "The injury will be done before he is aware of it, and when done, it can never be retrieved."[16] Samuel Miller was the only one to offer specific proscriptions regarding women:

> Every thing that approaches to fondling with females; frequently taking hold of their hands; leaning on, or over their persons; saluting them; retiring much with them into private apartments; often taking solitary walks with them; corresponding with them by letter, &c.—are all practices of which clergymen, young or old, ought to be extremely cautious, and more especially in respect to married females. In a word, in all your associations with the other sex, let your delicacy be of the most scrupulous kind. Shun not only the reality, but even the appearance of evil.[17]

Such specific counsel was very rare, however, because it contradicted the general pastoral advice to "associate freely and without restraint" with one's parishioners. Miller only obliquely acknowledged this dilemma and the trap it posed for the unwary pastor: "Remember that the very confidence, with respect to purity, which is commonly placed in a clergyman's character, while it is, in some respects, highly advantageous, may become a snare to him in a variety of ways easily conceivable." The fact that Miller did not elaborate on the "variety of ways" that pastoral confidence could become a "snare," but instead left his readers to imagine them, illustrates the process by which the discussion of women in the pastoral relation became "forbidden" and "forgotten." For fear of addressing frankly the sexual hazards of ministering to women, educators employed discreet euphemisms that conveyed the gravity of the threat without directly confronting and resolving it.[18]

Pastoral journals once again reveal the problems women posed in the pastoral relationship. If theological students often felt inadequate and ill prepared for their private pastoral work, consumed with doubts about their effectiveness and appropriate manner, then their anxieties were most acute when they encountered women face to face. Once outside the masculine sem-

---

16. Enoch Pond, *The Young Pastor's Guide: or, Lectures on Pastoral Duties* (Bangor, Maine: E. F. Durren, 1844), 330.

17. Miller, *Clerical Habits,* 343–44. A few explicit warnings appeared in Charles Finney's lectures. See William A. Westervelt, lecture notes on pastoral theology by Dr. Finney (1843–44[?]), Westervelt Papers, Oberlin College Archives; Fairchild, "Suggestions to Theological Students. . . ."

18. Miller, 343. For veiled references to the problem of women see Archibald Alexander, lecture notes on pastoral theology, "Ministerial Manners," n.d., Archibald Alexander Papers, Princeton Theological Seminary Libraries. There is evidence that young pastors received warnings about women from friends and family members. See Malcolm Douglass Papers, letters to and from David Bates Douglass, 1846–1850, Hobart and William Smith College; Shelton Family Papers, Philo Shelton to Rev. William Shelton, October 5, 1823, Shelton Family Ms. Collection 37, Box III, Folder 02, Fairfield Historical Society, Fairfield, Conn.

inary community, students invariably met many more women than men while developing their pastoral skills. The young men were often surprised and dismayed by interviews with women who failed to conform to the cultural ideals of piety and submissiveness. On his vacations from Andover seminary early in the century, Isaac Bird spent many weeks visiting and distributing tracts among the poor of Boston. In a journal he kept of the mission, he recorded the most singular impressions of his work in the field. He was appalled by the filthy houses and muddy streets, but especially by the "women (chiefly black) frequent in streets talking loudly, impudently, romping with men &c." He met many young women who resisted his message. Visiting in the "female compartment" of the prison, the women laughed at his missionary efforts. In a bawdy house, one young prostitute appeared "intelligent," he noted, and spoke "with much spirit." She explained to young Bird that her vicious profession was "not from choice," but forced upon her. She showed him her Bible "with a great deal of self-complacency," he wrote. Bird claimed he "endeavored to warn her faithfully," but was stunned by her parting words, "I think *my* chance for heaven as good as *yours*." Certainly none of the pastoral manuals or lectures that Bird might have read specifically prepared him for such an independent and corrupt young woman. On the other hand, an exceptionally warm reception also disturbed him. While visiting a sick young woman and her sister, Bird was impressed by their candor and tears. But when he and a fellow seminarian turned to leave, the girls "reached their hands & clung as if they felt themselves sinking & we could deliver them." Such scenes of deep emotion and physical intimacy were more distressing than rewarding for young men.[19]

At mid-century, when historians have claimed that "feminization" of the church was well entrenched, Edward Whiting Gilman still faced enormous problems with women in his first pastorate. In his Lockport, New York parsonage Gilman received women in his study and visited in their homes, often engaging in private conversation. Yet even though Gilman seemed to cultivate and encourage a warm and intimate relationship with his women parishioners, there is little evidence in the individual entries to indicate that he felt successful in his ministry to them or that he had formed any "alliance" with them. Gilman displayed little of the overt condescension toward women that marked other pastors' journals; he seemed to take their inquiries seriously. Yet he was repeatedly disappointed in his ability to influence them. His call on one sick woman found her "indifferent respecting the matter of the greatest moment & unmoved by all that I could say." A visit to

---

19. Many of these visits apparently were performed in the company of another seminary student. No doubt this helped to protect the young men from accusations of impropriety while they conducted their work among Boston's lowlife. Isaac Bird diary, May 31, 1814; Sept. 27, 29, and Oct. 25, 31, 1819.

another ailing young woman was equally unsettling: "She told me that her former interview with me did her no good[;] that she felt worse after it and was assured that it was not best for her to speak with me about religion[.]" Gilman had difficulty determining his own culpability in the failure. "[P]erhaps it was my manner of speaking with her," he reflected, "perhaps the subject matter." Despite such setbacks, Gilman persisted in his pastoral work with women. During interviews with one anxious young woman he "feared I could say nothing more to her, but yet have found words, and trust not in vain."[20]

Gender difference was a significant problem in several of Gilman's cases; yet, like most of his contemporaries, he never acknowledged it. Even though pastoral manuals insisted that women were as capable of rational discussion as men, numerous examples of interviews with women reveal that ministers often perceived women to be less rational and more emotional than men and, thus, unfit to engage in theological discourse. A revealing excerpt from Gilman's diary illustrates the problem. Gilman was "surprised" and dismayed to find that one of his female parishioners not only attended Roman Catholic services and participated in the devotions, but also defended Catholics as slandered and persecuted people. Unable to accept his first negative impressions of her, he returned a few days later and found his "worst apprehensions were true." The woman's manner toward Gilman had "wonderfully and painfully changed. Her language was full of sneers at my remarks: she was quick & snappish—extremely sensitive and unwilling to hear reason."[21] Gilman, bewildered and defensive, carefully recorded the details of the troubled interview in his journal. "No talking of mine seemed to have the least good effect," he protested. When he suggested she had "dust thrown in her eyes," the woman "took umbrage." When he tried to "explain and illustrate, she took offense at that." When he listed the "corruptions of the Romanism," she countered that there were "wicked people in any denomination." When he spoke of the Scriptures, she asked him "why Protestants had altered the Bible" from the Catholic version. Gilman could not see that, in fact, some of the woman's arguments were quite reasonable and were based on her own observations of the Catholic service and the prejudice of nativists. Nor could he see that his arguments were offensive to her as a woman. When he "reminded her of Eve's self confidence in temptation . . . she was piqued that she should be likened to Eve. . . ." When he failed to best the woman with his

<hr>

20. Gilman Family Papers, Edward Whiting Gilman diaries, July 1 and 12, 1851, Yale Manuscripts and Archives. For additional examples, see entries for Sept. 1849; Oct. 10, 1850; Feb. 16, 1851.

21. Gilman diary, Dec. 11, 1853. Tracts that replicated pastoral conversations with women reveal that pastors deliberately avoided theological discussions with women. See Archibald Alexander, *Practical Sermons; to be Read in Families and Social Meetings* (Philadelphia: Presbyterian Board of Publication, 1850); Ichabod Spencer, *A Pastor's Sketches: or, Conversations with Anxious Inquirers, Respecting the Way of Salvation* (New York: M. W. Dodd, 1855, second series, 1853).

arguments, he appealed finally to her feminine sympathy. But this strategy misfired too. "If I spoke of my pain at her position," he moaned, "there was no Christian response."[22]

Gilman tried, but failed, to fathom the workings of the woman's mind. Her suspected apostasy was "peculiar" because it lacked those familiar evangelical signposts for which he had been accustomed to look. He could discern no "single element of religious conviction" about her change of mind and "no intellectual process of enquiry and discovery." He could only ascribe her bizarre behavior to "a spirit of independent self-will," which was considered unacceptable in a nineteenth-century woman. Most likely, he concluded, her change of spiritual heart was merely a desire to marry a Roman Catholic widower. To Gilman, the woman was either perverse or deluded; she was not persuaded or convinced. Even if Gilman was correct in his assessment of this woman's motivations, however, he could neither understand nor sympathize with her position. A striking contrast to the woman's case appeared in the same long journal entry. Gilman faced a similar situation with a man who also appeared sympathetic to Catholicism, but whose case Gilman insisted was "entirely different." The man was "tolerably well informed; cool, close, and in some measure unstable in his plans." Gilman respected the man's character, especially since he had once studied for the ministry. Unlike his bewildering and upsetting conversation with the woman, though, Gilman had a long, even amicable, debate with the man about Catholic doctrine—a discussion in which he disagreed with, but still admired and respected, his adversary's theological reasoning.[23]

Gilman never admitted that sexuality was an impediment in the pastoral relationship, but several cases suggest that young women, especially, had difficulty speaking with him. One young woman admitted to him that she felt "rather embarrassed & restrained" in his presence, and he finally recommended that she speak instead to a pious young female friend. Similarly, another young woman "dreaded" to see Gilman, but he hoped that she would be able to "converse fully and freely with her sisters" and overcome her difficulties. Finally, still another young woman appeared to suffer a terrible conflict because of her visits with him. "To-day she hardly wanted to talk with me, yet would not let me go," worried Gilman. She admitted to him that she did not attend prayer meetings "on account of remarks from the other girls," who had "misconstrued" her motives and "accused her of caring more for the minister than for religion." Gilman prayed and spoke with her "for some time" (no doubt adding fuel to the gossip), but never acknowledged the problem of sexuality that inhibited their relationship.[24]

22. Gilman diary, Dec. 11, 1853.
23. Gilman diary, Dec. 11, 1853.
24. Gilman diary, Dec. 11, Sept. 25, Sept. 10, 1849.

Gilman's responses to these troublesome encounters with women were typical of many young ministers. His reactions showed he had assimilated the explicit and implicit lessons in pastoral manuals and lectures on women. Young men were surprised and shocked, often speechless, when women did not conform to contemporary cultural ideals of true womanhood nor display the requisite qualities of piety, purity, domesticity, and submissiveness. When women resisted or disagreed with a pastor's religious lessons, he often branded them irrational. Finally, if women felt uncomfortable with him, or the threat of sexuality intruded into the relationship, the prudent pastor transferred his charge to the care of another female. Pastoral journals recorded numerous unsatisfactory conversations, encounters that fueled feelings of inadequacy and ineffectiveness. Yet, even though the great majority of these pastoral meetings were with women, no young man ascribed the problem to gender difference.

The only indication that women in the pastoral relationship were a significant problem is evident in the general advice to pastors on marriage. Marriage miraculously eliminated sexual temptation and also strengthened the minister and his ministry. Samuel Miller argued that it was "not good for man to be alone," but also that marriage was a positive benefit for the man's pastorate.

> If he be married, his female parish[i]oners will have more confidence in him, and feel more freedom in approaching him. He will himself, also, in this case, be delivered from a great many embarrassments and temptations which would otherwise beset his ministerial intercourse with the younger females of his congregation.[25]

But even as Miller argued that marriage brought a pastor closer to his female flock, he maintained that the pastor's wife should serve as intermediary between the two. In addition to her duties as his companion and household manager, the pastor's wife must also be,

> *above all*, a happy medium of intercourse, and pledge of confidence, between you, and the other pious females of your congregation. I have often known the pious wives of clergymen exert an influence so manifest, so extensive, and so happy, within the pastoral charges of their husbands, that, in some cases, there were those who felt constrained to doubt whether the pastors or their companions, were, all things considered, the more useful.[26]

25. Miller, 322.
26. Miller, 330–331 (emphasis mine). When women were addressed in pastoral manuals, the discussion was almost entirely devoted to the question of the pastor's wife. See Leverett Griggs, *Letters to a Theological Student* (Boston: American Tract Society, 1863), 90–93; *Methodist Discipline*, 25–26 and Chapter XXI; Mather, 27; Park, 176. (This excerpt from Herbert's *Country Parson* is the only advice that recommends celibacy over marriage for a settled pastor.) Enoch Pond, 204–214, writes

Thus, the pastor could distance himself from the troublesome problem of women by marrying a surrogate pastor and delegating pastoral work *among* women *to* women. The ideal pastor's wife simultaneously satisfied his own sexual needs, signaled to young women that he was unavailable, and served his female parishioners as spiritual counselor and guide, making any further discussion of the problem of sexuality or the needs of women completely unnecessary.[27]

The significance of the problem of women in the pastoral relationship can once again be measured by the importance of marriage in the private writings of students and young pastors. Young men worried constantly over their marriage choices and the impact of the decision on their careers. Marriage sometimes seemed a burdensome prerequisite to a ministerial career. Ferdinand Clarke, a student a Princeton Theological Seminary, was forced to find a wife before he was eligible to leave for a mission in China. He wrote to family and friends seeking recommendations for a suitable candidate, but admitted that "I have never yet seen the lady to whom I had the most distant desire to pass the special addresses." Finally, the missionary board demanded that he devote all his time to finding a young woman to share his overseas duties. "I do not like it," he lamented, "I want time . . . for other things."[28]

Edward Gurney, studying at Rochester Theological Seminary, felt compelled to seek a wife, in part, because he was "still harassed by temptation and an unusual proneness to carnal sensual thought." No doubt, he hoped that marriage would relieve this annoying problem. He realized, however, that a spouse must satisfy not only his worldly desires, but his professional ambitions and spiritual aspirations as well. Gurney worried that, next to his conversion and call to the ministry, "this is the most serious question that ever came before my mind for consideration." Indeed, Gurney's prayer, introspection, and careful, even anguished, deliberation over marriage certainly mirrored his evangelical conversion experience. Desiring to be "submissive to the guidings of [the] Spirit" in the matter, he decided that one young woman was clearly the best choice by consulting both his "judgment as well as [his] religious feelings." But he confessed to his diary that his "worldliness would have sought another." Practical qualities, not beauty or charm, determined which young woman would "add most to my usefulness

---

extensively about delegating pastoral duties to the laity, both men and women. See, also, the Elam J. Comings Papers, notes on pastoral theology, diary, 1837–46, n.p.; William Westervelt, Finney lectures, n.p., n.d.; Archibald Alexander's lecture outlines, box 13, folder 5.

27. For examples, see Freeman-Clarke Family Papers, letters of Ferdinand DeWilton Ward to Henrietta Ward, 1833–35, University of Rochester, Special Collections; Edward F. Gurney Papers, diary, 1851–53, American Baptist Historical Society, Rochester, N.Y.

28. Freeman-Clarke Family Papers, Ferdinand DeWilton Clarke to Henrietta Clarke, July 2, 1833; Geoffrey C. Ward, "Two missionaries' ordeal by faith in a distant clime," *Smithsonian* (Aug. 1990): 118–32.

as a minister of Jesus Christ." Clearly, Gurney's marriage choice was determined by her fitness as a helpmeet in his calling. Whether she was also successful in delivering him from sexual temptation is not so obvious.[29]

The discussion of the minister's wife was merely a substitute for addressing the infrequently admitted problem of gender difference in the pastoral relation. Distancing the minister from women by placing the problem squarely on the broad shoulder's of the pastor's wife, however, prevented the clerical profession from resolving the contradictions of women's place in the church. The profession could not promulgate the notion of spiritual equality and promote the ideal of the "true woman," a model of Christian piety and submissiveness, and still deny such a paragon a useful role in religious institutions. Nor could the ministry confront the issue of sexuality and still encourage an intimate association between pastor and female parishioner. It could invest all the hopes and concerns for the success of the pastoral ministry to women in the minister's wife, without according her the respect and dignity of a real office in the church, and without offering her the education and support of the ministerial profession. Only one seminary, Oberlin, opened its doors to women, but without conceding any official place or recognition in the profession to women.[30]

In the end, professionalization of the ministry was a shield against the feminization of the church. It redefined the ministry as a masculine endeavor, moving away from the older paternal model of the pastor toward the professional, public, intellectual, and spiritual leader. In a professional milieu that constantly employed military metaphors for its work, preaching from the pulpit was literally man's work. Ministers utilized their scholarship and rhetorical skills in order to aim "big guns" at their congregations, defending from a safe distance their doctrinal positions but ill prepared and ineffective in close combat, especially with women. No wonder the brightest and bravest seminary students aspired to the romantic dangers of missionary work on the frontier or abroad, took up chairs in the theological seminaries, sought positions in the many benevolent and educational associations, or worked their way up to a very public and influential pulpit in a large city. By doing so, they were undeniably in competition with other male professionals and entrepreneurs in a masculine public sphere. By contrast, the pastoral or nurturing qualities of the traditional role were ignored or devalued; the simple

29. Edward F. Gurney diary, 1851–53, April 29, 1851; July 27, 1851; August 10, 18, 24, 1851; May 2, 1852.

30. Westervelt's notes on Finney's lectures at Oberlin are clearly addressed to both the young men *and* the young women in his class: "Let her try to elevate the society. Let her form societies. Let her have a weekly meeting with the young ladies. Keep a [wake?] to prayer. Inform yourself. promote female education. relieve your husband as far as possible from care. Pray for him as a minister. Be as useful to him as you can in every p[ossible] way. Be sure to pray that you may be profited by your husband" n.p., n.d.

pastor of a small parish was no longer a highly respected position. The *de facto* delegation of the pastoring *of* women *to* women contributed to the general devaluation of pastoral work, redefining it as women's work. Despite the lip service paid to the importance of practical theology and pastoral labor in manuals and rhetoric by professors, theological seminaries only contributed to the devaluation of the work. In large part, this devaluation was due to the profession's inability, first, to acknowledge that the work was primarily a service to women and, second, to resolve contradictions in pastoral theology regarding women's place in the church.

The unacknowledged problem continued to plague the ministry throughout the century. When Professor James H. Fairchild addressed the male seminarians at Oberlin late in the century, his advice echoed earlier warnings but made them much more explicit than the vague discussions of his predecessors. His remarks exposed the clerical assumptions about women's irrationality and sexuality. He admonished the students against "consciously or unconsciously" adapting their "ministrations" to women's tastes. "There is some danger that [the pastor's] preaching may become unduly emotional or esthetic, & that the intellectual element will be reduced to a minimum," he asserted. Without a "virile presentation of religious truth," the pastor would soon lose all his male audience. Women's "flattering & indiscriminate admiration" must be resisted, he warned, or the pastor "will sacrifice his manliness & his strength." If pastoral visits to the home could not be made by or with the pastor's wife, they had best be avoided. Even thoughtful and dispassionate relationships with women must be shunned. "I do not deny the theoretical possibility [of a platonic relationship]," he averred, one in which the pastor and a woman parishioner might exchange opinions and counsel on religious subjects and church business. "But considering all the liabilities of the case," there was only one "safe position"—"to leave it off before it be meddled with." At bottom, Fairchild argued, Christianity was distinguished from the pagan and false religions because it avoided the "strange commingling" of "religion and lust" that had characterized the earlier faiths. Unfortunately, the "strange commingling" too often characterized Christianity, as well as constantly affected the pastor's conduct. The Christian pastor must constantly strive to conduct his pastoral work with the strictest propriety, yet avoid the "stiffness and prudishness" that resulted from a conscious application of rules and maxims. He must display an "ease & freedom of deportment & of intercourse" that was "spontaneous & instinctive," yet offensive to no one. These were the paradoxes that continued to be imposed upon the pastor by the rarely acknowledged problem of women in the pastoral relationship.[31]

31. Fairchild, "Suggestions to Theological Students as to the Relations of the Pastor to the Women of his Church & Congregation," 6–8, 10–12, 15.

9

Learning in the Margins

Virginia Lieson Brereton

There is a very simple and, as far as it goes, accurate way to describe the relationship of women to theological education, which is to state flatly that very few Protestant American women ever got a theological education in any formal sense—and that goes for whatever Protestant traditions we're talking about and for whatever period of time, except the most recent decades. By "formal" theological education, I mean, basically, instruction in the core fields of systematic theology, church history, biblical studies—Old and New Testament—and, to a lesser extent, practical theology. Most instruction of this "bona fide" sort has been obtainable exclusively in theological seminaries, and until recently women have either been absent entirely in those institutions, or present only as second-class citizens.

There are, of course, many reasons why American women have traditionally been barred from theological seminaries and, hence, from formal theological education, but one of the most important is that for most of their history, seminaries have been conceived of as basically male institutions, no matter what the formal rules happened to be concerning the admission and matriculation of women. A brief review of the history of the theological seminary is enough to demonstrate its thoroughly masculine lineage. The seminary is mainly an *American* educational form, usually traced to Andover Theological Seminary, which opened up in 1808. It was soon followed in 1812 by Princeton Theological Seminary, which together with Andover, "set benchmarks for other theological institutions"[1] In its conception, the American theological seminary was freestanding and largely independent of other educational institutions. Ideally, it was intended to follow four years in a lib-

---

1. Glenn T. Miller, *Piety and Intellect: The Aims and Purposes of Ante-Bellum Theological Education* (Atlanta: Scholars Press, 1990), 147.

eral arts college. The curriculum was remarkably standard: It took three years to cover and fell into a fourfold pattern of theological, biblical, historical, and practical studies, with the practical field somewhat subordinated. After the mid-nineteenth century, women were admitted to theological seminaries here and there (Antoinette Brown graduated from Oberlin Theological Seminary in 1850; Anna Howard Shaw from Boston University School of Theology in 1878; Garrett's first woman graduated in 1887; Emilie Grace Briggs graduated from Union Theological Seminary in 1897), but never in enough numbers to alter the seminaries' essentially male identity.

In the early twentieth century came the first major alterations in this pattern. Many seminaries became related to the new universities but, more important for our purposes, the seminaries expanded their practical offerings to embrace such subjects as religious education, missions, Christian sociology, psychology, and field education. For the most part, seminaries didn't add the practical subjects because they were convinced to their importance, though some individuals within the seminary were; rather, they were pressured into this by the success of missionary training schools and Bible schools, and the expansion of vocations in the church—pastor's assistants, church musicians, YMCA and YWCA secretaries—for which some preparation was felt to be necessary. The presence in seminaries of studies such as religious education attracted women as students (and to a modest extent as faculty); they were, of course, usually expected to enter the tracks leading to degrees in the practical fields rather than routes leading to the ordained ministry. And because the practical fields, though expanded early in the twentieth century, were still clearly subordinated in the theological curriculum, women also remained safely subordinated—and somewhat segregated—in seminary student bodies.

One might have expected the seminary form to loosen up further as the twentieth century advanced—what with all the educational ferment of this century and particularly the widening acceptance of women in other sectors of higher education. But a couple of factors ensured that theological seminaries would continue to be relatively conservative and masculine institutions. First, ordination to the ministry remained pretty much a male prerogative. Even in mainline denominations where the ministry became a theoretical and legal possibility for women, the numbers of women entering the pastorate remained quite low, partly owing to a limited opportunity structure for women.[2] In some of the conservative groups originally most open to

---

2. In an unpublished essay, "Ordaining Women: The Diffusion of an Organizational Innovation," Mark Chavez of the Department of Sociology at Notre Dame makes the point particularly forcefully that though the Methodists and Presbyterians churches began to ordain women in 1952, very few women entered the pastorate in these churches until well into the seventies. The granting of clergy rights to women had less to do with the internal needs of the denomination than with pressures external to it.

women's leadership—those with Holiness and Pentecostal backgrounds, for instance—the opportunities for women actually diminished as those groups organized more formally as denominations.[3]

Second, the twentieth century movement to accredit theological education, which eventually resulted in the Association of Theological Schools, was essentially conservative in its impact on women. Accreditation of theological education got off the ground with a conference in 1918 and the standards for accreditation began to be formulated in the mid–1930s. The process spelled difficulty for women. To begin with, the accreditation movement defined (or one might say confirmed) the theological seminary as the basic form of the theological education and, therefore, put a damper on the luxuriant growth of institutions between 1880 and 1930 intended to prepare religious workers and those were the very places—the missionary school and the Bible school—that had welcomed women. Accreditation exacerbated the tendency, already present, to designate missionary training schools and Bible schools as outside the educational pale—"short-cut" institutions. Thus, when funds for religious education became scarce, as they did most notably in the thirties, these schools, now defined as "marginal," were the first to be cut off from diminishing resources. Furthermore, by applying pressure on theological seminaries to raise their academic standards and stabilize their finances, the accrediting movement—perhaps unwittingly—saw to it that the seminaries would continue to favor male students, faculty, administrators, and board, for that was traditionally the gender with the greatest academic prestige. In sum, the theological seminary, totally a male preserve in 1808, the year of Andover's founding, remained basically masculine well into the 1970s.

In Europe the situation was slightly different. Theology was taught in the graduate divisions of the universities, as well as in institutions specifically meant for the training of pastors; in America theology was almost exclusively the preserve of the theological seminaries. Thus, when American women were discouraged officially or unofficially from attending seminaries, especially as theological students, they had few options for obtaining either theological knowledge or credentials. Had theology been an interest of graduate departments in the American university, women might have gained access sooner to academic theology.

As my references to training and Bible schools may suggest, when I say that Protestant American women did not get a formal theological education in seminaries, I hardly mean to imply that they lacked any meaningful preparation at all for work in the churches. And work in the churches they certainly did, as both professionals and volunteers, especially from the 1880s

---

3. See, for example, Edith L. Blumhofer, *Restoring the Faith: The Assemblies of God, Pentecostalism and American Culture* (Urbana, Ill.: University of Illinois Press, 1993).

onward. They evangelized, taught Sunday schools, became deaconnesses, organized home and foreign missions organizations, played the churches' music, and authored devotional tracts and Bible studies. As long as the churches had a strong missionary interest, both home and foreign, they were willing to draft women for the missionary tasks—or, perhaps more correctly, they *permitted* women to commit their willing hands and hearts to missionary tasks. As preparation for this missionary work, women frequently attended training schools of a year or two in duration, some of them founded and supported by women's home and foreign missionary societies. In those schools women learned practical lessons: they studied effective methods of pedagogy; specialized in techniques of religious work with young people or children; practiced effective soul-winning approaches. They also learned their English Bibles with very pragmatic goals: they wanted to know which Bible verses would lead prospective converts to Christ, which would bolster their own faiths or faltering confidence, and which would give guidance for Christian activity in a changing society. In addition, training school students spent much of their time actually working—in settlements, in Sunday schools, in rescue missions, in homes for the aged, in street meetings, and in factories, hospitals, and prisons. Rather than acquiring bodies of formal knowledge, women learned how to *do* things; they learned the "how" rather than the "why" of Christian life and activity.[4] Not surprisingly, they often came to regard formal theology as beside the point, mostly the source of useless wrangling among Protestants who, many women thought, needed to be united rather than divided in performing evangelistic tasks if the world was ever to be won for Christ.

By the 1920s, women, while effusively praised for their contributions to the church, were also coming under criticism for being theologically unsophisticated. Margaret Bendroth in her book *Fundamentalism and Gender* comments that in the twenties fundamentalists tended to perceive women as "theologically shallow."[5] They were especially perturbed to notice that women in positions of leadership in the mainline denominations treated the theological claims of the conservatives with considerable impatience; to the fundamentalists it seemed that women like Helen Barrett Montgomery and Anna Canada Swain were far more interested in preserving organizational harmony than in recognizing or advancing theological "truth." As far as many conservative evangelicals were concerned, of course, this failure to take doctrine seriously enough was true of all theological liberals, but the charge seemed particularly justified when applied to women. Later, in the early days

4. Virginia Liesan Brereton, "Preparing Women for the Lord's Work: The Story of Three Methodist Training Schools," in Hilah F. Thomas and Rosemary Skinner Keller, eds., *Women in New Worlds: Historical Perspectives on the Wesleyan Tradition* (Nashville: Abingdon Press, 1981).
5. Margaret Lamberts Bendroth, *Fundamentalism and Gender: 1875 to the Present* (New Haven: Yale University Press, 1993), 56.

of the formation of the World Council of Churches in the forties and fifties, mainstream Protestant women, meeting the female leadership from the European churches, would accuse themselves of theological naivete in comparison to their sisters from across the ocean. But, as we have seen, there was no easy solution. Women did not go to seminaries in large numbers, and, having been underexposed to theology for so long, most of them tended to think of it as relatively unimportant and perhaps beyond their capabilities as well.

The handicap faced by conservative evangelical and other Protestant women in regard to theological education was exacerbated in the middle years of the twentieth century. Historians like Margaret Bendroth, Betty De-Berg, and Janette Hassey have argued convincingly that the strictures against women in evangelical institutions increased in these decades. Certainly this was true in religious education. Even within the Bible schools, traditionally hospitable to women and often enrolling a female majority, there gradually developed more of a tendency than in the beginning to discriminate between the men and women. Sometimes the sheer proliferation of courses in a well-established Bible school allowed for the creation of "female" and "male" classes (e.g., "Work with Children" for women, "Homiletics" for the men). Frequently in the teens or twenties a pastor's course was introduced into the Bible school curriculum, usually on a fairly modest scale. Often it was understood, sometimes without anything explicitly said, that this course was mainly intended for men. The explicit strictures upon women increased in the thirties. Bendroth has traced some of the quotas that seminaries, colleges, and Bible schools began to institute in that decade to limit the number of women in their student bodies. For instance, in 1930 the trustees of Gordon College of Theology and Missions voted to restrict the number of women students to one-third of the total. Bendroth observes that

> The quota effectively dried up the supply of women applicants. By 1944 the Gordon Divinity School, as a separate entity from the college, reported seventy-two incoming male students, and only three women. That year the trustees lifted the quota on female students, responding to the absence of male candidates during World War II; however, by the mid–1950s, the Gordon campus was entirely male.[6]

Similarly, William Trollinger reports that when Northwestern Bible School created a seminary in 1935, its pastoral training program was designated "men only."[7] And George Marsden tells us that at Fuller Theological

---

6. Ibid., 92. See also Beth A. DeBerg, *Ungodly Women: Gender and the First Wave of American Fundamentalism* (Minneapolis: Fortress Press, 1990); and Janette Hassey, *No Time for Silence: Evangelical Women in Public Ministry Around the Turn of the Century* (Grand Rapids, Mich.: Zondervan, 1986).

7. William Vance Trollinger Jr., *God's Empire: William Bell Riley and Midwestern Fundamentalism* (Madison: University of Madison, 1990), 107.

Seminary's founding in 1947, women were barred from classes, even as auditors. Once they were admitted a couple of years later, it was to candidacy for a degree in Bachelor of Sacred Theology, understood not to lead to the ordained ministry.[8]

Let me hasten to say that I don't detect any dark conspiracy here to keep women out of theological education. What happened, I think, is that as the new evangelical groups matured organizationally and as they commanded more resources, they could begin to think about upgrading the educational preparation they provided for their pastors and other religious workers. Upgrading usually meant that Bible *schools* were turned into Bible *colleges* and then just plain colleges, with less concentration on practical and Bible studies. Under pressure from the Association of Theological Schools, training for the ministry and for other church vocations was more and more consigned to a theological seminary or divinity school, which was expected to operate on a graduate level and needed to be separated from whatever "undergraduate" institution it had previously been related to. And, in general, the "higher" the academic level of colleges and seminaries, the less they welcomed women.

Even at the nadir of their access to formal theological education, however, evangelical women retained and in some cases created ways to prepare themselves for ministries in the church. As had Protestant women before them, they operated in the educational margins, but often quite effectively. One school that continued to welcome women in large numbers was Biblical Seminary in New York City (it had started out as Bible Teachers Training School at the beginning of the century), perhaps because its approach continued to be somewhat idiosyncratic in comparison to "standard" seminaries. An early leader in InterVarsity Christian Fellowship, Jane Hollingsworth, graduated from Wheaton and then Biblical Seminary. There she learned the distinctive inductive method of Bible study (originated by Wilbert White, taught during Hollingsworth's day by Robert Traina) and then through her classes and writings on behalf of IVCF went on to make inductive study the prevailing Bible study method at IVCF.[9] Hollingsworth was not unique as a Biblical alumna; whole cohorts of women graduates (and some men) of Biblical Seminary carried the inductive method to the church and parachurch agencies of evangelicalism.

Evangelical women sometimes benefited from briefer periods of training as well, in weekend conferences or in longer conferences and institutes. Though most of the first women staff members of IVCF mostly learned the

8. George M. Marsden, *Reforming Fundamentalism: Fuller Seminary and the New Evangelicalism* (Grand Rapids, Mich.: Eerdmans, 1987), 123–27.

9. Keith and Gladys Hunt, *For Christ and the University: The Story of InterVarsity Fellowship of the U.S.A., 1940–1990* (Downers Grove, Ill.: InterVarsity Press, 1991).

ropes by following an experienced worker around and then simply plunging in, after 1945 they could attend a four-week summer camp not far from Toronto. This as so successful that soon there were similar camps at strategic points around the United States.

Admittedly, parachurch organizations like IVCF and later Campus Crusade remained remarkably open to the ministry of women, so that Hollingsworth and her peers had remarkable opportunities to put their "theological" education to good use. But even as members of the faculties of more traditional evangelical colleges and seminaries, women sometimes managed to preserve or carve out places, albeit thoroughly subordinated. The influence of Rebecca Price and of the LeBar sisters, Lois and Mary, at Wheaton was real, though weakened by their identity as women and their location in the field of Christian education.[10]

But religious education and training programs of whatever kind were expensive to maintain and attend. Women chose still other forms of preparation, many derived from their own experiences in the faith. Ruth Tucker and Walter Liefeld have remarked on the kind of preparation that lay behind the ministries of the numerous evangelical speakers and writers of the fifties and sixties:

> In the mid-twentieth century a new breed of female speakers arose—women whose subject matter came primarily out of their own struggles in the Christian life. And in virtually every instance the speaking ministry was supplemented by a writing career—the one ministry that has always been safe for Christian women.[11]

In general, we historians have given very little systematic thought to this kind of "education," though the sources—personal narratives, Bible study books and pamphlets, magazine and journal articles—are abundant.

Relatively few of the women whose ministries began in the 1950s and 1960s had been to seminary or even to Bible school. In fact, many had simply been raised in Christian homes and Sunday schools and had started out in the approved role of wife and mother and had moved bit by bit into ministry. If they had married ministers, missionaries, or evangelists they often participated extensively in their husbands' enterprise. Besides (or, rather along with) their experience of successful struggle to become real Christians, these women were prepared usually by participation in testimony and prayer groups, sometimes by an informal apprenticeship under an already estab-

10. Paul H. Heidebrecht, "The Educational Legacy of Lois and Mary LeBar," unpublished paper, Wheaton College, Wheaton, Illinois, 1991.
11. Ruth A. Tucker and Walter Liefeld, *Daughters of the Church: Women and Ministry from New Testament Times to the Present* (Grand Rapids, Mich.: Zondervan, 1987), 394–95.

lished leader, and finally, and most important, by extensive and ongoing Bible study—either carried independently or in groups. The authority of these women usually came not from a diploma or a B.A. or B.D., but the state of their souls—their born again status and their personal knowledge of Jesus Christ. Thus, in the mid-sixties a middle-aged housewife named Millie Dienert had finally completely "yielded control of her life to God."[12] As a young girl, a rebellious daughter of a minister, she had studied to be an actress (and apparently to compensate had briefly attended the Philadelphia School of the Bible). Eventually she had settled into a rather ordinary if not particularly happy life as wife of a traveling salesman. After years of spiritual struggle and two serious automobile accidents, she had attained closeness to God and a "singleness of direction."[13] In 1966 she was asked to assist in the "Prayer Preparation Program" for the Billy Graham Crusade. The next thing she knew she was in England (and then elsewhere in the world) arranging teas, coffees, and lunches for women who would aid in Graham's campaign there.

However important personal religious experience was in evangelicalism, the urge to systematize and, to some extent, formalize the preparation of Christian workers was never far behind the experience. As one woman leader exhorted: "Women equip themselves for secular jobs through study and training. We should equip ourselves to serve the Lord too."[14] Thus, there emerged a whole genus of educative ministries geared exclusively to the preparation of women. The segregation along sexual lines was natural; women had traditionally prayed, studied, and worked together in their own groups, and women leaders were less likely to offend if they confined their efforts to those of their own gender. Marilyn Kunz and Catherine Schell, both former IVCF staffers, formed the Neighborhood Bible Study in 1960. In 1966 Jo Berry got the idea for Creative Ministries to equip Christian women to be "the moral and spiritual activists in their society, not complacent followers."[15] In 1967 in Seattle Jane Hansen, her eyes on the example of the Full Gospel Business Men's Fellowship, started what would become Women Aglow, a charismatic ministry that featured prayer and healing groups.[16] Some women's ministries instructed and aided groups with particular needs, for instance, female overeaters (Overeaters Anonymous and Overeaters Victorious). Joni Eareckson Tada began a ministry to the dis-

12. Helen W. Kooiman, *Cameos: Women Fashioned by God* (Wheaton, Ill.: Tyndale, 1968), 78.
13. Ibid.
14. Jo Berry, *Growing, Sharing, Serving* (Elgin, Ill.: David C. Cook, 1979), 32.
15. Ibid., 13.
16. Ruth Marie Griffith, "A 'Network of Praying Women': Negotiating Identities in Women's Aglow," paper delivered at conference, "Pentecostal Currents in the American Church," Fuller Seminary, March 10–12, 1994; Susan M. Setta, "Healing in Suburbia: The Women's Aglow Fellowship," *Journal of Religious Studies* 12 (1986): 46–56.

198   *Women and Theological Education*

abled, "Joni and Friends," after a 1967 diving accident that had left her par-
alyzed from the neck down. Some evangelical women educated largely
through their speaking and writing ministries, for instance, Catherine Marshall, Elisabeth Elliot, Eugenia Price, and Ann Kiemel Anderson, to name
only a few of the most famous. One female testimony after another has credited some particular volume as crucial in bringing her to her Lord and freeing
her to minister to others.[17]

At the core of many of these ministries has been inductive Bible study, a
rather inclusive label for a number of varied, but loosely related, approaches
to the Bible. What inductive Bible study has usually entailed has been the use
of an English translation or translations (often several sanctioned translations are compared) and the posing of a series of questions designed to elicit
the student's thoughtful response to the biblical text under consideration
(sample instructions: "Underline the important ideas and words," "Look up
the related passages in your topical Bible," "Look up key words in your con-
cordance") and to encourage the student to apply her reading to her own life
and situation ("What do each of the following verses say to you personally?"). One of the virtues of inductive Bible study that recommends it to lay
women is that it does not demand much expertise; all it requires is ordinary
care, intelligence, and, especially, a dedicated heart.

Few of these ministries I have referred to have developed formal educational institutions (one exception is Jo Berry, who established a center to
which women "from different churches throughout the United States could
come and be trained by qualified staff about how to develop their spiritual
potential and set up women's ministries in their home churches");[18] likewise,
few women's ministries had any formal connections with theological seminaries. The chief educational method was books, informal study groups, and
apprenticeships—or disciplineships, as women preferred to call them. Not surprisingly, given their history, some evangelical women have looked at formal
education with a skeptical eye. Berry, for instance, has argued that to do
Christian counseling, a woman needs only a Bible, not "a degree in psychology or a lot of worldly knowledge." Counseling, she cautioned, "is not
throwing the latest theories at someone."[19] However, since many of these
ministries continue strong, there is every reason to suppose that they will
have an impact on evangelical theological seminaries. Indeed, some tentative
alliances and connections have already occurred. Berry reported that one of
her disciples was a team teacher in a women's ministry course at Talbot Seminary. Beth Donigan Seversen received her M.Div. at Trinity Evangelical Di-

17. See also the *Women's Devotional Bible* (Grand Rapids, Mich.: Zondervan, 1990), which is
interlaced with meditations and prayers by well-known evangelical women.
18. Berry, *Growing*, 109.
19. Ibid., 54.

vinity School and went into women's ministries; in 1990 she was an associate pastor of women's ministries at Elmhurst Church in Waukesha, Wisconsin. In that position she also became writing assistant to Jill Briscoe, coordinator of women's ministries at the same church and a prolific author of Bible study books for women.

Slowly, but quite impressively, the numbers of women at evangelical theological seminaries are increasing, including those in the professional ministerial track. By an ironic twist of fate, the same agency—the Association of Theological Schools—that helped reduce or keep down the numbers of women in theological education earlier in the century is now urging its member schools—among whom number most of the major evangelical seminaries—to make their curriculums and their ethos more hospitable to women. This is reason for cheer, but not yet elation. Here the example of the liberal Protestant seminaries, where the greater presence of women students is three decades old, is instructive and also cautionary. In those seminaries the appointment of female faculty and administrators has not begun to keep pace with the rise in female students; indeed, the tendency has been for women's interests to be consigned to a part-time, untenured coordinator, whose responsibilities are immense, and whose authority within the institution is severely limited. Further, the coordinator's budget is likely to have come from temporary foundation funding rather than being accepted as a line item in the regular school budget. Hence, women's interests have tended to be "add ons," subject to the vagaries of fashion and funding. All this has been detrimental to women students; it has also been damaging to the seminaries, for in failing fully to integrate women's interests they have failed to benefit as much as they might from the influence of a feminist pedagogy: an emphasis on pedagogical practices such as team teaching and self-directed learning; a focus on the learner more than the instructor; and a tendency to downplay compartmentalization and dualisms in favor of a more holistic, collaborative, cross-disciplinary approach to knowledge.[20]

It will be regrettable if, in seeking to accommodate the needs of their growing body of women students, evangelical seminaries emulate their mainline counterparts too closely, for evangelical schools undoubtedly have much to learn from evangelical women's diverse and complex "ways of knowing."

---

20. Cornwall Collective, *Your Daughters Shall Prophesy: Feminist Alternatives in Theological Education* (New York: Pilgrim Press, 1980).

Part 4

Between the Church and the Academy

A perennial struggle in evangelical theological education has been one which pits the demands of academic performance and quality against a desire to serve the church. In recent years, as evangelicals have pursued graduate studies in Bible and theology in record numbers, the academic quality of evangelical seminaries has climbed precipitously. More evangelical seminary faculty have Ph.D.s than previous generations, and they produce a wealth of scholarly books and articles. Some, however, without denying the value of scholarship, wonder whether the newfound academic orientation of evangelical seminaries is entirely a blessing. For they sense that the stress upon academic professionalism has meant a lack of attention to the needs of the church. Evangelical professors may participate as full partners in the American Academy of Religion and the Society of Biblical Literature, but some wonder whether they are as active in preaching and teaching Sunday school in their local churches.

Yet, these are not new concerns. Addressing these two audiences, the academy and the church, has always been a dilemma facing evangelical theological educators, as the essays in the fourth section make clear. In the first chapter, Nina Reid-Maroney demonstrates how academic concerns motivated Presbyterians who promoted a conception of Christian experience that seemed to make intellectual pursuits less important. Her chapter on eighteenth-century New Side Presbyterian academies, which were founded to train ministers sympathetic to revivalism and which were criticized for lowering the academic qualifications of the clergy, illustrates the influence of Enlightenment philosophy and scientific method even on those Protestants crit-

201

ical of rationalism in the academy and formalism in the church. David Bebbington's essay on Charles Spurgeon and his Pastor's College, though covering a later period of evangelical history and a different culture, dovetails with Reid-Maroney's chapter by exploring the tensions between ministerial education and academic pursuits. Though British evangelical Baptists sorted out these tensions differently from eighteenth-century American Presbyterians, Bebbington nonetheless highlights the characteristic ambivalence that evangelicals have when making theological education conform to certain academic criteria.

James Bratt's chapter on Abraham Kuyper and the Free University, an institution which since its founding has attracted a fair number of American evangelicals for graduate training in theological disciplines, adds another wrinkle to the tension between the church and the academy. Critical to Kuyper's academic enterprise was a precarious balance between the antithesis and common grace, between a recognition of the profound spiritual differences that separate believers and nonbelievers in their pursuit of knowledge, and an acknowledgment of the traits or qualities that unite all humans in the scholarly enterprise. Bratt shows how, despite Kuyper's acrobat-like ability to balance these concerns, social and religious developments in the twentieth century have made such balance increasingly difficult.

In the final chapter of this section, George Rawlyk examines Canadian evangelicalism to reiterate Bratt's point about effects of secularization upon theological education. In a story which could apply just as well to the United States, Rawlyk shows how the strategy of liberal Protestant theological education to accommodate many of the assumptions of modern thought has contributed to seminaries' marginalization. He also underscores the importance of a commitment to historic Christian truths for the recent resurgence of evangelical seminaries in Canada. But lest evangelicals become tempted by triumphalism, Rawlyk adds that their good fortunes could become illusory if they are too deeply bound up with accommodating the forces of modernity.

10

Science and the Presbyterian Academies

Nina Reid-Maroney

An apocryphal story survives about Robert Smith, the Presbyterian minister who founded a small theological academy at Pequea, Pennsylvania in 1752. In order to demonstrate to a Quaker acquaintance that a trained minister could still be moved by the Spirit, Smith agreed to preach his next sermon on any Scripture passage of the Quaker's choosing, to be disclosed to Smith on the appointed Sunday in the interval between the long prayer and the psalm. The test was made. Smith preached with warmth and spontaneity, and the well-pleased Quaker made Smith the present of a small red cow—his best milker—for having proved his worth.[1] Circulated in the early twentieth century, the story plays on the tension between theological education and ministerial calling. The implication is that Smith could still preach, despite his training. Yet in his own time, Robert Smith maintained that a proper theological education could not separate piety from learning.

Between 1727 and 1752, four Presbyterian academies, including Robert Smith's, were founded in the hinterland of Philadelphia. Their existence, like the lives of their founders, was tied to the fortunes of the Great Awakening. William Tennent and his four sons at Neshaminy, Samuel and John Blair at New Londonderry, Samuel Finley at Nottingham, and Robert Smith at Pequea were all leaders in the New Side faction of the Presbyterian church, which left the synod of Philadelphia from 1741 to 1758. Together, the New Side academies filled an important role in the training of ministers to serve

---

1. "The Quaker and the Presbyterian Preacher: A True Story—Extracted from the History of the Westminster Presbytery," *The Presbyterian* (June 2, 1927): 9. The denouement to the story concerns the cow. Smith was given his choice from the Quaker's herd, and modestly chose the least-likely looking beast. The fact that it turned out to be the most valuable animal on the Quaker's farm suggested that in this instance, Smith was playing Abraham to the Quaker's Lot.

the rapidly expanding population of the Pennsylvania backcountry. At the same time, the academies' instructors worked out an approach to enlightened learning which affected both the process of theological education and the progress of the Enlightenment in the middle colonies.

The prospect of our discussing Enlightenment among the intellectual heirs of William Tennent would have puzzled his brethren on the Old Side of the Presbyterian schism. Born in the controversy over ministerial qualifications, the New Side academies were subject to ridicule, which even in its mildest forms centered on a questioning of academic standards.[2] Despite their critics' claims to the contrary, the Presbyterian academies offered a curriculum rich in the "new learning"—a point which has led more recent historians to concede that instruction at the academies was "critical of learning, but not contemptuous."[3] When the Synod of Philadelphia formed standing committees to ensure that candidates (and their examiners in Presbytery) were "well-skilled in the several Branches of Philosophy and Divinity and the Languages," the Tennents were among those who approved the measure "by a great majority."[4] Subsequently, at the New Side academies this demand was taken seriously. While Gilbert Tennent railed against the abuses of mere "letter-learned Pharisees" in the church, he used the same sermon to recommend to prospective ministers the academy of his letter-learned father.[5]

In some sense, both the revival and the Enlightenment addressed the same very old questions about the nature of human knowledge and the interaction between the created world and the divine voice that had called it into being. Those involved in the training of ministerial candidates were particularly pressed to find answers. As an intellectual community, the New Side leaders clearly saw much of their own authority in terms of their skill in the "several branches of philosophy." It is also true that the imperatives of the revival bent natural philosophy to evangelical purpose. This meant that the instructors at the academies judged the claims of enlightened science by the standards of a quickened faith; they would never have contemplated the reverse. With the Age of Reason they made no compromise. Their approach to the new learning ensured that the goals of Enlightenment would be consumed within the refining fires of conversion.

---

2. For one example of this kind of criticism of William Tennent, see *An Examination and Refutation of Mr. Gilbert Tennent's Remarks on the Protestation &c* (Philadelphia, 1742), 13.

3. Douglas Sloan, *The Scottish Enlightenment and the American College Ideal* (New York: Teacher's College Press, 1971), 52. See also Patricia Bonomi, *Under the Cope of Heaven: Religion, Society and Politics in Colonial America* (New York: Oxford University Press, 1986), 140–45; Glenn T. Miller, "God's Light and Man's Enlightenment: Evangelical Theology of Colonial Presbyterianism," *Journal of Presbyterian History* 51 (1973): 97–115.

4. Minutes of the Presbyterian Church in America, 1706–1788, ed. Guy S. Klett (Philadelphia: Presbyterian Historical Society, 1976), 291.

5. Gilbert Tennent, *The Dangers of an Unconverted Ministry* (Boston, 1742).

The strain of evangelical Calvinism, which dominated the New Side academies, was not unique. It had a strong corollary, for instance, in the work of Jonathan Edwards. Yet in terms of its effect on the course of enlightened thinking, this view enjoyed greater cultural significance in the middle colonies than in other places. Clustered about the scientific capital of Philadelphia, the Presbyterian academies were attuned to the possibilities proffered by the city's burgeoning scientific Enlightenment. Much of the character of Philadelphia's Enlightenment—particularly its openness to the sceptical method of Scottish science and its infusing ideas of progress with an evangelical zeal—can be traced to the New Side academies. By the 1760s, the center of Presbyterian theological education in the middle colonies had shifted from the academies to the College of New Jersey. Nonetheless, in those important years from the founding of William Tennent's small school to the reunion of Old and New Sides in the Synod of New York and Philadelphia, the academies built a wide circle of influence.

II

The Tennents' familiarity with the materials of the scientific Enlightenment reaches back to William Tennent's education at the University of Edinburgh in the 1690s. The timing is important. While the university did not shift from regents to a professorial system until 1708, the 1690s saw the old system of teaching enlivened by new texts and ideas.[6] Tennent would surely have sensed a change. Reworking their dictations to accommodate Descartes, Newton, and Boyle, the progressive Edinburgh regents spent the last decade of the seventeenth century laying the epistemological and theoretical foundations for the Scottish Enlightenment. The intellectual ferment of the period was part of William Tennent's inheritance. It was applied both in his sermons and in his teaching, as evidenced by the work of his four sons, all of whom were educated by their father.

It is equally important to remember Gilbert Tennent's theological studies at Yale. Although his degree, awarded in 1725, was an honorary M.A., Gilbert Tennent's time at Yale in the winter of 1724 to 25 certainly provided the opportunity to read and to reflect on the implications of enlightened learning for his newly chosen life as a gospel minister.[7] There is also evi-

---

6. Christine Shepherd, "University Life in the Seventeenth Century"; Eric G. Forbes, "Philosophy and Science Teaching in the Seventeenth Century," both in *Four Centuries: Edinburgh University Life, 1583–1983*, ed. Gordon Donaldson (Edinburgh: Edinburgh University Press, 1983); Roger Emerson, "Science and Moral Philosophy in the Scottish Enlightenment," in *Studies in the Philosophy of the Scottish Enlightenment*, ed. M. A. Stewart (Oxford: Oxford University Press, 1990), 11–36.

7. James Logan to James Greenshields, 2 January 1725, printed in *Documentary History of William Tennent and the Log College*, ed. Thomas C. Pears and Guy Klett, *Journal of Presbyterian History* 1950, 56–57; *Catalogue of the Officers and Graduates of Yale University in Connecticut, 1701–1924* (New Haven: Yale University Press, 1924), 571.

dence to suggest that his association with the college brought him into contact with Jonathan Edwards, who was a tutor from 1724 to 26. The prospect of Tennent's having known Edwards well before the revival of the 1730s invites a more thorough investigation of the link between their ideas. While it is difficult to establish the exact lines of influence, it is clear that the Tennents, and through them the other New Side leaders, came to adopt the epistemological stance toward the Enlightenment most commonly associated with Edwards. They shared Edwards' sense of the divine mystery pervading all natural processes—even those things which appeared on the surface to follow mechanical laws—and his insistence on the contingency of natural phenomena. Tennent's public alliance with Edwards and the private admiration for his scholarly life came to fruition, as we will see, in Tennent's commitment to the Enlightenment as Edwards had defined it and used it to his own ends.[8]

The development of New Side sermons and teaching is a further measure of the Tennents' engagement with the culture of Enlightenment. Their body of work, from William Tennent's oldest extant sermon preached in 1706 through the lecture notes used by Robert Smith between 1752 and 1790, indicates that natural philosophy and the study of its metaphysical and epistemological foundations supplemented training in divinity and classical languages, just as natural philosophy became increasingly important at the same time in other colonial colleges, in the English dissenting academies, and in the Scottish universities. The most complete record of the academies' teaching is found in the lectures of Robert Smith. By the time Smith took up his place in the academies' chain of influence (1752), a generation of New Side learning had accumulated. His students at Pequea discussed natural philosophy (Newton, Boyle, and Descartes); natural history (Buffon and Linnaeus); epistemology (Malebranche, Locke, Berkeley, Hume, and Reid), as well as elements of physiology and medicine. Smith's treatment of these subjects was both informed and critical. The New Side ministers valued these lessons not only because, as Smith pointed out, "the varnish of knowledge was an ornament to youth," but because they wanted to avoid what the Synod of Philadelphia had called the "formidable Train of sad Consequences" attending professional ignorance.[9] Smith linked progress of the revival to the planting of "schools of learning in the wilderness"; both would work together to bring the precious truths of Christ to "the poor people that sat in darkness."

8. Gilbert Tennent, "Eulogy on Jonathan Edwards," *Pennsylvania Gazette*, 6 (April 1758); "Prefatory Attestation" to Jonathan Dickinson's *A Display of God's Special Grace* (Philadelphia, 1743); *Jonathan Edwards: Scientific and Philosophical Writings*, ed. Wallace Anderson (New Haven: Yale University Press, 1980), 46.

9. Minutes of the Presbyterian Church in America, 291.

III

"The most likely method to stock the Church with a faithful ministry," Gilbert Tennent wrote, was to encourage "pious and experienced youths" to attend "private schools of the prophets." Tennent expected that the theological training in such places would differ from that offered by the traditional colleges not in content, but in evangelical emphasis. For guidance in the interpretation of natural philosophers' claims, the New Side leaders had only to look to the *Institutes of the Christian Religion.* Calvin recommended a diligent study of the natural world, even though the fallen powers of reason could offer only a "bare apprehension" of things. The place of natural philosophy in the training of a Presbyterian ministry was determined in part by Calvinist tradition, in part by particular circumstance.[10]

From the beginning, the fate of the new learning at the academies was bound up with the Tennents' willingness to use the terms of the science of the human mind to describe the operations of grace. In his earliest sermons, William Tennent emphasized the psychological connections among preaching, hearing, and conversion. For Tennent, it was important to distinguish between "external instruction"—the kind of knowledge derived from sensory impressions—and "Internal instruction"—the empowering or sanctifying of those impressions by the Spirit of God.[11] This position was strongly rooted in Reformed theology and was soon to be given a more complete American expression in the work of Jonathan Edwards. Like Edwards, William Tennent argued that reason was not really a separate faculty of the mind. Nonetheless, to speak of discrete stages in the transformation from external to internal instruction—from the spoken word to the ear, to the understanding, then to the will—made sense of an otherwise mysterious business. It was, as Robert Smith would later write, a matter of using an "assemblage of metaphors" to describe divine truth in human terms. The process of conversation was thought to restore the universal harmony "of all the soul's faculties first established by the God of order." That sense of unity was best conveyed by referring to true religious experience as "affective knowledge."[12]

Perhaps more striking was the definition of the new birth as a restoration of the powers of reason. Set in these terms, the question of natural philosophy's place in theological education was really part of a wider dialogue in which both the awakened and the enlightened participated. What were the

10. John Calvin, *Institutes of the Christian Religion,* trans. Henry Beveridge (London: James Clarke and Co., 1962), 1: 51–52.

11. William Tennent, sermon on unbelief, 1706; sermon on God's teaching, 1729, MS, Presbyterian Historical Society, Philadelphia.

12. John Blair, "Essay on Regeneration," in *Sermons by the Tennents and their Contemporaries,* compiled by Samuel Davies Alexander (Philadelphia, 1855).

limits of human knowledge and how seriously should we take arguments for the "reasonableness of Christianity"? One part of the New Side answer was to rework the language of moral science to accommodate a preoccupation with the nature of religious experience. Samuel Blair, for whom religion even in the midst of the Awakening was "solid and rational," said that the powers of reason required supernatural illumination—a "divine energy"—to restore their efficacy.[13] Accordingly, New Side sermons described the action of the Holy Spirit in conversation as a power which gave "lively impressions" to the mind of the convert, or as a physical energy which bridged the distance between object and observer to bring a "lively and affecting apprehension" of truth.

As historian Glenn T. Miller has pointed out, such language signaled that the Enlightenment and its powerful appeal to the reasonableness of humanity could be appropriated as a part of the revival.[14] If the New Side's insistence on a learned ministry and on the role of the rational powers in the conversion process guarded against the charge of enthusiasm, it was also designed to reclaim the psychology of the Enlightenment from the proponents of a rational religion. The Tennents' answer to the Deists was to seize the notion of the "reasonableness of Christianity" and define it in their own terms. Surely they understood the implications of Matthew Tindal's bold announcement that even the Holy Spirit "can't deal with men as rational creatures, but by proposing arguments to convince their understandings and influence their wills." The New Side countered by insisting that regeneration did not come through "moral suasion." Regeneration was a supernatural act, in which those things partially known through the "mere reports of the senses" were transformed into an affective understanding.[15] The rational powers were instruments which God deigned to use as part of an infinitely mysterious process. To say that they could be used as a means of grace in no way detracted from the mystery, nor did it mean that the standards of human reason were the measure of religious truth. It was simply a matter of God's harnessing the rational powers to achieve conversion.

The identification of the new birth with the renovation of reason opened the glorious prospect that study of the natural world might be an instrument through which the Spirit would reveal glimpses of God's character. Such a prospect was reason enough to encourage the contemplation of God's power in the natural order of things, not because the visible evidence of design was in some way necessary to prove God's existence, but because a careful attention to the marks of his glory might open mind and heart to a

---

13. Samuel Blair, *A Short and Faithful Narrative, of the Late Remarkable Revival of Religion in the Congregation of New-Londonderry, and Other Parts of Pennsylvania* (Philadelphia, 1744).
14. Miller, "God's Light and Man's Enlightenment," 115.
15. Matthew Tindal, *Christianity as Old as the Creation* (London, 1731), 179.

work of the Spirit. The proper stance toward nature was a constant reminder of the efficacy of grace alone, in the natural world, and in the moral universe. Smith made the connection explicit: "For it is by the almighty power upholding the frame of nature, and keeping all its springs in tune, that we are enabled to perform natural actions; so it is only by the Holy Spirit's maintaining and exciting the principle of grace implanted in us that we can perform spiritual actions."[16] Perhaps more than any other branch of learning, natural science could encourage an appropriate posture of humility before the power of God, and an aesthetic appreciation for the visible intimations of his glory and love. The transforming moment in which grace broke through the formal structures of study is suggested in Samuel Finley's poetic praise of Samuel Blair, who, we are told, studied the mysteries of Newtonian physics "'til cold Philosophy at length refin'd/ kindled to warm devotion in his mind."[17]

In the same spirit, Smith's students, versed in the Linnean system of classification and in the works of Buffon, were taught to appreciate the marks of design—the "large and legible characters" in nature which told of God's attributes. They were not expected to find in natural history the proof of things already known through faith. They were encouraged to use such study as part of an "elaborate religious ritual" which might issue in an aesthetic experience of grace.[18]

The distinction between this sort of "lively understanding" and "bare speculative knowledge" was sharpened by the revival's emphasis on the new birth. It reminded the New Side educators that the work of natural philosophers, unless transformed by grace, was concerned only with the "knowledge of externals" and said little about the essence of things. Similarly, the revival's debate about means and grace, human preparation and divine sovereignty, sharpened the New Side interest in conveying to ministerial candidates a proper sense of God's absolute power. All natural actions and all moral actions were but the effects of divine influence, which kept the frame of nature in tune even as it moved mind and heart toward conversion. An overemphasis on second causes in scientific systems might draw attention away from the immediate power of God. The result would be the natural philosopher's equivalent of the Arminian heresy.

Both the distinction between internal and external knowledge and the recognition that natural phenomena were contingent on the will of God offered a critical vantage point from which to comment on the conclusions of natural philosophers. The best example is found in Robert Smith's assessment of

16. Robert Smith, "The Principle of Sin and Holiness," in Alexander, *Sermons,* 319.
17. Samuel Finley, *Faithful Ministers the Fathers of the Church* (Philadelphia, 1752).
18. D. L. LeMahieu, *The Mind of William Paley: A Philosopher and His Age* (Lincoln: University of Nebraska Press, 1976), 31–53. LeMahieu argues that eighteenth-century natural theology served as religious ritual rather than as an apologetic or an attempt to prove rationally the existence of God.

Newton. Smith was drawn to the nonmechanical possibilities of Newton's natural philosophy. In his own work, Newton had posited the existence of "active principles"—the forces of attraction, gravity and the aether—which occupied an ontological position somewhere between the reality of God and the mundane world of matter and motion. For Newton, the active principles were the agents of the will of God in some immediate sense and were, therefore, not bound by mechanical laws, even though they might appear to act that way on the surface.[19] Smith recognized that the powers of attraction and the force of gravity had served an explanatory purpose in Newton's system, and that they were not propositions to be proven, but only useful hypotheses which could bear no further enquiry. They were important, however, because they represented what Smith called a "perpetual influx" of God's active powers.

Consequently, Smith taught Newton's laws of matter and motion, while entirely rejecting a mechanistic interpretation of those laws. He even went so far as to criticize Boyle and Newton for not having been clearer about the place of God in their systems of natural philosophy. He suggested that the English natural philosophers had been preoccupied with answering Descartes and had left their work open to misinterpretation in other ways. Smith rejected the oft-made comparison between the creator of the universe and a human artisan. The whole analogy was flawed, he argued, since God "cannot be absent from his works or an idle spectator of the universe and consequently by the perfection of his nature is incapable of enjoying that imaginary honour which these great men would attribute to him, viz., that of being absent from his workmanship and leaving it wholly to itself."[20]

It is important to note that while Smith was cautious toward Descartes and Malebranche because he thought their view seemed to deny the existence of material bodies as second causes, he was nonetheless close to their occasionalist position in other ways. "As the several parts of the successive existence of nature have no necessary connection with each other," Smith wrote, "therefore the continuance of the divine will must concur to the support or continuance of their existence."[21] If we are looking for similarities between the New Side foundations of natural philosophy and the thought of Edwards, the use of occasionalism as an evangelical strategy seems an obvious point of contact. Smith and the Tennents agreed with Edwards that the very springs of cause and effect, as John Blair pointed out, "always depend on the

---

19. The relationship between Newtonian voluntarism and the "active principles" is discussed in P. M. Heimann, "Voluntarism and Immanence: Conceptions of Nature in Eighteenth-Century British Thought," *Journal of the History of Ideas* 39 (1978): 271–82; J. E. McGuire, "Force, Active Principles and Newton's Invisible Realm," *Ambix* 15 (1968): 198–202.

20. Robert Smith, lectures on Metaphysics, MS, n.d., Presbyterian Historical Society.

21. Ibid.

divine pleasure. Means are effectual or ineffectual as he affords or withholds his concurrence."[22]

When applied in the New Side schools, this position created what I can only describe as a cheerful scepticism toward the fruits of human enquiry. How could we know anything of the natural world, given the contingency of even those things designated as the "laws of nature"? The problem was compounded by the obvious shortcomings of human reason—a power easily confounded, as William Tennent put it. We know nothing about the real causes of things, despite the efforts we might make to build up our "knowledge of externals."[23] In a similar vein, Gilbert Tennent reminded his enlightened audience at Philadelphia's Second Presbyterian Church that there would always be an extraordinary contrast between the "perfect intuition" belonging to the mind of God, and the knowledge of creatures "who can but guess and conjecture at things to come, according to the present appearances and probable tendencies of things."[24]

In drawing attention to the contingency of cause and effect and to the insufficiency of reason, the Tennents and their circle struck a Calvinist parallel to the scepticism of David Hume. Hume had also been quick to point out that "human blindness and weakness is the result of all our philosophy, and meets us at every turn, in spite of our endeavors to elude or avoid it."[25] And like the Scottish sceptics, the New Side leaders viewed the conclusions of natural philosophers in this light. The nature of human understanding dictated that we must construct a kind of imperfect knowledge from the "Images or Ideas of things" and from "deductions or reasonings about them." As Gilbert Tennent said, "It is the weakness of our understandings that renders these measures necessary."[26]

Thus, the key to the New Side's aggressive appropriation of enlightened learning was to recognize the hypothetical character of the scientific enterprise. The conclusions of natural philosophers were certainly treated this way in Smith's lectures. If we think back to his discussion of Newtonian forces, for instance, we find a willingness to see attraction and gravity as hypothetical parts of a scientific system. Science could hold practical consequences, and was to be valued for its tendency to counter what Smith called a "narrowness of mind." It was, nonetheless, constrained by its very defini-

22. John Blair, "An Essay on the Means of Grace," in Alexander, *Sermons,* 207. On Edwards' occasionalism, see Norman Fiering, "The Rationalist Foundations of Jonathan Edwards' Metaphysics," in *Jonathan Edwards and the American Experience* ed. Nathan Hatch and Harry Stout (New York: Oxford University Press, 1988), 73–101.
23. William Tennent, untitled sermon, 30 February 1731, MS, Presbyterian Historical Society.
24. Gilbert Tennent, *Twenty-Three Sermons upon the Chief End of Man, the Divine Authority of the Sacred Scriptures, the Being and Attributes of God, and the Doctrine of the Trinity* (Philadelphia, 1744), 187–89.
25. David Hume, *Enquiry Concerning Human Understanding* (Edinburgh, 1748), sect. IV, part 1.
26. Tennent, *Twenty-Three Sermons,* 187–89.

tion as a human activity in a fallen world. The evangelical, natural philosopher, then, had free access to the scientific method, but no pretensions about
its self-sufficiency. Smith told his pupils that "philosophy, when divested of
pride, affectation, deceit, and sophistry may be very usefully employed for in-
vestigating the laws of nature and the rules of life, so far as these are discov-
erable by reason."[27] Surely this was an evangelical Calvinist's view, focused
on the heart of the participant and hedged about with the hard realities of
human frailty.

The effect of this epistemology was to undercut the claims of a secular Enlightenment, even as it encouraged the pursuit of enlightened learning within
an evangelical context. To borrow from a sermon title of the younger William Tennent, God's sovereignty was no impediment to the natural philosopher's striving. In fact, an attitude of scepticism prevented the very reliance
upon unaided reason which was the mark of Deism, and which offered no
comfort, as the Tennents were quick to point out. In contrast, the New Side
approach to science freed students to explore the possibilities of the new scientific method without fear that this kind of contingent or probable knowledge could alter the affective truths of religious experience. For Smith, the
building of scientific systems on the foundation of "obscure ideas" and uncertain conclusions could work to human advantage. Sorting through such
obstacles actually developed finer qualities of mind and heart which might
have been neglected otherwise. Ministers and the laity alike were encouraged
to see this side of enlightened progress. The willingness to "act upon probable truths and to act wisely and providentially upon obscure ideas" made
room in the Tennents' intellectual world for the sceptical method of texts
such as Pierre Bayle's *Historical and Philosophical Dictionary*. Gilbert Tennent recommended Bayle's *Dictionary* ("a work equally instructive and de-
lightful") and was pleased to "own the mistery" [sic] of divine sovereignty
which he found acknowledged there.[28]

IV

The recognition that the materials of science were confined to the "present
appearances and probable tendencies of things" was an extension of the theology of the Great Awakening. But through the personal connections between New Side leadership and the enlightened culture of Philadelphia, the
lessons of the academies were applied in other settings, and in ways which
must have pleased the Tennents and their New Side friends. The academies
were soon accommodating students with professional aspirations outside the
ministry. Once established in Philadelphia, the academies' graduates found

27. Smith, lectures of Logic, MS, n.d., Presbyterian Historical Society.
28. Tennent's recommendation of Bayle is in his *Divine Government Over All Considered* (Philadelphia, 1752).

themselves not only under the continued influence of an evangelical approach to science, but possessed of the practical resources to make something of it.

There were particularly strong ties between the Tennents and Philadelphia's medical community.[29] The New Side interest in the progress of medicine centered on the relationship of spiritual trial to physical affliction. The calling of a physician was widely regarded with a reverence otherwise reserved for ministers of the gospel. It is then not surprising that the appearance of evangelical Calvinism in a scientific setting is most obvious in the work of men like John Redman, the first alumnus of the Tennents' school to apply a theological education to the study of medicine. To Redman, both fields of study were equally rooted in the circumstances of a fallen world. He brought to his enlightened medical practice the language and imperatives of religious awakening.[30] In the process of physical healing, he saw divine agency bringing human aspirations into line with the will of God, and directing human action toward the practice of true virtue.

Throughout his long career, including his duties as the first president of the College of Physicians of Philadelphia, Redman maintained a sceptical approach to human knowledge. The properly trained physician, while ineffective on his own, might prepare for physical healing in the patient much as a minister prepared for a work of grace in the heart of the prospective convert. While he encouraged his students of medicine to avail themselves of the best enlightened science had to offer them, he was not so sanguine as to believe that the enlightened physician had more answers than questions. The powers of human reason, he wrote "were neither to be depreciated, nor depended upon too much."[31]

The philosophical scepticism of the academies had a profound effect on the scientific work of other Presbyterian students like Benjamin Rush and the younger William Shippen. In particular, it seems to have prepared them to accept most readily the sceptical approach to the scientific method taken by their professors of medicine in Edinburgh. When William Cullen, professor of chemistry and of the practice of physics, urged his American students to assign causal relationships in medical theory on the grounds of constant con-

---

29. The Tennents' interest in medicine is reflected in Gilbert Tennent's early contemplation of a medical career, and in his brother William Tennent's "pointed attention to the particular circumstances and situation of the afflicted, either in body or mind" among the members of his congregation. Other connections between the Tennents and Philadelphia's medical community include the younger William Tennent's sons, John Van Brugh Tennent, who studied medicine in Edinburgh and Leyden, and Gilbert, who caught a fever and died while inoculating patients against smallpox. See Elias Boudinot, *Memoirs of the Life of the Reverend William Tennent* (Wilmington, Ohio, 1815).

30. A good example of Redman's blending of medicine and piety is found in his *Inaugural Address to the College of Physicians, Philadelphia* (Philadelphia, 1887).

31. John Redman to Benjamin Rush, 25 June 1802, MS, Rush Correspondence 22: 20, Library Company of Philadelphia.

junction rather than on the grounds of necessary connection, he unwittingly appealed to an evangelical sensibility. When he pointed out that scientific hypotheses were human constructs which do not make claims to ultimate truth, he made an argument familiar to those reared on the notion that human knowledge, for all its practical possibilities, could not be trusted.[32]

In the scientific work of Rush, the meeting of evangelical Calvinism and Scottish scepticism produced a powerful form of Christian Enlightenment. Cullen's use of hypotheses—his cultivation of a "slow-consenting academic doubt"—seemed to Rush to be the natural outcome of the mind's trying to stumble beyond the confines of sense experience toward a "distant resemblance" of divine knowledge. While reason did not presume to reach those secret springs of cause and effect known only to God, it could yield the best practical results in a world fallen from grace. As Rush told his students in physiology at the College of Philadelphia, truth was the perception of things as they appeared to the mind of an, as yet, inscrutable God. It would remain inaccessible to us, and yet our constitution dictated that we use the creative power of the mind to draw facts and ideas together in meaningful patterns for the moment.[33] By insisting that the best scientific hypotheses were those which left us "prostrate at the footstool of divine power," Rush turned the goals of the Enlightenment to evangelical purposes. Indeed, without its religious foundations, Rush wrote, the search for Enlightenment would be as "fruitless as the search for the philosopher's stone."[34]

V

The New Side leaders, likewise, tried to bring enlightened learning within the scope of their work for "our dear Lord's kingdom." Their identification of theological education and the progress of the revival invites comparison with the Old Side position. Both Francis Alison and John Ewing, who taught metaphysics and natural philosophy, respectively, at the College of Philadelphia, shared New Side scepticism. Although Alison tried to incorporate as much natural history and natural philosophy as he could in his lessons at his New London academy, he worried that "our Philosophers are too sanguine and draw too universal conclusions from their experiments that are too few

32. William Cullen's friendship with Hume and his commitment to Hume's philosophical scepticism is discussed in John P. Wright, "Metaphysics and Physiology: Mind, Body, and the Animal Economy in Eighteenth-Century Scotland," in Stewart, *Scottish Enlightenment,* 251–301; Arthur Donovan, *Philosophical Chemistry in the Scottish Enlightenment* (Edinburgh University Press, 1979), 59–60; J. J. R. Christie, "Ether and the Science of Chemistry: 1740–1790," in *Conceptions of Ether: Studies in the History of Ether Theory, 1740–1900,* ed. G. N. Cantor and M. S. J. Hodge (Cambridge: Cambridge University Press, 1981), 85–110.

33. Benjamin Rush, lectures on the mind, n.d., MS, Rush Papers, College of Physicians of Philadelphia.

34. Rush to Noah Webster, 20 July 1798, in *Letters of Benjamin Rush,* ed. L. H. Butterfield (Princeton: Princeton University Press, 1951), 2: 799.

to sustain their Fabricks."[35] However, without the same focus on the new birth as his evangelical brethren, Alison valued natural science for his own reasons. He praised science for its encouraging of "forbearance and moderation and benevolence." He said little about its relationship to the process of conversion. Old and New Side educators held similar views on the scientific Enlightenment, but were separated by their expectations about its theological uses.

With the reunion of Old and New Sides came the hastening of changes which had already pushed the academies beyond their peak. The schools at Neshaminy and Fagg's Manor more or less died away with their founders, although John Blair kept up his brother's school before moving on to a professorship at the College of New Jersey. Faced with the growing popularity of the College of New Jersey among ministerial candidates, Finley's academy operated as a grammar school rather than as a school for theological education. Only Smith's academy—a second-generation school of the prophets— continued to function as both an academy and as a training ground for ministers who often returned to Smith after taking degrees elsewhere. But the approach to science cultivated at the academies reached far beyond the debate about a qualified ministry which had engendered it.

The story of enlightened science at the New Side academies has much to tell us about the relationship between evangelicalism and Enlightenment. In particular, it raises the intriguing possibility that this relationship was played out quite differently in the American setting where the cultural prominence of the New Side leaders made their ideas influential in circles outside the immediate reach of school and pulpit. Again we are reminded of the importance of Calvinism, which operated here much as it did among the natural and moral philosophers of the Scottish Enlightenment.[36] In this respect, the New Side example also presents an interesting foil to the process described in D. W. Bebbington's work on the Tennents' English contemporaries. These evangelicals, Bebbington argues, shared the Enlightenment's optimism and applied the standards of the new scientific method—with its confidence in the certainty of sense experience—to religious belief.[37] In contrast, while our friends on the New Side were prepared to use the language and lessons of natural science as a practical guide, they were ever reluctant to speak of certainties. They mistrusted the "mere reports of the senses." They wrote of obscure

35. Francis Alison to Ezra Stiles, 14 March 1762, MS, Alison Papers, Presbyterian Historical Society.

36. Roger Emerson, "Natural Philosophy and the Scottish Enlightenment," *Studies in Voltaire and the Eighteenth Century* 242 (1986): 243–91; "Calvinism in the Scottish Enlightenment," in *Literature in Context*, ed. Joachim Scwend et al. (Frankfurt: Peter Lang, 1992), 19–28; Steward Sutherland, "The Presbyterian Inheritance of Hume and Reid," in *Origins and Nature of the Scottish Enlightenment*, ed. R. H. Campbell and A. S. Skinner (Edinburgh: Edinburgh University Press, 1982), 131–49.

37. D. W. Bebbington, *Evangelicalism in Modern Britain* (London: Unwin Hyman, 1989), 53–74.

ideas cast as obstacles to human understanding, of probable conclusions and the apprehension of partial truths. In the end they imparted these characteristic modes of thought to the enlightened world around them.

The Christian Enlightenment of the academies was never bound to the fate of arguments for rational religion. Consequently, it held no irony for its followers, and remained curiously separate from the version of Christian Enlightenment promoted by John Witherspoon at the College of New Jersey. While Witherspoon's encouragement of enlightened science in the college curriculum was intended to serve a religious purpose, his use of the Enlightenment had little scepticism about it. Unlike the Tennents, he placed considerable confidence in the fruits of moral and natural philosophy.[38] Ultimately, through the influence of students such as Redman and Rush, it was the non-denominational College of Philadelphia, and not the College of New Jersey, which inherited the evangelical Calvinist stance toward enlightened learning.

The New Side program of theological education thus reached its greatest cultural power outside the ministry, in a wider intellectual context. If a well-trained minister were to enhance the power of the evangelical message, what could be more appropriate than to reach out to the secular prophets of enlightened progress and beat them at their own game? The identification of the evangelical impulse with enlightened science was perfected in episodes such as that noted in Rush's commonplace book: A student was converted from Deism to Christianity, not by a sermon, but by Rush's lectures in physiology.[39] There is an appealing symmetry about all of this. The path leading from the theological academies to the College of Philadelphia—an institution which by 1765 was the epitome of enlightened education in the American colonies—marks the success of the New Side effort to lay claim to the scientific Enlightenment in the name of Christ.

38. Mark A. Noll, *Princeton and the Republic, 1768–1822* (Princeton: Princeton University Press, 1989) thoroughly discusses the fate of the Christian Enlightenment at the College of New Jersey, and the irony of its consequences.

39. Rush, *Autobiography of Benjamin Rush—His "Travels Through Life" Together With His Commonplace Book for 1789–1813*, ed. George W. Corner (Princeton: Princeton University Press, 1948), 291.

11

Spurgeon and British Evangelical Theological Education

David W. Bebbington

During the ministry of Charles Haddon Spurgeon, between the 1850s and the 1890s, three broad trends impinged on theological education among evangelicals in Britain. The first trend was for theology to become more liberal. The Calvinistic doctrinal system inherited from the past by Anglicans, Scottish Presbyterians, and the Dissenters of England and Wales was in an advanced state of decay. Looking to the Bible alone as their source book, evangelicals increasingly dismissed the Puritan legacy as an unnecessary additional burden. "Make your own system" was the constant advice to trainee ministers of Spurgeon's fellow Baptist James Acworth, the president of the Horton Academy around the middle of the nineteenth century.[1] Although the great majority of ministers educated in institutions discarding Calvinism retained a firm grasp of central evangelical beliefs, a few began to be touched by currents of more advanced teaching sweeping in from Germany. Three students were dismissed from the Congregationalist New College for unorthodoxy in 1851, four from the Baptist Regent's Park College in 1874.[2] Doubts began to surface about the views of some of the teachers. Samuel Davidson was forced to resign from the Lancashire Independent College in 1857 for holding broad opinions on biblical inspiration, and the most famous episode occurred when, in the years around 1880, William Robertson Smith was censured and then dismissed by the Free Church of Scotland for

---

1. William Medley, *Rawdon Baptist College: Centenary Memorial* (London: Kingsgate Press, 1904), 26.
2. R. Tudur Jones, *Congregationalism in England, 1662–1962* (London: Independent Press, 1962), 261; R. E. Cooper, *From Stepney to St. Giles: The Story of Regent's Park College, 1810–1960* (London: Carey Kingsgate Press, 1960), 64.

teaching German biblical criticism.[3] The Calvinistic framework of theology had been generally abandoned and its orthodox content, especially in relation to the Bible, now seemed to be called in question. The tide was flowing in a liberal direction.[4]

The second trend was for society to become more respectable. Industrial and commercial success created wealth in unprecedented abundance. Rising standards of living, even for the working classes, meant that order and decorum were more highly prized than in an earlier age. Increasingly middle-class families moved from the overcrowded urban centers to the newly erected suburbs where they could live in dignified seclusion. A tangible sign of the new spirit of the age among the Nonconformists, as Dissenters now preferred to call themselves, was the growing taste for new chapels to be erected, not as plain meeting houses but in the Gothic style of traditional parish churches.[5] In 1857 the Baptists' premier theological college transferred from an unhealthy spot in Stepney to a magnificent mansion in Regent's Park. The new building, Holford House, was a striking classical edifice complete with a central portico, urns at intervals on the balustrade and pavilions at the end of each wing. It was opened with a prayer meeting in the ballroom.[6] Theological colleges were clearly moving with the times. A new generation of the upward, socially mobile would be well satisfied that pastoral training took place in such elegant surroundings. A more urbane constituency had higher expectations of the colleges.

The combined effect of the theological and social trends was to make ministerial education more academic. Fresh doctrinal approaches had to be evaluated, even if it was hoped that they would be rejected, and rising social aspirations created a demand for more scholarly preaching. Although spiritual qualifications for the ministry were chief, conceded Benjamin Godwin at Horton's jubilee in 1854, they were not sufficient: "Qualifications of an intellectual character are needed, the power both of acquiring and imparting knowledge."[7] As the barriers to academic achievement by nonmembers of the Church of England at Oxford and Cambridge were steadily dismantled during the Victorian years, even the scholarship of the ancient English universities began to seem within the grasp of the Nonconformists. The trend

3. Jones, *Congregationalism*, 254–56; J. S. Black and G. W. Chrystal, *The Life of William Robertson Smith* (London: Adam and Charles Black, 1912), chaps. 5–10.

4. For an account of the liberalizing trend as a whole, chiefly within the Church of England, see B. M. G. Reardon, *Religious Thought in the Victorian Age: A Survey from Coleridge to Gore* (London: Longman, 1980); and for its impact on Nonconformity, M. T. E. Hopkins, "Baptists, Congregationalists, and Theological Change: Some Late Nineteenth-Century Leaders and Controversies" (Oxford D. Phil. diss., 1988).

5. Clyde Binfield, *So Down to Prayers: Studies in English Nonconformity, 1780–1820* (London: J. M. Dent & Sons, 1977), chap. 7.

6. *Baptist Magazine* (Nov. 1856): 678; Cooper, *From Stepney to St. Giles,* 58, 61.

7. J. O. Barrett, *Rawdon College: A Short History* (London: Carey Kingsgate Press, 1954), 48.

culminated in 1889 with the opening in Oxford of Mansfield College, a permanent private hall of the university that gave Congregationalists facilities for ministerial training and theological research.[8] The marked growth in the number of universities at this period meant that more evangelical Nonconformists could enjoy the distinction of a degree. Whereas in 1870 only 1 percent of Spurgeon's colleagues in the Baptist ministry were university trained, by 1901 the proportion had risen to 8 percent.[9] Stepney College had affiliated in 1841 to London University so that its students could participate in its arts courses; Horton followed its example ten years later.[10] Theological degrees, however, were still available only to Anglicans, and so, in 1879, there was established a "Senatus Academicus" to grant diplomas in the subject to Nonconformist candidates for the ministry.[11] It was a significant milestone on the road by which theology was turning into an unquestionably academic subject. Here was a third major trend affecting the training of ministers during the Victorian epoch.

Spurgeon cast himself in the role of stalwart opponent of all three trends. In theology he was robustly conservative, cherishing Calvinistic teaching and upholding verbal inspiration. In the Down Grade Controversy (1887–88) he denounced what he saw as the erosion of cardinal truths among his fellow ministers, breaking with the Baptist Union on the issue. "To us," he explained, "it was an imperative necessity that we should have no fellowship with Universalists and other parties of the New School of Doctrine."[12] Spurgeon held, with some justice, that liberal tendencies in the ministry were associated with rising social aspirations in pew and pulpit. Congregations were flattered by allusions to recent or contemporary thinkers such as Strauss, Goethe, Comte, Renan, or "our home-bred heresy-spinners, such as Maurice and Huxley." Away, roared Spurgeon, with preachers of "this superfine order," "eminent personages" who affected gentlemanly ways in order to ape the manners of their betters. Social pretensions always attracted the scorn of this champion of the common man. Accordingly, he told the supporters of the college he founded, he aimed to produce "men of the people, who feel with them."[13] Its training was to be practical rather than literary, a down-to-earth affair rather

8. *Mansfield College, Oxford: Its Origin and Opening* (London: James Clarke & Co., 1890).
9. J. E. B. Munson, "The Education of Baptist Ministers, 1870–1900," *Baptist Quarterly* 26 (1976): 321.
10. Cooper, *From Stepney to St. Giles*, 51; Medley, *Rawdon Baptist College*, 29.
11. E. A. Payne, "The Development of Nonconformist Theological Education in the Nineteenth Century, with Special Reference to Regent's Park College," in *Studies in History and Religion*, ed. E. A. Payne (London: Lutterworth Press, 1942), 244.
12. *Annual Paper concerning the Lord's Work in Connection with the Pastors' College, Newington, London, 1887–88* [hereafter *AP*, although titles vary slightly], Spurgeon's College Archives London (London: Alabaster, Passmore & Sons, 1888), 6. I am grateful to the Reverends Ian Randall, Michael Nicholls, and J. J. Brown, and to John Brown and Judy Powles for help with the records of the college.
13. *AP, 1870*, 7–8.

than an imitation of Oxford or Cambridge. There would be no attempt to compete for scholarly distinctions or to turn theology from a vocational into an academic subject. Spurgeon was prepared to swim against the tide.

He was admirably fitted for his self-appointed task. Born in 1834, Spurgeon was the son of a coal yard clerk who was also a minister of the Independent denomination in the East Anglican heartland of the Old Dissent. Converted at fifteen, he turned to the Baptists and was baptized as a believer four months later. After a short while he was exercizing a fruitful ministry at the Baptist church in Waterbeach, near Cambridge. While there, in a celebrated incident, a misunderstanding prevented an interview with Joseph Angus, the president of Stepney College, and so Spurgeon was denied a formal theological education.[14] Soon he was feeling glad that he had avoided college, and he was pleased two years later to discover that the deacons of the famous New Park Street Church in London actually regarded it as a special recommendation that he was not a college man—since, as they put it, "you would not have much savour or unction if you came from College."[15] Spurgeon's vivid preaching almost immediately stirred the capital. Was this country lad with his untutored style and native wit a fraudulent impostor or a new St. Ambrose? The crowds thronging to hear him rapidly outgrew the old meeting house so that he temporarily occupied first the Exeter Hall in the Strand, the center of the evangelical world, and then, to the scandal of some, the Surrey Gardens Music Hall. Eventually, in 1861, the congregation settled permanently in the purpose-built Metropolitan Tabernacle, a vast auditorium with space for almost six thousand hearers. Over the thirty-one years until his death, Spurgeon at the Tabernacle was numbered among the sights of London. A female admirer, who in 1857 had thought the face attractive, "the square forehead and magnificent dark eyes redeeming it from ugliness, and every line of his face and figure speaking of power," admitted by 1865 that he had become "coarse-looking even to grossness, heavy in form and features." Yet, she added, "as soon as he spoke, one felt the same power was there and that the man himself was unchanged."[16] Spurgeon reigned from his platform over the English-speaking world, his weekly published sermons penetrating to distant corners of the globe. He was without doubt the greatest preacher of the age.

In one sense his college was Spurgeon's personal creation. For the first fifteen years of the institution's existence, the apostrophe in its title, Pastor's College, was placed before the *s*.[17] Nobody questioned the word of the pres-

14. Spurgeon to his father, 24 Feb. 1852, in *Letters of Charles Haddon Spurgeon*, ed. I. H. Murray (Edinburgh: Banner of Truth Trust, 1992), 35–7.

15. Spurgeon to his mother, Nov. 1852, and to his father, n.d., in *The Letters of Charles Haddon Spurgeon*, ed. Charles Spurgeon (London: Marshall Brothers, 1923), 42, 45.

16. [Mrs. F. Curtis], *Memories of a Long Life*, privately printed, n.p., 1912, 141, 145.

17. *Historical Tablets of the College founded by Charles Haddon Spurgeon in 1856 and first called the Pastor's College*, ed. G. W. Harte (Thomas Seddon, 1951), 7.

ident. Yet Spurgeon regularly insisted that the college was "no project of mine, it grew without sound of my axe or hammer."[18] It was rather, he claimed, an inevitable, organic development from his ministry, unpremeditated and providential. Certainly the institution evolved gradually from small beginnings. During 1855 one of the Tabernacle converts, T. W. Medhurst, received weekly tuition from Spurgeon in preparation for ministry. Recognizing the potential of such close personal influence over future pastors, Spurgeon began to look about for "another to be my dearly-beloved Timothy."[19] In 1856 the first pair of students lodged with George Rogers, an Independent minister already nearing the age of sixty, who was to remain as principal until his gradual retirement around 1880. By 1861, when the students moved for tuition from Rogers' home to the basement of the new Metropolitan Tabernacle, they numbered 16. Two years later they had mushroomed to 66. Numbers stabilized at around 100 in the 1870s and 1880s.[20] By the end of Spurgeon's life, a total of 863 men had been trained at the college, and they constituted over 50 percent of the Baptist ministers in England and Wales.[21] What were the distinctive features of this remarkable achievement? The theological stance, the social role, and the educational position of the college can usefully be reviewed in turn.

First, as George Rogers put it in a manifesto of 1867, "Calvinistic theology is dogmatically taught."[22] Although there were a few exceptions, Calvinistic views normally formed a prerequisite for admission to the college.[23] The Reformed theology professed there, however, was not of a fossilized or rigidly exclusive variety. Spurgeon accepted, for example, the novel but growing popular tenet that overseas mission was best pursued on the faith principle.[24] Although he questioned the accuracy of much of John Wesley's Arminianism, he readily conceded that Wesley's Methodist movement had brought out vital truths of the gospel.[25] John Clifford, the distinguished General Baptist exponent of Arminian teaching, was a guest lecturer at the college, as was William Landels, who upheld the non-Reformed brand of revivalist theology known as Morisonianism.[26] Spurgeon valued Calvinism less for itself than for its preservative power over basic convictions. "I cannot

18. *AP, 1872–3*, 3.

19. Spurgeon to Medhurst, 22 Sept. 1855, in *Letters,* ed. Murray, 61.

20. *Historical Tablets,* ed. Harte, 26; AP, *1880–81*, 5.

21. *AP, 1891–92*, 342; K. D. Brown, *A Social History of the Nonconformist Ministry in England and Wales, 1800–1930* (Oxford: Clarendon Press, 1988), 33.

22. *Outline of the Lord's Work by the Pastor's College and its Kindred Organisations at the Metropolitan Tabernacle* [hereafter *Outline*] (London: Passmore & Alabaster, 1867), 13.

23. *AP, 1882–83*, 47.

24. Brian Stanley, "C. H. Spurgeon and the Baptist Missionary Society, 1863–1866," *Baptist Quarterly* 29 (1982): 319–28.

25. *AP, 1870*, 5.

26. Clifford: *AP, 1873–4*, 9; *AP, 1876–7*, 15; Landels: *The Sword and the Trowel* [hereafter *S & T*] (Dec. 1865): 515. Spurgeon to Landels, n.d., in *Letters,* ed. Spurgeon, 194.

sever Evangelicalism," he told his ex-students in 1884, "from Calvinism."[27] Rogers, as principal, gave a weekly lecture lasting one and a half hours that in the course of two years covered the whole Calvinistic system.[28] Spurgeon's brother, James Archer, who became vice president of the college in the mid–1860s, and who had been forced out of his first charge at Southampton for preaching too Calvinistically, used the Puritan Stephen Charnock's treatise on the divine attributes extensively in his early instruction.[29] David Gracey, who succeeded Rogers as principal around 1880, carried on teaching from Elisha Cole's *Treatise upon Divine Sovereignty* (1673), "notwithstanding," as he put it, "his antiquated style and endless repetitions."[30] In the early years Spurgeon compiled a handbook of the doctrines of grace that was read in the college, and in 1868 republished Thomas Watson's *Body of Divinity* (1692) to show what theology was taught there.[31] Charnock was superseded in 1869 by A. A. Hodge's *Outline of Theology* (1860).[32] Gracey believed the *Systematic Theology* (1872–73) by A. A. Hodge's father Charles, the American Old School Presbyterian, to be a great work, but he awarded the palm in divinity to Jonathan Edwards. In his lectures on systematics, Gracey preferred Edwards' method to Hodge's and aligned himself with Edwards against Hodge on the seemingly recondite point of the order of guilt and depravity in the fallen state of mankind.[33] In the last resort, therefore, the Calvinism taught at the college, though definite and structured, was a moderate, experimental version more than a self-consistent, intellectual system.

The natural partner of Reformed theology was common sense philosophy. This school of metaphysics, exported from Scotland since the later eighteenth century and enormously influential throughout the English-speaking world, was essentially empirical, but it held that certain first principles have to be assumed. Gracey voiced this position when, in the introduction to his theological lectures, he concluded that "those self-evident truths which arise, not from experience, but from the constitution of our nature, are to be implicitly trusted."[34] Originally from Ulster, Gracey had imbibed Scottish philosophy at Glasgow University before pursuing theology at the Pastor's College.[35] Sir William Hamilton's *Lectures on Metaphysics,* the latest (though modified) restatement of the Scottish school's position, were added to the curriculum

27. *The Freeman* [hereafter *F*], 25 (Apr. 1884): 270.
28. *Outline,* 1867, 21.
29. G. Holden Pike, *James Archer Spurgeon, D.D. LL.D.* (London: Alexander & Shepheard, 1894), 79, 58–9; *Outline,* 1867, 28.
30. *AP, 1876–7,* 16; cf. *Outline,* 1867, 24; *AP, 1884–85,* 8.
31. *Outline,* 1867, 28. *Outline,* 1868, 4.
32. *Outline,* 1869, 10.
33. David Gracey, *Sin and the Unfolding of Salvation* (London: Passmore and Alabaster, 1894), 28, 109–10.
34. Ibid., 16.
35. *Outline,* 1869, 9.

in 1870 and thereafter formed the climax of the course in metaphysics.[36] Other texts used consistently in philosophy were *The Elements of Moral Science* (1834), by Francis Wayland, the Baptist president of Brown University, Rhode Island, and Bishop Butler's *Analogy of Religion* (1736), the staple of nineteenth-century apologetics.[37] But it was the Scottish intellectual framework within which other studies were pursued. "Every teacher," wrote Spurgeon, "should know the laws which govern the mind on which he is to operate."[38] It was assumed that Hamilton and his like taught indubitable axioms. It was not until immediately after Spurgeon's death that a course on the history of philosophy, encompassing Descartes, Spinoza, Locke, Berkeley, and Kant, was introduced.[39] For the first time students were introduced to the idea that notions of human intellectual powers had changed over time; but the tutor responsible for the course was on the staff for less than a year.[40] In Spurgeon's own day, and no doubt after the tutor's departure, the common sense position seemed not a transient phase in the history of philosophy, but an impregnable redoubt of the truth. It contrasted with the vagaries of continental thought, what Spurgeon called "the cloudland of metaphysics,"[41] that appeared to foster airy Germanic heresies. Common sense philosophy served as a handmaid to Christian doctrine.

The teachings grasped in college had to be passed on from the pulpit. Spurgeon wanted to ensure that his men were effective preachers. Since, as he believed, training could not produce the gift of utterance, he normally insisted that candidates admitted to the college should already possess experience of preaching for at least two years. Their pulpit ministry, he added, should have brought souls to Jesus and have proved acceptable to believers.[42] The chief medium of training was the sermon class, which in 1867 occupied the first hour on Thursday mornings. One student would preach; he would be criticized by his peers; and then a tutor would summarize from the chair.[43] By the 1880s this task was the responsibility of Frederick Marchant, a Pastor's College trainee who had taken over the basic classical curriculum from Gracey and who continued to serve as Baptist minister at Hitchin.[44] The college assessment book reveals that his judgments tended to be more generous than those of his colleagues, yet his criticisms were dreaded by the students.[45] Spurgeon himself was particularly dismissive of preachers who indulged in

36. *AP, 1870*, 19; *AP, 1877–8*, 40.
37. Wayland: *Outline*, 1867, 23; *AP, 1884–85*, 10; Butler: *AP, 1873–4*, 11; *AP, 1884–85*, 10.
38. *AP, 1886–87*, 7.
39. *AP, 1892–93*, 8.
40. The tutor was J. C. Ewing, subsequently a distinguished Baptist minister, *S & T* (1892), 334.
41. *AP, 1886–87*, 7.
42. *AP, 1870*, 13.
43. *Outline*, 1867, 21.
44. *AP, 1882–83*, 27.
45. J. C. Carlile, *My Life's Little Day* (London: Blackie & Son, 1935), 58.

histrionics, those who "drove their finger nails into the palms of their hands as if they were in convulsions of celestial ardour."[46] Reading of sermons was forbidden[47] and simplicity of style encouraged. In 1870 Spurgeon asserted that elocution classes were of dubious value since no instructor could teach in the absence of aptitude, but already rhetoric figured on the curriculum and within a couple of years elocution training became standard.[48] The college had a practical preoccupation with preparing communicators.

It also gave ample opportunity for putting the lessons learned into practice outside the institution. "Ministers discover how to preach by preaching," remarked Spurgeon, "even as men learn to swim by swimming."[49] Most weekends during the course were spent on pulpit engagements. Seniors, in particular, were often absent from courses on Mondays, when they were returning from their visits, and the less scrupulous knew how easy it was to gain exemption from a class on the plea of taking a service at a distance.[50] All entrants to the college had to promise to undertake any work for Christ allotted to them during their studies,[51] and, by strategic deployment of his manpower, Spurgeon planted a large number of new churches in London and the southeast of England. Already in 1870 he reported that roughly forty had been launched in the growing suburbs of the capital alone.[52] Spurgeon had in 1864 set up a Chapel Building Fund, with himself as treasurer and his deacons as generous donors, to supply loans for erecting places of worship where his students were preaching.[53] The college spawned other agencies to help with outreach. For a while there was a Home Visitation Society under whose auspices students delivered copies of Spurgeon's sermons to houses in assigned districts. A Pastors' College Society of Evangelists, begun in 1874 at the time of the visit of Moody and Sankey to Britain, supported traveling gospel preachers cast in their mold. One pair, J. Manton Smith and W. Y. Fullerton, proved particularly powerful. A Pioneer Mission, started by E. A. Carter toward the end of Spurgeon's lifetime, carried his technique of launching new causes into a subsequent generation. A Missionary Association, founded in about 1888, gathered funds for assisting Spurgeon's men called overseas but lacking support from a regular missionary society.[54] Each bore witness to the evangelistic dynamic of the college.

If Spurgeon was committed to Calvinistic doctrines and their proclamation, he was also attached to a particular social vision. Ministers, he insisted,

46. C. H. Spurgeon, *Lectures to my Students* (London: Marshall, Morgan & Scott, 1954), 50.
47. *Outline,* 1867, 15.
48. *AP, 1870,* 13; *Outline,* 1869, 11; *AP, 1872–3,* 10.
49. *AP, 1884–85,* 6.
50. *Outline,* 1867, 28; Carlile, *My Life's Little Day,* 58.
51. *AP, 1870,* 17.
52. Ibid., 16.
53. *Outline,* 1867, 55, 60.
54. *Historical Tablets,* ed. Harte, 45, 39, 51, 37.

should be drawn from any socioeconomic stratum, not just from the better off who could afford to pay for a theological education. Wealth or poverty should not sway the selection of candidates for the ministry one iota.[55] Here was an emphatically egalitarian understanding of the role of the college. Accordingly, instruction, lodging, and maintenance were all given free. Even clothing and pocket money were supplied when necessary. Only in cases, few in the 1860s, where relatives or friends could afford to subscribe was financial support requested.[56] It has been established that there was an increase in the proportion of unskilled and semiskilled laborers entering the Baptist ministry in the later nineteenth century, and this enlargement of the social pool has rightly been attributed to Spurgeon's college.[57] The achievement was made possible by elaborate fund-raising. In the early years Spurgeon delivered weekday lectures in the provinces to raise money, and he devoted the proceeds of the sale of his sermons in America to the college. These techniques, however, were extremely risky, as he found when illness prevented him from lecturing and when his denunciation of slavery dried up income from southern states.[58] Although he continued to declare that the college finances depended on faith ("the Lord . . . is our bountiful Treasurer"),[59] the Metropolitan Tabernacle assumed partial responsibility for its daughter institution. A deacon, T. R. Phillips, organized an annual supper, and weekly offerings were taken up for the college.[60] From 1869 until 1886, the figure collected in pounds sterling was identical with the digits of the year. The sum must, therefore, have been topped up by wealthy Tabernacle laymen, and it is significant that over half of the college's annual income always came from donations.[61] The prosperity of Spurgeon's congregation made possible the generous admission policy of the college.

By far the greatest financial outlay was always on students' board and lodging. Members and friends of the Tabernacle boarded the young men in twos and threes at moderate rates. It may well be that this practice of home residence was sustained primarily on the pragmatic grounds of its cheapness. Spurgeon, however, exalted home residence into the principle that young divines "should continue in association with ordinary humanity." To abstract them from family life might breed artificiality, a clerical tone that he often called "officialism." If family incidents disturbed them, so much the better. In the future they would suffer disturbances "for they are not likely to be Lord Bishops." There were, he explained, further advantages. The associa-

55. *AP, 1870,* 11.
56. *Outline,* 1867, 9–10.
57. Brown, *Nonconformist Ministry,* 32–33.
58. *S & T,* (Apr. 1868), 178. *Outline,* 1869, 5.
59. *Outline,* 1868, 3.
60. *Outline,* 1867, iii, vi.
61. *AP.*

tion of young men, few of whom were married, courted great perils (no doubt meaning homosexual attraction) against which family life would inoculate them.[62] And, as Spurgeon memorably put it, young men living together were "too apt to fall into superabundant levity."[63] Youthful high spirits were not altogether tamed; one student with aspirations of being a poet wore his hair long, but was raided at night, presumably in his lodgings, and his locks forcibly cut.[64] Yet the lodging system, superintended by James Archer Spurgeon, allowed him to receive regular reports on the students' habits.[65] "When a young man resides in a Christian family," wrote the president, "not only is he under the most vigilant oversight, but he never ceases to be one of the people."[66] The first consideration, of restraining students, was significant for Spurgeon, but it was the second, with its antielitist thrust, that was fundamental.

Another unusual feature of the college was its integration in the life of the Metropolitan Tabernacle. Students were, therefore, constantly associated with Christian mission; they were not isolated in scholarly seclusion. Rather than being assigned to another church for an apprenticeship, in the manner of a curacy in the Church of England, students gained the equivalent benefits without leaving the Tabernacle.[67] The connection with a pastorate, Rogers observed, was in accordance with the method by which the gospel was to be preached. Jesus started no church convention or school for general education; "but he founded a Pastors' College," consisting of twelve disciples.[68] Certainly the great attraction of the link with the Tabernacle for students was the association with its pastor. Although Spurgeon carried the responsibility of weeding out men who turned out to be unsuitable for ministry, whether spiritually or intellectually,[69] a close rapport developed between him and the body of students. Their attitude toward Spurgeon was said to be "akin to the many-sided feeling of a clansman for his chief."[70] The president delighted to throw off his inhibitions among his trainees. His devastating capacity for wit, sarcasm, and mimicry, usually kept within bounds in the pulpit, was allowed full play in the college.[71] Especially on a Friday afternoon, when he spent two hours addressing the whole body before counseling individuals about their future work, he delighted to poke fun at mannerisms, pomposities, and pro-

---

62. *AP, 1870,* 15.
63. *Outline,* 1869, 8.
64. Carlile, *My Life's Little Day,* 61–62.
65. *Outline,* 1867, 26.
66. Spurgeon to Mr. Sawday, 12 Apr. 1862, in *Letters,* ed. Spurgeon, 191.
67. *AP, 1880–81,* 11.
68. *AP, 1883–84,* 3.
69. *AP, 1871,* 7. *AP, 1880–81,* 6.
70. *AP, 1876–77,* 13.
71. William Williams, *Charles Haddon Spurgeon: Personal Reminiscences* (London: Religious Tract Society, n.d.), 55.

prieties, "to put one's foot," as he expressed it, "through the lath and plaster of old affectations."[72] Students, weary from the week's work, revelled in such relaxation. They inevitably assimilated something of Spurgeon's knock-about unconventionality.

Their loyalty to "the Governor," as he was called, became lifelong. From 1865 onward the bond was expressed in attendance at a week-long annual conference for students and ex-students alike.[73] Members delivered papers on topics of common concern, but the star was always Spurgeon. Each conference closed with a communion service at which all joined hands to sing Psalm 122 and then each shook hands with his neighbor.[74] The sense of enduring brotherhood among college men was enhanced by several other practices. Because of their inability to afford many books, for instance, thirty-four library boxes were circulating among them by 1867.[75] From the following year there was a Pastors' College Assurance Society, probably the brainchild of James Archer Spurgeon, who was associated with the Star Assurance Society.[76] There also existed, from 1864, a College Total Abstinence Society (despite the president's disagreement with its principle) that further bound together ex-students.[77] They also continued to look to Spurgeon and his brother to arrange fresh pastorates for them.[78] During the later nineteenth century, the normal way for Baptist ministers to move to another church was to rely on mere hearsay of their availability. The Spurgeon brothers, however, acted much as area superintendents were to function in the twentieth century, trying to match personal qualities with opportunities for mission. Perhaps the prospect of a recommendation was the most powerful inducement for Spurgeon's men to remain loyal to their college and its chief.

Spurgeon's educational approach was a piece of his social vision. Just as there must be no financial barrier to training for the ministry, so there should be no academic obstacle. Consequently, prospective students were not required to show any educational qualifications whatsoever. Those lacking elementary skills in English were coached, whether for a shorter or longer period, sometimes never reaching the highest classes.[79] In addition, there were evening classes run by Archibald Fergusson, "open to respectable young men without distinction of sect or denomination," that trained even the illiterate with a view to greater Christian usefulness and operated as a feeder into the college. Alexander McDougall, subsequent pastor at Rothesay, avowed that

72. *AP, 1887–88*, 8; C. H. Spurgeon, *Lectures to my Students: First Series* (London: Passmore & Alabaster, 1875), vi.
73. *S & T,* (Apr. 1865), 178.
74. *F,* 27 (Apr. 1883), 264.
75. *Outline*, 1867, 43.
76. Pike, *James Archer Spurgeon*, 81.
77. *Historical Tablets*, ed. Harte, 44, 97.
78. *AP,* 1870, 18.
79. *Outline*, 1867, 22–23.

before the evening classes, "I had heard about mathematics, but knew not what that word meant."[80] Fergusson, a Scottish Presbyterian, was admirably qualified for the work because he combined a stern manner, making him "the terror of the College," with a personal warmth that brought him an annual Christmas present of books from the men.[81] The corollary of drawing in the educationally disadvantaged was to shun external examinations. There were internal assessments, conducted in earlier years rather impressionistically in the main by James Archer Spurgeon, and later rather formally by Gracey and the others,[82] but the college made a virtue of not submitting its men to public examinations. It was not bound, James Archer wrote in 1887, by "the arbitrary regulations of some secular authority, with its demands for studies adapted to meet the requirements of its examiners, rather than the duties of a pastor's life."[83] The scheme for a *Senatus Academicus,* when first mooted, was roundly dismissed as useless.[84] This stance was not a species of simple anti-intellectualism—James Archer had achieved some distinction when at Regent's Park College as a Syriac scholar and was to accept two honorary degrees from America[85]—but rather the result of an intensely felt sense of priorities. Theological education was designed to produce men for the pulpit. "Let them become scholars if they can," wrote Spurgeon, "but preachers first of all, and scholars only to become preachers."[86] A seminary was different in kind from a university.

Instead of the academic, Spurgeon emphasized the spiritual. In other colleges, he alleged, the fervor of the students might be far behind their literary attainments, but at the Pastors' College the devotional life was deliberately fostered. Spurgeon delighted to report that one student who had been warned against losing his spirituality at college felt once there that he could live closer to God than ever. Candidates for admission were carefully screened to ensure that they were truly devout.[87] At his preliminary interview, one college man recalled that Spurgeon had tried to deter him by stressing the lack of financial or social attractions to the ministry, but then his eyes had lit up when speaking of the joy of bringing people to Christ.[88] Once admitted, students were encouraged to pursue private spiritual reading, perhaps "productions of some great Puritan," and heard from Gracey that piety

---

80. *Outline,* 1867, 31–40.
81. J. C. Carlile, *My Life's Little Day,* 56, 65; J. C. Carlile, *C. H. Spurgeon: An Interpretive Biography* (London: Religious Tract Society, 1933), 172.
82. *Outline,* 1867, 21; *Outline,* 1869, 10; *AP, 1880–81,* 13; College Assessment Book, 1882–91, Spurgeon's College Archives, London.
83. *AP, 1886–87,* 12.
84. *S & T,* (March 1865), 132.
85. Pike, *James Archer Spurgeon,* 4.
86. *AP, 1870,* 7.
87. *Outline,* 1869, 4; *AP, 1870,* 15, 13.
88. Carlile, *My Life's Little Day,* 57.

must be combined with reason in the study of theology.[89] Most important were the prayer meetings. Each day students were expected to attend the college prayer meeting in the morning and the Tabernacle prayer meeting in the evening. In addition, there was an afternoon prayer meeting once a week and, at least for a while, a daily prayer cycle for missionaries.[90] Spurgeon took careful note of the devotional temper of his men. He claimed not to be surprised, for instance, when one who prayed, "O Thou who are encinctured with an auriferous zodiac," subsequently left the Baptists for the Congregationalists, took to playacting and deserted his wife.[91] There was considerable pressure for prayer to be heartfelt, unfussy, and free from trite phrases. "It is really a delight," declared Frederick Marchant, "to hear the brethren pray over Greek and Latin difficulties."[92] The college attempted to create a consistently spiritual atmosphere for Christian learning.

The curriculum itself was remarkably diverse, with no discipline being pursued to any great depth. There was too little time for advanced study during a course that in 1867, as a general rule, lasted only two years, by contrast with the four or even five years at other Baptist colleges.[93] But the real advantage in the system was that the curriculum was tailored to the needs of particular students. There were different courses for different men so that, for example, those possessing only a basic education were not expected to learn Hebrew.[94] Again, although mathematics, what Spurgeon called "the drill of the mind," was taught to all, the level attained in geometry ("Euclid") necessarily varied enormously.[95] Apart from biblical knowledge, doctrine, and philosophy, there was instruction in history, both of the church and of the nations, in English composition and style, and in the ancient languages. Geography, taught in 1869, disappeared in later years,[96] but Latin remained a mainstay of each man's training. "We need Latin," remarked Spurgeon in 1887, "that we may know the meaning of English, and may see how the regular and orderly speech of a civilized race is fashioned and ordered."[97] Science also found a place in the curriculum, though chiefly as a source of sermon illustrations. Fergusson used his philosophy teaching as an opportunity for polemic against the theory of evolution, maintaining his "protest against being considered a blood relation of the ape or the oyster."[98] In 1881 higher standards of scientific instruction were introduced by F. R. Cheshire, a minister, but also a lecturer at the

---

89. *AP, 1885–86*, 26; Gracey, *Sin and the Unfolding of Salvation*, 31–38.
90. *Outline, 1867*, 16; *AP, 1881–82*, 19.
91. Charles Ray, *The Life of Charles Haddon Spurgeon* (London: Passmore & Alabaster, 1903), 336.
92. *AP, 1888–89*, 12.
93. *Outline, 1867*, 11; Brown, *Nonconformist Ministry*, 71.
94. *AP, 1870*, 14.
95. *AP, 1886–87*, 7; *AP, 1883–84*, 8.
96. *Outline, 1869*, 11.
97. *AP, 1886–87*, 7.
98. *AP, 1881–82*, 17; cf. Carlile, *My Life's Little Day*, 56.

government-sponsored South Kensington Science Museum, who three years later reported proudly the acquisition of "a very excellent but peculiarly portable magic-lantern apparatus." But the reality that science was not taken too seriously was illustrated by the fact that the magic lantern was to be used chiefly by students for giving entertainments at churches.[99] It has to be concluded that, though Spurgeon's men did gain a smattering of a broad range of subjects, their training was not very thorough outside the core of theology.

Methods of teaching, too, were not overdemanding. The approach in the college, Rogers explained in 1867, was not formal and dictatorial, but familiar and fraternal. "The dry syllabus," he went on, "technical phraseology, laborious writing from dictation, and the necessity of consulting numerous authors upon each subject in hand, are avoided." It sounds like an ingenious attempt to defend a rather amateurish mode of instruction that evidently relied heavily on single textbooks in particular subjects, instead of encouraging the evaluation of different points of view. Although close private study was expected in classics and mathematics, Rogers concluded, "beyond these no severe efforts are required."[100] Ten years later, when Gracey's efforts were tending to raise academic standards, Rogers reported that the aim was "to maintain the happy medium between the scholastic and the familiar method of instruction."[101] Yet, when during the 1880s Marchant tested classical knowledge more thoroughly than usual, he discovered that grammatical forms were poorly grasped, and a student of that period recalled that work was "not over-serious."[102] Perhaps the most stimulating elements in the curriculum, at least potentially, was the weekly discussion class that drew together the whole college. This arena was where, as Rogers put it, free enquiry was encouraged and "discussion within reasonable bounds is permitted."[103] The surviving minute book reveals that several students would speak impromptu before the principal propounded the official line. Successive meetings in September 1867 considered the following questions: "Does morality increase with civilization?"; "Has love a greater power in the world than fear?"; "What is meant by the covenant of grace?" Some topics extended over several sessions, as when, in answer to the question, "What form of church government is most in accordance with Scripture?" several Scots opted for Presbyterianism before Gracey and Rogers concluded in favor of Congregationalism.[104] The discussion class did induce at least some of the students to think on their feet and express themselves clearly. Uniquely

99. *AP, 1881–82,* 15; *AP, 1884–85,* 9.
100. *Outline,* 1867, 14–16.
101. *AP, 1877–8,* 38.
102. *AP, 1883–84,* 8; Carlile, *My Life's Little Day,* 58.
103. *Outline,* 1867, 14.
104. "Discussion class, Pastor's College Metropolitan Tabernacle minutes commencing Sept. 12th, 1867, 5–19 Sept. 1867, 7 Oct. [for Nov.] – 5 Dec. 1867, Spurgeon's College Archives, London.

among college pedagogic agencies, it also revealed different views among the tutors. Thus although Rogers put faith before regeneration in sequence of time, Gracey reversed their order; and whereas Rogers and Gracey resisted state intervention in elementary education, Fergusson argued in its favor.[105] In matters that came up for discussion, there was room for variety of opinion. Although it occupied a small portion of the weekly round, the class was a partial exception to the general rule that issues were settled by authority.

The college was, therefore, designed to resist contemporary tendencies in the narrowly educational sphere as much as in the theological world and in society at large. It is not surprising that, especially in the early years, Spurgeon's novel institution was the butt of sharp criticism. It was charged, for instance, with training an inferior order of minister. The reply, after a short while, was that Spurgeon's men were proving entirely acceptable to churches of the denomination. By 1882 it could be pointed out that the two most famous Baptist pulpits in England, those of St. Andrew's Street, Cambridge, and Broadmead, Bristol, were occupied by pastors from the college.[106] Subsequently, of the twenty-nine ministers who became president of the Baptist Union between 1897 and 1933, ten had studied there.[107] Spurgeon's trainees could hold their own with their contemporaries from any other institution. A second objection was that the large numbers from the Pastors' College were overstocking the market. Existing colleges had been sufficient to meet the demand from the churches, and, as has recently been demonstrated, there was a high dropout rate from the Nonconformist ministry in the later nineteenth century.[108] The new institution, critics asserted bitterly, was responsible for high unemployment among ministers. Spurgeon's answer was that several students had already been pastors before admission; that many created new churches to serve; and that a large proportion settled outside of England. He estimated that more than half of his men occupied positions that did not affect existing ministers.[109] A third charge, publicly voiced by an American journalist in 1866, was that Spurgeon was laying the foundation of a new sect. His trainees were less attached to the Baptist denomination than to "Spurgeonism."[110] This criticism was wide of the mark during Spurgeon's early and mature years; at the college "undenominational" tendencies were actively discouraged, and as late as 1881 Spurgeon wholeheartedly endorsed the Baptist Union.[111] Seven years later, however, during the Down

---

105. Ibid., 10, 24 Oct. 1867; 13 Feb. 1868.
106. *AP,* 1882–83, 20.
107. Carlile, *Spurgeon,* 185.
108. Brown, *Nonconformist Ministry,* chap. 4.
109. *AP, 1871,* 8.
110. Mr. Tyler of the *New York Independent,* quoted by William Walters, *Life and Ministry of the Rev. C. H. Spurgeon* (Edinburgh: Religious Tract Centre, 1884), 114–15.
111. *AP, 1879–80,* 22; *AP, 1882–83,* 23; Spurgeon to the editor, *The Baptist,* 27 May 1881, in *Letters,* ed. Murray, 180–81.

Grade Controversy, he tried to carry his former students into a new body, the Pastors' College Evangelical Association, that, unlike the Baptist Union, was bound to orthodoxy by a creed. Yet eight of them refused to join,[112] and nearly all the remainder, including his brother James Archer, were still active in denominational life. Although Spurgeon was long to remain a beacon for those who became disenchanted with the Baptist Union,[113] he established no structures for a separate religious body other than the Evangelical Association. Spurgeon can be acquitted on each of the main counts urged against his college, but it is clear that his ways were controversial in his day.

When that has been said, it must also be recognized that the college was rather less distinctive than might be supposed. Spurgeon might, at first sight, appear to be standing in rugged isolation against the trends of the times, but others shared his perspective to various degrees. Thus the Wesleyans were still practical rather than academic in the training of their ministers during the later nineteenth century, and the course at the primitive Methodists' college lasted only a single year, as late as 1892.[114] Joseph Parker, Spurgeon's equivalent among the Congregationalists as a popular preacher, founded in 1860 a college in Manchester to train working men, including nonresidents, chiefly in Bible knowledge rather than classical learning. Transferred to Nottingham under J. B. Paton three years later, it offered a two-year course, containing a great deal of evangelistic practice and was soon turning out students in large numbers.[115] Even beyond the evangelical community, the Unitarians felt the need to open a Home Missionary College with a similar role in 1854.[116] Among the Baptists there was widespread sympathy for aspects of Spurgeon's approach. A group of strict communion Baptists in the north of England decided in the 1840s to organize the boarding of candidates for the ministry with existing pastors so that they could secure scriptural knowledge and practical skills. At the same time J. M. Cramp, the Baptist minister at Hastings who later became president of Acadia College in Nova Scotia, was propounding comparable ideas. The northern group eventually established a college at Bury in 1866. Some of the students were to be housed in Christian families; since they often lacked a previous education, high academic standards were not expected; time was allocated for town missionary work; and the teaching was professedly Calvinistic. The scheme was very like Spurgeon's. When the institution transferred to Manchester in 1872, it was ap-

112. Kruppa, *Spurgeon*, 443–4.

113. D. W. Bebbington, "Baptists and Fundamentalism in Inter-War Britain," in *Protestant Evangelicalism: Britain, Ireland, Germany, and America, c.1750 – c.1950: Essays in Honour of W. R. Ward*, ed. Keith Robbins (Studies in Church History Subsidia 7), (Oxford: Basil Blackwell, 1990), 303–4., ed.

114. Brown, *Nonconformist Ministry*, 84,82.

115. R. R. Turner and I. H. Wallace, *Serve through Love: Per Caritatem Servite: A History of Paton Congregational College, Nottingham*, n.p., n.d., 1–5.

116. Herbert McLachlan, *The Unitarian Home Missionary College, 1854–1914* (London: Sherratt & Hughes, 1915), 14–15.

propriate that the London preacher should be the chief speaker at the stone-laying.[117] Furthermore, the distinctiveness of Spurgeon's foundation was eroded when his innovative ideas were copied elsewhere. Thus conferences for ex-students were organized by Rawdon, Bristol, and Regent's Park Colleges.[118] So it is evident that there was considerable support, not least within his own denomination, for much of Spurgeon's vision.

There were also changes within the college that lessened its distinctiveness. Spurgeon held himself free to be entirely pragmatic—to extend, change, or even abolish the college if circumstances altered.[119] In 1874 there took place a major development, a move into more spacious buildings some distance away from the Metropolitan Tabernacle.[120] Now, with rather less physical integration in the life of Spurgeon's church, there was a greater sense that the college was a separate institution with an academic purpose. External developments drew it in the same direction. The creation by the 1870 Education Act of a national system of education meant that for the first time everyone enjoyed at least basic schooling. Spurgeon commented twelve years later that "the age of Board Schools will not be likely to listen to a preacher whose lack of knowledge even the boys and girls discover in an hour."[121] Every year, Gracey noted, the number of students entering the college without the rudiments was dropping, and soon attendances at the evening classes associated with the college fell away.[122] At the other end of the scale there were students who went on to study at Edinburgh and Glasgow, for the Scottish universities erected no barriers against English Nonconformists.[123] Most significantly, the normal length of course went up from two to three years. This alteration, which seemed desirable on pedagogic grounds, was also the result of outside circumstances. By the early 1880s, long-term agricultural depression was making it impossible for many rural churches to afford a minister. The demand for men from the college fell, fewer students were admitted, and so a longer course became natural.[124] "Our course of instructions being more extended," remarked James Archer Spurgeon, "will, we trust, better prepare our young brethren for teaching the truth to others. A higher order of scholarship, if sanctified, must surely produce corresponding results."[125] The justification sounded little different from those offered by

117. Charles Rignal, *Manchester Baptist College, 1866–1916* (Bradford: William Byles and Sons, [1916]), 10–36, 61.

118. Medley, *Rawdon Baptist College,* 35; N. S. Moon, *Education for Ministry: Bristol Baptist College, 1679–1979* (Bristol: Baptist College, 1979), 57–58; *F,* (27 Apr. 1888), 267.

119. *AP, 1871,* 6.

120. *S & T,* (July 1873), 291–93.

121. *AP, 1881–82,* 5.

122. *AP, 1880–81,* 12; *AP, 1887–88,* 3; *AP, 1888–89,* 13.

123. *AP, 1871,* 6; *AP, 1872–3,* 5; *AP, 1877–8,* 49.

124. *AP, 1880–81,* 5; *AP, 1881–82,* 9; *AP, 1882–83,* 23; *AP, 1886–87,* 11.

125. *AP, 1879–80,* 51.

other colleges twenty or thirty years before. The drift toward a more academic ethos implied that, even during his lifetime, part of Spurgeon's original
educational ideal was being modified.

During the two years 1891 and 1892, Rogers, who had continued to take
a benevolent interest in the college into extreme old age, died at last, Fergusson retired, Gracey died, and Spurgeon himself, as a memorial volume
quaintly put it, was translated "from the pulpit to the palm-branch."[126] Although James Archer Spurgeon, who succeeded as president, provided stability and continuity, he recognized that, without the resource of his brother's
reputation, the college's income would be permanently lower and so it must
contract to around fifty students.[127] The practice of home residence was sustained, though with some difficulty, until, in 1923, the institution moved out
to a large house in the suburb of South Norwood that provided accommo-
dation for most of the students.[128] The move severed theological training
from the Metropolitan Tabernacle, the college reaffiliating to the Baptist
Union in 1939, some sixteen years before the temporary return of its mother
church.[129] The college, now called Spurgeon's, still struggled to give a free
training to a few of those who could not afford to pay, but tacitly abandoned
its waiving of entry qualifications. Very little of the founder's social vision,
therefore, survived, and even less of his educational approach. What did continue was the conservative theological stance he had stamped on the college.
Although Spurgeon's Calvinism went into eclipse there, his institution remained a training center for evangelists and did not follow the path taken by
other evangelical colleges of accepting biblical criticism. Nonconformist
leaders had generally come to terms with the newer views of the Bible by the
early 1890s,[130] but Spurgeon's college had no time for them. It was one of a
handful of theological institutions approved by fundamentalists in the
1920s.[131] More than any other group, the men trained at Spurgeon's ensured
that the Baptists of Britain, unlike the Methodists or Congregationalists, remained preponderantly evangelical in the later twentieth century.[132] In the
theological sphere, though not in the social or educational sphere, Spurgeon
was successful in resisting the prevailing trends of his day.

---

126. *S & T*, (1892), 334; *AP 1892–93*, 3; *From the Pulpit to the Palm-Branch: A Memorial of
C. H. Spurgeon* (London: Passmore and Alabaster, 1892).
127. Pike, *James Archer Spurgeon*, 178.
128. *Historical Tablets*, ed. Harte, 21.
129. E. A. Payne, *The Baptist Union: A Short History* (London: Carey Kingsgate Press, 1958), 242.
130. W. B. Glover, *Evangelical Nonconformists and Higher Criticism in the Nineteenth Century*
(London: Independent Press, 1954), chaps. 7–8.
131. *Journal of the Wesley Bible Union* (March 1922): 59. Regent's Park, interestingly, was also
approved by this Methodist representative of fundamentalism.
132. Peter Brierley, *"Christian" England: What the 1989 Church Census reveals* (London: Marc
Europe, 1991), 164.

12

Kuyper and Dutch Theological Education

James D. Bratt

To understand the educational ventures of Dutch Neo-Calvinism, we need to consider the career of its founder, Abraham Kuyper; and to introduce Kuyper to an American audience we might begin with a comparison to his most famous evangelical Protestant contemporary, Dwight L. Moody. The comparison is inviting because Kuyper and Moody were born the same year, 1837. Both grew up in homes of tepid theological moderation, and both turned to more rigorous courses as young adults. Both found their life's work in broadcasting the old orthodoxy into the new order of their times, the urban-industrial world that alternately fascinated and disturbed them, but always commanded their attention. "Broadcast" is the key word. It was their gift for popular communication that distinguished their careers, that revealed their creativity and insight, and that would help, they supposed, heal some of the woes of the emerging order and renew the religious tradition besides. In this effort, both showed remarkable energy and organizational skill, founding—among other things—institutions of higher education.[1]

Here the difference between them emerges most starkly. Moody founded a Bible institute; Kuyper, a university. Their most famous statements tell why. In his sermon on "The Return of Our Lord" Moody declared: "I look on this world as a wrecked vessel. God has given me a life-boat, and said to me, 'Moody, save all you can.' God will come in judgment and burn up this world, but the children of God don't belong to this world; they are in it, but not of it, like a ship in the water." By contrast, Kuyper declared at the open-

---

1. James F. Findlay, *Dwight L. Moody: American Evangelist, 1837–1899* (Chicago: University of Chicago Press, 1969), is the standard biography. The most accessible English-language introduction to Kuyper's life is James D. Bratt, *Dutch Calvinism in Modern America: A History of a Conservative Subculture* (Grand Rapids: Eerdmans, 1984), chap. 2; and James D. Bratt, "The Public Career of Abraham Kuyper" and "Ranging Tumults of Soul: The Private Career of Abraham Kuyper," *Reformed Journal* 37 (Oct. and Nov. 1987): 9–12, 9–13.

ing ceremonies of the Free University of Amsterdam: "There is no part of our mental world that can be hermetically sealed off from the rest, and there is not a square inch in the whole compass of human life of which Christ, who is Lord over all, does not say: 'This is mine!'"[2]

Quite another contrast emerges, however, in the audiences the two attracted. Moody's lonely lifeboat proved to be exceedingly wide. To borrow current evangelical argot, Moody "touched the lives" of millions in the North Atlantic world. Kuyper had but his thousands—not just limited to the Netherlands and its emigrant diaspora, nor even to the Protestant sector thereof, but to a circumscribed set of Dutch Protestants, called out and walled off from the rest by his own program. Moody's heirs could well criticize the narrowness of Kuyper's arrangements; for their part, Kuyper's heirs noted how superficial Moody's touch could be. Perhaps at a century removed we can agree that, coming to their task with the same amount of water, Moody poured his out a mile wide and an inch deep, while Kuyper pumped his down a pipe a league deep and a foot across.

This comparison highlights three dimensions we need to explore in Neo-Calvinism's educational enterprise: its bold ideas, their institutional articulation, and the historical context that conditioned both. Put otherwise, neo-Calvinism's comprehensive intent and particular strategy of implementation were the response of a specific social audience to the challenge of late nineteenth-century modernization in society and culture. The response proved both quickening and constricting as times changed, but still offers insights for reimagining theological education in a post-modern world.

I

To sketch the historical context, let's focus on 1877, the year Moody published his lifeboat sermon, also the year when the Dutch Parliament secularized the state universities. Specifically, their faculties of theology were turned into departments of religion, with chairs in practical theology retained to train pastors for the Netherlands Reformed Church (*Nederlandse Hervormde Kerk,* hereafter NHK). Jonathan Z. Smith labels this act the birth of religious studies as an international academic discipline. Not coincidentally, it also catalyzed the founding of the Free University of Amsterdam.[3] The con-

---

2. Dwight L. Moody, "The Return of Our Lord," in W. H. Daniels, ed., *Moody: His Words, Works, and Wonders* (New York, 1877), quoted in William G. McLoughlin, ed., *American Evangelicals, 1800–1900: An Anthology* (New York: Harper and Row, 1968), 185. Abraham Kuyper, "Souvereiniteit in Eigen Kring" (Amsterdam, 1880), 32.
   3. Jonathan Z. Smith, *Imagining Religion: From Babylon to Jonestown* (Chicago: University of Chicago Press, 1982), 102–3; W. J. Wieringa, "De Vrije Universiteit als Bijzondere Instelling: 1880–1980," in *Wetenschap en Rekenschap, 1880–1980: Een eeuw wetenschapsbeofening en wetenschapsbeschouwing aan de Vrije Universiteit* (Kampen: J. H. Kok, 1980), 12–13; Jan Veenhof, "Hondred jaar theologie aan de Vrije Universiteit," ibid., 44.

servative Protestants behind this move denounced Parliament's action in some cases; in other cases legitimated it; but in all cases they protested the monopoly that liberal Protestants obtained over the practical theology posts. Practically speaking, then, the Free University had its origin in the need of the orthodox confessionalists in the NHK to train new pastors in their own perspective. The fledgling institution clearly showed this demand; in its first two decades some sixty percent of its students were theology majors.[4]

But another event in 1877 signaled a broader aim. In that year Abraham Kuyper returned from fifteen months in the Alps, whither he had retreated to recuperate from stress and depression.[5] Kuyper's breakdown was understandable. In the first half of the 1870s he had assumed a leading pulpit in Amsterdam (1870), founded and edited a daily newspaper (*De Standard*, 1872), and won election to Parliament (1874), all the while corresponding with the like-minded across the country on multiple topics of discontent. Why this frenzy of work? Partly because of Kuyper's personality, partly because of his sense that everything was hanging in the balance. The latter assessment was correct. The 1870s was the crucial decade of Dutch modernization—in technical innovation, economic reconfiguration, the popularization of communications, voluntary group formation, and the secularization of lower, as well as higher, education.[6] The old formulas of genteel Protestant hegemony, decrepit as Kuyper had found them in his youth, were now utterly passé. A new formula—clear, convincing, and distinctly Christian—had to be fashioned for every domain of society.

That Kuyper could not do all the refashioning himself was the lesson of his breakdown. Thus when he returned home in 1877, Kuyper gave up the pulpit and his seat in Parliament, contenting himself with the editor's chair. From there, however, he made the three moves that laid Neo-Calvinism's permanent foundation. First, he directed a massive petition campaign against lower-school secularization and organized the petitioners into an alternative, Christian school association. Second, he modernized the confessional Protestant political movement by instituting a central committee that aligned local chapters into a disciplined party. Third, he organized a nation-

---

4. Veenhof, "Hondred Jaar," 46; Cornelis Augustijn, "Abraham Kuyper," in Martin Greschat, ed., *Die Neuste Zeit, Gestalten der Kirchengeschichte,* 9/2 (Stuttgart: Kolhammer, 1985), 296.

5. The developments surveyed in the next two paragraphs are covered succinctly in Bratt, "Raging Tumults of Soul," 9–13; Augustijn, "Abraham Kuyper," 292–96, 300; and Jan Romein, "Abraham Kuyper: Klokkenist der Kleine Luyden," in Jan and Annie Romein, *Erflaters van Onze Beschaving* (Amsterdam: Querido, 1971), 169–70; J. C. Rullmann, *Abraham Kuyper: Een Levensches* (Kampen: J. H. Kok, 1928), 53–107, gives complete detail, though in hagiographic style.

6. These developments are aptly summarized in Dirk Th. Kuiper, "Het Nederlandse protestantisme in ontwikkelingsperspectief (1860–1940)," in J. de Bruijn, ed., *Een land nog niet in kaart gebracht: Aspects van het protestants-christelijk leven in Nederland in de jaren 1880–1940* (Amsterdam: Querido, 1987), 2–9; Dirk Th. Kuiper, *De Voormannen* (Meppel, 1972), 111–238, gives a very detailed analysis.

wide network of clubs to give moral and financial support to a Calvinist university; it opened three years later with Kuyper as rector and professor of theology. As might be expected, the three organizations had considerable overlap, tapping the same people in the same locations and run by an interlocking directorate of ideological (and often, blood) relatives. Together these bodies framed a new social world, a nation within the nation, that gave the orthodox their own power base, independent of local magnates' historic hegemony.[7]

Thus, the Free University was founded out of a social movement to serve a social movement. The school was financed voluntarily, by some wealthy patrons, but also by common folks who dropped their legendary *dubbeltjes en stuivertjes* (nickels and dimes) into the little tin banks, the *V.U.-busjes,* that dotted the mantels of orthodox homes across the country. These people honored the university for the place it gave them in the cultural discourse of the land, for defying the liberals' sneers at their social, as well as their theological, position. The university, in turn, served them with the solid commentaries on Scripture and social affairs that its faculty published well into the twentieth century. In their tireless debates on such writings, around the kitchen table or in church groups, common people could stay on the same page as their leaders, learned to grapple with the leading questions of the day, and, in effect, obtained a secondary education of no mean quality. Kuyper's journalism served the same purpose. Most of the world that was later bound in volumes as his systematic scholarship first appeared in newspaper columns. In sum, the professors and the pastors they produced were tribunes of the people, taking seats in Parliament and on association boards. The rank and file were exactly that, a consolidated army of supporters.[8]

For Kuyper, such close contact was vital for Christian scholarship. Theology, also academic theology, had to remain "the maidservant of the congregation," he insisted; heterodoxy, modern or ancient, always betrayed elitism.[9] To Kuyper, "the little people" were the natural custodians of the flame of true Calvinism, covered though it might be beneath the blanket of their own fears and the mists of liberal compromise. The Free University existed to stoke that flame into a bright blaze so that its constituents might walk out into the bright day of freedom and dispel the gloom of modern un-

7. Kuiper, "Nederlandse Protestantisme," 4; for details and charts on the leadership's remarkable kinship network, see *De Voormannen*, 613–41.

8. H. C. Eindedijk, *De Gereformeerde Kerken in Nederland: Deel 1, 1892–1936* (Kampen: J. H. Kok, 1990), 29–34, 41–43; J. Veenhof, "Geschiedenis van Theologie en Spiritualiteit in de Gereformeerde Kerken," in M. E. Brinkman, et al., eds., *100 Jaar Theologie: Aspecten van een eeuw theologie in de Gereformeerde Kerken in Nederland (1892–1992),* (Kampen: J. H. Kok, 1992), 14–15, 26–30; Wieringa, "Vrije Universiteit," 15–16.

9. Quoted in Eindedijk, *Geref. Kerken,* 53; see also Veenhof, "Hondred Jaar," 50.

belief. The university would redeem its people so that they might redeem modernity.[10]

All sorts of fault lines lay hidden beneath this ideal; time and crisis would expose them all. At its most hopeful, however, Neo-Calvinism was liberation theology of a sort, of a nineteenth-century sort, to be sure—the sort good for marginalized white males, less so for women, and least of all for people of color. Yet for its core clientele, Neo-Calvinism did spell emancipation. It proved their dignity, it lent them culture, it raised their status, and it brought them into full participation in national life. Further, this emancipation aimed at the grander liberation of modern life from the sin and error that held it in thrall.[11]

Here, of course, the fault lines begin to appear. For people on the outside, Neo-Calvinism raised questions of freedom and justice. What about those who did not want to be "liberated" on Christian terms? Within the movement loomed questions about means and ends. To recall the imagery of fire and light: Was the Free University to be a forge where materials from the Reformed past and secular present would be smelted together into tools to make a better future? Or was the school to be a "beacon on the coast," guiding pilgrims over the shoals into safe harbor? Or was it to train an officer corps for a Calvinist army, a Gideon's band whose torches would terrorize the heathen into flight? And what of the cultural booty the heathen left behind or, to invoke the Exodus liberation story, the gold that God's chosen took from the Egyptians? Could Christian scholars refine this for the Master's uses or would they inevitably be seduced into fashioning an idol of modern culture?

II

Questions like this (and put like this, in metaphors florid, militant, and biblical) formed the matrix in which Neo-Calvinists forged their core ideas. The answers they found in Scripture, too, particularly in the favorite passages that configured the whole of their Christian understanding. One was Colossians 1:15–20, which presents Christ as "the image of the invisible God, the firstborn over all creation," by whom and for whom all things were created and in whom all things hold together. Another was Romans 8:18–23, which

---

10. Eindedijk, *Geref. Kerken,* 53, puts this point very succinctly. It is also the overarching theme in Romein, "Kuyper de Klokkenist," and in W. Speelman, "Christelijk-conservatief, Christelijk-liberaal, Christelijk-radicaal," in C. Augustijn, et al., *In Rapport met de Tijd: 100 jaar theologie aan de Vrije Universiteit* (Kampen: J. H. Kok, 1980), 175–81. A fine summary statement from the close of Kuyper's life is his "De Kleine Luyden" (Amsterdam, 1917).

11. Perhaps owing to the recent secularization of Neo-Calvinism (as detailed below), this is the dominant motif in current Kuyper interpretation. For Kuyper himself, "emancipation"—important in itself—was ultimately a means to the further end of re-Christianization. See H. E. S. Woldring, "De sociale kwestie—meer dan een emancipatiestrijd," in C. Augustijn, et al., *Abraham Kuyper: zijn volksdeel, zijn invloed* (Delft: Meinema, 1987), 123–45; Speelman, "Christelijk-conservatief," 175–77; and Eindedijk, *Geref. Kerken,* 53–54.

speaks of "the whole creation . . . groaning as in the pains of childbirth," waiting "in eager expectation for the children of God to be revealed" so that it too might "be liberated from its bondage to decay and brought into the glorious freedom of the children of God."

Christ as the mediator of creation; redemption sweeping up not just souls, but bodies, institutions, the entire cosmos; the Christian's high calling to forward this process—these grand themes inspired the remarkable dedication which marked all of Neo-Calvinism's efforts, including its educational ventures. Kuyper etched the vision memorably in his Stone Lectures at Princeton (1898):

> The world after the fall is no lost planet, only destined now to afford the Church a place in which to continue her combats; and humanity is no aimless mass of people which only serves the purpose of giving birth to the elect. On the contrary, the world now, as well as in the beginning, is the theater for the mighty works of God, and humanity remains a creation of His hand, which, apart from salvation, completes under this present dispensation, here on earth, a mighty process, and in its historical development is to glorify the name of Almighty God.[12]

At the same time Neo-Calvinism was pervaded with tones of fear and strife. It feared the instability of modern culture, the disenchantment and relativism that secularist principles must spell. Kuyper decried the entire course of nineteenth-century history as a primer in bourgeois duplicity. The French Revolution, which had begun the process, had thrown out tradition and transcendent authority only to install a harsher regime. Its materialization of life was papered over by vapid sentimentality; its atomistic individualism required countervailing regimentation; its boastful capitalism begged for labor violence.[13] Theoretically, God was Lord over all but seemed, in historical fact, to be losing his grip.

Neo-Calvinism cannot be understood apart from this constant double mindedness. Sometimes the movement divided into two wings, each following one slant. Or its members might show either attitude on alternate days. Kuyper could manage both at the same time. It was to resolve this tension that Neo-Calvinism made its key move, the Copernican revolution it effected upon Kant, whereby it lodged reason squarely within the bounds of religion, debunked the alleged neutrality of scholarship, proposed a pluralistic academy, and made scholarship a—perhaps the most—vital of Christian callings.

12. Abraham Kuyper, *Lectures on Calvinism* (Grand Rapids: Eerdmans, 1961 [1898]), 162.

13. James D. Bratt, *Dutch Calvinism,* 20–24, further explicates Kuyper's sociopolitical critique. See also Dirk Jellema, "Abraham Kuyper's Attack on Liberalism," *Review of Politics* 19 (October 1957): 472–85. Two of Kuyper's seminal statements that address the theme from different angles are *Christianity and the Class Struggle* (Grand Rapids: Eerdmans, 1950 [1891]) and *De Verflauwing der Grenzen* (Amsterdam: Hooveker and Wormser, 1892).

The road to that revolution passed by several mileposts. First, Neo-Calvinists' praise of creation came along with keen awareness of its corruption. No part of nature, also human nature, escaped the span of evil; reason and education no less than emotion, sexuality, and the will were infected at the root. Secondly, God's purpose in Christ was to undo the fall; hence, redemption would be as comprehensive as creation.[14] Kuyper thus rejected the two principal options of his day: the Christian cause could be secured neither by identification with reason nor by isolation from culture. Instead, if the state universities would study religion from a secular, scientific perspective, the Free University would study the "secular sciences" from a Christian perspective and thus uphold the claims of Christ in the academy. In this light, the study of theology strictly taken was "scientific" (thus higher than the academy would grant), but no more godly than any other discipline (thus lower than the orthodox had thought).[15] Nor was study less of a "kingdom" venture than evangelism, preaching, or pastoral care. Scholarship *was* evangelism, bringing the gospel to, in, and out of a crucial sector of human life.

A third premise of his project was Kuyper's romantic sensibility. Kuyper thought about everything—including thinking—in organic terms. Every civilization had its "ground tone"; every thought a "root principle." Kuyper turned this approach to Christian purposes by defining these principles as religious, as commitments to, or defiance of, God's will, leaving every school of thought, indeed, all human action whatsoever, properly subject to religious critique.[16] Finally, for Kuyper, life and thought demanded system. One's ground commitment had to radiate through and integrate all activities, including education. True knowledge consisted not in the heaping up of data, but in discerning their source, purpose, and destiny, in answering the questions of whence, and why, and whither. In other words, scholarship was *necessarily* involved with paradigmatic issues. Either a theonomous or human-autonomous perceptual grid determined the place and trajectory one gave to the data collected. Thus, scholarship honored either God or human

---

14. See Kuyper, *Lectures on Calvinism*, 118. The theological approach as a whole is well explicated in Albert M. Wolters, *Creation Regained: Biblical Basics for a Reformational Worldview* (Grand Rapids: Eerdmans, 1985).

15. On theology as a science, see Abraham Kuyper, *Encyclopedia of Sacred Theology* (New York: Scribner's, 1898), 292–99.

16. Kuyper put it concisely in *Lectures on Calvinism* (p. 189): "As truly as every plant has a root, so truly does a principle hide under every manifestation of life. These principles are interconnected, and have their common root in a fundamental principle; and from the latter is developed logically and systematically the whole complex of ruling ideas and conceptions that go to make up our life and world-view." He explicates the point more broadly in "Calvinism a Life-System," ibid., 9–40. See also J. Klapwijk, "Abraham Kuyper over wetenschap en universiteit," in Augustijn, *Abraham Kuyper*, 63; and J. D. Dengerink, "Kuyper's Wetenschapleer," *Radix* 2 (1976): 90–91; W. Speelman, "De Democratische Kuyper," *Segmenten* (1978): 157–99, thoroughly delineates and evaluates the place of the organic in every dimension of Kuyper's thought.

pretension, either worked to advance the kingdom or acquiesced in the reign of evil.[17]

At this point many objections and exceptions leap to mind, as Kuyper himself acknowledged. We must, therefore, make his meaning precise. He did not think that Christians were inherently brighter than others; all evidence from the Bible to the pew argued the opposite. He did not mean that believers had nothing to learn from unbelievers. He emphatically did not want the righteous to squelch the free research of the opposition. He did believe, however, that with regeneration comes some restoration of that immediate apprehension of God and creation that had been lost in the fall; that through the thick fog of sin, which remains also before the eyes of faith, the Word of God revealed in Christ and Scripture outlines norms that the unredeemed cannot or will not see; that Christians, therefore, have some epistemological advantage in being open to the paradigms that frame the world as it actually is and in looking for details that promise best to fill in that frame.[18]

Thus Kuyper offered an interesting, sometimes perplexing, philosophical conjunction. At times he was a stout ontologist of realist bent: there is but one cosmos, God sees it as it is, and we should do likewise. But since the fall has corrupted reason and since regeneration does not restore us at once—or ever—to the divine mind, Kuyper at other times was drawn toward the orbit of Kant. Human viewers play a substantial role in perception, shaping reality by their first principles. Kuyper even brushed the shore of postmodernity at times in reflecting on how social position, ethnocultural heritage, and gender shape knowledge beyond any appeal to some supposedly neutral reason.[19]

Usually, however, he focused on religious a priori. Two peoples—or at least two systems of thought, variegated as they might be—stood in antithesis to each other, bearing forth fruit betokening their different roots. The "Normalists" take the present world as unbroken and undistorted and the human mind as ultimate authority. "Abnormalists," on the other hand, know how grossly sin has disrupted things and so take their start from the certainty of faith granted by grace, grounded in Christ, and confirmed by the testimony of the Holy Spirit.[20] The two schools might agree on many details, accept the same rules of logic, and follow similar research procedures, but

17. Klapwijk, "Abraham Kuyper," 75–76, 80–81; Jacob Klapwijk, "Rationality in the Dutch Neo-Calvinist Tradition," in Hendrik Hart, et al., *Rationality in the Calvinian Tradition* (Lanham, Md.: University of America Press, 1983), 98–102; Dengerink, "Kuyper's Wetenschapleer," 90–91, 98–99.

18. Klapwijk, "Abraham Kuyper," 75–76, 79–81.

19. Klapwijk, "Abraham Kuyper," 76–77; Dengerink, "Kuyper's Wetenschapleer," 95–100; Wieringa, "Vrije Universiteit," 19.

20. An apt summary is Klapwijk, "Abraham Kuyper," 65–67. Kuyper put it most succinctly in English in *Lectures on Calvinism*, 131–41; more extensively in *Encyclopedia of Sacred Theology*, 150–82.

they will not come to the same knowledge because knowledge involves inferred relations and implicit meanings, precisely the counts on which they disagree.

The disagreement would be pointed, as Kuyper thundered in his Princeton lectures: "Let principle . . . bear witness against principle, world-view against world-view, spirit against spirit." Christians could not think to avoid the fray, for a retreat to piety amounted to "saving your upper room when the rest of the house is on fire." Nor, he said literally in the face of B. B. Warfield and other Old Princetonians, would apologetics avail much; that is "trying to adjust a crooked window-frame while . . . the building itself is tottering on its foundations." No, "Normalists and Abnormalists . . . are both in earnest, disputing with one another *the whole domain of life,* and they cannot desist from the constant endeavor to pull down to the ground *the entire edifice* of their respective controverted assertions." Anything less would show "that they did not honestly believe in their point of departure, that they were no serious combatants, and that they did not understand the primordial demand of science, which of course claims *unity of conception.*"[21]

Such combat, however, was to proceed by words only. In public policy Kuyper advocated a genuine and principled pluralism, forbidding any school from silencing any other. That this posture served Christians' interest against the current secularist hegemony Kuyper acknowledged, but he also acknowledged that hegemony is just retribution upon the church's past and a challenge for the Christian future. Formerly, Christians had turned others out of the temple of learning; now "by God's righteous judgment" it was their turn to suffer. Indeed, "the energy and the thoroughness of our antagonists must be felt by every Christian scholar as a sharp incentive" for his own initiatives. These should begin with a return "to *his* own principles in his thinking, to renew all scientific investigation on the lines of these principles, and to glut the press with the burden of his cogent studies." As those of other convictions did likewise, the resulting pluralism would make the academy more diverse and inclusive and so more just. Quite as much, by being informed with consciously held values rather than uninvestigated premises, scholarship within and between schools might attain "progress—honest progress—and mutual understanding."[22]

For Kuyper, in sum, all education was theological education in the American sense of that adjective. And since ideas ruled the world, education held a lofty status. By articulating their own minds, Christians defended the faith in the public arena. They pushed creation toward its divine destiny in tense tandem with those who might deny creation and divinity alike. Separate organization amid pluralism allowed Dutch Calvinists to have it both ways: the

21. Kuyper, *Lectures on Calvinism,* 139, 135, 133.
22. Kuyper, *Lectures on Calvinism,* 139–40.

freedom of modernity without its anomie, scholarly engagement without the relativization of truth claims. Or so they hoped.

III

That the reality would be more complicated became evident already in 1901, when Kuyper left his theological chair in Amsterdam for the prime minister's chair in the Hague. However possible it might be in education, one could not rule a nation simply by antithesis. Instead Kuyper's years in office saw the publication of his three-volume, 1,720-page work on common grace (*Gemeene Gratie,* 1902–04), elaborating what had been a rising theme in Neo-Calvinism as the movement edged toward power.[23]

Common grace was not just tactical, but fundamental in the Neo-Calvinist cause. The doctrine was essential for maintaining the cosmic scope of redemption and served, in the words of a Marxian historian, as "the valve through which Kuyper pumped fresh air into his people . . . build[ing] Calvinism up from a one-sided dogma to a many sided life- and world-view. . . ."[24] The concept was particularly vital for scholarship. In the first place, said Kuyper, honesty demanded the recognition that "the unbelieving world excels in many things," in science and art and, often, the virtues of those who produced them. Such luminaries as Plato, Kant, and Darwin were undeniably "stars of the first magnitude," Normalists proceeding from unbelief though they were.[25] Second, people could learn from each other across the perspectival divide because God had graciously restrained the working out of sin in creation and human perception. Nature still showed its laws, and observers of all convictions could see something of its beauty and order. This did not deny human sinfulness; in fact, Neo-Calvinists cited common grace to maintain the doctrine of total depravity in the face of seeming evidence to the contrary. Heathen genius was still sinful, but produced truth and virtue by way of God's grace. But as works of grace, these were to be taken seriously by people of faith, just as grace could make the works of faith compelling outside the fold.[26]

But how could one know where the taint of sinful starting point left off and the fruits of common grace began? One could not tell in advance, a worrisome point for a group that craved safety. Common grace challenged both sociological and epistemological solidarity. Not surprisingly, then, Kuyper tended to focus this lens on long-term developments and large blocs, not on

---

23. Abraham Kuyper, *De Gemeene Gratie,* 3 vols. (Amsterdam: Hooveleer and Wormser, 1902–4). Kuyper summarizes the theme in *Lectures on Calvinism,* 121–26. For historical context, see Bratt, *Dutch Calvinism,* 18–22, 30–31.

24. Romein, "Kuyper de Klokkenist," 754.

25. Kuyper, *Lectures on Calvinism,* 121; "stars" quotation, *Gemeene Gratie,* vol. 3 supplement, 12, cited in Klapwijk, "Abraham Kuyper," 67.

26. Kuyper, *Lectures on Calvinism,* 121–24; Klapwijk, "Rationality," 99–101.

particular instances or individuals. Common grace served him more as a language of limit than of action, of order than of freedom.[27] That usage connected with what Neo-Calvinist progressives would later criticize as Kuyper's "scholasticism," his drafts upon ancient and medieval logos theory. Speaking in this vein, Kuyper defined the cosmos as the emanation of God's mind, giving scholarship the mandate to think God's thoughts after him, the better to disclose the ordinances by which the world stayed in being. Such laws, Kuyper thought, were easier to see in science and technology—in his words, the "lower sciences"—where common grace remained the strongest. The "higher" or more "human" the field of study (that is, the humanities and social sciences), the more the antithesis prevailed.[28]

But there was nothing principal about the point. What would happen if someone applied common grace also to individuals, to psychology, letters, even theology? The answer emerged in the quarter century after Herman Bavinck arrived to replace Kuyper as the Free University's premier theologian.

Bavinck brought to Neo-Calvinism a different experience and vision from his predecessor's.[29] The two men died only a year apart (Kuyper in 1920, Bavinck in 1921), but Bavinck was born half a generation after Kuyper (1854) and represented a younger spirit in the inner circle. Kuyper was raised in the national church and agitated for orthodoxy against it; Bavinck was born in a free church that had already (in 1834) seceded from that body and wanted to bridge sectarian lines. (The first step came in 1892 when Bavinck's denomination merged with the group Kuyper had led out of the national church in 1886 to form the Reformed churches in the Netherlands [*Gereformeerde Kerken in Nederland,* or GKN], the ecclesiastical home of Neo-Calvinism's various organizations.) Bavinck never waned in his love for the Reformed tradition and gave half his career (1883–1902) to the seceded church's theological seminary at Kampen, where he wrote a magisterial four-volume *Reformed Dogmatics.* But by the time he replaced Kuyper at the Free University, Bavinck was ready for a new conversation.

That required some reworking of Neo-Calvinist principles. Bavinck's was a romanticism that prized each of the individual parts that Kuyper hurried to weave into organic system. Bavinck recognized the antithesis, but found it warring within himself as within the modernist and Roman Catholic theolo-

---

27. See, for example, Kuyper, *Lectures on Calvinism,* 123–24. Simon J. Ridderbos, *De Theologische Cultuurbeschouwing van Abraham Kuyper* (Kampen: J. H. Kok, 1947, 192–213, evaluates this type of application; see also Dengerink, "Kuyper's Wetenschapleer," 93. Conservative reaction to the whole doctrine is described in Bratt, *Dutch Calvinism,* 29, 46–50.

28. Dengerink, "Kuyper's Wetenschapleer," 96–101; Klapwijk, "Abraham Kuyper," 67, 72–74; Klapwijk, "Rationality," 102.

29. For Bavinck I have relied on R. H. Bremmer, *Herman Bavinck als Dogmaticus* (Kampen: J. H. Kok, 1961), and *Herman Bavinck en zijn Tijdgenooten* (Kampen: J. H. Kok, 1966). See also Bratt, *Dutch Calvinism,* 30–31; Veenhof, "Geref. Kerken," 26–28; Eindedijk, *Geref. Kerken,* 90–99; and Johan Stellingwerff, *De Vrije Universiteit na Kuyper* (Kampen: J. H. Kok, 1987), 16–17.

gians with whom he liked to talk. He saw common grace to be real light shining in real persons, not just restraints embedded in structures. By the power of common grace, the particular grace of the gospel had been able in antiquity to transform paganism into Christian civilization; something similar, perhaps, beckoned in modernity. Thus Bavinck subscribed to Kuyper's manifesto that Calvinism not be repristinated, but rejuvenated, by coming into rapport with the consciousness of the age, only he saw another age at hand. Kuyper's was the late nineteenth century, when spirituality battled materialism and Calvinism had to fight foes. Bavinck looked at the young twentieth century, saw spirituality searching through the darkness, and thus called Calvinism to shed light on others' paths.[30]

In this spirit, Bavinck's doctoral students launched a "Young Reformed" movement (*Jong Gereformeerde Beweging*) in the 1910s. They wrestled with the theological implications of Einstein's physics and listened to Free University psychology professor Leendert Bouman's (favorable) lectures on Freud, the first in the Netherlands. They promoted ecumenical student organizations, women's suffrage, and a metaphorical reading of early Genesis. For some "little people" back home it was too much. Freud and Einstein might not matter much, but the place of women and of Eden did. The catastrophe of World War I made their anxieties worse. When the war's aftermath brought a new wave of hedonism instead of repentance, the GKN's 1920 synod decided to fortify the walls of Zion and issued formal warnings against ecumenism and worldliness.[31]

Bavinck could get away with sniping at those pronouncements. What about the worldliness already within the gates—the spiritual smugness, the militaristic spirit, the wartime, black-market profiteering that had made some of the "little people" rich? But death silenced his voice the next year, and the progressives' new leader, J. G. Geelkerken, could get away with less. Not that he tried. A young Amsterdam minister like Kuyper fifty years before, Geelkerken imitated the master in blasting away at a dormant church that knew neither the treasures it held nor the hungers of the age. He also invoked Kuyper's "organic" theory of biblical inspiration to harmonize Genesis with scientific thinking. And, like Kuyper in the 1880s, he responded to synodical reproof in 1926 by leading his followers out to form a church of their own.[32]

The Geelkerken affair exposed the tricky dynamics of Neo-Calvinism. Kuyper's example rose up to attack Kuyper's institutions; the fist of antithesis nailed the chin of common grace. To the progressives, the church

30. Klapwijk, "Rationality," 103–4; Veenhof, "Hondred Jaar," 65–67; Stellingwerff, *Vrije Universiteit*, 15–16, 28–31.

31. Stellingwerff, *Vrije Universiteit*, 18–21, 27–28; 77; Veenhof, "Geref. Kerken," 31–35; Ilse N. Bulhof, *Freud en Nederland* (Baarn: Ambo, 1983), 144–66.

32. Veenhof, "Geref. Kerken," 35–41.

seemed worldly and the world churchly; to the conservatives, the youth movement caved in to the age in the name of Christianizing it. Neither was the "rapport" Kuyper had sought. The 1926 divide was social, as well as theological. The founders of Neo-Calvinism had thrived as tribunes of the people in a system of mutual trust. Geelkerken and company were a self-conscious elite, more comfortable with outside intellectuals than with ordinary believers. But if his departure cost the GKN few members, his creativity was in short supply. On the question of the veracity of the Genesis account of the fall, for example, a Free University theologian could only say: "Snakes are snakes, trees are trees, words are words."[33] The tensions built into Neo-Calvinism demanded extraordinary leadership. Lacking that, the movement could lose the critical interaction with the age that was its reason for being.

IV

"Critical" in the preceding sentence has two senses. In 1926 Neo-Calvinists shortened the one meaning "essential to the vitality of" and so invited stagnation. Half a century later they shortened the other, connoting exacting judgment, and moved toward secularization. A capsule account must suffice to show the transit between the two poles and to raise questions about other options.

With the 1926 excision of its "left," Neo-Calvinism fell to the control of a cluster of leaders born in the movement, educated at the Free University, and committed to institutional self-perpetuation. The concept of routinization of charisma was coined for such men as these, and its formula of conformity, boundary maintenance, and central control described their agenda well. The theologians at the Free University did not extend the founders' vision, but burrowed down within it. Most indicatively, Bavinck's successor, Valentin Hepp, used scholastic concepts (the old in Kuyper) and apologetic methods (contra Kuyper) to revive natural theology (in the era of Karl Barth!) and give cosmic warrant to earthly institutions.[34] Hepp's motive was sound enough: He wished to defend a common Christian culture in a Europe descending into chaos and fascism. But his system palled on those hungry for Neo-Calvinism's original dynamism.

For that, new leaders emerged among the philosophers at the Free University and in a circle of preachers who often had a greater impact on the students than did the faculty. The philosophers were Herman Dooyeweerd (1894–1977) and his brother-in-law, D. H. T. Vollenhoven (1892–1978), who both joined the faculty in 1926 and worked for the next fifty years at

33. Veenhof, "Geref. Kerken," 38–41; quotation from G. Ch. Aalders cited on p. 39.
34. Veenhof, "Geref. Kerken," 42–46, 51–53; Veenhof, "Hondred Jaar," 74–78. Hepp's one work in English is *Calvinism and the Philosophy of Nature* (Grand Rapids: Eerdmans, 1930).

reforming their discipline on a consistently Christian basis. The preachers turned from the traditional systematic theology to the emerging biblical theology, which they conveyed with great power to their congregations. Soon the popular communications grid brought the news to local study circles, which experienced a new birth of zealous discussion.[35]

The project was exemplified by Dooyeweerd's use of Kuyperian procedures to criticize Kuyperian theology.[36] Rather than proceeding consistently according to the Word of God, Dooyeweerd charged, Neo-Calvinism had compromised with scholasticism, elevating spiritual over material, soul over body, and thought over everything. Scripture taught no such thing, Dooyeweerd insisted. It portrayed every domain of creation as good and of equal dignity, free from any hierarchy but the Lord's rule and commanded to develop according to its own purpose. For Dooyeweerd God did not set places, but ordained directions; this was the Kuyperian dream of free development. It was also a decolonization project fit for the mid-twentieth century; Dooyeweerd sought to free the world from the imperial intellect and to reground it with all its lovely variety in the religious heart.

But this liberation still came via law. Indeed, Dooyeweerd named his "the philosophy of the law-idea" (*de wijsgebeerte der wetsidee*). Every creature in the cosmos bore an innate purpose toward a divinely designated end. World history as an "opening-up process" was not to be a mere careening about amid the twisted order of the fall. Rather, proper Christian thinking would further God's work in Christ to restore every being in its proper function according to creational norms. Philosophy was to clarify such thinking and critique its works; theology was to reflect upon the faith that drove it all. Together they would deepen biblical wisdom into a reforming action-system.

For the moment, however, much of that action remained theoretical. Creational norms first had to be unpacked; that is, each of the various modes of being (biotic, economic, juridical, and so on) had to be differentiated by its distinctive grounds and concern. Then, too, for all its fresh energy, this philosophy still aimed its guns primarily at humanist and socialist proposals. Applied concretely, modal sovereignty militated against state intervention in

35. Veenhof, "Geref. Kerken," 48–53. Veenhof names Simon Gerrit de Graaf and his clerical mentor, J. C. Sikkel, as particularly influential Amsterdam preachers.

36. Dooyeweerd's major work was the four-volume *New Critique of Theoretical Thought* (Jordan Station, Ontario: Paideia Press, 1984); succinct presentations in English are *In the Twilight of Western Thought* (Nutley, N.J.: Presbyterian and Reformed, 1968) and *Roots of Western Culture: Pagan, Secular and Christian Options* (Toronto: Wedge Pub., 1979). The Free University context is summarized in J. Klapwijk, "Hondred Jaar Filosofie aan de Vrije Universiteit," in *Wetenschap en Rekenschap*, 553–62. Good English secondary introductions to Dooyeweerd are L. Kalsbeek, *Contours of a Christian Philosophy* (Toronto: Wedge Pub., 1975), and C. T. McIntire, ed., *The Legacy of Herman Dooyeweerd: Reflections on Critical Philosophy in the Christian Tradition* (Lanham, Md.: University of America Press, 1985).

the economy, in line with Neo-Calvinist political policy in the Great Depression.[37] Indeed, by lowering their gaze from the whole world to one specialized domain in it, and there—in the temple of pure Christian philosophy—seeking to ferret out the ill fit, the philosophers resembled the Neo-Calvinist establishment in no small part. The biblical theologians sounded familiar chords, too: God calls a people *out* to stand over against the world so that ultimately they might be a blessing to the world—or, in truth, to some part of it.[38]

Such venturous conservatism was redoubled in the movement led by Klaas Schilder (1890–1952), professor at the GKN's Kampen Theological Seminary. Schilder had once sympathized with the Young Reformed movement and always retained its contempt for institutional routine. But he pointed to Kuyper's common grace theory as the problem, and to a vital reappropriation of the old confessions as the cure. The existential angst of the 1930s, which Schilder felt keenly, he hoped would drive the Reformed from their customary ways to a well-earned faith that scorned complacency when it could and gave up the world when it must. Schilder proved as good as his word. While some older Neo-Calvinist leaders temporized, his ringing protests against Nazism drove him underground during the German occupation (1940–45). Nonetheless, from there he was called upon to answer charges that the GKN—no friend of the Nazis—brought against him for ecclesiastical insubordination related to his theological complaints. The 1944 synod found against him, prompting Schilder and 100,000 followers to leave the denomination. Many of those who remained had to wonder about a policy that divided the flock just when the worst wolves Neo-Calvinism could imagine were ravaging the flock.[39]

With excision on the left, excision on the right, and conformity and creativity in between, Neo-Calvinism spent the interwar years trying to shore up a system premised on a dynamic balance. It continued that approach for twenty more years after the liberation of 1945, although with a warmer heart and more supple hand. Setting the pace were two theologians appointed to the Free University in 1940: Gerrit C. Berkouwer (1903-) and Johan H. Bavinck (1895–1964). They restored the theology department to equality with the philosophers, in part by accepting the latter's critique. Berkouwer,

37. Kuiper, "Nederlandse Protestantisme," 19–20; Klapwijk, "Abraham Kuyper," 88–90.
38. S[imon] G[errit] de Graaf, *Promise and Deliverance* (English translation of *Verbondsgeschiedenis* [3rd ed., 1952]), deals especially with Old Testament materials. A classic New Testament treatment in this vein is Klaas Schilder's passion trilogy, *Christ in His Suffering, Christ on Trial,* and *Christ Crucified* (Grand Rapids: Eerdmans, 1938–1940).
39. Kuiper, "Nederlandse Protestantisme," 21; Veenhof, "Geref. Kerken," 47–48, 52–54. Schilder's position vis a vis Kuyper is clear from his *Christ and Culture* (Winnipeg: Premier, 1977). The only English-language studies are Rudolph van Reest, *Schilder's Struggle for the Unity of the Church* (Neerlandia, Alberta: Inheritance Publications, 1990), and Alexander C. De Jong, *The Well-Meant Gospel Offer* (Franeker: Wever, 1954).

in particular, hunted down "scholasticism" in its every lair through his eigh-teen-volume *Studies in Dogmatics*. He rid Reformed theology of any remain-ing body-soul "dualisms" and melted the distant "supernatural" into a Word of God that was transcendent, yet closely entwined with human life. Cosmic history became salvation history with Christ at its center and the kingdom of God as its destiny. All these phrases Kuyper, too, could say, but Berkouwer brought them emphatically down to earth by making their human faith their "contact point." Stern structures of law and sovereignty, he observed, would only drive people to doubt, apathy, or flight, but an existential recovery of Calvinism's dual sense of "call"—that is, a yearning for meaning and a vo-cation in the world—made God's will both hearable and doable. Berkouwer thus recovered the theme of justification by faith that Neo-Calvinists had let dim. At the same time, he instituted hope as a new norm for faith, demoting the Edenic ordinances and strict tradition that had served as the movement's cultural compass.[40]

One contact point deserves another. The faith that Berkouwer connected with God vertically, he also blazed across sectarian lines horizontally. He carried on lifelong conversations with Barthians and Roman Catholics and taught his students the rewards of dialogue. His colleague, J. H. Bavinck (Herman's nephew), cast the conversation world-wide as professor of missi-ology at the Free University. The common grace Kuyper saw in science and politics, Bavinck found in religion. From his reading of Romans 1 and his missionary experience in Indonesia, Bavinck concluded that all religions evince consciousness of God—better, reflect rays of divine self-disclosure. Since their followers twist or suppress those beams, Bavinck concluded, their faith qualifies as part idolatry, part truth. Still, that was one part more than earlier generations had been willing to grant, and later he helped launch the university's global development projects, and attracted Christian students from the third world.[41]

V

By the end of the postwar epoch, "contact" and "horizon" had gained vir-tual liturgical status in Neo-Calvinist circles. "Isolation" and "confine-ment" defined the state of sin from which they begged deliverance. Salvation came in a rush after 1965 in the "breaking through" (*doorbraak*) of the

40. Gerrit C. Berkouwer, *Studies in Dogmatics*, 18 vols. (Grand Rapids: Eerdmans, 1952–1976). His own concise overview of his themes and career is *A Half Century of Theology* (Grand Rapids: Eerdmans, 1977). On his church and academic contexts, see Veenhof, "Geref. Kerken," 57–60, and Veenhof, "Hondred Jaar," 82–84.

41. Primary works are Johan H. Bavinck, *Faith and Its Difficulties* (Grand Rapids: Eerdmans, 1959); *Introduction to the Science of Missions* (Philadelphia: Presbyterian and Reformed, 1960); and *Church Between Temple and Mosque* (Grand Rapids, 1966). Secondary summaries are Klapwijk, "Rationality," 104–5, and Veenhof, "Hondred Jaar," 81–82.

Netherlands' ideological pillarization. The Roman Catholic pillar was the first to go as the Dutch church changed from one of Europe's most conservative to its most liberal in a single decade. Sixties consciousness was at work, too, linking youth from all backgrounds in protest, pleasures, and pharmaceutical pursuits. But Neo-Calvinism responded so dramatically to the new environment that internal motives must also be adduced to explain the change.

On the ecclesiastical front the GKN, since the mid–1960s, has traced the same course as the American Protestant mainline. It has lost members and multiplied administrators, has shaded theological clarity and sharpened political urgency, has seen common ethos give way to a plurality of options. More "realistic" and "relevant," it seems less significant.[42] On the educational front, the Free University underwent the expansion typical of American campuses in the 1960s. Its enrollment nearly quadrupled from 3,169 in 1960 to 11,916 by 1976. At the same time, it received full state subsidy and democratized its governance structure to include students and staff. Both altered the constituency's influence. But the most radical change involved the composition of the student body. Fully 80 percent of its students in 1950 were of GKN background and 69 percent in 1960, but only 29 percent in 1976. The NHK share held firm at 18 percent over the latter two dates, while the Roman Catholic component rose from 4 percent to 18 percent. Most tellingly, students having no church affiliation increased from 6 percent of the total in 1960 to 32 percent in 1976, thus surpassing the GKN share.[43]

The impact of these trends was recognized when the university amended its constitution in 1971 to replace "Calvinistic principles" with "the gospel of Christ" as the grounds of its teaching and scholarship.[44] The new formula's ecumenical reach was obvious. Less clear was its precise substance. For with Berkouwer's disciples, Christ's traditional meaning as Lord and Savior came with heavy admixtures of the presence of good, the promise of liberation, or the simple humanity of all people. Berkouwer's vertical contact with God could now be understood also, or only, as human projection of God. The long assault on scholasticism approached the point of evacuating the supernatural altogether, while the grace of Christ seemed common indeed, in both senses of the term. Dooyeweerd's opening-up process could easily be taken as technical modernization, running on its own, liberated from law, but bereft of purpose. If their forebears had always said "yes" and "no" to secular culture, the post-'60s generation tended to give

---

42. Gerard Dekker, *De Stille Revolutie: De ontwikkeling van de Gereformeerde Kerken in Nederland tussen 1950 en 1990* (Kampen: J. H. Kok, 1992), gives a thorough profile and analysis based on survey data.

43. Wieringa, "Vrije Universiteit," 24–27; Stellingwerff, *Vrije Universiteit*, 407–8.

44. Wieringa, "Vrije Universiteit," 36–37.

it a "yes," reserving their "no" for the tradition and institutions that produced them.[45]

But this theological diffusion did not emerge from a vacuum any more than had Kuyper's original construction. The Free University now, as then, has been responding to a constituency, a constituency that lately, however, has been hungering for pluralism *within* the community. The GKN synods that refused to discipline such controversial theologians as H. M. Kuitert and Herman Wiersinga were elected in the same manner as in the days when the hammer of judgment fell. Memories of that shattering hammer, in fact, account for some of the new toleration. Berkouwer confessed his role in Schilder's excision as the worst mistake of his life and refused to countenance anything like it again. Many in the churches agreed.[46] Thus, attributing the new wave in Neo-Calvinism to a knowledge elite, somehow outwitting the rank and file, does not fully explain the transition. Either the movement has suddenly filled with "new class" types, or the rank and file's resistance has strangely waned, or—more likely—the rank and file has agreed that religion should be less intense, less defined, and simply more personal in orbit. In any case, Neo-Calvinism's theological muting has proceeded along with its sociological melting. For almost a century the Dutch Reformed world of separate institution formed as complete a plausibility structure as Peter Berger might prescribe for maintaining faith in a pluralized society.[47] Yet the plausibility *of* the structure became a question, which meant that the plausibility of the worldview *within* the structure became relative, requiring redefinition.

The Free University was thus struck by a social process that its Idealist assumptions could not fathom. More remarkable was its longstanding inconsistency in carrying out Kuyper's perspectival mandate. The university entered the post-'60s world without having in place a set of explicit statements to direct its academic work. Back in 1895 the university had constitutionally committed itself to "Calvinistic principles," but deferred discussion of how these were to shape education in general and the nontheological departments, in particular, for a later date. "Later" turned out to be fifty years later.

45. Veenhof, "Geref. Kerken," 67–83; Wieringa, "Vrije Universiteit," 35. The theologian at the center of these changes has been H. M[artinus] Kuitert, whose representative works in English translation include *The Reality of Faith* (Grand Rapids: Eerdmans, 1968), *Do You Understand What You Read?* (Grand Rapids: Eerdmans, 1970), and *Everything is Politics But Politics is Not Everything* (Grand Rapids: Eerdmans, 1986).
46. Veenhof, "Geref. Kerken," 70–77; Stellingwerff, *Vrije Universiteit*, 406–7.
47. Bratt, *Dutch Calvinism,* 233–34; Dekker, in *Stille Revolutie,* 203–6, 222–26, sees the GKN currently taking the third option (after a century of trying the first) for dealing with modernity laid out by Berger in *The Heretical Imperative: Contemporary Possibilities of Religious Affirmation* (Garden City, N.Y.: Anchor Press, 1979); that is, replacing its willed traditionalism with a blend of confessional tradition and contemporary experience. Kuyper's own project, however, followed the latter course as much as the former; he and his followers simply gave the liberal-secularist elements in contemporary experience much less normative weight than does the GKN today.

Only in the aftershock of World War II did the conversation resume, and then disclosed a wide range of positions among faculty, trustees, and constituents, on what the authority that Scripture, confession, church-historical experience, and disciplinary canons might hold for any field. In the 1950s a physicist and an economist at the Free University even argued their domains to be technical and value neutral, a position Dooyeweerd, Vollenhoven, and many others stoutly resisted, but whose very articulation betrayed either confusion in or innocence of Neo-Calvinist consciousness.[48]

For most of its history, then, the university seemed to draw its coherence not from a consistently applied set of principles, but from a shared ethos grounded in social homogeneity and perpetuated by the hegemony of the very philosophers who espoused the free and equal development of all domains. In this light, the new student profile after 1960 did not supply new clay for principial molding, but fundamentally altered the mold by diluting that ethos. The addition of two new faculties (medicine and social science) in the late 1940s had already strained communality; the proliferation of numbers, subdivisions, and specializations in the 1960s unraveled it further.[49] And so the university born out of protest against secularism underwent the metamorphosis of secularization. Put more poignantly, the momentum of technical reason swept the institution that knew how value laden and alienating that force could be, and did so at the very moment that the rest of the world was discovering the same, to its acute discomfort. The coincidence was symbolized by the sale of the university's original building on May 6, 1968.[50] The structure where Kuyper planted his dream for an academy to defy the logic of 1789 gave way to the cause of expansion in the same month that Paris again exploded in revolution.

That revolution signaled the birth of postmodernity, that is, of the context and cultural program with which Neo-Calvinist education must hereafter deal. To the extent that the two share a common foe they can cooperate. Both arose in protest of modernity, exploded the myths of value-free knowledge, battled the disenchantments of cold reason, and championed diversity. On the other hand, each carries on a part of modernity that—to put it politely—gives the other distress. The program of 1968 would extend the liberation process to domains it had not yet reached—to gender, sexuality, and erstwhile colonies of every sort. This logic profoundly suspects order, law, and hierarchy, values Neo-Calvinism has always held dear and whose rejection, it suspects, must lead to a harsher, more arbitrary domination. Furthermore, postmodernity is a Romanticism of the freed part; Neo-Calvinism, of the integrated whole. It is no accident that the Netherlands' pillarization started to

48. Wieringa, "Vrije Universiteit," 19–22, 26–28; Stellingwerff, *Vrije Universiteit,* 359, 363.
49. Wieringa, "Vrije Universiteit," 26–27.
50. Stellingwerff, *Vrije Universiteit,* 404.

dissolve in the '60s, nor it is likely that this form of pluralism will ever appeal to postmodern tastes. Neither will the elements of modernity that Neo-Calvinism incorporated: the elevation of print by which it negotiated with rationality, and the work ethic and nuclear family by which it made peace with industrial capitalism.

The challenge to Neo-Calvinism and its potential relevance for Christian education in the future thus lie in adapting its core insights to a new world. If the day of complete systems has passed, that of networks has arrived. If deductive principialism does not work, a carefully and communally cultivated sensibility might. Communality is of the essence. The history of Neo-Calvinism demonstrates that Christian consciousness fares only as well as its social sheathing. Yet carefulness is equally essential. The same history testifies that alienating outsiders soon alienates insiders; demarcating without divides within. Imagining a disciplined, charitable community remains the supreme test of this tradition. But carefulness must also apply to intellectual substance. Cultivating a sensibility, especially in a therapeutic world, might simply generate a muddle.

The insights this tradition bears are too important to be forgotten; its methods are too awkward to be followed. Just that perplexity challenged Kuyper in confronting Calvin one hundred years ago. We might, therefore, play Kuyper's move upon Calvin back upon himself and "go back to the living root of the . . . plant, to clean and water it, and so to cause it to bud and to blossom once more, now fully in accordance with our actual life in these [post-] modern times, and with the demands of the times to come." What lies in that living root? The conviction that all education proceeds in service to some master; the mandate to make ours a faithful education, freed from idolatries, including the idolatries of education and sometimes of our faith itself; the hope that education will be renewed when it again serves a popular audience; and the prayer that we thereby might help advance the liberation of the world into the order of the Lamb of God who claims it all as his own.

13

Canadian Protestant Theological Education

George A. Rawlyk

In their boldly conceived, disturbing, sprawling, my-thumb-in-your-eye kind of book, *The Churching of America, 1776–1990: Winners and Losers in our Religious Economy*, Roger Finke and Rodney Stark have some controversial things to say about theological education in North America. These two happy revisionist warriors, energized by an almost Manachaen approach to evidence and truth, argue, often with passion, that American theological education has been, and continues to be, the handmaiden of spiritual declension and denominational decline. As denominations become more preoccupied with scholarly respectability, whether in the nineteenth and twentieth centuries, they replace a Christianity permeated with the supernatural and mystery with an accommodating belief system free of logical ambiguities, but completely devoid of spirituality.

According to Finke and Stark, secularization, in general, becomes a significant corrosive force "whenever religion is placed within a formal academic setting, for scholars seem unable to resist attempting to clear up all logical ambiguities. "Rather than boldly celebrating mysteries," so-called Christian scholars are, and have been, eager to "create a belief system that is internally consistent."[1] And, consequently, as far as Finke and Stark are concerned, the essential Christian message "becomes more worldly and is held with less certainty" as religion, in general, and Christianity, in particular, becomes "the focus of scholarly critique and attention."[2] The American evidence seems

---

1. Roger Finke and Rodney Stark, *The Churching of America, 1776–1990: Winners and Losers in our Religious Economy* (New Brunswick, N.J.: Rutgers University Press, 1992), 45.
2. Ibid., 84.

compelling, according to the authors of *The Churching of America*, that whenever "religious doctrine" is significantly adjusted to modernity and whenever it is "delivered into the control of intellectuals," it is secularized and disemboweled of Christian energy.[3] Many of the well-educated clergy, especially those who teach in the seminaries, are the first to "support a lowering of the tension with the surrounding culture"[4] and are also the first to condemn, as primitive obscurantism, the "most cherished beliefs" of their coreligionists.[5]

Within the context of evangelical Protestant theological education of Canada, over the past century and a half, there may be found evidence both to support and to question the basic thesis about theological secularization advanced in *The Churching of America*. Moreover, and surprisingly, there is some evidence to back up the seemingly wrong-headed Finke and Stark contention that secularization is indeed a "self limiting process that leads not to irreligion but to revival."[6] Radical evangelicalism, which placed almost inordinate emphasis on the new birth, the emotions, and what has been called Christian anarchism, provided the leading edge of Protestantism in what is now Canada during the decades spanning the American Revolution and the outbreak of the War of 1812. This radical evangelical hegemony, however, was successfully challenged by a more moderate evangelicalism—one significantly shaped in the postwar period by intense anti-Americanism and the influx of hundreds of thousands of British immigrants into Canada who helped to neutralize the amazingly strong American demographic bias of the English-speaking colonies. The nineteenth century in Canada has been referred to, with some justification, as "The Evangelical Century."[7] This was an "Evangelicalism," as Goldwin French perceptively observed in 1968, shaped by a "Creed"[8]—a loosely constructed and yet pervasive body of orthodox and central Christian beliefs and assumptions—rather than by a common collective traumatic conversion experience. In the years prior to the War of 1812, in particular, but also during the third and fourth decades of the nineteenth century, even though there was "an evangelical element in the Anglican and Presbyterian churches," French has accurately observed, there were still "real differences between them and the genuine evangelical churches— the Methodists and the Baptists."[9] But by the latter part of the nineteenth century, however, these so-called genuine evangelical churches in Atlantic

---

3. Ibid., 158.
4. Ibid., 170.
5. Ibid., 185.
6. Ibid., 13.
7. See Michael Gauvreau, *The Evangelical Century: College and Creed in English Canada from the Great Revival to the Great Depression* (Kingston/Montreal: McGill-Queens University Press, 1991).
8. French, "The Evangelical Creed," 16.
9. French, "The Impact of Christianity on Canadian Culture and Society Before 1867," in Mc-Master Divinity College *Theological Bulletin*, No. 3 (Jan. 1968) 29.

Canada, Ontario, or the West, had become more and more like the evangelical Anglicans and Presbyterians. This new evangelical alliance, led by an emerging urban middle and upper class, began to place more stress on the religion of the head and less on the religion of the heart and, as has been noted, easily "succumbed . . . to the materialist delights" of late Victorian Canada.[10]

Increasingly, as Canadian society changed in the so-called progressive milieu of the late nineteenth and early twentieth centuries, the old orthodox evangelical religious language no longer seemed to articulate the changing experience and practice of a growing number of Canadian Protestants. In an attempt to find new wineskins for what remained of the old evangelical wine, the traditional conversionist piety was altered, some would say fundamentally, by key members of the denominational elites, especially those teaching in seminaries, and replaced by a new piety that no longer placed great emphasis on the new birth of the individual, or on the supernatural, or on transcendence, but rather saw its special mission in the immanence of God and the spread of scriptural holiness by reforming the nation.[11] Throughout key sectors of the major Protestant denominations, this accommodating Protestantism would become the essence of Christianity. Having lost faith in themselves and having abandoned the faith of their mothers and fathers, many influential Protestants sought salvation in the gospel of "inhibited scientific inquiry" and others in what has been called the "insidious antithesis to essential Christianity"—the gospel of narcissistic, therapeutic self-realization underpinning both North American consumerism and the social gospel.[12]

And as the twentieth century unfolded, especially in the post-World War I period, the forces of secularization began their almost inexorable advance from the elite levels of Canadian Protestantism into the rank and file denominations. In 1946 "some 60 percent of Protestants claimed they had been in church in the previous seven days."[13] By the early 1990s, this percentage had plummeted to a little over 20 percent—a level that has remained very stable for the past two decades.[14] This remarkable decline in Protestant church attendance, during the past half century or so, should be seen within the com-

10. French, "The Evangelical Creed," 16.

11. Phyllis D. Airhart, *Serving the Present Age: Revivalism, Progressivism and the Methodist Tradition in Canada* (Kingston/Montreal: McGill-Queens University Press, 1992), 144.

12. See George A. Rawlyk "A. L. McCrimmon, J. P. Whidden, T. T. Shields, Christian Education and McMaster University," in George A. Rawlyk, *Canadian Baptists and Christian Higher Education* (Kingston/Montreal: McGill-Queens University Press, 1988), 31–62.

13. Ronald Bibby, *Fragmented Gods: The Poverty and Potential of Religion in Canada* (Toronto: Irwin, 1987), 12.

14. See the Angus Reid/G. A. Rawlyk survey, Jan.–April 1993, in the possession of G. A. Rawlyk, Queen's University, Kingston.

parative context recently provided by Mark Noll. According to Noll, for virtually the entire pre-World War II period, Canada:

> despite a national history without the ideology of special divine blessing . . . has an even better objective argument for being considered a "Christian nation" than does the United States. The lists of comparisons with the United States is striking: Canada did not tolerate slavery, it has not thrown its weight around in foreign adventures, it has not done quite so poorly with its Native Americans, it has not puffed itself up with messianic pride, it has tolerated less social violence, until very recently its rates of church attendance were considerably higher, its believers have promoted missionary outreach at home and abroad at least as vigorously, its churches have had much more (Quebec) or considerably more (Ontario, Maritimes) impact on local public life, it has cared more humanely for the poor and weak members of its society, and its educational structures make some provision for teaching religion. In other words, if believers want to find a more convincing history of "Christian America," they should look to Canada.[15]

Much historical and sociological evidence is now being brought together to argue, quite convincingly, that for much of the twentieth century, because if has continued to be a more traditional, cohesive, and deferential society than the United States, Canada has "experienced rapid losses in church adherence as its political, economic, cultural, and educational leaders turned from traditional faith." The American republic, on the other hand, "a sprawling, diffuse society in which leadership remains largely a function of democratic appeal, has absorbed secularizing changes with fewer obvious changes in patterns of church attendance or adherence."[16] It should not be surprising, therefore, that as the twentieth century blurs into the twenty-first, there "is a form of secularization in the States that advances within the churches" while there is "another form in Canada that advances by taking people away from the churches."[17]

When this overarching secularization thesis is explicitly applied to Canadian Protestant theological education, during the past century and a quarter, the murky outlines of a potentially intriguing picture begin to emerge. For much of the Victorian period, it may be argued, the evangelical bias of most of the Protestant elite was faithfully reflected not only in theological education, but also in rank and file or popular religious beliefs and practice. By the end of the second decade of the twentieth century, however, most Canadian Protestant leaders—and what Antonio Gramsci has referred to as their intellectual "deputies"—in the seminaries, were determined "to win over the tra-

15. Mark A. Noll, *A History of Christianity in the United States and Canada* (Grand Rapids: Eerdmans, 1992), 547.
16. Ibid., 549.
17. Ibid., 550.

ditional strata" to support their new liberal and modern version of "social, economic, political" and, one might add, religious order.[18] In the 1920s and 1930s, virtually every academically recognized Canadian Protestant seminary or theological college, was now in liberal hands, as were the administrative bureaucracies of the mainline Protestant denominations. The evolving Protestant bureaucratic, academic hegemony was strengthened by what has been called "direct domination"—a complex process, which at its core was infused by an obsession with organizational structure and administrative connections.[19]

This liberal Canadian Protestant hegemony, however, perhaps because of its success in disemboweling mainline Protestant Christianity of its core orthodox beliefs, found itself, by the last decade of the twentieth century, pushing up against a largely hollow organizational structure and using meaningless administrative connections. The mainline administrative elite, especially in the United, Anglican, and Presbyterian denominations (three denominations that presently make up some 60 percent of all self-identified Canadian Protestants) has been confronted by the bitter logic and legacy of their own liberal theology. Few liberals today worship regularly in the mainline churches; and most of those Protestants who do are either evangelicals or fairly orthodox Christians who still possess a sense of loyalty to their denominations. The fastest growing churches in Canada (almost matching in their growth rate the exodus rate of those Protestants who are abandoning organized Christianity, but not necessarily Christianity) are the conservative and evangelical ones. On any Sunday in Canada, apart from Easter Sunday and Christmas Sunday, there are more evangelicals at worship than "liberals" broadly defined or even what *Maclean's* recently referred to as "Ardent Churchgoers"—those who hold orthodox Protestant beliefs but are not as likely as evangelicals "to say that the Bible is God's Word or that it is important to encourage non-Christians to convert."[20]

The collapse of the liberal Protestant hegemony is to be seen not only in the precipitous decline of liberalism in the pews and the growing strength of evangelicalism (almost by default it must be admitted), but also in its remarkable declension in the realm of Canadian theological education. Some key features of the rise and fall of liberal hegemony (or another way of putting it, the rise, fall, and rise of the evangelical tradition) may be captured by taking four fairly unfocused pictures of the state of Protestant theological education in Canada—one in 1867, another in 1890, one in 1930, and the final one in 1990.

    18. See Antonio Gramsci, *Selections from the Prison Notebooks* (New York: International Publishers, 1971). The specific quotations are from P. Craven, *"An Impartial Umpire:" Industrial Relations and the Canadian State 1900–1911* (Toronto: University of Toronto Press, 1981), 15.
    19. See Craven, *"An Impartial Umpire,"* 16.
    20. *Maclean's* (April 12, 1993): 46.

The year of Confederation was 1867—when present-day Canada came
into being—"Stretching from sea to sea." In Canada's first census, in 1871,
out of a total population of 3,689,257, 15.4 percent or 567,091 were Methodist, 14.8 percent or 544,998 were Presbyterians, 13.4 percent or 494,049
were Anglicans, 6.7 percent or 245,805 were Baptists and 40.4 percent or
142,029, were Roman Catholics.[21] The four leading Protestant denominations thus made up slightly more than 50 percent of the total Canadian population, and this Protestantism, as has already been mentioned, was dominated by its unique Canadian variant of evangelicalism. In 1871 virtually all
Methodists, Presbyterians, and Baptists, and a surprising number of Anglicans, would have been proud to describe themselves as evangelicals.

According to Donald Master's authoritative and groundbreaking, but
largely neglected, study, *Protestant Church Colleges in Canada*, there were
in 1867 fifteen denominational colleges in Canada, most of which were preparing men for the Christian ministry. Of the fifteen, eleven were clearly
evangelical institutions: Acadia College (Wolfville, Nova Scotia), and the
Canadian Literacy Institute (Woodstock, Ontario) were Baptist; Albert College (Belleville), Victoria College (Cobourg, Ontario), Mount Allison (Sack-
ville, New Brunswick), were Methodist; Queen's (Kingston), Knox (Toronto), Molin (Quebec City), and Theological Hall, Halifax, were
Presbyterian. Also, two Anglican institutions were definitely evangelical in
1867: Huron (London, Ontario), and St. John's (Winnipeg). Four Anglican
colleges—Bishop's (Lennoxville, Quebec), King's (Nova Scotia), Trinity
(Toronto); and Queen's (St. John's Newfoundland)—were definitely nonevangelical both in theological emphasis and style. In fact, it may be argued
that these four institutions were antievangelical and proud of the fact.
Clearly, if any one institutional reality underscored in 1867 the evangelical
hammerlock on Canadian Protestantism, it was the actual number of evangelical denominational colleges and the number of students serviced by these
often vibrant institutions.[22]

The evangelical hammerlock, despite Darwin, higher criticism, comparative religion, and an emerging industrial order, still remained in place in
1890—a little less secure and owing, perhaps, more to the past than to
present theological realities. Almost a quarter of a century after confederation, there still no new additions to the small constellation of nonevangelical colleges. On the other hand, despite the closing of Albert, Morin,
Theological Hall (Halifax), and the Canadian Literacy Institute as colleges,
eight new evangelical institutions of higher learning had emerged. McMaster

---

21. See Phyllis D. Airhart, "Ordering a New Nation and Reordering Protestantism 1867–
1914," in George A. Rawlyk, ed., *The Canadian Protestant Experience 1760–1990* (Burlington,
1990), 102–4.

22. This paragraph is based upon D. C. Masters, *Protestant Church Colleges in Canada: A History* (Toronto: University of Toronto Press, 1966), 29–88.

in Toronto became the major Baptist college in Central Canada; Wycliffe in Toronto was constructed to challenge the High Church preoccupation of Trinity; and Montreal Diocesan College performed a similar theological and academic function with respect to Bishop's. The Presbyterians built Manitoba College in Winnipeg, Presbyterian College in Montreal, and Presbyterian College in Halifax. Not to be outdone, the Methodists constructed Wesley College in Winnipeg and Wesley Theological College in Montreal.[23]

It should be noted that, according to the Canadian census of 1891, of the total Canadian population of 4,833,239, 17.5 percent were Methodist, compared to 15.4 percent in 1871; 15.6 percent were Presbyterians, compared to 14.8 percent twenty years earlier; the Anglican percentage was exactly the same in both years, 13.4 percent; while the Baptists had dropped to 6.2 percent from 6.7 percent. The Roman Catholics made up 41.2 percent of the total population—an increase of less than 1 percent since 1871.[24] The Methodist/Presbyterian/Anglican/Baptist demographic domination of Canadian Protestantism was obviously continuing as the nineteenth century blurred into the twentieth—as was that of the still powerful evangelical majority.

By 1930, however, at least at the level of Protestant theological education, the evangelical hold on Canadian Protestantism had been definitely broken by the significant forces unleashed by liberal Christianity and so-called modernity. According to Masters, during the 1890 to 1930 period, two conflicting views "of the Hebrew-Christian tradition were proclaimed" in Canadian theological education—the "old and conservative" and the "new and liberal."[25] By 1930 the latter had emerged dominant and victorious. It is Masters's contention, (some might criticize him for being too simplistic and Manichaen in his analysis) that according to the "conservative view":

> God had revealed himself directly to man [and woman] and had left the testimony to Himself in his law and in the written word. . . . Divine revelation was the ultimate test of human thought and conduct. All doctrine and action must be judged against the norm revealed by God concerning Himself and His Son.[26]

In sharp contrast, "the liberal view," was:

> based upon a fundamentally different view of Scripture. The Bible, instead of being God's revelation of Himself to man, became the product of man's gropings after God from animism through polytheism to monotheism . . . . In its extreme form it left the way open for the departure from old doctrines and even creeds as the search of man after God continued. The old norm became only a

23. See ibid., 89–132.
24. Airhart, "Ordering a New Nation," 102–4.
25. Masters, *Protestant Church Colleges*, 172.
26. Ibid.

stage in a process of upward development which had no place for the concept of "absolute truth."[27]

In 1930, apart, perhaps, from the Anglican Wycliffe College in Toronto, every Canadian Protestant theological college had abandoned much of what might be described as nineteenth century evangelicalism. The vast majority were now liberal Christian institutions and proud of the fact; a few were liberal evangelical—with the emphasis on liberal. In the former camp were the new seminaries of the United Church of Canada, Emmanuel in Toronto, Pine Hill in Halifax, Queen's in Kingston, the Co-operative Colleges in Montreal, Wesley College in Winnipeg, and United Theological College in Vancouver. Huron, Montreal Diocesan College, and St. John's, Winnipeg, had abandoned the Anglican evangelical side; Knox College in Toronto and Presbyterian College in Montreal were uncertain of their theological moorings, as were the three Baptist institutions—Acadia, McMaster, and Brandon. In fact, the evidence suggests that Brandon and Acadia had moved in the direction of liberalism to a far greater degree than the much maligned McMaster.[28]

If Michael Gauvreau is correct in asserting that the evangelical clergyman-professor was, without question, the single most significant influence in determining the shape of Canada's *Evangelical Century*,[29] the period from the Second Great Awakening to World War I, then it may be argued that the liberal clergymen-professor played a key role in transforming Canadian Protestantism in the post-World War I period. There was, in other words, a symbiotic relationship between the changing theological word of the clergymen-professors and much of mainstream Protestantism.

It would be distorting historical reality to suggest, however, that in 1930 there were absolutely no human evangelical conduits for the traditional evangelical perspective in the liberal-oriented Canadian Protestant seminaries. Many of the institutions, which in the nineteenth century had been evangelical but had become liberal by 1930, had at least one evangelical clergyman-professor on staff. There was, for example, the dour Calvinst-evangelical J. M. Shaw at Queen's (1929–1952)[30] or the extraordinarily able Abraham Lincoln McCrimmon at McMaster, where he would die in harness in 1935.[31] There would be other men, of course, but fewer as Canada entered the post-World War II period—as the liberal hammerlock was firmly and confidently applied to Protestant theological education.

27. Ibid.

28. Based largely on ibid., "The Modern Adjustment," 173–206 and David Marshall, *Secularizing the Faith: Canadian Protestant Clergy and the Crisis of Belief, 1859–1940* (Toronto, 1992), 156–248 and my work on Acadia, McMaster, and Queen's Theological College.

29. Gauvreau, *The Evangelical Century,* passim.

30. See George A. Rawlyk and Kevin Quinn, *The Redeemed of the Lord Say So: A History of Queen's Theological College 1912–1972* (Kingston: Queen's University Press, 1980), 769.

31. Rawlyk, "A. L. McCrimmon, H. P. Whidden, T. T. Shields," 44–50.

By 1931, 41.3 percent of the Canadian population was now Roman Catholic; 15.8 percent, Anglican; 19.5 percent, United Church; only 8.4 percent, Presbyterian, and 4.3 percent, Baptist—while 3.8 percent was Lutheran. The four largest Protestant denominations thus made up close to 50 percent of the entire Canadian population. Some sixty years later, however, the traditional Big Four have experienced significant hemorrhaging of members and adherents—and are now only about one-third of the total Canadian population; 15 percent of Canadians in 1993 "say they have no religion" and a little more than 2 percent are "Jewish, Hindus, Muslims and Buddhists."[32] The remarkable decline of the major mainline denominations, especially the United Church, Anglicans, and Presbyterians, has occurred at precisely the same time that millions of Canadians have totally abandoned Christianity and tens of thousands of others are moving into the burgeoning conservative evangelical and fundamentalist churches. For example, it had been recently noted that during the 1981 to 1991 period:

> Conservative congregational Christian groups, accounting for a much smaller percentage of the [Canadian] population, saw significant increases in numbers. Pentecostals increased by 29%, Mennonites by 19%, Evangelicals by 76%, Adventists by 26% and Alliance 75%.[33]

In sharp contrast, United Church members dropped 18 percent, Anglicans by 10 percent, and Presbyterians by 22 percent. Only Baptist numbers have remained fairly steady over the decade—largely because of the growth of more conservative Baptist churches and the decline of the liberal accommodating ones.[34]

In the immediate post-World War II period, Canadian Protestants seemed to be on the verge of entering yet another "Golden Age"—perhaps not an evangelical one, but one characterized by remarkable numerical growth and an almost palpable sense of confidence. Hundreds of new churches were built—mainline and nonmainline—and it has been estimated that in the late 1970s, six in ten Canadian Protestants worshipped each week. It was an era—characterized by what Pierre Berton, the Canadian writer, disparagingly called, *The Comfortable Pew*.[35] Within a few decades, however, the so-called comfortable pews of Canadian mainline Protestantism were largely empty, that is, those not occupied by fairly orthodox believers, while those of the many so-called conservative churches were often filled to overflowing.

The further secularization of Canada and the decline of Canadian mainline liberal Protestantism, particularly during the past three decades, has

32. See Bob Harvey, "A Nation of Believers," *Ottawa Citizen* (April 17, 1993).
33. *Western Report* (June 21, 1993.)
34. Ibid.
35. Pierre Berton, *The Comfortable Pew* (Philadelphia: Lippincott, 1965).

been accompanied, as has already been pointed out, by the relative growth, almost by default, of Canadian evangelicalism. This evangelical growth may be graphically seen in student enrollment figures for the 1988 to 1992 period in accredited Canadian Theological seminaries.[36]

In 1990, there were four more full time equivalent (F.T.E.) M. Div. Students enrolled in evangelical institutions, than in nonevangelical ones (521 to 517) and 1,079 students overall, compared to 974. Furthermore, of the seven largest seminaries, each having F.T.E. total enrollments in 1990 of 100 or more—Emmanuel, Ontario Theological Seminary, Regent College, Providence, Canadian Theological Seminary, Wycliffe, and Trinity—five are clearly evangelical, and the two largest by far, Regent and OTS are conservative evangelical flagship institutions. It is also noteworthy that some observers have estimated that at least 25 percent of the students enrolled in liberal mainline institutions like Knox, Queen's and Emmanuel are self-proclaimed evangelicals.[37] What these figures and percentages appear to indicate is that as the twenty-first century approaches, at least at the accredited seminary level (excluding Bible schools and unaccredited seminaries, almost all of which are conservative evangelical in style and substance), Canadian evangelicalism, in its various guises and manifestations, is returning to its former position of dominance—but with a fundamental difference. This dominance is one exerted by a largely leaderless, defensive, and morbidly introspective movement over a rapidly declining Canadian Protestantism. It is, for some, a Pyrrhic victory; the spoils of battle are mere whiffs of what might have been and what once was, but are now meaningless theological shibboleths hurled about by the deaf at the deaf in an age characterized by a lack of loyalty, and by an obsession with the self at the expense of the community, whether Christian or secular.

There is, of course, another way to try to trace the murky outlines of the apparent transformation of Protestant theological education in Canada during the past century and a half. The move from an evangelical consensus in Victorian Canada to a liberal accommodating stance in the interwar years and then to a revitalized evangelicalism of the last two or three decades may also be discerned by explicitly examining the histories of a select number of theological institutions. During the past three decades I have been particularly interested in the theological developments of Acadia. Its history reveals the larger trends in Canadian evangelical theological education.

It is clear that from its early nineteenth-century origins, Acadia College was, without question, an evangelical institution. Acadia existed in order not

36. These tables are based upon *Fact Book on Theological Education, 1991–1992* (Pittsburgh: A.T.S., 1993), 4–13, 43–79.
37. Angus Reid survey of a variety of university seminary students, January 1993, in the possession of G. A. Rawlyk, Queen's University, Kingston, Ontario.

only to train men for Christian ministry but also to convert the unconverted. For example, "The revival of '40 and '41 was one of the great power" it was noted. "Every student in the academy and college, with one exception, professed to be savingly converted to God."[38] "1848" was another "wonderful year," when "Of all the students in college and academy not one remained without a hope in Christ."[39] Nor would "The year 1855 soon be forgotten."

In the early 1860s, Acadia also experienced a series of intense revivals, most of which were student inspired and student-led. There would be other Acadia revivals during the last three decades of the nineteenth century but the fires sparked by "these religious awakenings"[40] would be virtually extinguished on campus as the first decade of the twentieth century unfolded. The nineteenth-century New Light revivalism which had been accompanied on the Acadian campus "by evidence of uncommon spiritual power"[41] had by World War I been replaced, at the core of the institution, by an accommodating, liberal evangelicalism. It was a theology which owed a great deal to important intellectual developments occurring in key Baptist seminaries in the United States, especially at Newton in Massachusetts, Rochester and the University of Chicago. By the 1920s, it is clear, the so-called forces of Christian liberalism had had a far greater impact upon Maritime Baptists than upon their counterparts in Central Canada and the West. And this was particularly the case at Acadia. The liberal theological bias of Acadia was nicely captured in the infamous Kingston Baptist Parsonage Case which was heard in the Supreme Court of Nova Scotia in May 1935. From the beginning of the case, everyone in the Maritime Provinces of Canada realized that the real issue was not that involving the ownership of an obscure Baptist parsonage but the battle between modernism and fundamentalism—especially at Acadia.

On Saturday, 25 May, Professor Simeon Spidle, Dean of Theology at Acadia, was called to the witness stand. A native of Nova Scotia, Spidle had graduated from Acadia with a B.A. degree in 1897, and then served two Nova Scotia Baptist pastorates. He then went to Newton Theological Seminary, where he received his B.D. in 1903; in 1911 he was awarded his Ph.D. from Clark University in Worcester, Massachusetts. In 1911 he was also appointed professor of philosophy, systematic theology and church history at Acadia and then in 1922 its Dean of Theology, a position he held until 1936 when he retired. Spidle was the general factotum in the Maritime Baptist Convention during the 1920s and early 1930s.[42] He was a key member of

38. A. C. Chute, *The Religious Life of Acadia* (Wolfville, N.S., 1933), 26.
39. Ibid., 26–27.
40. Ibid., 33.
41. Ibid., 23.
42. *Acadia Bulletin*, Nov. 1954. See also Simeon Spidle, *An Outline of Theology*, 2 vols. (Privately printed, 1953).

the Examining Council and almost singlehandedly determined who would and who could not be ordained as ministers in the convention. An ardent believer in the importance of an educated ministerial elite, he attempted, often without much success, to impose his high academic standards on the convention. He accepted much of the critical Biblical scholarship but without abandoning totally his belief in regeneration, and immortality. As a scholar, he refused to see things solely in black and white terms but rather frequently saw huge grey patches. He did not perform particularly well in Kentville on 25 May 1935, perhaps because of his tendency to avoid answering certain questions directly and honestly.[43]

In his cross examination, Spidle was asked what he meant when he stated that the "Old and New Testament Scriptures were written by men divinely inspired by whom?" "By the spirit of God," Spidle responded. "Is that not, in all fairness, the doctrine of verbal inspiration?" he was asked. "No, not by any means," Spidle replied. "I say verbal inspiration means this, that the very words and ideas were dictated to the minds of the writers; that the writers themselves had nothing to do with creating the ideas or the language." Spidle was then asked whether he believed there was an actual "dictation to Moses." "Cite the case" Spidle retorted. " What I have reference particularly to is the making of the ten commandments." "There's nothing said there about dictation," was the curt reply.

After reiterating that a premillennial belief had never been a prerequisite to membership" in any Maritime Baptist Convention church, Spidle was urged to clarify his view of inspiration. "Do you accept the scriptures from Genesis to Revelation as being verbally inspired and of God yourself?" "No, certainly not," Spidle answered. "What do you say?" "I hold to the historic theory of the inspiration of the Bible," Spidle replied. "How do you define that?" Acadia's Dean of Theology quickly retorted: "Co-operation of the spirit of God and the mind of man arriving at the religious truth incorporated in the Bible." Before Spidle could get himself any deeper in difficulty, his lawyer jumped to his feet and argued that "the individual views of the witness are immaterial." He was sustained and the cross examiner shifted to a few seemingly irrelevant questions about Acadia before returning to theological issues by asking, "Do you preach and teach the virgin birth of Christ?" Once again, Spidle's lawyer, George Nowlan, the future Federal Conservative Cabinet Minister, objected to the line of questioning, and it was agreed not to "press the question." But the lawyer who represented the Fundamentalist Baptists did press Spidle on the question of whether he believed "that Christ was divine. Certainly do," answered Acadia's Dean of Theology.

Q. Do you believe and teach he was the Deity?

43. This section is based upon Court Records, Acadia University Archives.

A. He was divine in the sense that there was in him the divine quality of life.

Q. Do you believe that the death of Christ upon the cross was by way of atonement of sins?

A. I surely do, but you must remember there are no fewer than twelve different theories. The substitution is one of them, which is that the sufferings of Christ were a punishment inflicted on Christ the innocent in place of the guilty; that the innocent was punished for the guilty and the guilty were allowed to go free.

Q. Do you believe in the physical return of Jesus?

A. That is a doctrine that is held by Baptists, that there will be a return of Christ to this earth.

It was clear to everyone in the courtroom that Spidle had tried to avoid the question. So he was asked again, "Do you preach and teach a physical return?" "I never use that in any of my preaching because I don't think it is an important matter to emphasize in teaching; our business is to carry on the work and when the time arrives he will come." Spidle was asked on a number of occasions to define modernism and fundamentalism but he stubbornly refused to do so. He was then asked if he knew the University of Chicago theologian, Dr. Shirley Jackson Case. Spidle did. He was then asked if he considered Case a modernist or a fundamentalist?" "I am not labelling any man," he shot back. Spidle was asked why Case had been given an honorary doctorate by Acadia in 1928. It was, suggested Spidle, because of Case's close association with Horton Academy, the Baptist school, where he had once taught. Spidle was then requested to listen to a statement to be found on page eighty of Case's *Jesus Through the Centuries.*

The spark that ignited the tinder of a new faith for Peter was the need felt within himself during the crucifixion, for his former leader's reinstatement in divine favor. The notion of Jesus' apotheosis, so readily suggested by popular Gentile religions in Peter's environment, brought to him too valuable a relief from his perplexity and too vivid an assurance of future help to leave any room for questioning the propriety of his procedure. Peter did not actually believe that a deceased man had become a god. No Jew, however unschooled, could have assented to any such affirmation. It remained for his Greek successors in the new religion to recognize in Jesus a full fledge Christian deity . . . . Strictly speaking, this risen Jesus was not an absolute deity; he was only a messianizsed hero.

"Would you say that was in any way fundamentalistic?" Spidle was asked. "I will let the fundamentalist say whether it is or not," was the curt reply. Similar responses were given to questions about three other quotations from Case's writings.

The lawyer representing the fundamentalists wondered how any orthodox Baptist university could confer an honorary degree on a person like Case, whose modernist views were so well known. In reply Spidle stressed that "The degree was not conferred upon him for his theological views but because he was a teacher in the academy whose centenary was being celebrated." Again, the lawyer endeavored to pressure Spidle into admitting that Case was a modernist. There was, understandably, a biting edge to the lawyer's question "Do you mean seriously to say, as an educationist of this province, you do not care to answer a simple question in regard to extracts I have read as being the work of a fundamentalist or modernist?" "I make no pronouncements on the matter," was Spidle's response. The final question was "Does Acadia, as a university, teach organic evolution?" "That belongs to the Department of Biology. I am not a member of that Department," answered Spidle. This was obviously not Dean Spidle's finest hour.

The "thick history" of the Kingston Parsonage Trial is of critical importance because it reveals what Spidle actually said, under cross examination, after swearing to "tell the whole truth and nothing but the truth." What Spidle said about theology accurately reflected what was being taught in the interwar years at Acadia. By the 1950s, Acadia, had, without question, become even more liberal; the legacy of nineteenth century populist evangelicalism had been largely marginalized by a faculty obsessed with so-called academic respectability and modernity. When, in the 1950s, Dr. Gordon Warren, the Dean of Acadia's Faculty of Theology was asked by some New Brunswick Evangelical leaders what "he believed about the virgin birth," Warren replied "I believe it but there is a great many strands to the thing which cause some doubt and I would not definitely say yes." William Lumsden, another theology professor, was asked the same question. "Yes, I believe in the virgin birth," he answered "but I believe that there could be some knowledge or facts, such as archaeological discoveries, come to us later which would lead us to see that we were wrong in accepting that position." Professor Fraser, a philosopher, threw oil on the "flickering flames of controversy" when he declared "I don't know which virgin birth you are talking about, the one in Matthew or the one in Luke. There are two virgin births and I do not know which one you want me to respond to . . . I do not know which one to accept."[44]

It is not surprising that Baptist conservative evangelicals in the Maritime Convention discouraged potential theological students from attending Acadia. Instead these men were sent either to Gordon College in Massachusetts or to Toronto Bible College. When they returned to the Maritimes, they were determined to take over control of the Convention and Acadia.

By the early 1960s the conservative evangelicals, making shrewd and effective use of their New Brunswick base, took effective control of the Con-

---

44. R. S. Wilson interview with Dr. A. C. Vincent, 15 March 1988 in possession of G. A. Rawlyk.

vention and its mouthpiece—the *Atlantic Baptist*. But before they could effectively organize themselves for the battle over Acadia—to make it a truly Christian university—they found themselves cleverly out-maneuvered by a besieged liberal minority. This minority made brilliant use of the Acadia Alumni Association and its contacts in the Nova Scotia Legislative Assembly to ensure that legislation would be introduced which would effectively secularize Acadia and remove it from possible conservative evangelical control. This bold preemptive strike, placed the conservative evangelical majority on the defensive and eventually it would have to be satisfied with control over a separate seminary—the Acadia Divinity College. Within a decade of its creation in 1969, the College had a majority of conservative evangelicals on staff and, moreover, the flow of conservative students to ADC had begun in earnest—not only from Atlantic Canada but also from Central Canada and the West.

Acadia University and Acadia Divinity College had, over a period of less than 100 years, moved from an evangelical position to a liberal evangelical and then a largely liberal one and then back to an evangelical position. This movement reflected changing theological realities in the region as well as a fascinating power struggle between leaders of two very different theological perspectives.

Scores of future Canadian Baptist Convention ministers received their education not at Acadia but at Ontario Theological Seminary and Regent College—the two dominant Canadian Protestant seminaries. Since its founding in 1976, under the effective leadership of Ian Rennie, OTS has attracted scores of Convention students—many of whom have helped to reshape the contours of the church's theology and practice. The same is true, with somewhat smaller numbers, with respect to Carey College, the Baptist Convention of Western Canada seminary loosely linked with Regent College in Vancouver. Since its creation in 1976, Regent has become "one of Canada's most influential seminaries." According to John Stackhouse:

> On the campus of one of Canada's premier secular universities was a major evangelical school. A denomination well-known for a strong streak of anti-intellectualism, the Christian Brethren, founded a graduate school, fully accredited by the Association of Theological Schools, with a faculty among the most distinguished in North American evangelicalism.[45]

Both Regent and OTS have pointed in the direction of evangelical growth and evangelical potential. New religious market forces shaping market shares, thus determining the outreach of competing denominations, appear

---

45. John Stackhouse, *Canadian Evangelicalism in the Twentieth Century: An Introduction to its Character* (Toronto: University of Toronto Press, 1993), 154.

to be blending with a continuing search for the pristine purity of a religious past to pump new life into an evangelical movement which many observers had described as virtually dead—sixty years ago. But this same almost inexorable movement may, as Finke and Stark have contended, have at its core a fundamental weakness—the powerful tendency to adjust the sacred to meet the demands of modernity especially in the realm of theological education.

In our gnostic and antinomian world, at the interface between the spirituality of neo-evangelicalism, the therapeutic interests of New Age thought and practice, and the black bleakness of postmodernity, traditional theological education, even that of a conservative Christian variety, appears to be very much on the defensive. It is not uncommon for bright students, obsessed by the inner glow of spiritual hubris, to declare that all theological education is nonsense, especially if real truth is communicated directly to the individual by the Spirit of God. Moreover, with the growing privatization of faith, and the exodus of tens of thousands of Canadians from the churches, theological education, nonevangelical and evangelical, appears to be growing increasingly irrelevant. There is growing body of evidence suggesting that in the U.S. the megachurches are determining what the conservative seminaries should be actually teaching. Market demand is obviously shaping curriculum reality. Is this the Canadian future?

Public and Private Religion

On the surface, Canada appears to be a very secular nation shaped only by a very hazy recollection of a distant Christian heritage, and largely oblivious to what seems to be an increasingly marginal minority of committed Christians. Hidden beneath the surface of the seas of secularization are to be found another part of the iceberg—many Canadians with a surprisingly strong *private* religious conviction and commitment.

In the 1990s in Canada there is a huge gap between those who believe *and* practice their Christianity, and those who have little faith in traditional Christianity. In the nineteenth and early twentieth centuries, the Christian church could be used by the Canadian elite to impose its values on society in general—and to impose a form of social control. This alliance, however, collapsed in the interwar years. The elite having little really contact with the Canadian grass roots, believed that Christianity was a spent ideological force and that God was indeed dead. Their world was a secular one, devoid of any sense of ultimate meaning other than that shaped by the shibboleths of consumerism, progress, and so-called scientific truth. In disemboweling Canadian Christianity, they alienated many Canadians whose religiosity remained orthodox and, moreover, they failed to realize that Christianity had not, in fact, died in Canada. Thus, when religiosity in Canada is studied from the bottom up, a radically different picture begins to emerge from that projected for decades from the top down. Obviously, any funeral planned for Canadian Christianity is premature. In fact, the evidence is suggesting that Canadian Protestantism is beginning to look more and more like American Protestantism and Canadian Catholicism, though largely secularized, is becoming more Protestant, even more evangelical in its style and emphasis. This is indeed a religious revolution. There may be more hope than some of us who are professional pessimists seem to realize.

Part 5

The Future of Evangelical Theological Education

This book concludes with some reflections by several leaders in the seminary world about what the history of evangelical theological education means for the future. What is the health of evangelical seminaries, and do these institutions have a stable foundation on which to build? Or are there problems in evangelical theological education that arise from the history of the movement and that faculty and administrators need to address both to be faithful to the evangelical tradition and to be effective in their educational endeavors? Also, the authors reflect on the particular strengths and weakness of evangelical theological education in the light of the history presented in these studies.

In the essays that follow the answers to these questions display variety and yet are almost unanimous in making sound and careful theology a priority. Gabriel Fackre, who teaches at Andover-Newton Theological Seminary, a mainline Protestant institution, sees many of the strengths of evangelical theological education, particularly its willingness to be faithful, its loyalty to the church, and its responsiveness to people in the pew. But Fackre also warns that these strengths can turn into weaknesses and suggests some ways that greater involvement from congregations in theological education can guard against these problems. R. Albert Mohler, president of Southern Baptist Theological Seminary, is more cautious than Fackre about the future of evangelical seminaries. Mohler believes that evangelical institutions need to work harder than ever to retain their theological identity while also recovering their churchly and spiritual dimensions. His is a warning against the dangers of academic as well as ministerial professionalism. Many of the concerns that Mohler voices about evangelical theological education, according to

273

Richard J. Mouw, president of Fuller Theological Seminary, have a long life within the evangelical tradition, are legitimate, and need to be kept in mind constantly. At the same time, Mouw believes that the changing demographics of the student body, the rapid development of new education-related technologies, and the increasing demand from seminaries for spiritual formation are matters that will greatly affect the future of evangelical theological education. He offers no predictions about that future but concludes, not unlike Mohler, that seminary faculty and administrators will have to be more explicitly theological as they negotiate the changes underway. The section concludes with the reflections of David F. Wells of Gordon-Conwell Theological Seminary about the perils of this particular cultural moment and how these perils are influencing the education offered to the students studying at evangelical seminaries. If these schools are going to serve churches faithfully, Wells believes they need to be much better grounded in theology, especially a theologically critical understanding of modern culture that will prevent the kind of schizophrenia that he sees throughout much of contemporary evangelicalism.

Wells' essay may strike some as a less than inspirational way to conclude this book and to think about the legacy of evangelical theological education for future generations. Yet the recent rapid growth and prominence of evangelical seminaries mentioned in the introduction make the seriousness of Wells' reflections all the more urgent. Indeed, in different ways all of the authors in this section reinforce the point that evangelical seminaries need to attend to the theological task of their educational mission even more than to their enrollments, number of degree programs, library holdings, or endowments. As necessary as these matters are to the health of a seminary, Fackre, Mohler, Mouw, and Wells stress that evangelical seminaries need to be watchful constantly about the solidity of their theological foundations.

To be sure, readers will have different perspectives on the future of the task of evangelical theological education in the light of its history. But as we hope the stories represented in the previous pages make clear, without some awareness of the history of evangelical seminaries' projections about the future will surely miss the mark.

14

Educating the Church

Gabriel Fackre

What are the learnings from this book? My answer comes against the background of the history of Andover, the first evangelical venture in seminary education in this country, and the institution in which I teach.

Two responses to evangelical educators, and a footnote: (1) build on your strengths; (2) beware of the temptations that go with the strengths, the corruptibility of good things. The footnote has to do with a modest proposal on the role of congregations in theological education.

Strengths

First, the institutions discussed in this book have a commitment to "keep the faith"—the historic faith, espoused in evangelical idiom. Many establishment institutions like my own, in spite of their origins, develop long flirtations with cultural orthodoxies. Mainline seminaries and divinity schools, perhaps to demonstrate their intellectual credentials within the academy, are regularly tempted to take their signals from the surrounding culture. Evangelical institutions, as we have heard, define themselves as countercultural, as "cognitively dissonant." At their best, therefore, they are prepared to resist the allurements of society's conventional wisdom.

Second, evangelical institutions are unswervingly loyal to the church in one or another of its manifestations—congregations, denominations, evangelical subcommunities. Andover, at its inception, and when faithful to its original purposes (now as Andover-Newton), describes itself a "school of the church." Evangelical seminaries are born and raised in the bosom of the Christian community, exist to prepare its leaders, rely on its resources, and thus are schools *of the church*. At the same time, they aspire to academic excellence, calling the church to "love God with the mind." They are schools of the church, willing to challenge the church when threatened by anti-intellectual frenzies or cultural captivities.

Third, evangelical institutions love "the folk." As populist (in the best sense), they are committed to serve ordinary people, are not scornful of grassroots humanity, and are not given to intellectual hauteur. Humanly speaking, this may account for their growth at times when elitist mainline institutions suffer decline.

The underside of the strengths are the weaknesses, temptations attendant to the gifts. First, evangelical stewardship of the gospel has meant "keeping the faith" in a highly subjectivist mode, the priority of the "born again" experience. This can issue in a simplistic fideism and anticultural obscurantism, as has been noted. With it comes loss of credibility. Worse, it entails defection from the evangelical theological tradition of common grace and general revelation. The latter constitutes the need for cultural dialogue, and for the critical appropriation of the good, true, and beautiful expressions God chooses to grace upon a fallen world.

A second minefield, hidden in the green fields of "keeping the faith," is the Manichaean temptation. This is again related to the experiential piety in which evangelicalism houses its commitment to historic faith. The sharp juxtaposition of light to night in the experience of conversion has a tendency to move from its legitimate place in Christian beginnings to an omnipresence that breeds both an "us" and "them" separatism and a self-righteous fury. Better a deeply affective but self-critical faith, aware of the sin that persists in the life of the redeemed. Such a piety brings with it openness to other gifts in the body of Christ, the avoidance of sectarian polemic, and the possibility of the role of loyal opposition within ecclesial institutions that desperately need the evangelical witness.

Second, the welcome commitment to the church has its shadow side. Beware of the temptation to accede to the ways of supportive ecclesiastical givens. "The churches love us. They pay our salaries and send us students, and so we thrive and grow." All this invites captivity to the way things are. A faithful seminary is not, finally, accountable to its ecclesiastical tribe, but only to its Lord. Indeed, just as the discipline of theology is said to be the self-scrutiny of the church's preaching and teaching, so the theological school, at best, is the church's loving critic-in-residence.

Third, and related to the foregoing, the commitment to the people can easily turn into conformity to the vox populi. The social, economic, and political world can make its way into the seminary through the back door of its supporters. The price of growth and popularity can be walking in lockstep with the values of the folk. The captivity to consumer attractions and the political agenda of right-wing politics of prominent TV preachers is a case study in these things. The more ambitious seminary plans are for the future, the more the need for biblical sobriety about who is paying the fiddler and for what tune. Once again, the history of both mainline seminaries with their trustee boards and funding sources, and university divinity schools with the pressure from their academic environments, is worth remembering.

My footnote (a supportive word for the attention here and there to the role of congregations in theological education): The congregation, with its workplace-attuned laity, provides a unique location for the theology/culture encounter. But we have to find a way to do it in which the laity can bring their own gifts to the table.

For thirteen years, the Eliot Church in Newton, Massachusetts has been experimenting with the "evangelical academy" approach developed in post-World War II Europe. A group of from ten to fifteen scientists has met each month for thirteen years to explore the relationship of Christian faith to workplace issues (from scientists at MIT, Boston City Hospital, research corporations on Route 128, and so on). What is the morality of commercializing gene research? What would a code of ethics for a cancer research laboratory entail? What perspective does a Christian bring to the cleanup of Boston harbor?

In this exchange, with laity providing the problematic and principal arena of discourse, the pastor and a teacher (for twelve years myself the latter) enter the conversation with the church's historic resources. Here is the bearing of the Christian doctrine of human nature; that is where the understanding of the divine mercy—or divine justice—points; this is what the doctrine of creation holds; here are the points of view in the debate on this in the history of Christian ethics.

Our experience has been that the much-sought, intellectual encounter with contemporary culture can take place this way in the congregation through its own pastors and people, as well as in more formal academic settings. Indeed, the congregational habitat, with its special sensibilities and commitments, may make for a different and deeper impact by faith on culture on such a one as a Phil Sharp, a member of our group and a 1993 Nobel Prize winner, than a comparable effort at communication in his MIT locale. Of course, it is not a case of either-or.

15

Thinking of the Future

Evangelical Theological Education in a New Age
R. Albert Mohler

"I never think of the future. It comes soon enough." Thus spoke Albert Einstein, reflecting a recognizable mood of scientific aloofness from the concerns of lesser mortals. This statement could not truthfully be made by most theological educators, for we are constantly scanning the horizon to catch a glimpse of the future shape of theological education.

Within American Protestantism, our concerns are often justifiably linked directly to the institutions we serve and about which we care deeply. It is likely that several of the seminaries and divinity schools currently in existence will not survive long into the twenty-first century.

Denominations in the old Protestant "mainline" are now considering the consolidation of some seminaries and the closure of others. Declining enrollment and denominational downsizing have left several long-established seminaries in a very precarious position. Other well-endowed institutions, such as Princeton Theological Seminary, are almost certain to endure.

Among evangelicals, the picture is less clouded by numerical decline, but remains complicated by the social and cultural transformation of the evangelical movement—a transformation that has raised serious theological issues and will certainly influence theological education.

What, then, are the critical issues facing evangelical theological education? What are the pressing questions that are even now apparent?

First, evangelicals must recover and reaffirm the essentially theological character of theological education.

The history of theological seminaries, especially among evangelicals, indicates the tension between the academic and churchly worlds—a dichotomization brought about by the culture of modernity. Lacking the Christianized culture that barely survived into the twentieth century, theological seminaries increasingly found themselves pulled in two, often opposite, directions. The churches thought of seminaries as training schools for preachers. The larger academic culture, with the rise of the culture of professionalism and modern research universities, saw seminaries as graduate schools with a theological specialization. The divide is now so wide that no single institution can serve both of these masters. Most have attempted a middle way between these two publics, but with mixed results.

A theological seminary has no right to exist apart from its charge to train, educate, and prepare ministers for service in the churches. This is an inherently theological task, for this ministry is, biblically defined, kerygmatic in character.

On the Protestant left wing, the secularization of the civic culture and the vandalizing of the academic culture have left little tolerance for theological concerns. At Yale, for example, some faculty within the university have publicly questioned the existence of the Yale Divinity School as a part of their purportedly "secular" university.

Among evangelicals, the danger is less a resistance to theology in the name of secularism and more a marginalization of theological concerns in the wake of pragmatism. Evangelicals are certain that theological seminaries are to train ministers; they are uncertain that serious theological engagement is necessary—or even helpful—for this purpose.

Evangelical theological educators must make clear that ministerial education is inescapably theological and that serious theological engagement is neither an accessory nor a threat to ministerial education.

Second, evangelical theological education must be confessional in character.

Confessionalism sets evangelical theological institutions apart from the larger world of theological education. Evangelical ministerial education must be theological, but a further distinction must be made. The theological character of evangelical seminaries must be safeguarded by confessionalism.

This confessional character—in terms of a confession that is both declarative and regulative—is the evangelical seminary's warrant for its theological mission. The most significant divide in theological education is not between the Protestant and Roman Catholic schools, or between the schools of the Free Churches and the connectional churches, nor is it a matter of geography or demography or ethnicity. The great divide is between the seminaries that are confessional and those that are not.

Thus, we now face a landscape with two opposing cultures of theological education. The confessional culture understands its primary public of accountability to be the churches. The nonconfessional culture sees its primary public as the academy. The issue comes down to this: Who sets the norms and establishes final accountability? Evangelical institutions must stand ready to declare their theological convictions and maintain unapologetic fidelity to their confessions and churches. This is the scandal of particularity, but it is a scandal we must bear.

Evangelical churches are rightly concerned that theological education severed from confessional accountability is immediately vulnerable to the accommodationist pressures of modern secular culture. The mainline Protestant denominations have largely been secularized, and the dominant academic culture generally shapes the worldview of those institutions serving these historic denominations.

Evangelicals have overtly resisted the modernizing acids of the secular culture, but covertly we have imported modernity in worship, doctrine, and lifestyle. As sociologist James Davison Hunter and theologian David Wells have demonstrated, evangelicals have become skilled at disguising modernity through what Hunter describes as "cognitive bargaining" and what Wells traces as the self-referential character of modern evangelicalism.

A recovery of confessionalism is now taking place in many evangelical sectors, including the Southern Baptist Convention and evangelicals in the mainline denominations such as United Methodism.

Authentic confessionalism is a necessary corrective to these trends, but it is not sufficient. Confessionalism must be guarded by sustained relationships with identifiable churches, who hold the seminary accountable.

Third, evangelical seminaries must forge new working relationships with the churches—and learn from the congregations.

For evangelical institutions, distance from the churches means abstraction from the task and risks alienation from the faith. Evangelical theological education was born in the churches, who understood their responsibility to train and educate ministers of the gospel. Over the past two centuries, theological education has been increasingly removed from the congregation to the seminary.

This trend will be reversed—and the reversal has already begun. Among evangelicals, the megachurches are increasingly setting the pace and shaping the culture. Though the pastors or senior ministers of most megachurches hold seminary degrees, these churches often educate and train their own staff ministers, who may be called out of a secular business background and trained within the context of the megachurch congregation.

The antebellum tradition of "reading theology" with an older and learned minister is also returning, often in the form of staff experience under a megachurch pastor or minister. Churches seeking pastors are often more impressed with the congregational ministry experience a candidate has received under a recognized senior minister than with formal theological education received through a seminary.

The megachurches are not the only issue, however. New models of congregational theological education and ministerial preparation are emerging.

Some seminaries will see these models as threats to their existence and prosperity. Other institutions will seize the opportunity to forge healthy and creative partnerships with those churches.

In any event, we must learn again to listen to the congregations and to gain from them the knowledge necessary for seminaries to prepare ministers "well furnished" for ministry in the local church.

Fourth, evangelical seminaries must seek to regain curricular focus out of the current confusion.

In the years since World War II, most seminaries have experienced a radical expansion of degree options and course offerings, and evangelical institutions have often led in this expansion. The basic degree for ministry, generally the Master of Divinity (M.Div.), has now been joined by a plethora of degrees, degree tracks, and options. Furthermore, within the M.Div. itself, a vast array of courses—many with minute areas of specialized study—compete for student enrollment.

This confusion, the unintended consequence of well-intended innovations, has not well served the churches, the students, or the seminaries. A review of recent editions of the *Fact Book on Theological Education,* published by the Association of Theological Schools, reveals that seminary M.Div. enrollment has been shrinking as a percentage of total head count enrollment within many seminaries—and within the seminaries taken together. What does this say about theological education and its future? Most of the competing programs are less demanding in terms of both duration and cognitive disciplines. (Most non-M.Div. programs do not require biblical languages, for example.)

This pattern threatens the core mission of the seminaries, because some students are clearly choosing non-M.Div. programs in order to save both time and effort. Seminaries that allow this trend to continue unabated will find themselves in a very difficult position. Churches have other means of securing and supporting programs of study in counseling, administration, communications, and the various areas of specialization now common to the larger seminaries. I am not suggesting that these specialized programs should not be offered. I am sounding a word of caution against the trend.

Competing degree programs are not the only confusing and dangerous trend, however. The M.Div. curriculum has itself been transformed as the core theological and biblical disciplines have been weakened and, at times, marginalized. Today's seminary graduate is less prepared in terms of exegesis, doctrinal knowledge, theological formation, and historical backgrounds than graduates of recent generations past. Modern graduates are often formed by a myriad of superficial survey courses and electives of dubious value.

Curricular recovery and clarity are essential if evangelical seminaries are to remain true to their central vision and mission. The academic catalogue is a critical document of institutional accountability and a barometer of purpose.

Fifth, evangelical seminaries must avoid conceiving themselves as mere professional schools and understand that authentic seminary education requires the establishment and nurture of a faithful community of scholars.

For over a century, theological educators have debated the design and purpose of seminary programs, but the general trend of seminary development has been consistent with the professionalization of the culture. The minister is often understood as a religious professional in the same sense that a physician is regarded as a medical professional.

Theological education may thus be conceived as a program of professional training and education that can transform any person into a minister. This is a reversion of the biblical pattern. We believe that God calls ministers for the church and that this spiritual calling is matched by spiritual gifts and qualifications.

We must never apologize for the spiritual dimension of our task or the spiritual foundation of our calling. We must also see our seminaries as communities of faith, where consecrated scholars are gathered for studies that are inherently both cognitive and spiritual.

This communal character of theological education raises yet another issue facing seminaries. The development of new educational technologies and delivery systems raises new considerations. Some educators point to the development of a "virtual university," and thus of a "virtual seminary," whereby theological education is transmitted over the Internet from the host institution directly to the student's personal computer.

Though some disciplines and vocations may lend themselves to such technologies, this is not a proper or adequate means of providing theological education. We should avoid becoming neo-Luddites even as we refuse uncritically to join the latest technological bandwagon. The relational and ecclesial character of ministerial education defies reduction to bits and bytes.

Finally, evangelicals must not be surprised to find themselves and their theological institutions more and more characterized as a cognitive minority. This status is very real, and it is to be expected, given the increasing secularization of the culture.

As we consider the future, the heritage of evangelical theological education must be more than a trophy or an issue for historical investigation. This heritage establishes critical markers for accountability. Would those persons who founded and nurtured our seminaries recognize what we are doing in the name of theological education? Would they recognize in us the same passions, convictions, visions, and commitments they saw in themselves? Are we possessed of the same hopes and concerns for our students and graduates as they were?

Quite obviously, the answers to these questions cannot be reduced to matters of degrees, delivery systems, courses, and catalogues. These issues are matters of the heart. And of all persons, evangelicals should be the first to recognize matters of the heart.

Einstein was right—the future does come soon enough, God willing. We are called the look to the future with hope and with care.

16

Challenge of Evangelical Theological Education

Richard J. Mouw

A strong commitment to theological education cannot be taken for granted in the evangelical community. Indeed, there are several unique reasons why evangelicals are somewhat suspicious of the enterprise of theological education. As a movement with affinities to the pietist movements of the past, evangelicals have long nurtured some rather overt suspicions of the academy.

These suspicions have been reinforced by two major historical struggles. The first is the reaction on the part of many of the early post-Reformation pietist groups against what they saw as the "dead orthodoxy" of scholastic Protestantism. In seventeenth century Germany, for example, pietists expressed a deep dissatisfaction with university-related theological education. Theological faculties, they insisted, promoted a religion of the "head" and not of the "heart"—a language that is still preserved today in evangelical circles. They formed house churches and other spiritual renewal associations to provide an alternative to worship settings that were dominated by lengthy doctrinal discourses.

The second struggle was initiated when the "dead orthodoxy" of Protestant scholasticism was replaced in the universities by the "live heterodoxy" of Enlightenment modernism. Here was a new kind of rationalism, one that celebrated a secularizing anthropocentrism. While this form of rationalism called for the formation of new defenses, it was yet another stage in evangelicalism's painful struggle against the mindset of the academy. Even when conservative Protestants established their own academic institutions, they often did so with considerable caution and suspicion.

When the twentieth century came along, North American evangelicals found some new reasons for maintaining this longstanding attitude. The struggles against mainstream theological liberalism were often waged on academic battlefields, the goal being the control of denominational seminaries. Evangelicals were regularly defeated in these battles, with the result that many of evangelicalism's most painful memories focus on the loss of theological schools. Evangelicals know what it is like to cry out in despair, "They have taken away my seminary, and I do not know where they have laid it."

It is important for those of us who are deeply involved in evangelical theological education to name this pain. I find this necessary in my own academic context. I must admit that I find it very distasteful when evangelicals worry that the institution I lead is on "the slippery slope," or has allowed "the camel's nose in the tent." While I consider these metaphors inappropriate as applied to Fuller Theological Seminary, I also feel the need to acknowledge the real experience of vulnerability that goes along with a predilection for that kind of imagery. As people who live with vivid memories of seminaries that have been lost in the struggle against modernism and other heterodox forces, our penchant for the metaphors of vulnerability are not mere exercises in the paranoid style. They are worries that stem from real historical experiences.

For these and other reasons, evangelicals find it easier than most other Christians to ask the poignant question, "Why have seminaries at all?" That question is not voiced much among mainline Protestants and certainly is not a natural one for Roman Catholics to ask. It is never far, though, from the lips of many evangelicals.

I came across abundant evidence of this a few years ago when I read Virginia Brereton's fascinating historical study of the "Bible institute" movement, *Training God's Army: The American Bible School, 1880–1940*. The Bible institutes usually presented themselves as a complement to the theological seminaries. They asserted that their goal was to train lay workers as missionaries and evangelists. As A. J. Gordon, founder of the Boston Missionary Training School, put it, the purpose of these institutes was not to produce gifted preachers or profound theologians, but "men and women, who know enough of their Bible to lead souls to Christ, and to instruct converts in the simple principles of the Gospel." There was often, as the deconstructionists would put it, a subtext to this surface rhetoric: A. J. Gordon himself observed on at least one occasion that he was "perpetually chagrined to see how much better many of the unschooled lay preachers of our time can handle the Scriptures than many clergymen who have passed through the theological curriculum."

The histories of many of these Bible institutes provide a vindication of sorts for the continuing existence of theological seminaries. Many of them *became* seminaries: A. J. Gordon's institute, for example, is now Gordon-Conwell Theological Seminary. But these sentiments expressed in Gordon's lament about theological education still persist. Not long ago I talked with a minister who spoke with much enthusiasm about a "megachurch" institute he had attended. At first his language was complementarian: what he learned there was a good addition to what he had studied in seminary. As the conversation moved along, though, he began to sound more and more critical of seminaries; maybe, he wondered, short-term training sessions in the outreach and discipling methods of the megachurches was *all* that was needed for successful ministry.

Evangelical Christians have a penchant for raising basic questions about the rationale for theological education. We do not take it for granted that Mother Teresa—or Chuck Colson or Corrie Ten Boom—would have been better off with a seminary degree. Indeed, some evangelicals are not fully convinced that anyone really needs to engage in the formal study of theology.

It would be wrong simply to dismiss these concerns as wrongheaded. I am convinced that there are some good instincts among those who question the value of theological education. One instinct is embedded in a deep commitment to effective ministry. Evangelicals are shaped by pietist and populist passions, and we know that study in a seminary has often had the effect of dampening spiritual ardor. Theological schools have sometimes fostered a clerical elitism that is out of touch with the spiritual needs of ordinary Christians. When evangelicals have questioned the need for formal theological education, it has often been out of a devotion to a high, rather than a low, view of the ministerial calling.

The question, then, of "Why seminaries at all?" is a constant one on the agenda of evangelicals. And it's a good question. I think one of the things that shock some people about the work George Marsden is doing is that he is willing to consider, in ways that American intellectuals aren't used to considering, a fundamental restructuring of the relationship between religion and higher education. That is an evangelical gift. We are sensitive to those realities because education has to be subordinate to the religious calling. Evangelicals are a people who are committed to the gospel, but we must be willing to think radical thoughts about what it takes to promote it through education.

There are a number of concerns that need to be addressed as evangelicals look to the future of theological education. One of those concerns deals with the important issue of student demographics and the geography of theological education. New students coming to seminaries these days are, on the average, older than they used to be. Gone are the times when the typical Protestant seminary student body consisted of males in their early twenties just out of college and preparing for ministry in a traditional one-person staff parish. More and more seminary campuses are filling up with women and older persons, many of whom are now considering a vocation in church-related ministries after having spent time in a different career. Another reality of student demographics is that some students only come to seminary part-time or commute, while others even want the theological curriculum brought to them via extension programs. Obviously, these are important factors to consider when thinking about the future of theological education.

A closely related second concern has to do with the new technologies that are forcing educators to rethink the way that theological curriculum is taught. For example, language learning can often take place, at least on an introductory level, with an individual student working at home with the aid of computer software, rather than in the classroom with a teacher writing conjugated verbs on a chalkboard. Another formative technology is the introduction of interactive video programming along fiber-optic lines. Now, through videotaped lectures, prominent theologians and theological educators can teach individuals who do not belong to the student body of the institutions where they are faculty members. Technology is definitely altering the patterns of learning, as well as the geography of theological education.

A third issue for consideration deals with new opportunities and challenges to be faced in the area of spiritual formation. The theological school has always considered itself as more than simply a classroom experience. Seminaries have also been viewed, and rightly so, as communities where the classroom learning and research activities have been complemented by, and integrated with, worship, devotional study of the Scriptures, and prayer life. One of the most stimulating developments in the area of spiritual formation involves a new ecumenical awareness. In North America more and more Protestants are drawing on the resources of, say, the desert fathers and the desert mothers. People in even very conservative evangelical churches are reading Catholic writers like Henry Nouwen and Thomas Merton. There is also a new visibility of the spiritual traditions of Eastern Orthodoxy. We are all learning from each other about issues of spiritual formation and the spiritual disciplines. This not only will, but should, have an important impact on the patterns of theological education.

In many ways, people are coming to seminary today specifically for the purpose of enhancing their spiritual formation. Often they are not at all interested in working within the boundaries of the parish as traditionally understood. There are more and more lay people who are coming to seminary from the marketplace simply to enrich their understanding of their vocation in, for instance, law, medicine, or social services. Others are preparing for the ample parachurch ministries that have been spawned by the growing evangelical presence in North America.

Another significant concern of theological educators deals with role proliferation. Several essays in this volume illustrate this historically. There can be no question that clergy function differently today than they have in the past. Previously, the job performance of pastors was often evaluated by their ability to preach a good sermon and carry out a limited variety of activities, such as visitation of the sick. Today team ministries have become essential. The very idea of a team ministry recognizes the diversity of the work of the parish. Much more explicit attention is being given to such areas as youth outreach and ministry to single persons. The complexity of issues facing church leaders today has increased considerably to include such interests as marriage and family counseling, church administration, and budget management. The parish ministry currently embodies a rich variety of roles, many of which were only implicitly acknowledged in traditional ministries, and some of which are new facets of ministry that have emerged as significant in the last few decades.

It is very difficult for seminaries to take on these important challenges at the same time as they attempt to preserve the strengths of the traditional theological curriculum. There is no doubt in my mind that we need more courses in areas such as counseling, church administration, and conflict management. We also need courses that deal with the various specialized foci of ministries in diverse congregations. We will not perform any of these tasks well unless we continue to preserve a solid foundation in the study of the Scriptures, systematic theology, and church history. So many of the things that we may see as innovations could very well be replays of mistakes made in the past. But we can also learn from the blessings and the successes of the past. Thankfully, a historical consciousness continues to be extremely important for the evangelical churches. Consequently, this enables us to maintain a very strong emphasis on systematic theology, in order to think clearly and carefully about the scope of Christian teaching as it bears on the life of the witness of the people of God.

Theological education must also acknowledge the important class shift in evangelical Protestantism that has occurred in recent decades. The cultural position of evangelicals is very different now than it was a half a century ago. Pentecostal and Holiness congregations, which once stood on the wrong side of the tracks, are now often flourishing ecclesiastical enterprises that occupy the best real estate in town. Evangelicals can be found in positions of leadership in politics, higher education, the entertainment business, and the marketplace. Our older theological formulations which reflected an experience of cultural marginalization, do not sit comfortably with today's prospering, upwardly mobile evangelicals. It should not surprise us that the very Christians who once thought of themselves as a faithful fundamentalist remnant and whose theme song was, "This world is not my home, I'm just a-passing through," came to describe themselves without embarrassment in the 1980s as a "moral majority." The more progressive entrepreneurial groups in the contemporary evangelical community are taking up new challenges. For example, many congregations, especially those influenced by "megachurches," are asking fundamental questions about the nature of a worship service, a sermon, and ministry in general.

Seminaries are being asked to take up these challenges, as well as face a few new ones. These new challenges are ones that I referred to previously:

What is a campus? What is a theological curriculum? How can psychology, sociology, and anthropology help us respond better to our rapidly changing cultural environment? How can we put new communication technologies to good use in our educational mission? These are questions of renewal that continually rest on the minds of theological educators today. They have much to do with the social and cultural—even economic—context in which evangelicals find themselves at the end of the twentieth century.

My sense of what theological educators will face in the future is tied to the conviction that we are going to have to be much more intentionally and self-consciously theological than we have been before. The distrust of the intellect I have addressed has been so common in the evangelical tradition that it has often led us into an unreflective pragmatism. This emphasis on "getting the job done" or "getting out there and reaching the world with the gospel" has obviously been linked to some important evangelical strengths. But, the evangelical community cannot survive long as a healthy spiritual and evangelistic presence in the world without thinking very carefully about the theological foundations for what it is doing. This is an important time for all of us who care deeply about the cause of theological education to emphasize the absolute necessity of conscientiously considering, on the basis of the authoritative Word of God, what kind of world we live in and what God is calling us to do in that world, with a sound and comprehensive theological perspective.

17

Educating for a Countercultural Spirituality

David F. Wells

There was a time when I thought that most of the answers to the church's perplexities and weaknesses in the present could be found somewhere in the past. I imagined the church's movement through time to be like that of a person climbing a spiral staircase, in which he or she kept passing over the same spot again and again, only at a different elevation. That was what I thought then, at the time when I was a practicing church historian, but what I think now, as a theologian, is a little different.

What I have come to see more clearly and what, in fact, I should have known all along, is that the question as to what can be learned from the past is one that can be answered only after a careful assessment has been made of the elements in continuity and in discontinuity between the two ages in comparison. What is *continuous* through all ages are matters of God and human nature. It is the same God, the same divine revelation, and the same gospel the church holds to in every age. And it is the same human nature and the same predictable furrows along which its corruption flows, which, in every age, is the object of God's grace. It is because of what continues that church history is so important. Augustine and Luther, Calvin and Edwards should be perennial reading because they have expounded and addressed the unchanging realities of God, his Word, his grace, and our sin with great profundity and abiding pertinence. These theological themes, then, are the threads that pass through every succeeding generation, linking one to the other.

The *discontinuities* arise from culture, from the assumptions in any given society about what is normal and normative in belief and behavior and these, by contrast, do change, as do the resulting habits and appetites that flow from them, as well as the cognitive horizons that they generate, for these shift with the moving cultural terrain. These are what make one age different from another. I once paid scant attention to these cultural discontinuities, thinking that they were irrelevancies in comparison to what was continuous in God and nature, but some of our sociologists of knowledge have persuaded me to give these cultural disjunctures far more weight than I once did.

In some ages, the elements in discontinuity are minor and, therefore, the ages are dominated by what they have in common. In those times, the church borrows easily from the past. In other ages, however, the elements of discontinuity loom larger, especially when civilizations are either unraveling or are building upon the ashes of a prior and fallen world. Then these discontinuities emerge starkly and may assert themselves in discomforting tension against what does not change. Borrowing from one age for another becomes an altogether more complex matter. Today, I believe, we are living at one of those transitionary moments because our civilization is beginning to unravel. As the West sinks beneath the weight of its own modernity, as the evangelical church wobbles and disintegrates with it, the discontinuities with the past become ever larger. At times they almost obscure what links human life in all ages.

Today, it is one of these fissures, one of these cultural breaks, that seems almost to place past eras of theological education on one side of a divide and our own on the other. Perhaps that states the matter too starkly. It is, nevertheless, true that before the virtues of what was done in the past can be brought into the present, our own cultural context has to be thought about very carefully, for without this the past efforts will have only an awkward and tangential relationship to what we are attempting to do in the present.

The Severed Past

It is, of course, true that in very general ways, the objectives of theological education, whether this has been considered formally or informally, carried out on the road or in institutions, by a minister with an apprentice or by professors with students, have remained largely unchanged. The church, at least in its better moments, has known that its ministers need to be people of godly character, knowledgeable of the Word, competent in its proclamation and application, and people who have the requisite personal skills to be shepherds of God's flock. But if the goals have not greatly changed, their realization today has been made considerably more difficult by the circumstances of modernity.[1] Indeed, so intrusive and novel are these circumstances that

---

1. The nature, ligaments, and dynamics of modernity are too complex to describe in this brief essay. I have sought to do this at greater length in my *No Place for Truth: Or, Whatever Happened to Evangelical Theology?* (Grand Rapids: Eerdmans, 1993), 55–94. I have elaborated on the connections between modernity and postmodernity a little further in the sequel, *God in the Wasteland: The Reality of Truth in a World of Fading Dreams* (Grand Rapids: Eerdmans, 1994), 46–50, 93–4, 216–24.

one is tempted to say that the church has faced nothing like it before. Consider just some of the most obvious institutional, cultural, and intellectual changes that have occurred in our time in relation to the places where men and women now receive their theological training.

First, think of the institutional changes. Perhaps the importance of institutional ethos is overestimated in its impact upon what is taught and what is learned,[2] but ethos should not be overlooked entirely. To begin with, seminaries must reckon, in a way that has never been so in the past, with the demands of the federal and state government, which, since the end of the Second World War, have become increasingly intrusive and have inserted into seminary life a growing body of rules, demands, and regulations.[3] In concert with this, seminaries must always be in a defensive legal posture because even the most ephemeral of student grievances can become a costly lawsuit. And student needs, needs of every kind, have grown exponentially. They have become insatiable and bottomless and they are voiced with all of the insistence of consumers who have a right to be served. In combination, these new forces have turned many seminaries into top-heavy bureaucracies and it is far from clear that their muscle-bound nature enhances the quality of the education they are offering.

As important as these changes are the ways in which seminaries are being changed structurally. Although a few seminaries still retain the nineteenth century practice of filling their boards with pastors, most today look for board members among the professions and, in particular, the business community. The reason for this is obvious. Seminaries are increasingly dependent on outside sources of revenue for their survival.

The influence of the business community on education, in general, is a well studied theme, and the consensus is that while there is something to be said on both sides, what is negative in its influence actually far outweighs what is positive. This is especially true when the attempt is made to model seminaries after corporations, when the students become the product, the churches become the market, and efficiency becomes the dominating ethic. The difficulty with this, of course, is that while institutional processes can be made more efficient, the rate at which learning occurs cannot and to expect of learners efficiencies of which only organizations are capable inevitably

---

2. In its Quality and Accreditation Project undertaken in 1993 and 1994, the Association of Theological Schools, the accrediting agency for seminaries, has been asking itself what a good theological education looks like. The nature of ATS clearly militates against its ability to give clear prescriptions with respect to the content of what is taught, the theological commitments of those who teach, and the specific theological and spiritual outcomes toward which educators should work. On these matters, it is mute. That means, then, that specificity has to be reserved for matters such as structure and governance and this skewers the understanding of what constitutes a good education, biblically speaking at least. See the whole edition of *Theological Education*, XXX, No. 2 (spring 1994).

3. Robert Wuthnow, *The Restructuring of American Religion: Society and Faith Since World War II* (Princeton: Princeton University Press, 1990).

produces a shallow experience of learning. Not only so, but this mentality also makes seminaries extremely vulnerable to what may be passing fads and fashions in the culture, which become the market to which they are obliged to adapt their product.

Seminaries experience cultural change in many ways, but one of the most direct is through this "market" which they seek to serve. In times of pared budgets, such as today, even the slightest twitch here becomes a convulsion in the seminary. The fact that it might be the negative and destructive values of modernity which are the strings that jerk around the seminaries apparently is not a thought which alarms us too much, so completely have many seminaries become enraptured by the model of the corporate world—with its markets, CEOs, and profits—and so completely intent are they upon surviving, regardless of the consequences. It surely would have alarmed many of our forebears, however, who had a keen sense, as the apostles did, of the great perils of worldliness.

But this is not the only place where developments in culture wash against the seminaries. With the multiplication of denominations, and with the growing enculturation of the churches, has come great confusion as to what a minister should be like and what he should do. This confusion is rooted in the fact that as churches have been affected by modernity their theological character has rapidly eroded. As they have become hollowed out, the emptiness has then been filled with a multitude of competing and conflicting beliefs as to what the Christian ministry is all about. Now the pastor is not simply a godly person intent upon caring for a flock by feeding them from the Word of God, but an institutional manager, a psychologist, a CEO, a denominational politician, an entrepreneur, a personality, and perhaps even an entertainer. This transformation of the minister is without precedent, unless we think back to the clerical decadence in the Middle Ages where we might find some parallels.

There are also enormous intellectual changes that are afoot and which leave us in an awkward and ambiguous relationship to the past. Despite our society's breathtaking technological gains, for example, our students are less educated than they were a century ago and the moments of great learning, such as in the scholastic period which Richard Muller has described, are so far removed from what is typical or attainable today as to be barely comprehensible. At the same time, seminaries are already having to experiment with new modes of delivering education, and whatever else can be said about it, the fact remains that watching a TV screen or listening to tapes in solitude is a little different than learning about the ministry by living in Jonathan Edwards' house. And seminaries have had to adapt themselves to a widening array of academic desires and now offer many master's degrees, not to mention the D.Min., their own thin version of a doctorate. One can scarcely imagine what the Puritans would have thought about that!

Then there is the factor of women in theological education. Most seminaries have actively sought to have women in the student body and on their faculties, but we have yet to see how far and in what ways the raising of gender issues, and the defining of ministry around such issues, is going to affect theological education. It can be said with certainty, however, that this does mark a departure from what was typical in the past.

Those who teach in the seminaries, both men and women, are the products of the learned guild and this, too, means that what is learned for ministry, what is considered important in that learning, is by its very modernity greatly at odds with most of the past. This learning is now completely professionalized. In the process, the field of knowledge has been shattered into hundreds of small pieces over which these professionals preside, pieces that would be unrecognizable to most of our theological forebears.

Therefore, today seminaries are at the confluence of two very troubling streams. On the one hand, there are numerous forces from government, from student demand, and from our admiration for corporate America which are coalescing to produce institutions which are increasingly top heavy and bureaucratic in their ethos. Consequently, the educational experience is changed for students and the costs are escalated. On the other hand, while the seminaries have become more musclebound in their organization, they have become more anemic in their internal life. Modernity has not only left its prints upon how learning is perceived and how it works, but also upon those who teach and those who learn, and the results are not always friendly toward serious thought or toward the preservation of Christian orthodoxy.

Each of these differences warrants the kind of careful and nuanced analysis that is impossible to provide here. What I can do, however, is to summarize briefly the findings of a major new study on evangelical seminarians.[4] It is all too common to think of theological education only in terms of the institutional structures in which it occurs, the curriculum design which is followed, and the faculty who deliver it, the kinds of things to which I have just briefly alluded. What is omitted all too often are the students who are taught. What are they like today and what major challenges will they pose to educators in the future? The answers to these questions in the years ahead may prove to be quite as important as any of the issues touched upon so far be-

---

4. The empirical research for this study was done in fall, 1993, by Rodger R. Rice, Director of the Social Research Center at Calvin College and by Ann W. Annis, Assistant Director. Seven evangelical seminaries participated in this study. They were: Asbury Theological Seminary, Bethel Theological Seminary, Calvin Theological Seminary, Denver Conservative Baptist Seminary, Fuller Theological Seminary, Gordon-Conwell Theological Seminary, and Talbot School of Theology. Of the 2,355 students eligible to participate, 1,591 were sent the questionnaire. Of these, 730 completed and returned it. This was a response rate of 45.9% and constituted 22.4% of all those eligible in the sampling pool. The sampling error is estimated to be plus or minus 3.2%. The full study, from which these findings are drawn, can be found in my *God in the Wasteland*, 186–213, 228–56.

cause they prescribe what can be achieved practically, and they sharpen our focus on what should be taught.

A Contemporary Portrait

This study of contemporary seminaries was quite extensive and sought to discover what the correlations were between the theological beliefs the students professed and the actual values by which they lived. Most of the findings, in fact, cannot be recounted presently because of space considerations, but what is at the heart of these findings can be sketched briefly.

We begin with an uncomplicated definition of theology as "the reflection on the truth of God's Word and application of that truth to ourselves and our world." In other words, it had three components. Foundationally, theology must begin with the truth of God's Word and, therefore, with the God of that Word, the God of unchanging truth. Theology, secondly, has to do with the interior life—with reflection, moral culture, intellectual formulation, and spiritual maturation. Third, it has to do with working out the intersections between that truth and the norms, values, hopes, and failures of American culture. With this definition, 47.3 percent agreed strongly and 43.9 percent simply agreed, for a total of 91.2 percent.

What we then discovered was that while the doctrinal substance of theology has been taught and is believed by the students, seeing the reality of that doctrinal truth, both internally and in the contemporary world was, despite their good intentions, largely lost on these students. They understand the doctrine of sin, for example, but do not always see how this plays out, either inwardly or in the culture. This is no small lacuna when one remembers that in the New Testament the "world" is that system of values in any given society which is erected by fallen human nature, which places the sinner at its center and God at its periphery and which, in consequence, makes sin look normal and righteousness look strange. One cannot love God and be worldly at the same time (James 4:4). Seeing sin in ourselves and in the culture is, therefore, of the essence of godliness, and in its absence the effectiveness of Christian ministry will be scuttled as certainly as was the Titanic upon encountering the submerged iceberg.

We, therefore, asked what images the students had of themselves and their world. We used a series of scales with contrasting images at each end and seven points between them. These scales had also been used in the 1980s by the National Opinion Research Center at the University of Chicago. This enabled us to make comparisons of our students with the general population.

On the matter of human corruption, our students were somewhat clear. Nationally, only 16.6 percent held positions on the continuum that asserted that nature is perverse and corrupt, but 79.4 percent of our students stated this. However, when the comparable question was asked about the outside world, our students' visions became quite cloudy. Although 79.5 percent saw the world as a place "of strife and disorder," rather than harmony and goodness, yet only 38.4 percent saw the world as filled with sin. What we seem to have encountered here is what we saw elsewhere. It is that culture is viewed as harmless and neutral, even if human beings are considered perverse and corrupt.

This, however, leads into a larger ambiguity. While the students affirmed that human nature is perverse and corrupt, they believed the self is mostly innocent. Our findings very closely replicated those of James Hunter in his survey of evangelical seminarians done in 1982. In 1993, 40.2 percent asserted that "realizing my full potential as a human being is just as important as putting others before myself," a proposition which, had the Son of God believed it, would have eliminated the possibility of the incarnation (cf. Phil. 2:5–12) and which, in any case, demolishes at a single stroke many of the matters the apostles insisted were central to the practice of Christian virtue. A large majority, 86.7 percent, think self-improvement is important and they are devoting themselves to it and 52.3 percent say that they spend a lot of time thinking about themselves.

It would seem rather evident, then, that the sea change in cultural attitudes plotted by Daniel Yankelovich in 1981 has deeply affected our students.[5] They, too, are defining life in terms of finding and fulfilling the self, the self being understood as a hierarchy of inner needs, which must simply be identified so that they can be satisfied. The fact that these needs might very well reflect the perversity and corruption believed to lie in human nature is not apparently a thought that has occurred to many. So what is the explanation?

Using some questions developed by Robert Wuthnow,[6] we were able to establish that there was a strong likelihood that these students operated with multiple worldviews. The most likely system of meaning, with 90.3 percent in the two highest categories, was theistic, namely, that meaning is given by the God who has created and sustains all of life. At the same time, 48.8 percent were also in the two highest categories of an individualistic worldview, which sees the individual at the center of life and believes that the outside world does not impinge upon their own interior reality. Finally, 51.6 percent were also to be found in the two highest categories of the mystical worldview, which sees meaning in life coming from its peak experiences of being at one with the universe, and in which intuition charts what direction the person takes.

Thus it is that these students navigate through life, probably using multiple worldviews, between which they move amphibiously. It would appear

5. See Daniel Yankelovich, *New Rules: Searching for Self-Fulfillment in a World Turned Upside Down* (New York: Random House, 1981).

6. See Robert Wuthnow, *The Consciousness Reformation* (Berkeley: University of California Press, 1976), 136–42.

that when speaking of matters of biblical doctrine, they think within a theistic worldview, but when engaging matters of the self, and when encountering our cultural obsession with what is therapeutic, they then move into an individualistic or mystical worldview. Therefore, that biblically they can affirm the corruption of human nature and society because they are speaking within a theistic worldview, but this corruption largely dissipates when they are looking at themselves and culture from within the individualistic or mystical worldview.

To the Future

How, then, can the best insights from the past be brought into the present? It seems to me that three matters of importance stand out above all others.

1. Education for ministry in the past, whether this was undertaken in seminaries or under the older apprentice model, was always education for a church, understood biblically and theologically. The church then called for a ministry that matched its own biblical and theological character. Today this character is eroding in the church and loud calls are now being made for a different kind of ministry for which a different kind of preparation will be necessary. So radical are the changes now afoot, that seminaries as we know them today may well disappear in a short period of time if the church is not able to recover its theological character. If this character continues to erode, then it will make sense to move the preparation of the next generation of ministers out of the seminaries and into schools of psychology and business.

2. As the West sinks into more pervasive and pernicious forms of modernity and postmodernity, the matter of Christ and culture looms larger and larger. We, today, are in a missionary context in which our host culture is as alien to the interests of biblical faith and sometimes as hostile, as are many societies in Africa and Asia. By contrast, evangelical faith has lost much of its own sense of being a "stranger and alien" in this culture. In fact, it is often quite comfortable and at home in modernity. Where a justification is offered for this kind of capitulation, it often comes in the form of an argument for Christ's connectedness to culture through natural revelation and common grace. This argument, however, is misconstrued if it is not accompanied by the clear understanding of Christ's moral and cognitive antithesis to modernity. Those at ease in the culture take unkindly to any suggestion of antithesis, but without this common grace simply becomes common worldliness. Not only so, but without this antithesis, we will, however unwittingly, set ourselves to duplicating the older Protestant liberalism, at the center of which was a Christ-of-culture motif. Or, to put it dif-

ferently, what we will produce for our time is simply secular evangelicalism where what is secular cohabits not simply with its more customary bed partner, humanism, but with one that is now religious.

It is this cognitive and moral antithesis that evangelical seminary students have sometimes missed entirely, and it is what most threatens the effectiveness of their education. It is this issue of Christ and culture, I believe, which should form the background of virtually every course that is taught. If seminaries fail to educate effectively within their own cultural context—as they expect all missionaries to do!—then they will continue to graduate students who may be doctrinally correct, who may believe in human depravity, but who, nevertheless, think that the self and culture are essentially innocent. Is it any wonder, then, that the evangelical church is now drowning in its own worldliness?

Seminaries are typically assuming either that their students will themselves know how to discern what is injurious to faith in the culture or that no such discernment is necessary, given the neutrality of culture. Is it likely, though, that students will do on their own what they know their professors have either been unable or unwilling to do for themselves? In the absence of a clear, sustained insistence that what is normative in culture is by no means what is normative for the church, evangelical Christianity will become indistinguishable from modernized American culture and that is simply the back door into theological liberalism. The preservation of biblical Christianity in the coming years, I believe, will be directly tied to our ability to distinguish Christ from culture.

3. The professionalization of learning has had both good and bad consequences for theological students. On the one hand, it has produced a mass of learned specialists in the seminaries whose microscopic knowledge of their fields is admirable and whose learning is prodigious. On the other hand, it has also produced an experience of learning for the student that is disconcertingly fragmented and disjointed, for all of the inner connections between subjects have now been lost. In this circumstance, it is then left to the theologians, if they can, to put Humpty Dumpty back together again. Unfortunately, they can have no more success than did all the king's men and all the king's horses in an earlier day.

The answer to this peculiarly modern problem is to begin by looking for a different kind of faculty, for those who, regardless of their discipline, are able to think theologically and to think of their own discipline within a larger theological frame. What is needed are not more specialists to break down further the coherence of what is learned, but for those who can once again build up this coherence within their own detailed knowledge of their specific field. The only way this coherence will be found again is if it is built upon biblical and theological foundations. Faculty of this kind are uncommon. What we have more typically are specialists who are highly proficient within a narrow scope of learning, but who are adrift in matters of theology and who see no particular need to remedy that deficiency since, in their view, it is not their field. The recovery of a unified field of knowledge, despite the massively corrosive effects of specialization, is an urgent need. And if the seminaries fail here, they will not only graduate students who resemble magpies who have simply collected unrelated odds and ends of knowledge, but they will also seriously undermine the church's real interests. The church needs as its leaders not simply those who are proficient in the language and interests of the learned guild, but those who can think biblically and theologically about themselves and their world, and to do so out of godly commitment. Rediscovering our focus may take a generation; failing to do so will leave the next generation without serious, biblically centered and culturally astute leadership in the church.

Bibliographical Essay

D. G. Hart

In a book whose point, in part, is that very little historical study has been done on evangelical theological education, some readers may think it strange to conclude with an essay on the literature that already exists on the subject. Just as bad is the standard admission at the start of bibliographical essays that what follows can only cover the highlights of a body of work—in this case, the history of evangelical theological education. Yet, despite the existing literature on this topic, some of which is solid, theological education, whether evangelical or not, has not received serious consideration from historians. Much of the extant literature consists of institutional histories, which occasionally make more general points about theological education and its relationship to the churches that educational institutions serve or the cultural values that they often reflect. For this reason, many of the references included here have more to do with subjects related to, but not directly covering, theological education, thus making good on our claim at the beginning of the book that our subject has not received sustained study.

The place to begin is with the good institutional histories that exist for prominent seminaries or divinity schools. Here the history of theological education has followed the lead of the history of American higher education, with the schools connected to respected universities receiving the most sustained attention. Glenn T. Miller's *Piety and Intellect: The Aims and Purposes of Ante-Bellum Theological Education* (Atlanta: Scholars Press, 1990), a comprehensive study of Protestant theological education before the Civil War in all its variety and denominational settings, is the starting point for studies on the origins of formal ministerial training and also raises important questions about the character and purpose of American Protestant theological education.[1] Among the old theological institutions, Harvard, Yale, and Princeton have generated the most interest. *The Harvard Divinity School: Its Place in Harvard University and American Culture,* ed., George H. Williams (Boston: Beacon Press, 1953), despite its age, offers a good overview of developments at Harvard, the shift from Trinitarianism to Unitarianism, which prompted the founding of Andover Seminary by conservative Congregationalists, and the changing status of theology in university education. Perhaps because of a larger constituency than Harvard, Yale Divinity School has generated more notable studies. Roland Bainton's *Yale and the Ministry: A History of Education for the Christian Ministry at Yale from the Founding in 1701* (New York: Harper & Brothers, 1957), aside from its value because of the author, is a good example of an institutional history that also answers larger questions about a school's relationship to the church and the broader public. Another book about Yale by a respected historian is Ralph H. Gabriel's *Religion and Learning at Yale: The Church of Christ in the College and University* (New Haven: Yale University Press, 1958), a work which focuses more on the university but also relates directly to the history of the divinity school and its connections to New England Congregationalism.

Of all the Ivy League related divinity schools or seminaries, Princeton has received the most scrutiny, in part, because of the influence of the Presbyterian Church (PCUSA) that it served, but also because it was, despite its Reformed confessionalism, open to non-Presbyterians. Much of the literature, however, is confined to dissertations and articles in periodicals. The best overview of Princeton remains Mark A. Noll's introduction to *The Princeton Theology: Scripture, Science, and Theological Method from Archibald Alexander to Benjamin Warfield* (Grand Rapids: Baker Book House, 1983). Noll also treats well the tensions within American Protestantism and culture in the early nineteenth century that led to the founding of Princeton Seminary in *Princeton and the Republic, 1768–1822: The Search for a Christian Enlightenment in the Era of Samuel Stanhope Smith* (Princeton: Princeton University Press, 1989). David B. Calhoun is currently working in a two-volume history of Princeton from its founding until 1929, the first of which, *Princeton Seminary: Faith and Learning, 1812–1868* (Edinburgh: Banner of Truth Trust, 1994), has recently been published and provides a readable and informative study of the seminary's faculty, theology, curriculum, students, and church ties. Also of value is Lefferts A. Loetscher, *Facing the Enlightenment and Pietism: Archibald Alexander and the Founding of Princeton Theologi-*

---

1. Despite the lack of an index, *Piety and Intellect* does provide annotated bibliographies which are useful not only for theological education before the Civil War, but also throughout American church history more generally. It should be added that Thomas C. Hunt and James C. Carper, *Religious Seminaries in America: A Selected Bibliography* (New York: Garland Publishing, 1989) is another valuable source for the study of Protestant theological education in the United States and covers the dissertations and periodical literature not included here.

cal Seminary (Westport, Conn.: Greenwood Press and Presbyterian Historical Society, 1983), a study of the school's first professor and the development
that led Presbyterians to adopt the seminary pattern of theological education.
Another useful study of Princeton, this time pertaining to its understanding
and study of Scripture, is Marion Ann Taylor, *The Old Testament in the Old
Princeton School (1812–1929)* (San Francisco: Mellen Research University
Press, 1992).

Another important evangelical seminary early on because it was the first
free-standing seminary in America was Andover, founded in 1808. H. K.
Rowe, *History of Andover Seminary* (Newton, Mass.: n.p., 1933) provides
a good narrative of the founding and development of the institution. Daniel
Day Williams, *The Andover Liberals: A Study in American Theology* (New
York: Octagon Books, 1970 [originally published 1941]) assesses the theological changes within New England evangelicalism in the late nineteenth
century that changed Andover from an institution founded in opposition to
the theological liberals of Unitarianism into one of the pacesetting seminaries
for liberal Protestantism. John Barnard, *From Evangelicalism to Progressivism at Oberlin College, 1966–1917* (Columbus, Ohio: Ohio State University
Press, 1969) is another solid study on the unraveling of New England theology that makes relevant points about evangelical theological education.

Another important institution for understanding liberalizing developments within evangelical theological education is Union Seminary in New
York, a school whose independence from ecclesiastical control (even though
it began as Presbyterian) bears many similarities to contemporary evangelical
seminaries. Robert T. Handy, *A History of Union Theological Seminary in
New York* (New York: Columbia University Press, 1987) is the best study of
Union's past and also offers a model for historical writing on a specific theological institution. Henry Sloane Coffin's *A Half Century of Union Theological Seminary, 1896–1945: An Informal History* (New York: Scribners,
1954), is more partisan in its rendering of Union's progressive posture but
still gives insights into the period of the schools' greatest influence, as well as
the character of theological education in mainline Protestantism before more
radical developments in the 1960s.

Baptists have written on the history of their own institutions, but not always with an eye to wider developments or a broader public.[2] For developments at the two largest Southern Baptist institutions, the following should
be consulted: William A. Mueller, *A History of Southern Baptist Theological
Seminary* (Nashville: Broadman Press, 1959): and Robert Andrew Baker,
*Tell the Generations Following: A History of Southwestern Baptist Theolog-
ical Seminary, 1908–1983* (Nashville: Broadman Press, 1983). Histories of

2. Readers should also consult the citations in Timothy George's, David Bebbington's, and George
Rawlyk's chapters above.

Northern Baptists are hard to come by. Herrick Everett Carleton, *Turns Again Home: Andover Newton Theological School and Reminiscences from an Unkept Journal* (Boston: Pilgrim Press, 1949) provides an informal history of Newton Theological School and Andover's 1925 merger with it. Warren C. Young, *Commit What You Have Heard: A History of Northern Baptist Theological Seminary, 1913–1988* (Wheaton, Ill.: Harold Shaw Publishing, 1988) is a retrospective history of the institution over its first seventy-five years.

Historians of Methodist theological education face similar difficulties to those studying Baptists.[3] Anson Watson Cummings, *The Early Schools of Methodism* (New York: Phillips and Hunt, 1886) covers Methodist developments in theological education at Boston University, Garrett, and Drew. Frederick Abbott Norwood, *Dawn to Mid-Day at Garret* (Evanston, Ill.: Garrett-Evangelical Theological Seminary, 1978) explores the 125-years history of Garrett-Evangelical Seminary and the theological shifts that shaped that history. Because Methodist seminaries provided the foundation for the creation of universities, their histories are often part of larger studies of particular institutions in American higher education. Three that should be consulted for Methodist theological education are: Charles Fremont Sitterly, *The Building of Drew University* (New York: The Methodist Book Concern, 1938); Earl W. Porter, *Trinity and Duke, 1892–1924: Foundations of Duke University* (Durham, N.C.: Duke University Press, 1964); and Mary Martha Hosford Thomas, *Southern Methodist University: Founding and Early Years* (Dallas: Southern Methodist University Press, 1974).

The origins and development of institutions founded in the nineteenth century are instructive for students of evangelical theological education because of the general theological consensus among American Protestants prior to the struggles associated with the modernist-fundamentalist controversy. But in the wake of the disputes that polarized liberal and conservative Protestants, the formation and history of seminaries whose theological identity was in tension with, if not opposed to, mainline Protestantism is of more direct bearing upon contemporary estimates of evangelical theological education. Here the histories of such independent seminaries as Dallas, Gordon-Conwell, Westminster, and Fuller are especially important. Of these institutions, only Fuller has received close scrutiny. George Marsden, *Reforming Fundamentalism: Fuller Seminary and the New Evangelicalism* (Grand Rapids, Mich.: Eerdmans, 1987) situates the seminary in the wider context of conservative Protestantism and does more than simply recount the history of the institution. Beyond uneven articles and dissertations, Gordon-Conwell Theological Seminary and Dallas Theological Seminary have not received the

---

3. Again, readers should examine the citations in Russell Richey's and Melvin Dieter's chapters above.

treatment they deserve. And no institutional history of Westminster Theological Seminary exists though John C. Vander Stelt, *Philosophy and Scripture: A Study in Old Princeton and Westminster Theology* (Marlton, N.J.:
Mack, 1978) explores important themes in the history of that school.

While these seminaries have not received careful scrutiny, some of the individuals associated with them have. Thus several biographical studies are
useful for understanding twentieth-century evangelical education. Ned Bernard Stonehouse, *J. Gresham Machen: A Biographical Memoir* (Grand Rapids: Eerdmans, 154) and D. G. Hart, *Defending the Faith: J. Gresham Machen and the Crisis of Conservative Protestantism in Modern America*
(Baltimore: The John Hopkins University Press, 1994) explore the founder
and issues that led to the creation of Westminster Seminary and the constituency it served. Rudolph Nelson, *The Making and Unmaking of an Evangelical Mind: The Case of Edward Carnell* (New York: Cambridge University Press, 1987) provides an engaging study of the president and influential
professor of theology at Fuller Seminary. Also valuable for developments at
Fuller is Carl F. H. Henry, *Confessions of a Theologian: An Autobiography*
(Waco: Tex.: Word Books, 1986). On Dallas Theological Seminary, Jeffrey
L. Richards, *The Promise of Dawn: The Eschatology of Lewis Sperry Chafer*
(Lanham, Md.: University Press of America, 1991) is one of the few books
of that institution's founder and guiding light. Also helpful is the *Handbook
of Evangelical Theologians,* ed., Walter A. Elwell, (Grand Rapids: Baker
Books, 1993), which includes biographical sketches of leading twentieth-
century evangelical theologians, many of whom taught at independent seminaries and were influential in the direction of those institutions.

In addition to independent seminaries, twentieth-century evangelicalism
has also been heavily indebted to the preparation of minister and missionaries provided by Bible colleges and institutes. The definitive study of these institutions, both for their religious and educational significance, is Virginia
Lieson Brereton, *Training God's Army: The American Bible School Movement, 1880–1940* (Bloomington, Ind.: Indiana University Press, 1990). Because dispensationalism sustained the religious convictions of many such
schools, Ernest R. Sandeen's *The Roots of Fundamentalism: British and
American Millenarianism, 1800–1930* (Chicago: University of Chicago
Press, 1970) is essential to understanding the theological education provided
by Bible colleges. Also helpful are biographies of some of the founders of
these schools. Among the best are James F. Findlay Jr., *Dwight L. Moody:
American Evangelist, 1837–1899* (Chicago: University of Chicago Press,
1969) and William V. Trollinger Jr., *God's Empire: William Bell Riley and
Midwestern Fundamentalism* (Madison, Wis.: University of Wisconsin Press,
1990) which examine the founders of Moody Bible Institute and Northwestern Bible School respectively, and their broader significance in American
Protestant history.

Focusing on theological education in the United States has obscured developments in Canada, which are often instructive for understanding the aims and purposes of North American evangelical seminaries more generally.[4] For specific studies of schools whose task focused upon the training of clergy, D. C. Masters, *Protestant Church Colleges in Canada: A History* (Toronto: University of Toronto Press, 1966), Arnold Edinburgh, *The Enduring Word: A Centennial of Wycliffe College* (Toronto: University of Toronto Press, 1978); George Rawlyk and Kevin Quinn, *The Redeemed of the Lord Say So: A History of Queen's Theological College, 1912–72* (Kingston: Queen's Theological College, 1980); *Canadian Baptists and Christian Higher Education*, ed., G. A. Rawlyk (Montreal: McGill-Queen's University Press, 1988), and Brian J. Fraser, *Church, College, and Clergy: A History of Theological Education at Knox College* (Toronto: University of Toronto Press, 1995) yield good histories and judicious analysis of Canadian developments. On the contributions and traditions of Bible schools and related educational initiatives in twentieth-century Canada, readers should consult John G. Stackhouse Jr., *Canadian Evangelicalism in the Twentieth Century: An Introduction to Its Character* (Toronto: University of Toronto Press, 1993). For penetrating assessments of the relations between evangelicalism, higher education, and Canadian intellectual life, the following are essential: Michael Gauvreau, *The Evangelical Century: College and Creed in English-Canada from the Great Revival to the Great Depression* (Montreal: McGill-Queen's University Press, 1991); and Marguerite Van Die, *An Evangelical Mind: Nathan Burwash and the Methodist Tradition in Canada* (Montreal: McGill-Queen's University Press, 1989).

Important for considering the place and function of formal theological education in American evangelicalism are books that treat the effects of the populist and egalitarian impulses of the movement on theological studies and those that assess the contributions of evangelical theological educators to the life of the mind more generally. Books that examine fruitfully the difficulties that evangelicalism poses for developing robust theological scholarship include: Nathan O. Hatch, *The Democratization of American Christianity* (New Haven: Yale University Press, 1989); George M. Marsden, *Fundamentalism and American Culture: The shaping of Twentieth-Century Evangelicalism, 1870–1925* (New York: Oxford University Press, 1980); Mark A. Noll, *The Scandal of the Evangelical Mind* (Grand Rapids: Eerdmans Publishing Co., 1994); *The Bible in America: Essays in Cultural History*, ed., Nathan O. Hatch and Mark A. Noll (New York: Oxford University Press, 1982); and *Evangelicalism and Modern America*, ed., George M. Marsden (Grand Rapids: Eerdmans, 1984). Not many books have assessed the contributions of evangelical theological and biblical scholarship. But Mark A.

---

4. Here again, readers should consult the citations in George Rawlyk's chapter above.

Noll, *Between Faith and Criticism: Evangelicals, Scholarship, and the Bible in America* (San Francisco: Harper & Row, 1986) is extremely valuable for understanding the academic world in which twentieth-century evangelical theological educators work and sets a high standard for theologically informed history.

Finally, a number of works in intellectual and cultural history are very helpful for understanding the place of theology and theological education in America intellectual life. Important books for exploring the demise of theology as a significant voice within intellectual circles include: Bruce Kuklick, *Churchmen and Philosophers: From Jonathan Edwards to John Dewey* (New Haven: Yale University Press, 1985); James Turner, *Without God, Without Creed: The Origins of Unbelief in America, 1880–1930* (Baltimore: The Johns Hopkins University Press, 1985); Conrad Cherry, *Hurrying Toward Zion: Universities, Divinity Schools, and American Protestantism* (Bloomington, In.: Indiana University Press, 1995); *Religion & Twentieth-Century American Intellectual Life*, ed., Michael J. Lacey, (New York: Cambridge University Press, 1989); and *Knowledge and Belief in America: Enlightenment Traditions and Modern Religious Thought*, eds., William M. Shea and Peter A. Huff (New York: Cambridge University Press, 1995). Another aspect of the declining status of theology, related theological disciplines, and the institutions which sponsor such scholarship is the increasing marginality of religious concerns within American higher education. Valuable studies of this subject include: Louise L. Stevenson, *Scholarly Means to Evangelical Ends: The New Haven Scholars and the Transformation of Higher Learning in America, 1830–1890* (Baltimore: The Johns Hopkins University Press, 1986); George M. Marsden, *The Soul of the American University: From Protestant Establishment to Established Non-Belief* (New York: Oxford University Press, 1994); Douglas Sloan, *Faith and Knowledge: Mainline Protestantism and American Higher Education* (Louisville: Westminster John Knox Press, 1994); and *The Secularizaiton of the Academy*, eds., George M. Marsden and Bradley J. Longfield, (New York: Oxford University Press, 1992).

Index